# Dog Dinners &
## Breaking Bread & Convent.

Authored by Alan Christ

Edited by Rachel Doug          ........ton

Cover design by David Beadle

# Dog Dinners & Snake Wine
## Breaking Bread & Convention in Southeast Asia

*Pen & Ink Publishing*

First published 2016

This book is a work of non-fiction.

ISBN (paperback) 978-1539805403
ASIN (ebook) B01MA1495A

# For Ranjit

Without your unwavering belief and support,
this book would have remained an idea without pages.

**Introduction: Flying Without Wings** CONTENTS

**Part 1: The Socialist Republic of Vietnam**

**Part 2: The Kingdom of Cambodia**

**Part 3: The Republic of the Union of Myanmar**

*The more that you read, the more things you will know. The more you learn, the more places you'll go.* (Dr Seuss)

## Introduction: Flying Without Wings

There's no place quite like Southeast Asia. Enchanting, carefree, impulsive, enigmatic, visionary and flamboyant, it is a global hot spot. This book will take you on a journey across the Indochinese Peninsula and maritime expanse of a beguiling subcontinent that is so compelling and culturally diverse, I made it my home. In Vietnam, Cambodia, Myanmar, Laos, and Thailand, it searches for answers to some of the region's greatest and smallest questions: Who is the Buddhist Osama bin Laden? What is a penis shrine? Why did the US lose the Vietnam War? What should you pack for a picnic in a Buddhist hell garden? Stopovers in the Philippines, Malaysia, Indonesia, Singapore, and Brunei present a miscellany of experiences against a backdrop of bloody killing fields, crumbling kingdoms, sinful cities, and tinkling temple towns. But first, the small matter of getting there.

Everyone has wished, at some point or another, that their life came with a page refresh or a reboot option. I wasn't afraid of starting over - throwing caution, convention and common sense to the wind - when I listed the components of my life 'for sale' at auction. While we are all creatures of comfort, we crave experience. It required a significant leap of faith, but I could part with worldly possessions in exchange for a paperless, one-way relocation to the other side of the world. If procrastination is 'the thief of time,' 'opportunity's assassin' or a grave in which to bury one's hopes and dreams, I have nothing in common with Shakespeare's most frustrating character - Hamlet - as I would have put a sword through his uncle's heart in Act One.

Better an *oops* than a *what if*.

Scholarly studies into stress and stressful situations usually cite the act of moving to a new house as a trigger, even when that move is from a squalid shack in Hackney to a palatial apartment in Mayfair. Racing against the clock to secure a visa and work permit, the capital city of the Kingdom of Thailand, Bangkok, was waiting to provide me with a new and fixed address between the Tropics of Cancer and Capricorn. An uneven, equanimous smile masked my fears, but there was a method to my madness: I wanted to explore Southeast Asia.

All of me, all of it.

The Internet is the world's greatest open marketplace where shoppers can submit bids for the sublime and the ridiculous, which includes virginity, cherished collections of belly button lint and a fifty-five-gallon barrel of lube. I couldn't believe how quickly my junk and jumble was snapped up by keyboard enthusiasts as old broken toys, worn-out shoes with flapping soles and rusted nuts and bolts all found new homes. My trash was another man's treasure. I used to enjoy bidding for vintage vinyl records on eBay, but I never imagined putting 'my life' up for auction. With everything sold, dismantled, boxed and delivered to the highest bidder, furniture-marked carpets remained, loose satellite cables and the washing machine's waste hose and standpipe.

To relocate to a far-flung and exotic elsewhere was only a romantic notion I harboured, until the moment I saw an advert for a teaching post in Thailand. It just felt right. Fate and Fortune were friends, with my appointment as the new Secondary Head of English - at Amnuay Silpa School - confirmed in time for a happy Christmas (the Thai school year begins in April, not September). My teaching degree found a greater purpose as a universal passport, and with the English language a global lingua franca, my subject knowledge was in high demand in Thailand - a serial underachiever in the English Proficiency Index. All the world's a stage, and I had a role to play in Southeast Asia. A multiple-entry visa and work permit granted access to the cultural spinning machine, but I also had the wherewithal to sustain my wanderlust.

Covered in scuff and black sticker marks, my suitcase joined me on the pavement as snow started to fall and dust sleepy Canterbury. As my former life disappeared in a taxi wing mirror, the poignant philosophising of an unlikely philosopher came to mind. When Ferris Bueller (*Ferris Bueller's Day Off*) skips school for a life-affirming journey of his own through the streets of Chicago, he explains his reasoning to Cameron Frye, his uptight friend: 'Life moves pretty fast. If you don't stop and look around once in a while, you could miss it.' Repeatedly bitten by an ever-thirsty travel bug, I was ready to break bread with strangers in an unfamiliar land full of challenges and surprises, rabies and earthquakes.

A flight distance of some 5,900 miles separates the harvested lands of Southeast England from the scorched plains of Southeast Asia. Sitting perfectly still in an aluminium purgatory - somewhere between thirty and forty thousand feet - I found time for quiet reflection and nervous tension. The impact jolted me back to life, like the efficacious joules of a fully charged defibrillator, when the wheels of Finnair Airbus Flight AY89 touched down at Bangkok's

Suvarnabhumi International Airport. But it was a different life, unburdened and renewed. My eyes were sewn shut with iron wire over the Caspian Sea or Central Asia, while a pool of syrupy drool leaked from my mouth and clung to the coarse bristles on my chin with all the tenacity of an expert climber on an overhanging cliff. With a cursory glance about the cabin, I narrowed my death stare on two sniggering teenage boys seated, for their convenience, in the geometrically perfect position for a sneaky selfie with the man-dog hybrid I had become.

While contemplating whether pimpled narcissists should be allowed to survive adolescence, I found some solace in the fact that as we all produce a litre of saliva every day, a little spillage is forgivable and probably necessary to prevent us from drowning in our sleep. I wiped away viscous strands with an ill-adjusted sense of humour and hoped no one noticed as I reapplied the unpleasant residue to a dandruff overlay that had formed on a headrest an inch from my face. There was, however, nowhere to hide my embarrassment: the hardened-plastic design of economy seats restricted movement to within two hundred cubic centimetres of suffering. My father told me that we are put on this Earth to be tested by God, and I believed him; I had, after all, passed the Master Sommelier Diploma in Confinement Endurance in twelve excruciating hours.

Having acquired an acute form of restless legs syndrome, I couldn't stop my lower limbs from twitching, or my feet playing air drums, as the cabin stirred to life like Frankenstein's monster with an apocalyptic hangover. The flight crew busied itself with mannequin smiles and practised politeness as one of the male attendants, apparently delighted by the prospect of landing in Bangkok, danced a merry slip jig along the narrow section of the aisle. His uniform was military-pristine and full of perfect angles, while his arched and over-manicured brows gave him a look that was both surprised and strangely predatory at the same time. He was evidently looking forward to his next international layover, but this was no ordinary landing: I was alighting on the darker side of the moon. My first challenge was to learn how to pronounce the name of the city airport I had just landed at when even the name of my new school presented a phonetic conundrum as 'Silpa' is pronounced 'sin.'

The aircraft taxied into its designated bay and the pedestrian tunnel attached to the front passenger exit like a jumbo-sized iPod with a docking station. It reminded me of my present disconnectedness as I no longer had a house and home. For the first time in my life, I was homeless. Unplugged. The secure and contented existence I had known for nearly four decades evaporated in the clouds. This changing state was confirmed by the captain's sunny disposition when he announced an outside temperature of thirty-five degrees Celsius. *Bangkok*. The only security left to ground me was a teaching contract, which was more important than my passport because it doubled as an access key to an alternative reality, and trebled as a permit enabling me to work, travel and live with legitimacy in the Kingdom of Thailand.

Summer getaways usually lasted for three to four weeks, but a two-year contract granted 104 weeks of extended stay in Southeast Asia. The stress that I had managed to postpone finally caught up with me, and I was a Death in the Afternoon cocktail of uncertainty, nervous excitement, and jet lag. I repeated the reassuring words of Mark Twain in the quietest chambers of my mind, as these were a comfort during the darker hours of self-doubt: 'Twenty years from now you will be more disappointed by the things you didn't do than by the ones you did do.' It was my time to explore, dream and discover; intrepidness should come before fear and regret. Carpe diem, and all that.

My journey of a thousand miles began with a single, tentative step at London Heathrow, but my priority upon landing in the Thai capital fell short of the romantic philosophies of Lao Tzu. Running my tongue over teeth to clean and redeem my neglected enamel, fellow passengers readied themselves for that customary scramble for the exit. Had I packed my toothbrush? My teeth were as furry as a fluffy-breed dog and I was close to barking too, having been rigidly confined within a monotonously beige and ivory canister. Looking through the nearest oval Plexiglas window, I was startled by the reflection staring back at me: the air conditioning dehydrated my reliably oily skin to cardboard, and I was a specimen ready for carbon-14 dating. I looked like the protagonist in Anthony Horowitz's *The Man with the Yellow Face*, but I desperately hoped for a future without a tragic derailment of some kind.

Patrick Smith claims in *Cockpit Confidential* that the average cabin temperature - at 12% humidity - is drier than most deserts. I had no reason to doubt him, so 'moisturiser' was added to the invisible shopping list compiled in my head. I remembered a strange tabloid story - about an even stranger woman - who hadn't smiled for nearly forty years as she wanted to prevent the onset of wrinkles and preserve her youthful looks. Had my frightening reflection been her own, she may have headed straight for the propellers of those Rolls-Royce aero engines and a close encounter of the *unkind* kind.

Surrounded by claustrophobic triggers, I tried in vain to fight the side effects of cabin fever and pressurisation, and when my ears popped, I refocused my eyes on the chair pocket and tidied away the in-flight magazines and safety instruction leaflets no one ever bothers to read. Attempting a rational explanation of the miracle of 'landing on water' (unless, of course, you happen to be Captain Sully) is an act capable of losing even the most captive of readers. My desire to escape that Airbus was becoming desperate - comparable to that uncontrollable urge to urinate the closer you get to a toilet. As belts unbuckled like the removal of starting blocks, passengers rushed to snatch their hand luggage as if the plane was about to burst into flames, before staking claim to inches of soiled carpet tiles (which disappeared under shuffling feet moving forwards in millimetres). I have never understood this behaviour or the stampede that follows, as I usually find myself waiting patiently with the very same people when we all arrive together at the luggage carousel.

With my visa bearing the official triangular stamp of the Kingdom of Thailand, I passed through the airport's border security area to be greeted by an acid green 'Nothing to Declare' sign which filled me with a smuggler's sense of dread. Was it too late to declare a temporary loss of sanity? I started my journey across Southeast Asia on April Fools' Day *of all days*, so the immigration officials were unlikely to believe me, and besides, I couldn't see any smiles on show in the fabled Land of Smiles. I remained tight-lipped and grim-faced. My former life weighed precisely 23kg (my luggage and 'new life' allowance) and could be pulled along on wobbling, uncooperative wheels. I resisted the opportunity this presented for a moment of existential angst and hurried to the nearest exit, fearing those stony, dour and humourless officials might change their minds and send me back home to the house I no longer owned.

I congratulated myself for having resisted another impulse and immigration no-no, which is to buy one of those novelty luggage stickers with images of a ripped suitcase packed with cocaine, or a bound-and-gagged flight attendant. It wasn't worth the risk of being led to a small room for an impromptu strip show and body cavity search, complete with the snapping sound of latex gloves and a splash of KY Jelly. Thailand is one of twenty-two countries that advocate the use of capital punishment as a deterrent, and the no-nonsense Thai Penal Code allows judges to issue death sentences to Thai drug traffickers, and a lifetime of incarceration to foreigners (ironically, a fate worse than death). I decided it would be wise to get to know my audience first and to test their sense of humour gently. The stickers remained unstuck, and so did I.

Having spent three whole summers holidaying in Thailand in 2006, 2011 and 2012, I was no stranger to Bangkok. I knew what I was letting myself in for and it was a subconscious fait accompli that I would take that next step and relocate. I was in for a penny, in for a baht. My new employers booked a double room in a hotel with a reassuring name (The Hopeland Hotel) and I clung to that *hope* as a good omen for the journey ahead. Generously, they covered the cost of my flight and a whole month's accommodation, but beyond those four weeks, I was on my own. No longer a ship moored in a safe harbour, I managed to arrive in one piece (despite the onset of old age) and avoid the fatal outcomes of an episode of *Air Crash Investigation*. I just hoped the airport taxi driver wasn't a dangerous driver or a serious speed freak.

By *speed freak*, I mean the methamphetamine type. 'Yaba' sounds like something Fred Flintstone might take when Barney's daughter Bamm-Bamm Rubble gives him a headache, but in the Thai language it translates to 'crazy medicine.' Yaba is produced in prodigious quantities in Southeast Asia and is more popular than heroin and cocaine in Thailand; it is widely available and cheaper than most legal and illegal highs. It used to be licit during the good ol' days of moderate lawlessness and was popular with long-distance lorry drivers who could grab a few pills with their petrol and cigarettes and keep on driving, *forever* if they wanted to. With close to 40% of the tourists arriving in Southeast Asia aged between fifteen and thirty-four years of age, Yaba is also quite popular with the international backpacker crowd and thus presents a strange case for cultural anthropologists to study.

Yaba was invented and manufactured by the Nazis to help keep exhausted troops awake and alert for days on end, as conflicts intensified on the German-Soviet frontier, but in today's Thailand, it is the drug of the poor and the perfect antidote to long and unsociable working hours. It is also the drug of choice for some Bangkok taxi drivers and can be held accountable for their unpredictable, irrational and occasionally violent behaviour. It's called 'the crazy medicine' for a good reason, because the drug floods the brain with dopamine which, in turn, creates intense feelings of exhilaration before psychosis sets in. Having had some colourful altercations with Bangkok taxi drivers, I resisted using their services until they were necessary, such as transfers to the airports. When a driver killed a foreign tourist with a samurai sword in July 2013 (allegedly, over a disputed fare), I vowed to be a model passenger and as polite as Mother Teresa at an Ann Summers party.

Upon my arrival in Bangkok for a summer holiday in 2012, my taxi speedster had already convinced himself that he was a champion of the Asian Touring Car Series as he weaved through traffic and cranked through gears. He was a marriage of man and machine, fully synched with his Champagne-pink Toyota Corona. A Charlie Kwan wannabe, he didn't seem to be too concerned when he mounted kerbs to get an advantage, but the pedestrians he narrowly missed *did mind* as they scurried from the paths of his personal racing circuit. My 'conversations' with Bangkok taxi drivers were like Bill Murray's rehearsed interactions in *Groundhog Day*, and I may as well have been in Punxsutawney, Pennsylvania, myself for all the good they did me. Fares from the city airports, advertised as 'metered' and 'regulated,' reassure tired and fretful first-time visitors, but as soon as the passenger doors close and click, that concept often gets left behind on the pavement (with your luggage too, if you are not mindful of it).

I started the lost-in-translation pantomime with a sincere and polite greeting in Thai, but it frequently went south from there as I had to dodge an awful lot of krap. 'Krap' and 'ka' are polite particles added to the end of almost every sentence in a Thai conversation. They are two of the most commonly used words in the Thai language, not surprisingly, but they are also stand-alone utterances and a standard response to any speaker, in virtually any social context. They may sound like simple enough words, but they are practically untranslatable. As the male response (krap) shares the same pronunciation as the British slang *crap*, every time I tried to be polite only resulted in awkward embarrassment:

'Sir, have you marked my homework?'

'Yes, krap.'

When my Bangkok dentist answered her smartphone (using her free hand to work on my teeth), I had a New Zealand kaka bird sitting on my shoulder. Robotically repeating 'ka, ka, ka' in response to a talkative girlfriend, she could have been perched on the branch of a kauri tree in the forests of Kapiti, Codfish or Little Barrier Island. Thais prefer to use their nicknames instead of their birth names, and this is a linguistic blessing for Johnny Foreigners since some of their full names are as long and complicated as Welsh towns (where they have an aversion to vowels and always win spelling competitions). My dentist's nickname - pinned to her blue scrub top - was inappropriately sweet for someone of her profession. Her name was Pancake.

Some of my students had unusual nicknames, others were bizarre or simply unfortunate, so I enjoyed taking the register which was no longer a chore of Johns and Janes but a challenge to maintain my professional composure: Pooh, Pee, Pong, Pepsi, Cola, Meow, Guitar, Fifa, Porsche, Beer, Wine, Champagne, and Brush. Brush loved to paint, but Meow didn't like cats. I even had a student whose name was *Name*. How lazy is that? Seriously, you couldn't make it up if you tried, but at least I was spared some of Thailand's more 'unique' and socially awkward names, such as *Fukmee*.

As Charlie revved his engine to a chorus of vrooms but no hurrahs, I thought it pertinent to establish some rudimentary details of our journey together, such as where I wanted to be taxied to in Bangkok. With a false sense of self-confidence, I initiated the conversation:

'Sawadee krap!'

'Krap,' Charlie replied, completely indifferent to my attempt at cultural assimilation.

'Do you know Somerset Lake Point Hotel, Sukhumvit Road?' I continued, my knowledge of the Thai language prematurely exhausted.

'Krap.'

'Brilliant! Take me there!' I rejoiced.

I hoped his repeated expression wasn't a succinct review of my chosen hotel, but as soon as the engine started and my common sense registered that I was communicating with a *Bangkok* taxi driver, I reconsidered my initial delight at the geographical impossibility that he would know - in a nanosecond - one hotel from all the thousands of indistinguishable hotels, guest houses and hostels in the city. And besides, the Sukhumvit Road is the longest road in Thailand. He had lots of gadgets on display as wires created race circuits of their own, but I couldn't see any sign of the one that mattered: a device with GPS navigation. It also occurred to me that he hadn't switched on that all-important dashboard taximeter, so I politely reminded him:

'Meter. Is it opened?'

'Krap.'

The taximeter wasn't switched on at all, as the digital red digits remained fixed on the starting tariff of thirty-five baht. With my grammar suffering as I had deliberately substituted 'opened' for 'switched on' (Thais *open* lights and other appliances, they never *switch* them on), the driver did at least make progress on his own as he attempted an ambitious six-word phrase in broken English:

'Three hundred baht, you pay, krap.'

'Krap,' I replied, despondently.

I finally understood why 'krap' is such a common word in Thailand, but I also mastered the workings of the Thai taxi system: he drove, and I paid whatever fare he wanted me to. And like Chinese water torture, Charlie returned to his slow-drip method with another *krap* response to my *krap* reply.

I was feeling emboldened and wanted to regain the advantage or, at the very least, make light of being ripped off on arrival.

'Take me to moon, krap?'

'Moon? Krap,' he returned, with a look of mild inquisitiveness gathering at the corners of his eyes, which blinked excessively the more seriously he considered whether this was a value-for-money request and the fastest route to get us there.

'Krap,' I continued, nodding my head with a triumphant smile, 'but first, take me to Somerset Lake Point Hotel on Sukhumvit Road.'

Charlie's taxi doubled as a purpose-built mobile techno party, and I was the special but *only* guest. As multi-coloured, multi-function LED lights flashed, twinkled and irritated, the party mix blasted with spontaneous choreography from coaxial speakers while a twin-active subwoofer thumped my head from behind. My host was having a smashing time on his own, but I suspected he was high on something. He was so wired and over-alert, I thought I was going to witness a rare episode of spontaneous human combustion. And then he did the unthinkable: he tossed a box of energy-red pills into the air (between gear changes), bounced it off his left shoulder and caught it again with his free hand. Popping it open with chipped and blackened teeth, a single pill was sucked into a black hole. He had a need for speed, and I half expected him to offer me a complimentary hit of Yaba. I was impressed by his assured dexterity, and I was confident he could race for McLaren or Mercedes if given a trial, but his disregard for my safety had my heart rate racing.

The Supreme Buddha believed it is better to travel well than to arrive. I agreed with him as his tiny head bobbed up and down on a dusty dashboard covered with talismans, magical charms, amulets, statues of monks, toys, coins, and an obligatory photograph of the late King Bhumibol Adulyadej. There was even a small bowl of rice, a kind and generous offering to the spirits, should they get peckish (clearly, the driver needed all the blessings he could get). The Buddha may well have been the first wise and awakened being, but I prefer to travel well *and survive*.

Returning to Thailand nine months later, I arrived at my temporary 'hometel' (on the day of fools in April 2013) and it was more *Hopeless* than Hopeland, if truth be told, but at least it was clean. I gave the taxi driver explicit directions from the airport to leave him in no doubt whatsoever that I knew my way around the Thai capital almost as well as he did. As I crossed the outdoor pool area to my pre-booked chamber of air-conditioned darkness, oversized Americans cheerily relived their youth as they splashed about with

Thai 'girlfriends' who were small enough to fit inside their attaché cases. I couldn't face humanity through the foggy haze of jet lag or the psychological unrest caused by displacement, so I retired myself to bed (even though it was still early in the afternoon) wondering what on earth I had been *drinking* when I decided that moving to Southeast Asia was a sensible idea. I had the first and only panic attack of my life as I lay naked on thin, damp sheets and stared wide-eyed at the ceiling fan; I was alone in a city full of strangers and some of them were strange.

When I awoke the next morning, the world was a different place. The fog had cleared. I opened the curtains to let the sunshine in, and a shit-brown wall greeted me for a view, but I knew beyond that lay a whole world of possibilities. Southeast Asia is an expatriated Wild West, a travel and cultural twilight zone and an opportunity to relive the awe and wonder of early childhood years. Like a snowman on the beach, it flips the coin of conventionality from heads to tails with ease; dog is sometimes preferred over chicken or pork and snakes are the new grapes turned into wine. In the Gospel of John, Jesus impresses his disciples when he performs his first miracle by turning water into wine at the Marriage of Cana, but snakes have scales, bones, and poisonous fangs so kudos to the Thais and Cambodians who can out-miracle Jesus on an industrial scale.

In his *Letters from the East* (1898), Rudyard Kipling expressed his sense of wonderment when he reflected on his time exploring Burma (modern-day Myanmar), observing that it is: '…quite unlike any land you know about.' His observation is still relevant today and encapsulates the region's enduring appeal for twenty-first-century travellers. There is simply no place like it and that's why I was there, flying without wings.

Using Thailand's capital as a regional hub, I rented a modest apartment on Luea Suk in the Klong Toey District, which is home to the country's largest slum area and a biblical plague of rats and cockroaches. I turned my living space into a bug fortress to keep determined invaders out, sealing every hole I could find with blu tack or duct tape, but nature is a tricky, wily adversary and always managed to find a way inside. My kitchen cupboards were an armoury of bug repellents and a dedication to pest control (I had insecticidal lacquers, power foggers, proactive dust, sprays, and traps). Every product had bold print and a brightly coloured name, with instructions written in Thai, and they all shared a familiar image: dead roaches, belly-up inside a circle with a red cross. I found a new hobby and purpose: I was the Cockroach Killer of Bangkok.

My apartment had a panoramic view of my neighbours' apartments and overlooked a canal that doubled as an open sewer, but I was living in one of the most vibrant cities in the world, and that was the silver-brown lining. When I heard the crazed barking of dogs late one evening, curiosity got the better of me, so I peered over the balcony to observe a scaly four-legged monster emerge from the fetid waters below. As it flicked its tongue to taste the air (which I am sure it regretted), its predatory instincts marked two stray dogs as potentially chewy, bite-size snacks. I hoped it would put an end to their excessive barking and do us both a favour.

The creature from the deep was a common monitor lizard, but whatever had been poured into or was still floating on those canal waters had much the same effect as nuclear waste on Godzilla. Had it escaped from Fukushima Daiichi after the 2011 nuclear meltdown? Had I chanced upon the Son of Godzilla? The dogs were frightened by this unexpected reversal as they were hunter-turned-hunted, so they retreated to a safe distance, and I returned to the hissing, huffing and humming of air conditioning. Serenity returned when the barking ceased, and I could only surmise that man's best friends found acidic beds inside the belly of that beast. Whatever their fate had been, it was the perfect result: *Son of Godzilla 2 - 0 Soi Dogs of Bangkok*.

I could never escape Bangkok's traffic, no matter how hard I tried, as a busy expressway ran alongside my apartment building and the spartan box of dry air I occupied on the fifth floor. The consolation was convenient access to the city's international airports, and the continuous engine noise was motivation to hit the road myself. But as a springboard into Southeast Asia and a surrogate 'home' of sorts, I will always have an affectionate regard for the city, the country's people and the stranger-than-fiction reality I adopted for two years. When my shower water brought with it the occasional scent of surfing raw sewage, I was less than enamoured with it all (to say the least). Pigs may be happy to bathe in the brown, but humans are the only animals smart enough to install air fresheners in their toilet areas. People often make mountains out of molehills, but showering in someone else's sewage is a mountainous molehill. And yet I had chosen to stand at the top of that hill, and I quite liked the view.

The Chinese Crested Dog might be one of the ugliest breeds known to man, but their owners adore them and even dress them up in cute pink dresses, transforming them into the stuff of nightmares. Bangkok is ugly on the eye too - especially at street level - and it doesn't even try to hide its glorious imperfections, but still I skipped along the oily grime of its uneven pavements, and I grew to love it unconditionally. It was the best of times and the worst of times; Bangkok was a begrimed window on Southeast Asia.

Memories of extraordinary places where remarkable experiences were shared with strangers who went on to become friends, inspired me to write this book. And I learnt a valuable lesson in the process: the most important things in life are *people* and *experiences*, not 'things.' When I returned to the UK, I was not the same person; a part of me remains in the tropics, basking in the sun, while a small piece of paradise shelters from the rains of Manchester.

Life's not meant to be lived in one place.

# Part 1: A Country, Not a War

## The Socialist Republic of Vietnam

*Travelling - it leaves you speechless, then turns you into a storyteller.* (Ibn Battuta)

### Chapter 1: Phoenix from the Ashes

The Socialist Republic of Vietnam, the country easternmost on the Indochinese Peninsula, is the subregion's surprise cultural package and that is why it features as the opening section of this book. Vietnam is the epitome of all that is still mysterious, exotic and wonderfully strange about Indochina and yet, for decades, it was a no-go zone for international tourists. Now *everyone* seems to be planning a trip to Vietnam. Thailand is a strutting, precocious peacock so its charms are immediate and rather obvious; it doesn't have to play hard to get because the tourists always come back for more. Vietnam, on the other hand, is a subtle and more cultured creature.

Like a phoenix rising from the ashes of war, Vietnam is rapidly transforming itself into Southeast Asia's destination of choice with its extraordinary and unique cultural heritage, beautiful beaches and awe-inspiring natural scenery. Despite certain connotations of conflict and war, Vietnam is a safe and welcoming country for travellers to explore. With a population close to ninety million, the Vietnamese are an unusual mix of cultures, languages, and historical backgrounds and they are an affable, easy-going and hard-working people. Vietnam is an ambitious, forward-thinking country that has set its sights on becoming a developed nation by 2020, which is a goal fuelled by one of the region's fastest-growing economies. Since the turn of the century, Vietnam's tourism industry has developed at a staggering and unimagined pace, but some travellers remain sceptical and discouraged by its past and wartime associations. The Vietnamese have a simple saying that neatly captures their country's predicament: *Vietnam is a country, not a war.*

With my trusty backpack bursting with readiness and a plentiful supply of toilet tissue, I journeyed to all four compass points and a variety of land and seascapes. My wanderings took me to the northern capital, Hanoi, Sapa District and the Lao Cai Province, Halong Bay, Hue, the Demilitarized Zone, Tam Coc and the Hoa Lu District, Hoi An, Ho Chi Minh City (formerly 'Saigon'), Cu Chi, Tay Ninh Province and the many rivers, canals, and streams that form the magnificent Mekong Delta. While a visit to Vietnam will, inevitably, be a journey into past conflicts, there is more to Vietnam than a legacy of war and recovery.

My generation's introduction to the country came through the medium of film. When the Vietnam War came to a bloody end on the 30th April 1975, it gave birth to a unified country and a new cinema subgenre. With my brother beside me, I watched the Vietnam canon on repeat, the mostly one-sided telling of war stories about a conflict the Vietnamese call 'The American War' (I guess it depends on which side of the fence you happen to stand or squat). We enjoyed the films for their explosive action, but we could have been reading comic books as we made no distinction between *Rambo* and *Apocalypse Now*. We were blissfully unaware of the real-life horrors of such a catastrophic encounter, and as napalm rained over rural Vietnamese villages, we tapped our toes to the loose rhythms of *The End* and Jim Morrison's baritone voice.

Michael Cimino's *The Deer Hunter* (1978), Francis Ford Coppola's *Apocalypse Now* (1979), Oliver Stone's *Platoon* (1986) and Stanley Kubrick's *Full Metal Jacket* (1987) were the first wave of films that tried to find some moral perspective from one of military history's long-drawn-out conflicts. They all left an indelible impression on me (even the much-maligned *Rambo*), and a travel seed took root. Fast-forward twenty-five years and I found myself visiting Vietnam for the very first time, scrambling my way through the extensive and claustrophobic Viet Cong tunnel networks at Cu Chi, driving the far-reaching freeways that were once the logistical system of the Ho Chi Minh Trail, and visiting the legendary battlegrounds of Quang Tri Province. I came full circle with my childhood and face-to-face with the horrors of modern warfare. To complete the experience, I practised my John Rambo blank stare, grew my hair long, pumped some iron and wore a black sweatband and jade Buddha pendant. The only puzzle piece missing was that iconic Bowie knife, but I didn't want to stir up a hornet's nest and start another war.

Vietnam is the perfect battleground for indulging in dark tourism, which is a global phenomenon and preference for sightseeing in the world's most unlikely holiday destinations; it's a macabre form of voyeurism that involves travelling to places associated primarily with death, disaster, and suffering. Dom Joly's *The Dark Tourist* introduced me to this concept, his travel memoir featuring a weekend in Chernobyl and day trips to North Korea and the killing fields of Cambodia. It is an amusing read, and it inspired me to find dark places of my own which are more thought-provoking than white-sand beaches. Places such as Auschwitz-Birkenau in Poland, an absorbing historical site and Holocaust memorial, which I enjoyed without an ice cream and Cadbury Flake in hand. Auschwitz is a lesson in the fragility of human existence; it is a warning from history that should never be forgotten or repeated, and everyone should visit the camp at least once in their lifetime.

The Agent Orange Exhibition, inside Ho Chi Minh's War Remnants Museum, is another dedication to darkness, despite its rather zesty title. Directly above the entrance, an orange sign with block capitals 'welcomes' visitors and wastes no time positioning their sympathies: 'AGENT ORANGE AFTERMATH IN THE U.S. AGGRESSIVE WAR IN VIETNAM.' The exhibition disturbs and overwhelms as it presents, without restraint, the consequences of herbicidal warfare. Decades have passed, and the world has refocused on new conflicts in the Middle East or Western Asia, but Agent Orange continues to claim victims in Vietnam today.

Outside the museum, I stopped to listen to a small band of the afflicted play traditional Vietnamese instruments, such as three-string lutes and bamboo flutes. Their disfigurements were a terrible reminder of the genetic legacy that continues to affect post-war generations. Euripides, the classical Greek tragedian, observed that experience and travel 'are an education in themselves' and, certainly for the first time in my life, I was beginning to understand the other side of Vietnam's story. For some Vietnamese survivors, their victory over the US must feel like a consolation prize as it's hard to imagine there was ever a winning side in such tragic circumstances.

I found it impossible to visit Vietnam and not engage with its past and this controversial war. I enjoyed learning about the spirited resilience of the Vietnamese people who, aptly, compare their national characteristics to the qualities of bamboo. While thin and seemingly frail, bamboo can withstand a tremendous amount of pressure before showing signs of strain or impairment; stronger than oak, it is the most durable of hardwoods. Its appearance belies its character, and the Vietnamese, often against the mightiest of odds, successfully repelled a succession of better-equipped foreign invaders. The Americans came to a hard understanding that you should never agitate the Vietnamese; you may as well pick a fight with a single bee in a hive and see how well that turns out.

With progressive modern cities, UNESCO World Heritage old towns, the remnants of war, diverse ethnic minority groups and spectacular land and seascapes, Vietnam is a miscellaneous and irresistible travel choice. Thailand is Southeast Asia's tourism Goliath, and it rests on its laurels, but Vietnam is emerging as the regional rival to challenge its status. It could be the true, future king of Southeast Asia; it would certainly wear the crown well. It might not be the easiest country to travel, but there is always reward for hard work.

## Chapter 2: Hanoi Rocks

With teenage dreams of rock superstardom, I purchased a vinyl copy of the Hanoi Rocks debut album *Bangkok Shocks, Saigon Shakes, Hanoi Rocks* but never imagined visiting those mysterious cities myself and, stranger still, in that exact order. The album is a glittering bubble-bomb of fun and mayhem, perms and spandex, so it was apt this Finnish hard rock band introduced me to some of the wildest cities in Southeast Asia.

I heard torrid tales about Vietnam's capital from fellow travellers, who seemed to regard Hanoi as a mere transit gateway to more desirable places. I met a teacher who relocated from London to Hanoi on an initial three-year teaching contract at the United Nations International School of Hanoi, only to return home three weeks later with her tail tucked. She loved the school but claimed her 'quality of life' had suffered (traffic, pollution, yadda, yadda, yadda) which hardly sounds like the ringing endorsement of a hard rock set. Hanoi is a Marmite capital and love it or hate it, any yeast extracts that are a by-product of the beer-brewing process are usually fine with me. And what is there not to love about an Asian city where the people live out their lives on the streets?

With most international flights landing at Noi Bai International Airport (which included my budget AirAsia flight from Bangkok), I decided to take a closer look for myself and form an unbiased opinion of this ancient capital, heavily influenced by both the French and the Chinese. As I waited in line and processed through immigration, I flicked through the pages of my impractical, unwieldy guidebook and noticed that it made an excellent impression of a geography textbook. I tried to be as invisible as I could while observing strict immigration etiquette, shuffling forward one step at a time to meet cold and enquiring eyes, before collecting another passport stamp on a full-page visa. The guidebook promised a colourful glimpse into a tropical kaleidoscope, but I was reminded that chronic pollution is monochromatic grey when I exited the terminal. Experience has taught me to regard travel guides with the same suspicion as online dating services: full of impossibly beautiful pictures, they often make exaggerated claims.

Noi Bai International Airport is twenty-seven miles north of Hanoi's popular downtown area, and with little in the way of public transportation, I found myself sweating profusely inside the wretched bowels of a Mai Linh Taxi. But at least there was no risk of being digested by the Son of Godzilla who, I imagined, was still chewing his way through my barking neighbours back in Bangkok. My first impression of Vietnam was filtered through dusty and lethargic windows that could no longer be troubled to wind up or down.

The previous occupant of my seat had evidently fallen asleep in transit, leaving behind a perfect impression of their face on the passenger window like a greasy *Shroud of Tourist*.

Fraught with apologies, the driver hurriedly pulled away from the concourse. He used improvised sign language to inform me that his air conditioning system was faulty, by frantically waving a hand in front of his face, and I wondered whether he was preparing me for the side effects of a chronic flatulence problem which only time would tell and the air reveal. To delay my anticipated discomfort, he forced the passenger door window wide open to allow the city's construction dust, and a swarm of starving mosquitoes, to share the ride. I couldn't decide which was worse: Bamm-Bamm Rubble's techno fever in Bangkok, or tropical malaria in Hanoi. Perhaps I would tuck tail and run myself.

You know you have arrived in Southeast Asia when sweat patches form in places you've never had them before, and as the taxi crawled through ill-tempered traffic for the next two hours, I evolved into a slow and excruciating bowel movement. I could have filled an Olympic-sized swimming pool with sweat and had a glass to spare, had I not flooded the reception counter on my arrival at a hostel hastily booked that morning.

'Glass of water, Mr?'

A rhetorical question, surely? I noticed an adult cockroach laying belly-up beside the reception desk, but I was too tired to give a damn as I had developed a deadly combination of jet and car lag. Jar lag. My first impressions of Vietnam jarred with all those glossy guidebook images of verdant rice terraces and conical hats.

In the past twenty years, Vietnam's post-war tourism industry has exploded (for want of a better word) and enjoyed a prolonged period of boom, peaking with nearly eight million arrivals in 2014. But nobody seems to care about the consequences, such as pollution and congestion. I was quite relieved when I exited the city stage left after my first brief visit in 2013, as I needed a break from Bangkok and Hanoi is a smaller, angrier version of it. Two days were more than enough in the way of an introduction, so I shook hands, made my excuses and escaped to the serenity of Halong Bay with my white flag held unashamedly high.

Arriving in Hanoi as a first-time visitor is an orientation that is anything but gentle; the city seems to delight in taking a mallet to already fragile senses. There is no denying its endless energy, and for me, that is one of Hanoi's greatest appeals. Vietnam's capital is a multisensory assault, and the cacophony of its streets made me question why I was there as I tried in vain to listen to a classical violinist, while drums and cymbals clashed and crashed around me. Perhaps those local tour guides know better, scooping up their arrivals at the airport before scuttling off to luxury cruise ships waiting on the calm and gentle waters of Halong Bay, or the clean and refreshing climate of Sapa's mountain resorts.

I try to resist my first impressions of a city by making every effort to tap into the rhythm of local life which, I discovered in Hanoi, always plays to the fastest beat. I passed the test on my second trip and became a city convert when I returned for a third stay in 2014. I was right to give Hanoi another chance(s) as it is one of Southeast Asia's unique and stimulating cities. Whenever I arrive in new capitals, particularly if that arrival follows a long-haul flight, my modus operandi is to locate my guesthouse, check in as swiftly as possible, dump my bags and get straight out on the streets *moving* and *doing* as much as possible. Hanoi changed my habits on my second and third visits as I went straight to my rooms, locked the doors, closed the curtains and hit slumber mode. To fully appreciate Hanoi, even after a short-haul flight, you need just as much energy as the city.

I like to search for cultural differences when I travel, and time and again I find them in the most unlikely of places or the simplest of acts. When crossing roads in Hanoi, instinctively I followed those sensible rules I obeyed all my life back home (look left, look right), only to realise (and quickly too) that those standards no longer apply. Had I bungled my first attempt, it could have resulted in serious injury or an unscheduled appointment with the Grim Reaper. Crossing the road is performance art, but once I had mastered the skill, I was one step closer to cultural immersion and, more importantly, still alive. The rules of the *Green Cross Code* are doomed to a quick death in Vietnam, but I had no plans to join them.

For many visitors, the simple act of crossing a road in the capital is a daunting experience, as dozens of motorbikes roar past with casual indifference and seemingly little regard for pedestrian wellbeing. You must force yourself to step out and go with the flow, letting traffic pass like water around rocks. If I were to create an alternative *Seven Wonders of the Road*, Hanoi would come in at the top of that list. As an English teacher, I model the skills I want my learners to master, but in Hanoi I switched roles and became the apprentice, carefully watching what the local Hanoians do effortlessly and mimicking them. A hostel I stayed at took the unusual measure of issuing leaflets to guests on arrival with the following road safety advice:

*1. Relax, show confidence.*

*2. Look both ways.*

*3. Make eye contact with drivers.*

*4. Walk slowly with purpose, never pause.*

*5. Never step back!*

With a reported thirty-seven million registered motorbikes and two million registered cars on Vietnam's roads, I wasn't convinced that I would be able to make eye contact with all those motorists, but I was determined to follow one rule to the letter: *Never step back!*

The capital's roads are an absolute menace, but the local cuisine can be a trifle daunting too, especially for animal lovers. If I were to offer a first-time visitor advice, I would tell them to keep their dog on a leash or, better still, leave little Buddy or Bella at home.

## Chapter 3: Bon Appétit! Dog M*eat*?

The consumption of dog meat in Vietnam is less a matter of cultural difference, and more a case of culture shock, much like that memorable banqueting scene in *Indiana Jones and the Temple of Doom*. I can still remember my parents' reactions to the 'silly nonsense' (as they described it) when, as an inquisitive child, I asked them: 'Do people actually eat that?' As the feeding frenzy unfolded with 'snake surprise,' live eels, goat-eye soup and chilled monkey brains, the comedy of the main female character's over-acted reactions suggested my parents might have been right all along. And it was nonsense, as the opening sequence was more far-fetched than any I had ever seen as Indiana Jones, his Chinese sidekick Short Round, and nightclub singer Willie Scott escape from a plane (which is about to crash into the Himalayas) on an inflatable raft. To compound the absurdity, they live and breathe against the longest odds for survival by journeying down a raging river and plunging over steep waterfalls. The director, Steven Spielberg, had, quite literally, suspended my disbelief.

My mother and stepfather had no interest in travel (aside from their local Chinese and Indian restaurants) so never ventured beyond the borders of their town and country. I have since discovered that fiction is a poor substitute for reality. The best way to explode a myth is to travel, but I still found it hard to believe that any man could put the barbequed pieces of a butchered dog to his lips. And then I went to Vietnam. When I travelled the Indian subcontinent, I discovered in Kolkata that child slavery and ritual sacrifice to the goddess Kali are as much a part of the real world as they are the fantasy one, and as the opening song of *Indiana Jones and the Temple of Doom* forewarns: *Anything Goes!*

I have encountered all kinds of exotic 'eats' and 'meats' on my travels around the world and China, naturally, comes to mind when I think about some of the strangest foods. I am fascinated by what other cultures consider 'edible,' and I enjoy shocking friends with some of the vulgar victuals that have passed my lips (usually, I must add, following the consumption of questionable local brews). It's all part of the travel experience. If I wanted to eat roast dinners or fish and chips every day, I would have stayed at home for that. When I travelled to China in 2010, I discovered that the philosophy behind Chinese cuisine is quite simple: *If it moves, it will be eaten*. It seems that having a pulse is a sure-fire route to a flaming wok and the belly of the Red Dragon.

Beijing is a memorable banquet of the exotic, bizarre and all things outlandish. Scorpion kebab? *Got that*. Penis hot pot? *Got that too*. Sheep spinal-cord stew? *Did you need to ask?* Whatever strange you can imagine or combine, *they'll have that too*. If insects were tourists, I would advise them to avoid the streets of Beijing where most bugs find themselves skewered and roasted over charcoal with a touch of char siu sauce. China converts the exotic into the inexplicable, and you can even order a steaming bowl of canine casserole on a bitterly cold day in the capital. For the Chinese man, it's a simple case of substituting 'best friend' with 'best entrée.' Had he visited Beijing, Roald Dahl could have written a gastronomical version of his *Tales of the Unexpected*.

Vietnamese cuisine comes second to Chinese regarding its unusualness, though the manner of its presentation is often inconsiderate of western sensibilities. The mass media is, rightfully or wrongly, accused of desensitising its audiences, but I would argue that travelling in Southeast Asia has much the same effect. One should expect the unexpected in a region where anything is possible, especially when it comes to culinary matters. If I was feeling peckish and wanted to taste cobra, I could take a hearty stroll to Hanoi's Le Mat in Long Bien District, which is the 'Snake Village' (*Snake Cemetery* would be more accurate) where many of the restaurants serve all manner of snake-themed treats. I could stop and ask for a glass of refreshingly warm cobra blood, and watch as the snake is killed, its viscid blood drained into a glass. The daring or disgusting, or daring *and* disgusting, can impress or repel their recoiling partners and friends by gulping down the snake's still-beating heart to claim a badass moment. *Rambo* enthusiasts can kill and drink, and restaurant owners provide step instructions:

*Step 1: Insert a knife under a snake's head.*
*Step 2: Kill it.*
*Step 3: Squeeze its blood into a small glass.*
*Step 4: Scoop the heart out, eat it.*

Tellingly, none of the restaurants included a polite salutation:

*Bon Appétit!*

In many of Le Mat's restaurants, this surprising tipple of choice is accompanied by snake wine, a bottle of rice wine or grain alcohol with a whole snake inserted inside (instead of the customary ship, which is cliché here). It is a rite of passage and must-drink trend for backpackers and western tourists, and its surge in popularity is attributed to *The Beach*. The film features a bar scene with Leonardo DiCaprio's character, a twenty-something backpacker named Richard, downing a series of shots of snake blood. *The Beach* inspired a whole generation of backpackers to head eastwards, and I have met travellers who claimed that very scene encouraged them to travel to Southeast Asia in search of strange adventures (augmented, no doubt, by a glass or two of blood and beating hearts). I guess it presents a persuasive case for the media effects debate; Mary Whitehouse must be turning in her grave.

For the Vietnamese and the Chinese (at least before the tourists arrived), snake blood has special healing powers and is claimed to enhance virility. The locals drink it raw, but holidaymakers prefer a splash of vodka to compensate for its metallic taste. Nothing goes to waste in Vietnam, so while the tourists gulp down their Bloody Marys with scales, the bodies of the dead snakes are gathered up like old belts, taken to the kitchens and turned into all manner of unpalatable unpleasantness, including fried snake backbone, snakeskin salad, and entrails soup. For a deadly nightcap, I was offered a glass of scorpion wine which is the perfect response to the bartender's question: What's your favourite poison? *Strange* is something I got used to seeing, eating and drinking in Southeast Asia, when the oddest dish I consumed in Europe was a plate of raw beef in Budapest.

The first time I visited Bangkok - in the summer of 2006 - I was initially amused when I passed a busy stall at Klong Thom Market selling hundreds of Siamese fighting fish, displayed in the most unlikely of aquarium spaces: recycled Hong Thong whisky bottles. I could understand the need to separate this breed as they are characteristically aggressive (hence their rather literal naming), but I couldn't help but notice that they all looked jaded in their Hong Thong cells. In England, jars of pickled onions and gherkins filled supermarket shelves, but as Southeast Asia has a habit of turning convention on its head, I became accustomed to bottles of pickled scorpions, snakes, and all manner of god-knows-what.

When I visited the Siriraj Medical Museum in Bangkok (nicknamed 'The Museum of Death,' which is a catchier and more accurate title), the ceiling of strangeness and dark tourism was pushed a little higher to break through the rafters. In the first 'exhibition room,' I was greeted by a grisly collection of medical exhibits Hannibal Lecter would have been proud to procure. Nine bottled babies, all preserved and floating in formaldehyde, were presented on pedestals at eye-level with names such as Gastroschisis (its intestines burst out of its stomach) and Cyclopia (a baby with no eyes). In Southeast Asia, *anything* can be bottled, and dead children are fair game.

The Siriraj is a world of glass, horror, and inappropriateness that is devoid of physical and ethical limitations, with collections of pathological, forensic, parasitological and anatomical specimens masquerading as 'science.' But it is fascinating nonetheless. Medical 'experts' have inserted a decapitated head (the victim of a helicopter propeller incident) inside a vacuum-sealed bottle, even going so far as to encase the mummified remains of a serial child killer named Si Quey. Si Quey is a notorious murderer and a modern bogeyman for Thai children; parents tell their children to behave themselves, or else they'll call for Si to visit. That's a useful parenting tip for us all. If it is indeed 'science,' it could be the weirdest form to exist.

For Si Quey, death was a delicacy as he reportedly ate the livers of his victims, but I am not sure if there's any truth to the rumour that he also liked fava beans and a nice Chianti. His corpse is secured in a standing position which allows visitors to gawp and peer straight into his eyes (what remains of them) as they contemplate the physical, moral and metaphysical nature of evil. I would like to believe that's the reaction the doctors hoped for, but I suspect the museum is a freak show surviving the Victorian period. My suspicions were confirmed when excited Thais adjusted their hair and sunglasses to pose for serial-killer selfies. By the look of him, Si wasn't too impressed either and didn't want to have his photo taken as he was having yet another bad hair day. He looks like the livers he ate as his skin is a reddish-brown, but while the liver is a potent superfood, Si Quey is no longer a potent life force.

Like the Chinese, the Vietnamese enjoy the traditional street eat called 'balut,' a fertilised duck embryo which is boiled in its shell and sold as a 'tasty' street snack. Add a pinch of salt, chilli or a splash of vinegar and, hey presto, lunch! It looks as disgusting as it sounds, and if there was ever a case for an acquired taste, it must be balut. Duck embryos were a mouthful too much for me, and the moment my vomit reflex becomes active, instinctively I take that as an early warning system to leave well alone. I do sometimes wonder whether I should petition for the word 'delicacy' to be redefined. Giant water bugs are another popular street grub, but as they closely resemble the common cockroach, I couldn't even touch one, so chewing was entirely out of the question. Without a McDonald's or a Starbucks, I may have died of starvation or dehydration.

On the Thai island of Ko Samet, I ordered a cheeseburger at one of the beachside restaurants, and it came with an unexpected but ghastly garnish. As the waitress plonked the plate on my grimy table (customer service is a foreign concept), I noticed a strangely docile cockroach poking its posterior from the side of the bun. Whether it had overindulged, the food was off, or squashed by a careless cook, it was still alive and had a mouthful of the beef (if that's what it was) that I had paid to eat. When I presented it to the waitress, she shrugged it off and barely registered a reaction, casually motioning that I should pick it out myself and throw it on the sand. Had this happened in a restaurant anywhere else but Southeast Asia, it would have emptied in seconds. I could sense there was no point asking the manager if I could send the dish back, as the waitress would return with the same plate preceded by a quick rearrangement of chips and salad. The concept of food hygiene standards is a lost cause in much of Southeast Asia.

In the Filipino capital, Metropolitan Manila, I spent a day with a slum resident - Remy Cabello - who guided me through one of the most deprived neighbourhoods in the world, visiting slum schools and recycling sites. Tondo, infamous for its Smokey Mountain (a mountain of burning trash, now cleared by the government), has been popularised by Andy Mulligan's *Trash*, which is a fictional and inspiring story about three slum boys hoping for a better future by daring to spring themselves from the capital's poverty traps. Pausing at an improvised food stall, Remy asked me if I would like to try 'pagpag' which, she explained, is a slum 'treat' formed from the leftover foods of fast-food restaurants, scavenged from the city's garbage sites and dumps.

'Pagpag' is a Tagalog term which means 'to shake off,' and it describes the actions of the rubbish pickers who shake the dirt from the food they find so it's 'cleaner' to eat. It is often eaten when and where found, but as a profitable business of the slums, salvaged meat is reformed into patties, refried and resold. When faced with extreme poverty and hunger in a daily fight for survival, Tondo's beggars really can't afford to be choosers. To consume recycled food demonstrates the practical challenges of hunger, and the Philippine Statistics Authority reported in 2014 that 24.9% of the country's population lives in poverty, with unofficial estimates for the capital coming closer to 50%. Even though no one has reportedly died while eating it, and it was refried to kill off any lingering bacteria, I declined the offer of pagpag and vowed never to take supermarkets for granted again.

The backstreets of Hanoi, away from the traditional tourist trails, transform cultural myth into shocking reality in the flash and sizzle of an oiled pan. They might not eat pagpag, but a controversial 'delicacy' (that word again) in the Hanoi area is dog meat (thit cho), which is more popular in northern Vietnam and the poorer regions than it is in the south (I was surprised by the fact that it's popular *anywhere*). I wanted to learn some useful Vietnamese words and phrases, so started the process with 'thit' and 'cho.' The consumption of dog meat in western countries is a taboo, and for some religions, it is considered one of the forbidden meats. Cultural differences are more apparent when it comes to diet and cuisine, and they are explicit on the streets of the northern section of the Old Quarter in Hanoi where whole dogs are smoked and chopped into chewable pieces.

I had a regular habit of getting lost in Hanoi, but one evening I took more wrong turns than usual, much like the victims of that slasher horror film, so it was quite by chance that I stumbled upon what is, effectively, an open-air street market for dog meat. This unexpected unearthing was both ethically disturbing and culturally fascinating, but as a stranger in a strange land, it was not my place to judge the culinary habits of my hosts, so I observed, but declined, the samples of dog that were offered to me as I passed stalls covered in freshly squeezed blood. The vendors formed a gallery of puzzled faces when I motioned with my camera that I would like to take pictures of their roasting mutts and pups, but this was the equivalent of a Vietnamese tourist photographing a turkey roasting on Christmas morning.

As I made my way through this macabre area (resembling what I imagined a zombie apocalypse might look like), I tried to imagine how a dog owner from the West might react to the grim scenes unfolding before me. I seriously doubted whether my friends and family would ever believe me as I described bloody buckets stacked with hounds ready for skinning, evisceration, and splitting. It was a gruesome inversion of the boucheries of France, replacing primal cuts of meat and giant wheels of Comté cheese with bloody platters of dogs' heads and fried and lightly spiced feet. Whenever I ordered at a restaurant popular with the locals, I carefully skimmed and scanned the menu for 'thit' and 'cho,' especially on Nhat Tan Street in Tay Hoo District, where most of the restaurants serve dog in preference to chicken or pork.

In Thailand's capital, it has been estimated that there are more than 100,000 street dogs (called 'soi dogs' locally). The management of these strays has become a serious problem, as they occasionally attack people (quite often sympathetic tourists trying to befriend them) and few are vaccinated against canine diseases. In Vietnam, I was surprised to see only a handful of dogs on the streets of any town or city. Perhaps they have all migrated to Thailand to escape the butchers' knives or have already met their canine maker. In Vietnam, the street dogs have been turned into ghosts.

I must add that Vietnam and China are not alone in their consumption of dog meat, as it's eaten - quite surprisingly - on most continents, with many developed nations having picked up a taste for the pooch, including South Korea and Japan. It is both a food of the poor and desperate and a delicacy of the uber rich and, quite possibly, one of Bangkok's monitor lizards. Vietnam does, however, attract a disproportionate amount of negative international press, so they should put the platters away and focus more on the art of food presentation.

The dogs should beware of the people.

## Chapter 4: Taking the Tourist Trail

Taking the tourist trail in any foreign town or city involves hours of staring at fine-looking public buildings. Buildings can be a fascinating subject and I enjoy admiring their architecture from time to time, but unfamiliar people and their unacquainted habits are more appealing and endearing.

Hanoi's tourism trail has a range of cultural highlights which include the city's traditional and colonial-era architecture. The Old Quarter is the city's cultural core, with a thousand years of history. It used to be known as 'The 36 Streets,' formed initially by a group of workshop villages surrounding the Royal Palace of King Ly Thai. Skilled artisans migrated to work together in guilds, with each street representing a different craft in a cooperative system. The maze of tubular houses is indicative of dense population and limited urban space, and it reminded me of the housing conditions of the Industrial Revolution, in cities such as Manchester and Liverpool. Scattered haphazardly about these thoroughfares are interesting but difficult-to-find heritage homes, where I could get a historical sense of mercantile life in well-preserved buildings.

In Bangkok, I was surrounded by modern steel and glass behemoths, but in Vietnam's capital, tradition and culture have not only survived, they are also prospering with the city's colonial and post-war era infrastructure still in use. Quite unlike progressive Ho Chi Minh City to the south, Hanoi has a rustic and old-world character, so I stepped back in time when I walked the streets of its Old Quarter and observed the local people maintain the traditions of their past. Every time I visited Hanoi, I booked a room in one of the Old Quarter's hostels to be as close to the tradition as possible, and far from the recent construction boom that has overwhelmed the city. It is an exhausting area, a challenge to moods and minds, and I found it impossible to visually map my way around it as I had to keep my focus on passing motorbikes, cyclos and hawkers with shoulder poles carrying local produce.

I enjoyed visiting the Old Quarter for its history, vibrant street life, the diversity of its products and to witness the hectic lives of its residents. The traders maintain well-presented, specialised shops but earthenware and pottery have long been replaced by the usual counterfeit repertoire. Some streets still have traditional wares for sale, such as China bowls on Bat Su, but I bought myself a pair of knockoff Nike trainers. The streets are narrow and crowded, and part of the fun is getting lost down dark alleys and wondering where on earth all the people went. There are many excellent restaurants to be found in this area, and their cuisine is as diverse as the street vendors' products, with an impressive range of traditional Vietnamese and Western options. Whenever my stomach rumbled, I remembered to beware of the dog.

The legacy of French colonisation announces itself from the facades of Parisian-style buildings and boulevards, elegant villas and tree-lined avenues, which signalled my arrival in the French Quarter. My budget couldn't withstand the European prices in this area, but the vibe was laid-back as the wide streets make for a pleasant stroll compared to the tangled streets of the labyrinthine Old Quarter. The Opera House is one of the distinct architectural highlights (with grey slate tiles shipped in from France), but I have been to France, and I have seen Paris, so my legs returned me to the Old Quarter where the heart and soul of the city resides.

A couple of days are enough to complete Hanoi's tourism highlights, which include the resplendent and iconic Red Bridge to the Ngoc Son Temple. I had already seen its printed form a dozen times, as it is a popular city symbol. A picture of the bridge adorned the cover of my travel guide which, I suspected, had been heavily photoshopped as the sky was a perfect, cloudless blue which was something I had not seen hanging over Hanoi on three separate visits. Hoan Kiem Lake is a favourite scenic and picnic spot that surrounds the temple, and it serves as a focal point for Hanoi's public life. The West Lake is the city's secondary watery escape and boasts the prepossessing Tran Quoc Pagoda, a Buddhist temple located on a small island near its south-easterly shore.

Walking around Hanoi is fatiguing and the humidity, exacerbated by the pollution, is a severe test for even the most intrepid of explorers. When it dawned on me that I was close to collapse as my head was pounding, my throat was sore, and my feet had turned into cumbersome blocks, I flagged down a taxi and made a strategic retreat to the relative comfort of my hostel. I would die another day. The climate of Southeast Asia can be defeating, and sometimes there is no alternative other than to raise your hands and surrender to it. I should have packed a white flag with my socks and antimalarial medication.

Returning to the theme of dark tourism, the Ho Chi Minh Mausoleum is a popular attraction for foreign visitors and can be found in the centre of Ba Dinh Square. It is an ugly, imposing marble building that would look more at home in Cold War Russia which is appropriate, given that the Vietnamese government regularly transports Ho Chi Minh's corpse to Moscow - first class of course - for embalming services and maintenance. Ho Chi's dead body has taken more first-class flights than I ever will. The mausoleum looks like a public toilet, replete with concrete cubicles, but it is the very spot where Ho

Chi Minh, former Chairman of the Communist Party, declared Vietnam's independence in September 1945.

I resisted the opportunity to go inside and view his body, but I was clearly in a small minority as a lengthy queue of strangely fervent tourists trundled past in the opposite direction. I made the same decision in Moscow (Lenin) and Beijing (Mao), but this is a matter of personal choice. I would rather see a masterpiece in painting or sculpture at the Vietnam Fine Arts Museum than a propped-up-on-ice corpse. I like to partake in dark tourism adventures, but I will never understand the appeal of deceased politicians. I don't even like the ones that are living. For a revered national hero, there is something quite distasteful about Ho Chi Minh's continued service to Vietnam as a tourist attraction, as he was very specific about being cremated upon his death. Seeing those butchered dogs was enough unpleasantness for one weekend, but I had stumbled upon that grim scene by chance.

Instead, I took a short walk to Ho Chi Minh's modest wooden house next to the opulent Presidential Palace, where I explored his private chambers and learnt about his role in Vietnam's history. Ho Chi held an impressive record of military success, leading the Vietnamese nationalist movement for more than three decades against the Japanese, the French colonial powers and finally, the US-backed South Vietnamese Army. The red of the national flag symbolises the bloodshed of revolutionary struggles, with the five-pointed gold star representing the five main classes in Vietnamese society (soldiers, peasants, workers, traders, and intellectuals) upon which the foundations of socialism are built. I combined this visit with a short walk to the Ho Chi Minh Museum, where I discovered more facts and insights into Vietnam's wars against persistent foreign invaders. Ho Chi Minh deserves to have a city named after him, of that I am in no doubt, but I am sure a simple cremation would have done him just fine.

I found my way to other sites of interest such as St Joseph's Cathedral, the excellent Vietnam Military History Museum, the One Pillar Pagoda, the Taoist Quan Thanh Temple and the Confucius Temple of Literature. There was barely any tourist information at any of these sites, but there was always a busload of tourists. The infamous 'Hanoi Hilton' is a former prison used first by the French colonists for political prisoners, and later by the North Vietnamese Army for captives of the Vietnam War. Its official name is Hoa Lo Prison, and its most famous 'guest' was a US Senator, John McCain, who was captured when his helicopter was shot down over Hanoi. With so much to see and do in both quarters, and with the weather and pollution formidable and persistent foes, I managed to see all of Hanoi's points of interest spread over three separate stopovers.

Hanoi introduced me to Vietnamese coffee. Whether hot or iced, it is distinct in its use of condensed milk and has a thick and creamy texture. It is served with a filter and a small coffee pot, and you can buy these containers at most local and tourist markets (a practical souvenir too, as I continue to make the coffee when I am at home). I have made thousands of ordinary cups of instant coffee in my lifetime, but travel always seems to find a way of introducing new ways of doing the very things you take for granted, like the everyday act of crossing a road. As I fumbled with the lid and filter like a virgin with a bra on date night, a waitress approached, sympathetically, and asked:

'You need help?'

While she demonstrated, nonchalantly, how the contraption worked, I remembered Bill Bryson's introduction to *The Best American Travel Writing 2000* in which he captures this unique aspect of world travel:

> *To my mind, the greatest reward and luxury of travel is to be able to experience everyday things as if for the first time, to be in a position in which almost nothing is so familiar it is taken for granted.*

Eating with a fork and spoon is the cultural norm in Thailand, so having lived there for two years, I wondered why I ever used a knife in the first place as spoons are far more practical (if you've ever tried to eat soup with a knife, you'll know what I mean). When travelling in Southeast Asia, I discovered that it is the smaller and unexpected details that leave a lasting impression. I may not be able to recall what the Opera House looks like unless I Google it or look at my photographs, but I can distinctly remember that sweet taste of Vietnamese coffee like a liquid first love.

When my lungs needed a break from Hanoi, I made my way eastwards to Halong Bay or westwards to Sapa Province. Both are incredible destinations, but with Hanoi equidistant between the two, it's a choice between rugged mountains on the mainland or karst formations in the bay. Getting to Halong Bay is the easier option to organise as the tour providers do all the hard work, collecting tourists from their hotels or hostels and driving them to coastal Haiphong, which is Vietnam's third largest city. Haiphong is northern Vietnam's most important seaport with its deep-water anchorage and extensive maritime facilities, but it is also one of the country's ugliest cities. It does, at the very least, provide contrast to the offshore splendour of Halong Bay and that, perhaps, is the point. For Sapa, travellers must rely on their wits by taking one of the overnight trains to Lao Cai Province, and public bus to the Hoang Lien Son Mountains by the Chinese border.

Hanoi, I discovered for myself, is so much more than a transit city.

## Chapter 5: Tropical-Siberian Express

The mountainous Sapa District in Lao Cai Province was the high point of my travels in Vietnam. I try to get out of Southeast Asia's major cities as often as I possibly can, as they are all guilty of trying to emulate the great metropolises of the West, or those closer to home in East Asia such as Taipei, Shanghai, Seoul, and Tokyo. They are often so eager to develop and modernise, they discard and destroy centuries of heritage like sand castles and, essentially, what made them unique for visitors in the first place. Boey Kim Cheng's *The Planners* is a poetic lamentation about Singapore and the cultural cost of progress, but I would apply its sentiments to every major city in this region. To get to the heart of any country in Indochina or maritime Southeast Asia, you must leave the comforts of their major cities behind. Departing Hanoi for Sapa was like listening to the radio and hearing an unexpected change of a record, with the rasping sounds of a rock vocalist replaced by the soothing tones of a soul singer.

My research quickly revealed that Lao Cai Province doesn't have an airport, and that was the first indication that I was heading in the right direction. If a destination is too easy to get to, its cultural authenticity has probably been trampled into dust. There is also a reduced sense of adventure or reward in boarding a convenient modern flight, so I was pleased to learn that the only way to reach Sapa is through a combination of trains and public buses from Hanoi. Sapa doesn't even have a bus or train station. In *Planes, Trains and Automobiles*, Steve Martin's character - Neal Page - battles the elements as he attempts to get home for Thanksgiving in Chicago. He is forced to do it the hard way, but the outcome is more satisfying for it. To earn your travel stripes and backpack patches in a foreign country, especially in Southeast Asia, travel like a local.

Sapa's fresh mountain air promised the perfect remedy for Hanoi's pollution, so I was initially glad to board that overnight train to Lao Cai. I protected my diminishing budget, prudently saving a night's accommodation expenses as the train departed Hanoi's Railway Station - Ga Ha Noi - at nine o'clock sharp. The service I booked was 'scheduled' to take just under ten hours, and I was advised to book ahead as the demand for tickets is consistently high. I was warned by my hostel receptionist (she was also the cook and cleaner) to be vigilant at the train station, as dishonest loitering locals have, purportedly, tricked tourists by asking them to present their tickets, only to disappear with them in hand and cheekily take their seats. Are some travellers that gullible? If they are, they should never be allowed to leave their home nations.

At the top of my ticket, I noticed three words written in English: 'Tourist,' 'Sleeper' and 'Train.' They had the intended effect, I am sure, of reassurance, but they also carried connotations of cosiness and perhaps even the luxuries of clean, flushing toilets and a carriage dedicated to gourmet dining. There was no harm to be had in hoping that I was about to board the Vietnamese equivalent of The Orient Express, but when I arrived at the tracks, I really couldn't distinguish one dusty-red carriage from another. While observing other passengers as they stepped, unconcerned, over live tracks, my eyes narrow focused on heavy-looking backpacks. They were tourists, of that I was sure, and they were all boarding the same train. I concluded that tourists, plus a train, must surely equate to a 'Tourist Train.' The only item awaiting discovery was the promise of 'sleeping,' but it was still too early in the evening to worry about that small matter and a potential misnomer.

As I climbed aboard the rusted and foreboding steps to my Orient Distress, as it turned out, it immediately dawned on me that I had fallen afoul of yet another tourist trap as the stale and pungent smell of ammonia greeted me on the corridor like an odious, unwelcoming conductor. I held my breath with Olympic stamina and made my way along a narrow corridor with greasy nicotine-yellow panelled walls. Oversized backpacks fought for space and bumped against my forehead as I searched for the reserved cabin compartment that would be my place of 'rest' for one night (and hopefully not the final type). When I eventually found it, I understood that 'reserved' doesn't necessarily mean 'private' as it had four identically spotted, grubby sleeper berths and my thoughts wandered off to consider (and fear) who my bedfellows for the night might be.

I hadn't slept on a bunk bed for nearly thirty years, so I couldn't resist that childhood reflex to climb immediately onto the top berth. I placed some personal items (deodorant and toilet paper) on a small ledge behind the pillow and settled down to eat my dinner, which consisted of a packet of out-of-date Oreo biscuits and a box of cheese and chive Pringle crisps. I was having flashbacks of the summer I travelled the vast Indian Railways Network, and I hoped the journey would be kinder to both my dignity and sanity. I learnt some hard transport lessons in India where I was forced to use water (and just water) to 'wipe' my backside on a rocking train, presenting a hand-eye coordination challenge on a mission impossible scale, as unfussy mosquitoes buzzed about my nether regions in search of their next free meal. That's why I now carry toilet tissue with me *everywhere* I travel in Southeast Asia.

Once bitten, twice shy.

I have also learnt from experience and travel's hard knocks to ignore all those guidebook clichés about idyllic train vistas, and I was right to do so: it was a bumpy ride and all I could see out the window was pitch blackness. Sapa is, however, rich reward for somnolent travellers and the perfect escape from Vietnam's major cities, so I imagined forgiveness would come quickly. Fortune was again my friend as I shared the cabin with an amiable couple from Birmingham, England. I was privately delighted that I wouldn't have to spend the duration of the journey sleeping with one eye open, praying for the Sandman to sprinkle some magic dust in my eyes. Instead, we whittled away the hours sharing tales of travel woe and joy (as travellers do), while devouring tubes of cracked Pringle crisps - the one product you are guaranteed to find *everywhere* in Southeast Asia, but always cracked.

Despite the valiant efforts of my new cabin friends to conceal them from me (I had already shared my entomophobia), a cockroach scampered across the cabin's ceiling, inches from my nose, to foreshadow a sleepless night. I had taken another 'Sleeper Train' that failed to live up to its namesake. As the motion of the train had a somewhat soporific effect on us all (but the opposite influence on the toilets), drowsiness entered the cabin to take its place on the fourth bunk as we settled heads on discoloured pillows. The train driver was not the only person on board guaranteed not to sleep, and he was determined to break all land-speed records. As the train bounced off the rails and shook from side to side like a cocktail mixer on methamphetamines, visions of derailment entered my mind while the presence of cabin cockroaches continued the nightmare.

Full of hope but with little expectation of sleep, I found myself recalling the story a traveller told me about the near-arctic conditions of a sleeper train she had taken from Mandalay to Bagan. I could relate to her experience as the cabin's air conditioning unit was fixed to the ceiling instead of a wall, and just like that bothersome cockroach, it was only a few inches from my face. The temperature was controlled centrally by the driver, who evidently wanted to broaden our experiences by demonstrating to his passengers - with as much precision as he could muster - what it is like to travel on the Trans-Siberian Express. We all made perfect impressions of cold meat storage when we arrived at Lao Cai Station in the early morning hours, and I finally understood the conundrum of all those scratchy blankets.

Partially thawed and half frozen to death, I connected by public bus from Lao Cai to Sapa Town. It is a forty-minute journey up and through the mountains and it presents a fabulous introduction to Sapa Valley. It was a struggle to stay awake, but the incredible rice terrace vistas were the early morning double espresso I needed. The north-west environs of Vietnam are living, cultural landscapes of unparalleled beauty that have been handed down from one generation to the next. I didn't expect the driver to share my silent wonderment, or pull over for a quick photo stop, as their goal is more rudimentary: to get their passengers to Sapa Town for the highest fee they can convince them to pay, and as quickly as possible.

I parted with some Vietnamese dong and reclined on a sticky seat (putting all thoughts of what had caused that stickiness to the back of my mind) to enjoy a snaking, rickety ride into the mountains. A group of enthusiastic backpackers, meanwhile, light-heartedly debated whether the Vietnamese ever have a destination in mind as they seem to spend their days scooting about on ramshackle motorcycles.

I smiled and considered the question, but I didn't have an answer.

## Chapter 6: Trekking in Sapa Valley

Having watched a nature documentary in ultra-high definition through the widescreen windows of a public bus, I arrived at the frontier town of Sapa. The engine chugged to a stop to take a deserved break (before the wheels fell off), and my first thought was to query why my guidebook had used the word 'frontier' to describe Sapa Town.

As weary passengers said their farewells to bring the briefest of friendships to an end, my eyes were drawn to bobbing backpacks that seemed to be fleeing a persistent entourage of hill tribe women selling handmade but unwanted handicrafts. It was like watching an episode of *The Benny Hill Show* without the canned laughter. Stepping out of the van, I was besieged by Hmong women and met with a chorus of enquiries: 'What is your name?' 'Where you from, Mr?' 'You buy something from me?' It is probably just as well that I try to resist my first impressions on arrival, as I could have been greeted by crowned mermaids or golden arches advertising the latest extra value meal.

Vietnam is home to fifty-four different racial-ethnic groups, with the most colourful represented on the glossy pages of travel guides and souvenir postcards. Once nomadic, the diverse ethnicities of Sapa District remain culturally independent of Vietnam and live together peacefully in the mountains of this region. As the principal market town in the area, Sapa is home to several ethnic minority groups including Hmong (the dominant group), Dao, Giay, Pho Lu and Tay. It is a small town with a population of forty thousand people, and while it floats like a cloud in the mountains, its traditions are holding on for dear life.

For decades, tourism has drawn the valley villagers into Sapa Town in ever-increasing numbers as selling handicrafts is a profitable and less toilsome industry than working the land. The provincial government has great difficulty persuading parents to keep their children in school, as they're often sent in fearsome packs to hunt and gather foreigners. Prominent signs advise tourists not to purchase souvenirs from children, but they are hard to resist as they are *everywhere* (and persistent to the point of bullying). This situation is, of course, a marriage of convenience as one of Sapa's primary attractions is the opportunity to get close to - and photograph - these ethnic groups, with costumes distinguished by tribal patterns and striking colours. I always aim to be a polite, respectful photographer, asking my subjects for their permission before I photograph them; some travellers assume it is their right because they bought a ticket, shoving large lenses into strangers' faces as if they are shooting a different species altogether.

Sapa Town has a reputation for the hard sell, and I fell victim to this when my patience was pushed to its absolute limit. Having spotted an elderly Hmong lady selling traditional ethnic fabrics - a colourful backdrop to her already distinctive face - I pointed to my camera and motioned to her that I wanted to take her picture. She replied with a smile and a friendly nod of the head, and I wondered whether I should receive a nomination for the international award for cross-cultural communication. I took a hurried photograph as I didn't want to overstay my welcome and besides, I don't think too many people enjoy having strangers take pictures of them. Si Quey was standing dead still in his box back in Bangkok, and he didn't seem to like it very much either.

Before my brain could signal for my feet to move, my portrait subject stopped me in my tracks with a bold and direct statement:

'And now you must buy.'

I had, incorrectly, assumed she had no English whatsoever, so I was initially bamboozled by five clearly enunciated words and a monosyllabic phrase that had an almost hypnotic effect. My composure recovered, I politely declined and inched away while thanking her for a second time with all the awkward courtesy of an Englishman abroad. Like a magician's trick, her teeth disappeared, and her smile became a frown as she started to pack up a makeshift stall with some haste. That direct marketing approach had evidently worked on others, but I wasn't susceptible to Jedi mind tricks. I had a budget to protect.

Scurrying away and around the nearest corner I could find, I retreated to an appealing French restaurant named Le Gecko, feeling quite pleased with myself and my latest great escape. But it was a victory short-lived. It was cool enough to dine on the open terrace so I opted for a table with a street view, so I could indulge in a spot of people watching while waiting for my food. 'People watching' is the second hobby I acquired in Southeast Asia (when I wasn't killing cockroaches), and there is no better place to indulge this interest (even Shakespeare would have struggled to imagine some of the colourful characters I have witnessed walking - or crawling - along the streets of this region). I ordered a local beer, a glass of fruit juice (for effect), steamed spring rolls and sweet potato fries, but before my food arrived at my table, along came an entrée I neither ordered nor expected: Darth Hmong, with an arsenal of handicrafts.

Having tracked me down like a stealthy apex predator, Darth Hmong was not going to give up so easily on a sale. She set up her stall again - next to my table - and insisted on showing me every item she possessed as I chewed and swallowed. It was one of the most awkward scenes I can recall in a restaurant (and I've had quite a few of those), but I remained resilient and let my body language communicate the force of my indifference. When she couldn't bully me into a sale or embarrass me into submission, she took her quest to find a gullible fool elsewhere, cursing me as she did so.

I had to leave the town and its tourist-tormentors behind me to find the alluring charm of this district and discover the picturesqueness of its landscapes. Sapa District appeals to international travellers because it is one of those treasured bastions of cultural authenticity in Southeast Asia; a landscape where you can connect with local people through food and shared experiences. In Cat Cat Village, Ta Phin Village, and Ta Van Village, I could mix with different ethnic groups and experience first-hand the traditional lifestyles of the hill tribe people. Trekking opportunities are nonpareil in Sapa, and the valleys are an open invitation that's impossible to resist. Away from the tourist hot spots and Sapa Town especially, the people are friendly, welcoming and still curious about their foreign guests.

Trekking my way across the valleys of Sapa, I independently explored the villages dotted along the Muong Hoa River. I made the effort to see the indigenous people in their traditional communities, finding reward in a backdrop of magnificent rice terraces that dress the impressive mountains. It was the Sapa I had hoped to see, and it fully justified that bumpy-cold night on the Trans-Siberian Express. I was invited into strangers' homes and offered traditional food and drink, and I was touched by the unexpected generosity of families with so little to share while I, by contrast, had so much. A Hmong lady pointed to the crest on my Manchester United football shirt with a puzzled expression, and I realised, in that very moment, that I had succeeded in finding a place both remote and isolated.

Some of the hill tribe villagers had limited English, but they were eager to learn key phrases and pose for photographs in return. It was the perfect cultural exchange. They helped me navigate some difficult terrain, which included a bamboo forest when I tried to locate a hidden waterfall (whoever had hidden it would be a useful companion on an Easter egg hunt). The experience was travel and comedy gold, as it provided endless amusement for the tribal mothers as they watched me struggle to climb muddy banks, while they casually carried babies strapped to their backs.

Sapa District is a looked-for and celebrated location in Vietnam as nature has been more than generous, bestowing upon it an abundance of breathtaking scenery. Vietnam's highest mountain, Fansipan, keeps a watchful eye on proceedings below where over-development is the only threat to culture and tradition. Some travellers I met in Hanoi and Ho Chi Minh City surprised me, as they had skipped Sapa altogether due its out-of-the-way location. Vietnam has vibrant cities to the north and south, white-sand beaches along its eastern fringe and the world-renowned tourism icon of Halong Bay to the northeast, but Lao Cai Province offers the traveller a unique opportunity to meet and mix with ethnic minorities and observe their traditional way of life, culture, and religion, as well as sample some of their local dishes (each ethnic group has its speciality, such as sour noodle soup). American author, James Michener, succinctly captures what a visit to the Sapa Valley should not be: 'If you reject the food, ignore the customs, fear the religion and avoid the people, you might better stay home.'

The Sapa valleys reminded me of the Tegalalang rice terraces in Indonesia, in the village of the same name on the island of Bali. There are three terraced landscapes in the central Ubud region, but Tegalalang is visually striking as its undulating slopes reach upwards to caress the clouds and downwards to dip their toes in tranquil river valleys. With Asia being one of the world's essential rice bowls, it naturally has its fair share of rice terraces carved into the land by an artistic giant or the very hand of God. They are, understandably, a huge global draw for travellers and landscape photographers as they present striking patterns in implausible settings.

Terraced agriculture is not exclusive to Southeast Asia, as the Incas of South America used this farming method to adapt their agriculture to the mountainous landscapes of Peru. China is famous for its Longsheng rice terrace in Guangxi Province and Nepal for its terraces on the lower Himalayas. The natural wealth of rice terraces in Southeast Asia is the commonly used image to represent the landscape of this region. The Banaue terraces in the Philippine Cordilleras are, undoubtedly, the farmlands of choice for most travellers, and I visited these myself in 2014. Their deserved listing as a UNESCO World Heritage Site in 1995 confirmed their special status, which is even more impressive when you consider that they were carved into the mountains of Ifugao on Luzon Island some two thousand years ago, using primitive tools. They are living, cultural landscapes that demonstrate ancient man's engineering prowess, craftsmanship, and creativity. Filipinos refer to them as the 'Eighth Wonder of the World' for a good reason, as they form stairways to heaven and showcase a blueprint for a sustainable relationship with the environment.

Only the rice terraces of Sapa can rival Banaue's prestige, as they look magnificent when set against the imperious Hoang Lien Son mountain range near the Chinese border. Bali has such a diversity of attractions and distractions, the wonders of Tegalalang tend to get lost in the cultural ether and, more literally, the dense tropical valleys of Tegalalang Village. The terraces, and the villagers who depend on them for survival, are the perfect examples of a traditional Balinese settlement with much of the indigenous people working in the rice fields to this day. They are a critical agricultural resource, and they utilise the traditional 'subak' method of water management which was developed and passed down - per local legend - in the eighth century by a revered holy man named Rsi Markandeya.

There are many natural viewing platforms from which to view the emerald splendours of Tegalalang, whose terraces sparkle as the sun reflects off irrigated water. The panoramic views are remarkable and dramatic, and the village ancestors' reworking of the natural landscape presents an award-winning slideshow. One of the village elders, topless and carrying a woven basket on her head, casually passed by and in that fleeting moment, I caught an unexpected glimpse of the ancestry and surviving lineage of the terraces.

Sapa District is the face of Vietnam the government is rightly proud to present to the outside world. Sapa Town is a former hill station established by the French in 1922, and its location is romantic for being remote, but tourism is booming rather loudly these days, and there is no doubt that it has been 'discovered.' The town should not be dismissed out of hand as it has a few highlights of its own, such as modern Quang Truong Square with its vibrant markets and the delightful Holy Rosary Church, which is illuminated at night by alternating colours.

Ham Rong Mountain, which is adjacent to the town and opposite Fansipan, offers superb views of the valleys, and the climb is relatively easy by hiking standards (footpaths lead to the summit). I walked through beautifully landscaped sculpture gardens and made my way up several hundred steps to find a viewing platform hidden behind geological formations. The more daring and adventurous climb Fansipan, but after all that exhausting trekking, climbing, some failed attempts at communication and a battle with a Sith Lord, the chilled comfort of a bottle of Lao Cai Beer and the relaxed walkways of Sapa Lake restored my equilibrium.

And I didn't even mention THAT war.

## Chapter 7: Follow the Ho Chi Minh Trail

It was inevitable that my travels would lead me, like a yellow brick road, to Vietnam's Demilitarized Zone (DMZ). A tour of the north, south or central regions is likely to brush against the Vietnam War; it would be like trying to cross a field barefoot in spring and not touching grass. The rusted remnants of combat are inescapable, with tanks and military aircraft positioned outside government buildings, including the Presidential Palace in Ho Chi Minh City. The scars of the past might be fading, but no other country can claim to have been so readily defined by war. Dedicated museums make it their business to present 'the other side' of the Vietnam story, and my understanding of the Vietnam War shifted from the American war films of my youth to a sobering Vietnamese version that offered balance to the many misconceptions I brought into the country with me.

The superb Vietnam Military History Museum in Hanoi covers the republic's past conflicts and presents a national perspective through impressive collections of photographs and model displays, with the main exhibition building housing the most-visited collections. It is dedicated to the war with the US and details the clever tactics of the Viet Cong, with presentations of original Vietnamese uniforms, homemade firearms, bamboo spikes and other innovations improvised by soldiers who were ill-equipped to take on the military strength of their better-supplied opponents. The pièce de résistance is an extensive collection of preserved military wreckage, which includes a Soviet-built Mig-21 jet fighter, the wreckage of French aircraft and a US F-11 Tiger. An arsenal of tanks and B-52 bombers complete the set, and there's a great view of it all from the top of the Hanoi Flag Tower.

Ho Chi Minh City's War Remnants Museum is unrestrained in its coverage of the brutality of the Vietnam War. It once carried the forthright and provocative name 'Museum of Chinese and American War Crimes,' but it has since bowed to international pressures to adopt a more politically neutral title (no doubt aided by the threat of trade and economic sanctions). The museum is a brilliant but harrowing portrayal of the conflict, and it is very popular with western tourists, Americans especially. A visibly distressed woman - inside the Agent Orange Exhibition - needed cheering up so I approached her, hoping my T-shirt would do the work for me. Purchased at a Hanoi street market, it had a split-framed portrait of George Bush and a close-up of a woman's pubic hair, with the slogan: *Good Bush, Bad Bush.* She noticed the T-shirt and smiled, before surprising me with an admission I did not expect.

She was an American tourist on her first trip to Southeast Asia, and she was deeply upset by her country's actions as the shocking exhibits confirmed her worst fears. Everything she learnt in Vietnam's museums (and it's hard to argue with supersized photographs) conflicted with her parents and high school teachers' accounts of the war. I wondered what kind of school she had attended and whether she had ever heard of a concept called 'propaganda.' In her defence, though, Westerners rarely learn about the atrocities the US soldiers committed in Vietnam so many of the photographs carry a heightened sense of horror on first viewing. They are compelling evidence of America's 'burn all, destroy all, kill all' policy, supported by casual accounts of disembowelments and beheadings. A framed quotation from Curtis Lemay, former Commander of the Strategic Air Command, presents his November 1965 'proposal' for a solution to the conflict: '...tell them (the North Vietnamese) frankly that they've got to draw in their horns or we're going to bomb them back into the Stone Age.'

Some depictions of America's war in Vietnam have taken on iconic proportions, especially those taken at the infamous My Lai Massacre or photos of children consumed by the ravaging flames of US bombing. The photograph that defined the war, the image of a nine-year-old girl named Phan Thi Kim Phuc (taken in 1972 and referred to as 'the girl in the picture'), went on to win the coveted Pulitzer Prize. Kim Phuc was severely wounded by napalm and was caught on camera - by Vietnamese photojournalist Nick Ut - running naked from her village in Trang Bang District, where a misplaced air strike had detonated above it. A disturbing image, few are prepared for pictures of US soldiers posing with the decapitated heads of their enemies, or laughing at the charred remains of Viet Cong soldiers scorched by incendiary devices. Politicians can make eloquent speeches full of carefully crafted rhetoric, but a single picture will always paint a thousand words.

Hanoi and Ho Chi Minh City's dedicated museums of war are well organised, informative and present an impressive collection of mangled wreckage. Visiting the Demilitarized Zone, the tunnels of Cu Chi and Vinh Moc brought me closer to an appreciation of the unabating resistance the US forces encountered, and to an understanding of the character of their woefully underestimated foe. That bamboo comparison was becoming more relevant by the day. Vietnam is not alone in having a designated Demilitarized Zone, but unlike the DMZ that separates North from South Korea, Vietnam's DMZ (or 17th Parallel) now functions as a famous historical and touristic zone. The irony, of course, is that any such area instantly becomes obverse to what it proclaims to be, as Vietnam's DMZ was one of the most militarised areas in the world. It is a scar that stretches from the Cambodian border in the west, all the way to Vietnam's eastern shores where the impressive Vinh Moc Tunnels are located (though they are often overlooked for Cu Chi).

Vietnam's provisional military demarcation line was established by the Geneva Accords in 1954 and stretches along the banks of the Ben Hai River. In 1967, *Time* magazine referred to the DMZ area as 'a running sore,' but the wounds of war have mostly healed in present-day Vietnam. I could walk across the Hien Luong Bridge unhindered into what was once North Vietnamese territory, from the South Vietnamese side. It was an unusual and slightly unnerving experience, as this once heavily fortified area basked in the quiet peace of a summer's day in a country reunified and at peace. But the legacy of suffering endures decades later, as unexploded ordnance claims the lives of the innocent. Cambodia's landmine troubles continue to attract international headlines, but little is ever said or done about Vietnam's present situation. Princess Diana's anti-landmine campaigns focused the world's attention on Africa in the 1990s, but some of Southeast Asia's beleaguered countries suffer in silence in these post-conflict settings.

The years 1955 to 1975 marked a period of intense hostilities after the First Indochinese War ended (or the 'Anti-French War' as the Vietnamese call it). The DMZ resumed its military function and became the staging area of the Second Indochinese War. In a Cold War era, America was compelled to neutralise the 'threat' of communism with its potential to expand all over Southeast Asia. Worldwide audiences played the role of distant voyeurs, as families watched the drama of each bloody episode unfold on television screens. The films followed like sequels and put many of the real-life battle sites on the world map, including Hamburger Hill, Khe Sanh, The Rock Pile and Quang Tri Province. Tour providers deliver their eager troops to these sites in a single day (although that can be a little rushed), but the caveat is realistic expectations. The war was a traumatic experience for the Vietnamese, despite their victory in the north, so every effort has been made to remove painful reminders; land that was laid to waste by chemicals is reforested and flourishing.

DMZ tours are an opportunity for veterans to reconnect with their past and for history and military enthusiasts to get beyond dry textbooks, but without the context a knowledgeable guide can provide, visitors will find themselves staring at rubble and open fields and wondering why they skipped their complimentary hotel breakfast. There are numerous tour operators in the cities of the central regions, but it is always sensible to do a little research first, so I matched a tour itinerary to my personal interests. The DMZ area is vast and has an abundance of significant war-related locations to visit and a few of milder interest, such as the graveyards of Viet Cong soldiers. I chose the private guide option because larger tour groups can be infuriating, with each nationality determined to keep to their time zone. The tour guides habitually warn their groups that if anyone is late, they will not wait, but they always do. I have been tempted to tip the driver to pull away and let the latecomers be damned.

I booked a tour with a seventy-one-year-old war veteran who fought for the South Vietnamese Army. He had all the croaky credentials which included original war documents and identification papers, and he provided insightful context on all the locations we visited, his words filling the blanks of my imagination. I did some late-night research on the DMZ area using Google Images to find old war photographs, and could appreciate what this area looked like before the grip of war took hold, and once the tanks had finally rolled away (the ones that could). There is little remaining *physically* within the DMZ, so I made the decision to pack some imagination with my camera, toilet paper and bottles of water, knowing all those American war films would play out in my mind as I moved from one historic site to the next. Some locations have an impressive array of war remnants (the Khe Sanh Marine Base especially), and my guide advised me not to fall asleep or else I would miss some DMZ-strange along the highways, such as an abandoned US tank sitting by the roadside since 1975.

The first stop on my tour was the infamous Highway of Horror (also known as National Highway Number One) which was a scene of carnage, tragedy, and convenient propaganda. Civilians were shelled alongside soldiers when they fled southwards from the North Vietnamese Army (NVA) and took the route of the highway, as the Truong Phuoc and Ben Da bridges had been bombed extensively and thus collapsed. The driver pulled over to stop briefly at a memorial to the victims and Dung, my guide, shared some facts and dramatic pauses before we continued north to the Ho Chi Minh Trail. He must have noticed the barely concealed smirk on my face, as he went off-topic to explain that his name means 'courageous' in Vietnamese, before quipping that he wasn't 'full of shit.' He had a sense of humour, and I liked him, which was just as well, as we would be spending two whole days together.

One of the more interesting but lesser-known stops on a tour of the DMZ is the heavily bombed Long Hung Church (a Catholic church) in Hai Phu Village, Quang Tri Province. It was shelled continuously for eighty-one days as it was the regional headquarters of the Viet Cong (VC) and a strategic position for protecting the town. The VC soldiers naively believed the Americans wouldn't dare bomb it, but they did. To ruin. Many tour itineraries feature a stop off at this church which now stands incongruously at the roadside of a modern town. As a symbol of national heroism and endurance, Long Hung Church is a protected but charred monument full of bullet holes and shrapnel. By contrast, the area of Hamburger Hill found international fame once the film of the same name was released in 1987, portraying the tumultuous battle of May 1969 during which hundreds of NVA soldiers and dozens of US soldiers lost their lives. I could follow a trail that leads up the hill as Dung organised a permit for me (in return for a generous tip), and reaching the top of the hamburger, I was left alone with my imagination to eye my way across the landscape to the border with Laos.

Both sides suffered greater losses at the Khe Sanh Marine Base where limited imaginations have support from muted tanks and abandoned American aircraft. Reconstructed US bunkers are eerily quiet, and portions of the airstrip are still visible (there is a small museum with historical pictures and the original US and NVA weapons). The base is notorious for a seventy-five day NVA siege that resulted in the loss of five hundred US soldiers and a staggering ten thousand NVA. It is a powerful symbol of the calamity of war, and it marked a political turning point in Vietnam. As America's faltering hopes turned to desperation (they faced unrelenting NVA attacks as committed as Japan's kamikaze pilots), they responded with force by dropping 100,000 tonnes of explosives on the region to complete the clusterfuck. A famous photograph of the war features the black humour of an anonymous Marine, with a message penned on the back of his combat jacket: 'Caution: Being a Marine in Khe Sanh may be hazardous to your health.'

In terms of spirited resilience, the Vietnamese were a force to be reckoned with and, more significantly, they succeeded in doing what others had failed to do: they duped the US troops and commanders and out-thought them strategically. The primary aim of those unremitting NVA attacks was to provide a tactical smokescreen, as NVA commanders wanted to distract and draw away US forces from important South Vietnamese urban areas, before launching their TET Offensive. The NVA soldiers made enormous sacrifices to achieve their country's ideological goals, and I am sure Abraham Lincoln paid quiet tribute from his grave.

Some tours include the Vinh Moc Tunnels which are a symbol of defiance and testimony to the local people's heroism. They are easier to explore than the more famous Cu Chi Tunnels to the south which, in comparison, are minuscule in their height and width and a tight squeeze for an average-sized westerner. The Vinh Moc Tunnels are a fascinating rabbit warren where - incredibly - ninety of the local Vinh Linh families defied the odds and common sense to survive below ground, despite the constant bombing overhead. It was blatantly obvious that the US forces had discerned they were hiding there, but they refused to retreat to safer grounds, preferring to relocate their village below the dust, shrapnel, and soft clay to live like moles in a subterranean world for years.

There is probably no better proof of the bamboo-like resilience and endurance of the Vietnamese people than Vinh Moc. They prospered against the odds as seventeen babies were born in the tunnel network, with one of the twelve exits leading directly onto a glorious beach facing the South China Sea. With no crowds, vendors or parasols, it wasn't a bad place to hide out. Above ground, I noticed some of the crawl passages the villagers used to retreat to safety when the sirens sounded and warned of incoming US bombing raids. Incredibly, it has been estimated that seven tonnes of bombs - per village inhabitant - dropped on this area which, no doubt, kept the gears of the US munitions factories turning.

The Vietnamese were adept at digging tunnels and establishing underground communities, and Vinh Moc is the largest complex of its kind in the whole DMZ area. The tunnels, which have been maintained in their original condition since the day the Vinh Linh families relinquished them, are built over three levels. Modern alterations include some necessary lights to guide tourists through damp, convoluted passageways. The dense clay they are carved from hardened on contact with air, so the tunnel network provided shelter from continuous bombardments. It is hard to imagine undertaking a project like this today, and yet the villagers often used their hands as simple digging tools.

In total, there is more than a mile of tunnels to explore with the deepest set at twenty-three metres. Further exploration of the compound revealed a seated hall, family quarters, wells, kitchens and clinics (even a maternity wing) as no detail went unnoticed (they even fashioned a ventilation system). There was no chance whatsoever that such dauntless people were ever going to give up their independence without a fight; they were a strong and unbreakable community and much like bamboo, they could survive in bad soil.

To complete my understanding of the conflict, I planned a visit to Cu Chi's famous tunnel networks near Ho Chi Minh City. Needing a break from all that war and ruin, I took to the nearby beaches of Quang Tri Province for some light relief, a cold beer, and to reflect on the absurdity of such a location and the madness of war.

And then I went to the ultimate non sequitur at Cu Chi, which marries tourism with farcicality and tragedy.

## Chapter 8: Get the Phuc Outta Here

I had been looking forward to visiting the legendary tunnels of Cu Chi for some time. Having read an excellent book with a title as long as the passageways it describes (*The Tunnels of Cu Chi: A Harrowing Account of America's Tunnel Rats in the Underground Battlefields of Vietnam*), I hoped Cu Chi would provide the final puzzle piece in my understanding of the Vietnam War.

Following the Fall of Saigon in 1975, the Vietnamese government recognised the symbolic significance of Cu Chi and its inherent tourism potential, so launched preservation campaigns to protect what is one of the most extraordinary battlegrounds in military history. Tourists can relive its horrible history by crawling through the 'original' tunnels in designated safe areas. Some sections collapsed into ruin and decay, others have been widened and reinforced to allow western tourists to access them, but without that foresight, none of this would have been possible as heavy monsoon rains would have washed history away.

The extensive underground networks of Cu Chi differ from the tunnels of Vinh Moc because Cu Chi's primary purpose was military and strategic: the tunnels enabled the communist VC to sidestep the advanced technology of the US war machine. Crucially, they allowed VC forces to take the tactics of guerrilla warfare to the Americans in a terrain that was not only unfamiliar, but it was also tipped to favour America's tunnel foes. The VC adapted their methods to survive, taking their cause below the surface as they were all too visible and vulnerable aboveground in what was a throwback to the trenches of World War One. Having ascertained that US success depended heavily on aerial bombing campaigns, it was a shrewd move. US soldiers were neither trained nor prepared for face-to-face guerrilla combat, so the superior technology they relied on to win previous wars was neutralised by the VC. Resourcefulness, ingenuity, and physical courage were the winning weapons of this war.

The tunnels of Cu Chi enabled the freedom fighters to facilitate strategic control of a large rural area eighteen miles from Ho Chi Minh City. The VC had a head start, establishing the tunnels in the 1940s during Vietnam's successful war of independence from the French colonialists. They returned to their tunnels and extended them over a combined distance of 155 miles, from the outskirts of Saigon to the Cambodian border. It was an incredible achievement that relied on peasant farmers to use their bare hands and fingernails to reshape the landscape. Repeating a past success and learning from experience, Cu Chi was a stubborn splinter. The network was so important to the VC cause, an estimated 45,000 Vietnamese men and women sacrificed their lives to defend it. They were an advantage they would not surrender, and peasant cunning prevailed.

The VC used their tunnel networks to launch deadly surprise attacks, only to disappear out of sight in the flash of a grenade. They provided shelter for soldiers who could transfer locations undetected, care for their wounded and transport supplies and munitions. The local people, who farmed the lands of this region, joined the VC in the tunnels to form underground villages like those in the north at Vinh Moc. As a base for combat operations, the VC could plan and launch devastating attacks on Saigon and return to hide in their secret tunnels, hoping to entice the US soldiers into jungle battlegrounds. With American frustration mounting, operations Crimp and Cedar Falls were launched as counterattacks, and both were unsuccessful. In their growing desperation, powerful herbicides were dropped on the area but still the VC endured.

The VC were innovative too, protecting their tunnels while destroying their enemy by setting creative booby traps to lie in wait for the unsuspecting, using only makeshift resources. US soldiers were reminded not to leave behind anything the Vietnamese could utilise, which included their ration cans. The specially trained US and South Vietnamese soldiers were tasked to locate these booby traps and scout for the presence of enemy combatants and were, consequently, nicknamed 'the tunnel rats.' The first-person accounts in *The Tunnels of Cu Chi* detail the conditions the tunnel rat survivors encountered, and they are a frightening read as they reveal the collaborative horrors of claustrophobia, deadly booby traps and silent enemies waiting in the dark. Oliver Stone's *Platoon* features horrific scenes of US booby trap victims, and he was applauded for the realism of his portrayal, the director having served as an infantry soldier during the war.

Getting to Cu Chi is straightforward enough from Ho Chi Minh City, as District One's Pham Ngu Lao Street is the epicentre of the city's tourism industry and is brimming with bars, restaurants, souvenir shops and tour operators (providing work for Vietnamese veterans). My guide to the tunnels was named Phuc, and he was quick to explain that his name means 'blessings' and 'luck.' As he recounted exaggerated tales of his heroism, I concurred that his survival was a mixture of blessings and luck but with a liberal sprinkling of falsehoods. The frequent mispronunciations of his name were far from being fortuitous, and he reminded me of crass Mr Chow from *The Hangover* films.

Phuc's name was, appropriately, the four-letter manifestation of his inappropriateness. Having shared this to break the ice with his tour group, he detailed his personal history through loud speakers while the bus crawled indifferently through slow-roasted traffic. Phuc explained how he fought as a proud patriot alongside his VC brothers, and he seemed to take great delight when informing his latest captives (those who hadn't already nodded off to sleep or closed their eyes to suppress his presence) that he had killed several US Marines. His attitude, decades later, showed little sign of remorse as he expressed thinly veiled anti-American sentiments throughout the Cu Chi tour. His grating, amplified voice detailed the conditions and suffering of the VC and its sympathisers, before he asked the open-eyed to imagine what they would do if a foreign invader landed on their shores: 'Would you defend your home and family at all costs?'

Phuc was loud and ridiculous and spent most of the tour making inappropriate comments about Americans, so we all felt rather *blessed* when we eventually escaped his verbal clutches, and he was indeed *lucky* not to have been mobbed by his tour group, which included American tourists.

When I organised my trip, I was advised to book with a company that goes directly to the tunnels in the early morning as the larger tour groups tend to visit the Cao Dai Temple first (to coincide with the midday service) and Cu Chi in the afternoon. I use a simple equation to determine how to get to places of popular interest: the cheaper the rate, the larger the tour bus. I was unable to organise a private tour, so I booked with an agency that advertised *Small groups, BIG experience*. The fee was suspiciously reasonable, so I asked the model of apathy tapping on the counter how many people would be sharing the ride. 'Dozen, just dozen,' he rep*lied*. Reassured by his repetition, I paid the fee and claimed my tour voucher, but his was a dirty dozen or at least a baker's dozen to the multiple of ten. As the bus stuttered to a stop, at least one hundred sad and perspiring faces peered out at me like a scene from a liberated concentration camp. With little choice, I boarded a greasy, thermally insulated chamber to contribute unpleasant aromas.

The journey lasted two torturously long hours with obligatory stops at roadside cafes and a Handicapped Handicrafts workshop and factory. I didn't mind visiting the latter as it's a genuine cause, providing employment for Vietnamese men and women born with physical and mental handicaps due to their parents' exposure to Agent Orange. Their products are crafted with care, reasonably priced, and there's no attempt at a hard sell. I was also relieved that it allowed me the opportunity to stretch cramped legs, answer the call of nature and dry myself out, but the delays continued like the slow reveal of a Hitchcock classic. And the moment we arrived at Cu Chi, so did the rain.

Before entry to the tunnels, I first had to sit through an 'information' film which was careful to focus the viewer on how many 'enemy' Americans the VC successfully killed or maimed during the 'American War.' It provided some context for Cu Chi, and the crackling old war footage helped to bring the tunnels to life, but as we all gathered around that flickering screen, we shared an unvoiced thought: we had come to see tunnels, not poorly made documentary propaganda.

Phuc showed the group some of the original tunnel entrances before guiding us to the ones we would be entering and exploring, the tunnels widened, as he so politely explained, for 'fat American asses.' To enter and navigate the shadowy tunnels of Cu Chi was an unsettling experience, and as I crouched and crawled in airless tropical heat, the feeling of claustrophobia was exacerbated by the dankest of conditions. Making awkward progress, I raised my eyes and noticed a rather plump lady in front of me (she was making even slower advances) and narrowly avoided being turned into a human chimney sweep. The further along I crept (into the tunnel, not the plump lady), the more I was convinced that I could hear voices from below as knee joints screamed for space. I could barely move forwards, and it was the same in reverse.

I feared Plump Lady would get stuck like an oversized letter in a pneumatic mail system, so I crossed my fingers as she created a total eclipse I would have preferred not to have witnessed. I was glad Phuc wasn't down there with us, for her sake. How the Vietnamese endured for so long in conditions such as these is baffling, and that bamboo metaphor came to mind once more as rivulets of sweat dripped from my brows and stung my eyes.

Exploring the tunnels only takes a few minutes as the conditions are overwhelming, both physically and psychologically. Perhaps that accounts for why there is a shooting range so close to the main tunnel entrances, where Rambo hotheads can busy themselves shooting AK-47s into sandbags. Despite the distastefulness of its opportunism, the *bratatat* of those assault rifles was a suitably discordant soundscape for the Cu Chi tunnel experience. If this heightened realism wasn't already enough, a sudden deluge forced a hasty retreat into the tunnels where we cowered for cover and re-lived history in an instant. When the rain eased, the sun resumed its duties, and the humidity forced us all above ground to rub backs as we complained about kinks and cramps. Tourists are less bamboo and more brittlebush plant.

Phuc enjoyed showing his captive audience the replicas of the traps the VC set for unsuspecting US soldiers, which included concealed bamboo spikes coated in excrement. For those with little imagination or bloodthirsty leanings, there are colourful paintings of US soldiers - spiked and bloodied - with mouths wide open in pain, covered in the brightest hue of blood-red the artist could find. The style of the paintings and Phuc's animated manner conveyed a sense of dark pleasure in the suffering and brutality of the past. Our guide's gallows humour was the blackest shade, and he asked us if we wanted to have a go on the booby traps ourselves, before wisecracking: 'The VC made ladyboys of US Marines!'

Phuc continued the 'tour' and his chain-smoking habit by taking us to see a US tank that had been successfully targeted and destroyed by the VC ('Destroyed by a delay mine in 1970' was painted on its rotating gun turret). He was quick to point out that its tank crew had also been *taken out*, and he showed us some lazy reconstructions of VC kitchens and munitions factories, complete with creepy-looking animatronic soldiers. He concluded his insightful analysis by declaring that the NVA won the war simply because: 'The Vietnamese know better than you how to shit!' By mastering the technique of the squat toilet, he claimed the NVA troops could crouch behind bushes for prolonged periods, before launching surprise and deadly attacks of their own on passing US soldiers. Toilet habits, it seems, can win wars just as effectively as strategic cunning and the technology of modern warfare.

As we were readying ourselves to return to the dreaded bus, it seemed the final joke was always destined to be on us: Phuc informed us that the tunnels we explored were *reconstructions* of the famous Cu Chi tunnels, not the originals. The disappointment of the group was palpable and showed itself involuntarily as lips pursed, eyes contracted and brows furrowed. The decrescendo played out its final clumsy notes.

Cu Chi is one of those places where you should 'see it to believe it' and putting my disappointment aside, this former frontline of the Vietnam War did at least bring all that context in the War Remnants Museum to animated life. I tend to spend my travel days chasing culture, history, unusual experiences and dark tourism as beach life is all too sedentary for my liking. At most historical sites (and the 'darker' ones especially), visitors intrinsically know how to behave, often getting lost in the silence of their thoughts. Places such as Auschwitz. At Cu Chi, there wasn't much reverence on display for the fallen as selfie sticks fought for space and dominance in cramped tunnels, like some bizarre modernist re-enactment. Our guide had, of course, set the tone and my time at Cu Chi felt like a day trip to a military fairground for adults where the tunnels were the rides. The words 'Cu' and 'Chi' should be substituted with 'tourist' and 'trap,' but the tunnels are, nonetheless, worth visiting.

With reconstructed tunnels, shooting ranges and souvenir shops, Cu Chi has undoubtedly become another trap on Southeast Asia's tourism trail. It is the original jungle location of the conflict, and there is no escaping that fact as bomb craters scar the land like acne pockmarks. I left with mixed feelings. I was pleased that I had visited the vastly superior Vinh Moc tunnels first, as they are a far more authentic experience with original shafts and passageways and modest tourist numbers, but Cu Chi should be more than what it presently is and less about amassing dollars and dong.

It was time to get the Phuc out of there.

## Chapter 9: Dining with Culture Vultures

Central Vietnam is the crown that holds Vietnam's finest heritage jewels, which include Hoi An Old Town and Hue Imperial City. The region appeals to travellers of the seasoned and wrinkled variety foremost, as sophisticated travel cases come with weatherproofing technology and hold an absolute majority over backpacks; a place where serene temples and art galleries take precedence over beer-bar neon and white-sand beaches. Life moves at a snail's pace in unhurried Central Vietnam. The DMZ and My Son complete the tourist set and, quite conveniently, form a cultural cluster like the type of bomb the US dropped all over this area.

Hue is the preferred base from which to explore the military history of the DMZ and from Hoi An, I visited the ancient jungle ruins of My Son. How travellers journey to this region will depend on a preference for comfort or discomposure (airlines, boats, buses, trains, taxis and motorcycles ply the route). Hiring a motorbike and taking to the palm-fringed highways holds a romantic and free-spirited appeal, but it is an urge I resisted like a bungee jump without the rope. Southeast Asia's roads laugh in the face of *The Highway Code*, and there's no such thing as lane discipline; the drivers may as well wear blindfolds. Vietnam's motorists are made from bamboo, don't forget, so they are quite casual about personal safety. I have witnessed whole families atop a single motorbike, precariously balancing groceries, babies, pets and grandma. If they were to perform such a scene on the streets of Montreal, they'd be booked to appear in the next Cirque du Soleil tour. Some daredevils challenge the laws of physics altogether, strapping ridiculous loads to their seats while hovering over half an inch of leather. Like a scene from *Mad Max*, Southeast Asia is a vehicular Wild West.

I have listened to the countless tales of easy expat riders as they excitedly shared their near-death experiences and biking mishaps, proudly showcasing their scars like a club tattoo. The wise tend to hide their stupidity and resist impulsivity, but in Southeast Asia, they are more likely to embrace and flaunt it. It never ceases to amaze me how first-time visitors, having never ridden a motorbike in the country of their birth, take to the roads of this region like extras from *Sons of Anarchy*. The catalyst for such an endemic failure of common sense is accessibility: you can hire a motorbike quickly and easily like buying a carton of milk at a 7-Eleven (and without proof of identification or a valid licence). The only 'licence' that seems to matter is the one printed on greasy bank notes.

Riding home late one evening from downtown Phnom Penh, a friend fell afoul of Southeast Asia's roads when his bike was clipped by a passing lorry, and he took a hard knock and fall. The driver didn't stop, perhaps not noticing the accident 'his' carelessness had caused. Rendered unconscious, he lay by the kerb like bloated roadkill. Unlike many of Cambodia's indigenous riders, he took the sensible precaution of wearing a helmet and that decision saved his life. When he regained consciousness, the sharp pain in his left leg indicated it would take longer to recover, having taken the brunt of the fall and suffering multiple fractures. Upon arrival at a local makeshift hospital, the doctor presented him with a choice he never imagined having to consider. To amputate, or not to amputate? *That was the question.*

Several surgeries later (including some clumsy efforts by Cambodian and Thai doctors), my merry mate was back on his feet with a world of pain, recovery and medical bills behind him. He will always carry a reminder of that incident, as he now walks with an unsteady gait and a pronounced limp. When I joined him for drinks one evening in Bangkok, I listened politely to stories of excess like a series of cautionary tales. As I quietly contemplated the motivation for his gung-ho antics and the inanity of his boozy existence, he admitted what I suspected all along: he had been drinking in a Phnom Penh bar the night of his 'accident.' After years of trying, he finally had a story to tell and a few X-rays to share, but more importantly, he had that club pass permitting full membership to the *Sons of Stupidity.*

With the fatigue of months of travel hanging over me, I flew in the face of my principles: I booked a budget flight with Vietnam Airways and took to the clouds, closed the window shutter and pretended to sleep. Having visited the diverse land and seascapes of Northern Vietnam, I chose Hoi An as my first central springboard, and with so many positive reviews shared by fellow travellers, I was more than ready to dine with the culture vultures.

In Hanoi, I met a retired New Zealander who couldn't stop talking about Hoi An, Hoi An, Hoi An. As she extolled its many virtues, describing it as a mythical city for pensioned hippies, she reminded me of the rambunctious Margaret 'Molly' Brown, socialite and survivor of the RMS Titanic. As the assembled ears gathered around her words at the bar, clutching cold cans like loved ones, we listened intently to tales of a golden age of travel. I admired Liz's commitment to the travel cause - she was inspiring. Her body had aged without her consent, and she was approaching her seventh decade, but her mind was still that twenty-something explorer full of the joys of discovery. She was a first-generation backpacker, one of the children of the flowers and the embodiment of the phrase 'young at heart.' Her finger and toenails were a rainbow of colours, and she maintained the traditions of her past by wearing a thin yellow ribbon tied at the back of her head. I wondered whether Liz owned a pair of shoes as her heels were black as coal.

Liz made the decision to settle in Hoi An and commit her final years to charitable works. With every word she uttered another superlative ringing in my ears, I had all the endorsement and invitation required. Liz shared her Hoi An address, broke the travellers' circle and retired to bed, insisting that we were welcome to visit her (though not at the same time) if we ever found ourselves in Hoi An. She offered a hobbit's welcome but wanted to avoid a company of dwarves. I lost her details by carelessly scribbling them down on the back of a wet beer mat, and in the process discovered that unlike travellers, ink and stale beer do not mix well. I was yearning for ancient history, culture and a slower pace after Hanoi, and having skipped both Hoi An and Hue on my first trip to Vietnam (when I explored the north and south), they were top of my must-see destinations in the central region. I hoped Liz was still enjoying her retirement, and I imagined her surrounded by enthralled backpackers as she regaled them with the same tales she shared in Hanoi.

Hoi An Old Town (also known as 'The Lantern City') is a small settlement in the central coastal region of Quang Nam Province. Historic, delightful, graceful and atmospheric, it is a timeless version of Vietnam and a stunning representation of all the ancient beauty of this intriguing and captivating country; it is also an exceptionally well-preserved example of a South-east Asian trading port, dating from the fifteenth to the nineteenth century. Its buildings and street plan reflect both the indigenous and foreign influences that have combined to produce a beautiful UNESCO World Heritage town. Hoi An is small enough to navigate on foot, and its clashing architectural styles were a joy to behold as I strolled and clicked and soaked up the Euro-Asian ambience. When I returned to Bangkok, I debated with a friend which city in Southeast Asia holds the greatest charm for European visitors; we agreed that Hoi An should come second only to Luang Prabang in The Lao People's Democratic Republic.

With Hoi An possessing so many cultural treasures secreted away down narrow lanes and zigzagging alleys, I was confronted by a mammoth task - complete with tusks - when I returned to Bangkok to edit my notes and photographs. It may be an anagram of the capital city, but Hoi An doesn't share its clutter and pollution. The cheerful blue of its sky is occasionally interrupted by discourteous, floating cotton balls and streets are pleasantly pedestrianised, but after four days of sauntering around the town on a tourist loop, I was trapped in a chapter of Edgar Rice Burroughs' *The Land That Time Forgot*. Hoi An is lovely, but it is a sedated kind of loveliness (without, of course, those dinosaurs and prehistoric creatures). That first impression impressed, but I found myself itching to get away (though that sensation was probably the result of hostel bed sheets). My grandmother maintained a fine-looking garden full of favourite flowers, but I never felt the urge to stand in it for days and admire it like she did.

My Hoi An highlight was the small but elegantly emblematic Japanese Covered Bridge, which was built over a stream by the Japanese (no surprise there) to connect their community with Chinese neighbours. Despite coming under heavy siege by day and night as tourist hordes jostle for space and position, their selfie sticks perpetually poised and at the ready, the bridge has an old-world charm that is strong enough to hold the focus of even the ficklest of cultural admirers. When day becomes night, the bridge is irradiated by the glow of changing colours which reflect in the water to lure tourists as cameras flash like fireflies.

The Old Town has charming heritage homes (including the Tan Ky Old House) and beautiful temples, such as Quan Cong, and while they are all worth visiting, there comes the point when enough is *enough*. I enjoy admiring both modern and ancient architecture, but the experience is passive. That's why I prefer travelling in countries such as South Africa where I can pull over at the side of the road to cage dive with crocodiles, or race against a friend on the back of an ostrich. I had already decided to be selective with my sightseeing in Hoi An, so rather than trying to see everything, I visited a handful of Chinese temples with beautifully decorative details such as inner-courtyard door paintings, or historical rooftop scenes. I bought a tourist pass upon entry to the Old Town, discovering that it was valid, generously, for ten days. There was no chance that I would be lingering longer than the four nights pre-booked; I was fearful that time would forget me in the land of Hoi An.

Tourist passes permit access to the Old Town and six of its twenty-one visitor attractions. Ticking and crossing attractions from a list of sites on a card, I had been tricked into entering an outdoor bingo hall where all the prizes are cultural, and the jackpot is the exit. My ticket explained, in shattered English, that the proceeds are reinvested in the Old Town and help to finance renovations, general upkeep, and tourist facilities while supporting the families who open their antique homes to the public. The admission fee covers a range of street 'entertainment' (folk dancing, singing and traditional games), but I would have gladly paid ten times the value of the ticket price to remove that kind of touristic nonsense from Hoi An's streets. They should use a portion of the funds to hire a reliable translator and reprint the tickets.

Despite that initial wow factor, I couldn't shake off the feeling that Hoi An is an over-sanitised version of Southeast Asia, carefully sculpted like a museum piece for middle class and ageing tourists. There was little in the way of surprise or adventure to be found on its streets, but I vowed to keep the glass half full (with red wine, not snake blood) and try to appreciate its gentler charms. I preferred Hoi An at night when lantern lights reflected off the Thu Bon River as tourists and locals strolled arm-in-arm, intoxicated by their drinks and partners as the town's charm, soothing tranquillity, and meditative pace did their work. The word 'picturesque' is applied much too liberally for my liking but was, evidently, coined for places such as this.

The best way to enjoy Hoi An is to walk its streets unguided, ticketless and without a tourist map in hand. Passing scores of restaurants along the river which presented the same menu, I wandered into art and handicraft shops selling the same overpriced textiles, pottery and lacquerware. It was like watching a repeat pan from an episode of *The Flintstones* when the characters are animated to move, but the background is a static repeat. Promenading along riverside pathways on my penultimate evening, I bumped into the couple with whom I shared a sleeper cabin on the journey from Hanoi to Sapa. We were following the same tourist trail, and we arranged to meet up for dinner and drinks before I departed for Hue. Hoi An might be one of Southeast Asia's most attractive towns, but it proved Robert Browning was right: *less* of something is sometimes *more*.

Hue is another favourite stop on the central region's heritage trail, but it pales in comparison to Hoi An's vibrant strokes. It is the capital city of Thua Thien Hue Province, and between the years 1802 and 1945, it was the imperial capital of the Nguyen Dynasty. At least that's what my guidebook told me as it detailed, quite unnecessarily, a family's rise to prominence and the succession of its rulers. Having purchased a small library's worth of voluminous travel guides, I have noticed that their publishers are guilty of padding out the contents with chapters on flora and fauna, arts and crafts and sport and leisure. My guidebook for South Korea has a whole section dedicated to the culture of business and is filled with jargon suited to an economics textbook. As I had never heard of the Nguyen Dynasty before, they couldn't have been *that prominent*, and I suspected my fellow travellers had not heard of them either, as we formed lengthy queues in the midday sun to enter their temples and tombs.

Had my time been limited, I would have chosen Hoi An over Hue. Hue has a handful of moderately interesting cultural attractions, and two days were more than enough to visit these and sail the Perfume River. It is a convenient base from which to visit the DMZ, and that was the primary purpose of my stay. Tourists marvel at the Thien Mu Pagoda, dawdle along the streets of the Forbidden Purple City and walk among the tombs of the Nguyen emperors, but as I had already spent several days visiting Beijing's vast and impressive Forbidden City in 2010, I was naively expecting more of the same here. The Forbidden Purple City, a UNESCO World Heritage listing, suffered more than most from the US bombing raids. It is a rather sorry-looking mixture or ruin and restoration, and with most of its inner structures flattened, my expectations were similarly crushed.

Hue gained notoriety during the Vietnam War when it was captured by the North Vietnamese Army (during the TET offensive) and held out for nearly a month. The US forces bombed it into pre-history as they attempted to recapture the city (with its important strategic placing in Central Vietnam), and an estimated 80% of historical Hue was lost. The irony and absurdity of war dictated that the US forces had to destroy the town to save it from the enemy, and with it went centuries of history. Despite the tragedy of such a cultural and ancient loss, it is hard to forgive the lazy restoration efforts of the city's modern tourism board.

Hue was full of disappointments, run-of-the-mill experiences, and misleading headlines. The river was polluted with sewage and chemicals and did not smell of feminine fragrance at all; the Forbidden Purple City was neither purple nor forbidden, and it wasn't much of a city either. There are ongoing renovation and rebuilding projects, but there is no sense of urgency as the tourists keep on coming, regardless of its state. By Vietnamese standards, the entrance fee is expensive, and with barely any of the original architecture surviving and even less helpful information, I saw it for what it is: a money-grab. Perhaps they should redirect their efforts to reconstruct a title worthier of its current, dilapidated state. The 'Overpriced and Empty City' is a far more accurate representation of this 'attraction.'

I was in and out of the Forbidden Purple City in twenty minutes, my jaw aching from incessant yawning. I tried to salvage the day with a boat trip on the Perfume River, and as I passed 'floating restaurants' (which were not floating at all), the lights of the Phu Xuan Bridge cast their reflections like fishing nets while small boats stirred the contamination to life. I visited pagodas and the tombs of the Nguyen emperors, which were a pleasant enough distraction from the aggressively modern, commercial centre of Hue.

When I sat down to my last supper at La Carambole restaurant in the tourist area of Le Loi Street, I asked the waitress if they sourced their fish locally before placing an order. I was feeling restless, my batteries drained by all that half-hearted traipsing over temple grounds and imperial tombs. With my Vietnamese dong depleted and my wallet getting thinner by the day (having sustained relentless attacks from Hue's inflated prices), it was time to move on, and Halong Bay offered the perfect escape from cantilevered, concrete monstrosities.

## Chapter 10: Bay of the Descending Dragon

I was tempted by glossy guidebook images of Halong Bay (which doesn't need airbrushing) and the unfathomable beauties of this distinct coastal region in the Gulf of Tonkin, before I embarked on a seascape escape. A worthy UNESCO World Heritage site, its Vietnamese name translates to 'where the dragon descends into the sea' as karst formations form a still image of the mythical spine of the dragon, which protrudes ominously from the bay's waters. It was the Jade Emperor of Chinese mythology who sent the dragon to protect Vietnam from Gulf invaders, and the dragon duly obliged and descended, spraying a thousand pearls from its mouth from which emerged a protective karst fortress. Halong Bay is one of Vietnam's most-visited tourist attractions, and like Sapa, it is the perfect getaway from the main cities.

The Halong Bay experience is all about the boating and sailing, so I booked myself aboard an Indochina Junk, designed in the style of an ancient Chinese sailing ship, and set sail. I switched off my mobile phone and zipped it away in an invisible compartment at the bottom of my rucksack, with the bay warranting total disconnection as it is the ideal divertissement from modern life. Some tour providers offer day cruises, but I wanted to explore the floating fishing villages of Cua Van, Ba Hang, Cong Tau and Vung Vieng, hidden in an archipelago made up of 1,969 islands and islets.

The Giant's Causeway (in Northern Ireland) was underwhelming when I separated truth from local legend - that an Irish giant named Finn McCool built a causeway across the Sea of Moyle to challenge a Scottish rival. I explored the site for thirty minutes, admired its polygonal columns of layered basalt, and returned to the bus wondering why it deserved UNESCO World Heritage status. Halong Bay would have been the perfect crossing for those mythical giants, and I could have sailed the bay's papaya-green waters and explored its rocky outcrops for months on end. I have not experienced that sense of escape and serenity since the boat returned me to port at Haiphong.

I shared my Halong experience with a cosmopolitan crew of travellers from across the globe and every moment was memorable, from boarding to departure. Our host's nickname was Happy, and he did everything he could, with the support of his staff, to ensure we were exactly that. He was the living, breathing antonym of Phuc. You can sense when a tour guide has had one day too many in the field but Happy - despite having sailed the bay with hundreds of tour groups - behaved with all the fresh enthusiasm of his first expedition. There are a growing number of competing operators with varying price tags, but I put reputation before cost, knowing that 'health and safety' is a concept loosely applied in Southeast Asia, where currency matters usually matter first. I was pleased with my choice, as Indochina Junk's standards of service are among the very best I have experienced in this region (they have a small fleet with contemporary cabins and modern safety facilities).

There is a history of tragic incident attached to Halong Bay, which shouldn't be discounted, with the more superstitious pointing the finger of blame at the dragon. Tourist boats capsized in 2002 and 2006, claiming the lives of both local crew members and international visitors, and another submerged like a coffin in 2009, taking five tourists with it. As recently as 2011, twelve more drowned while they slept in below-deck cabins, but there are greater efforts by the tourism authorities to check weather conditions and improve safety standards. There are times for penny-pinching, but this was a time for due diligence. The price for peace of mind may be steeper, but at least I got to wake up and see the next day, with May to September the region's unsettled period as these months are interrupted by frequent tropical storms.

One of the highlights of my trip was the dining-of-a-lifetime opportunity to have a candlelit dinner in a cave shared by stalactites that hung like nature's chandeliers. I had spent the day kayaking and swimming, visiting a floating village and relaxing on the sundeck, but this was the singular experience I looked forward to most. The kayaking almost brought on a hernia and heart attack as I partnered a sloth who could only fumble with the paddles, leaving all the hard work to me as I battled the bay's strong currents. The cave wasn't easy to access, but an apron of creamy sand on one side of the island allowed a foothold without getting soaking wet. Happy led the way by torchlight, whistling an unfamiliar tune like the Pied Piper of Halong, as we followed and stumbled over boulders and rocks to a cave entrance we would never have found on our own.

The opening was small but passable, and candlelight guided us to a long table with intricate decorations carved from exotic fruits, which included a sculpted dragon. Our feast was a banquet of traditional Vietnamese dishes, which had been superbly prepared and tastefully presented. The pho bo (a beef and rice noodle soup) was the best I have ever tasted, and my tongue somersaulted to the flavours of fresh ginger, radish, fish sauce, cloves, and cinnamon. Bay cuisine embodies the Taoist philosophy of balance and harmony, with grilled scallops served with helpings of dragon fruit. Happy sang a few songs as conversation waned like the moon, surprising us with the power of his tenor voice. With my eyes closed, I imagined the spirit of Luciano Pavarotti had joined us in the dark recesses of that cave.

I enjoyed getting to know my fellow passengers and learning about their varied lives and experiences. We dined heartily and shared course-after-course of exotic treats from the sea, briefly returning to a golden age of piracy. Our group was sociable, so the rum and conversation flowed freely until stuttering sobriety retired us to our private cabin quarters. As the boat made its gentle and leisurely way, its bow kissed the still waters below, fearful of awakening the bay's mythical dragon as huge green dragonflies hovered and darted in the dark.

Halong Bay is a unique seascape dotted with primaeval islands; it looks like a child's fantasy world filled with magic, adventure, and awe-inspiring vistas and it could pass as a still image from James Cameron's Pandora in the fictional, alien world of *Avatar*. It is one of those destinations that inspires people to travel across the globe enduring long, uncomfortable flights while wearing the mile-high fashion faux pas of flight socks. To get away from touristic channels, I booked a tour option permitting access to Bai Tu Long Bay with its pristine natural landscapes and unexplored islands. I enjoyed visiting the floating fishing village of Vung Vieng, learning about the traditions and aquacultural life of the fishermen and the fine arts of sailing and casting fishing nets. Stopping to watch fisherwomen carefully prepare pearls at oyster farms (used for jewellery, cosmetics, and medicine), I wondered whether I had set foot in the Vietnamese version of the British sitcom *The Good Life*.

The paradox of the poor has always fascinated me, as the humblest people in Southeast Asia are some of the happiest I have ever encountered on my travels. It is a continental paradigm. Social scientists have researched 'happiness statistics' by comparing developed and undeveloped nations, generally concluding that people living in poorer countries find happiness beyond material goods and attain greater moral satisfaction from the meaningful bonds that hold their families and communities together. As the girl with a pearl earring caressed farmed pearls with a cloth, her face was a portrait of contentment as gentle waves lapped against the stilts of floating houses while bedraggled children played about her feet. I hadn't used my phone or IPad for three whole days, and I was happier for it.

Southeast Asia has a rich diversity of extraordinary landscapes but the topography of Bohol, an island in the Central Visayas region of the Philippines, defies geological common sense. I travelled by boat across the Cebu Strait to view the spectacle of the Chocolate Hills near Carmen. They are a unique, natural wonder with the horizon presenting 1,268 grassy hillocks formed of limestone, shale, and sandstone in an area that was once covered by the Mindanao Sea. Their confectionary-inspired title comes from their appearance during the summer months, when conical summits turn brown, while legend claims they were formed by two quarrelsome giants who threw boulders at each other for days on end, before succumbing to exhaustion (leaving their mess behind for nature to tidy away).

The physiography of mainland Southeast Asia, with its string of archipelagos, is an incredible sight to behold. With five million square miles of mountains, plains and plateaus, river valleys, deltas and shallow seas, the region effortlessly captures the hearts and minds of its visitors.

I wondered how long it would take for my return to Halong.

## Chapter 11: Ninh Binh Province

I almost didn't make it to the Hoa Lu District in Ninh Binh Province. Having hit the snooze function on my alarm clock at least a dozen times (before switching it off altogether), the sound of a flushing toilet alerted me to the presence of a stranger in my bathroom. With neurotransmitters jump-started, I managed to prop myself up on one elbow as a female form emerged from the shadows wearing a white gown, latex gloves, and a stern countenance. Startled and confused, I tried to recall whether the check-in welcome had mentioned complimentary prostate checks. As awkward as a joke about death and dying at a funeral, Latex Lady made enough apologies to restore world peace while repeatedly bowing her head like a bobblehead toy. I was very much *disturbed*, despite the claims on that sign hanging outside my door.

My motivation for visiting this region came to the power of three: Tam Coc, the Perfume Pagoda and the ancient capital of Hoa Lu. Tam Coc Bich Dong is a tourist destination near the city of Ninh Binh in northern Vietnam, popular with backpackers as a budget version of Halong Bay. The French film *Indochine* put the region on the international travel map, and numerous coach companies ply the route from the capital. Tam Coc ('Three Caves') was the more remarkable of the three sites as it allowed me to get closer to nature when I was paddled down the Ngo Dong River in a sampan rowing boat, admiring karstic formations and limestone caves sweeping up from serene fields of deep-water rice. Tam Coc is a landlocked miniature of Halong Bay and the languorous ride down the river, to the tune of water slapping against the sides of the boat, was another one of those cherished travel episodes played on memory repeat back home.

Arriving at the point of embarkation at Pier Van Lam was, however, entirely forgettable. It was also immediately apparent just how sought after this natural attraction has become. I joined a small group of backpackers in Hanoi for a ride to this district, with the romantic notion that I would find peace and solitude in the company of nature like Wordsworth, Byron, and Blake before me. And then I saw the buses. Dozens of them. And behind the buses, souvenir stalls stretched all the way to Shanghai and beyond to eternity. Every stallholder sold the same 'traditional' handicrafts, but closer inspection revealed that they were all *Made in China*.

As humidity wrapped its arms around me, persistent vendors followed suit, circling like witches at their incantations. I had hoped for a quick escape downriver, with a route planned from inside the minivan, but sorceresses have greater powers of anticipation. Having travelled Southeast Asia for ten years, I have perfected the technique of a glazed expression coupled with resilient muteness. To verbally engage a vendor with a simple 'no thank you' is a sign of vulnerability, almost pre-contractual, and they will force the susceptible to repeat the phrase over and again. It is better to say nothing at all. In Southeast Asia, rudeness is a survival skill.

Having escaped the vendors and negotiated a fair fare with one of the boatmen (most are, in fact, boatwomen), the Ngo Dong River delivered me to the three caves. I was more impressed by the unique rowing technique of my oarswoman, as she preferred to use her feet instead of her hands. They all did. Like a proud biologist, I observed and discovered the trigger for this evolutionary change. The boatwomen sell embroidered goods to their floating hostages and, not wanting to miss an opportunity to make a slow sale, they keep their hands free to serve.

They also seem to understand western tourists like the sacred words of the Buddhist Tipitaka. When I politely declined the offer of an embroidered table cloth (explaining that I didn't own a table), she raised herself up, opened her plastic seat and revealed a cooler box packed with ice and bottles of Huda Beer. We were in business, and I didn't care about the exchange rate: I had a boat bar all to myself. Feeling as decadent as a Roman emperor, I put my feet up and raised a bottle to every passing vessel. The only snack missing, which would have completed the pastoral scene, was a bowl of salted KP Peanuts.

A trip to and through the three caves (Hang Ca, Hang Giua and Hang Cuoi) is a calmative experience, and as I passed other travellers waving or smiling (I was still in emperor mode), I noticed our faces all shared the same satisfaction as we quietly delighted in the encompassing natural world. We were a gallery of counterfeit copies of Eduardo Forlenza's *The Contented Man*. The joy lingered on as we passed timeworn pagodas, while fishers cast their nets and birds took flight from exotic river flowers. Had one of the Romantic poets visited the landscapes of Tam Coc, elegant stanzas describing sacred lotus flowers would have supplanted fluttering, dancing daffodils.

The Ninh Binh Province is also home to the Perfume Pagoda, which is a vast complex of Buddhist temples and shrines built into - and set against - the Huong Tich Mountains. It attracts religious pilgrims and tourists in equal number, so I took another boat along the Yen River to Thien Tru Pagoda, before reaching the spiritual crescendo of Huong Tich Cave. At least that's how the Vietnamese regard it. Temple caves and grottoes are important places of cultural, religious and historical value in Southeast Asia, but I have visited more damp caves than I care to remember.

The Huong Tich Cave does, however, have some impressive statues of deities and unusually shaped stalactites and stalagmites, from which the pilgrims claim to receive blessings. For a foreign visitor, it offers only passing interest, and that is not a good enough return on a long and haemorrhoid-inducing boat journey. At least getting up to the cave was straightforward enough, as a modern cable car has been installed to take devotees all the way to the top of the mountain and back down again. Drunk on either altitude or Huda Beer, I decided to use my feet for the return journey, but I soon wished otherwise as it took longer than I anticipated and the pathway down had nothing of note nor interest. Just vendors. And lots of them. I couldn't quite grasp the logic of setting up a stall on the side of a mountain, and I couldn't understand why I would be tempted to stop and purchase a decorated paper umbrella. Arriving at the foot of the mountain, I remembered conventionality is a stranger to Southeast Asia, and smiled as local women shaded themselves from the glare and intense burn of the sun. The penny had dropped; my forearms were lobster-red.

In Hoa Lu District, I visited the temples of King Dinh and King Le at the site of an ancient Vietnamese capital of the tenth and eleventh centuries. A few ruined ruins remain, but at least Yen Ngua Mountain offers a scenic backdrop to all the rubble. I engaged with a local guide for some meaningful context and regretted my decision immediately (a protracted chronology of the Vietnamese monarchs, and the individual achievements of each dynasty, followed). As he continued talking, my polite smile was impossible to hold in place as his words had the effect of verbal g-force. With my thoughts wandering off and trying desperately to escape my head, I imagined that I looked like a manic-faced circus clown and burst out laughing. My guide mistook this outburst for encouragement and continued his commentary. Had I tried to suppress another yawn, my face would have split in half.

The highlight of my trip to this province was not the attractions themselves, as you would expect, but the characters met. I clicked instantly like a shutter release with a friendly couple from Germany and Mexico, and we shared stories over plates of sticky rice and Export 333 (a traditional rice lager). I asked Heppi if that was his real name, and he explained that a 'Heppi' is a 'magical being' and an incredibly rare phenomenon. I liked him immediately. People tend to be a little reserved when you first meet them, but Heppi broke the ice over tales of Nazi relations when he revealed his grandfather was a member of Hitler's Schutzstaffel. Who needs small talk when you can open a closet and drag out skeletons such as these? Packed full of carbohydrates, malted barley, and memorable stories, we hired some rusty bikes and surmised that they probably belonged to the village grandmothers. We cycled past a thousand rice fields and along the pathways of the local communities of Ninh Binh Province, dodging stubborn cows and their sticky cow pats and high-fiving excited children as they passed and chased behind us.

Just like my newfound friends in Sapa, I met Heppi and Oyuki again - by chance - in Ho Chi Minh City. Sitting at a table outside a greasy spoon on Pham Ngu Lao Street, I was busy indulging an insatiable desire for imported Heinz Baked Beans. With my stomach gorged on stewed beans, I looked up from my plate for the first time that afternoon and in that split second, Heppi and Oyuki walked past with heavy, scoliosis-inducing backpacks. They had just arrived in the city following a long and arduous journey by public bus, so I called out to them and held up a bottle of cold Beer Saigon. They understood at once. They never made it to their hostel, joining me for a night's merriment and laughter in one of Ho Chi Minh's liveliest nightlife spots and their backpacks joined us.

It always amazes me how easy it is to turn strangers into friends when travelling. Travellers have a love of travel in common, and they can inspire you to visit places you may not have considered or knew existed. During the summer of 2009, for instance, I was sitting cross-legged on the floor of a traditional Turkish restaurant in Istanbul's historic area of Sultanahmet when a couple with strange accents sat beside me. I couldn't work out where they were from, but I detected the Afrikaans accent and deduced they were from South Africa. The UEFA Champions League football fixtures were announced on a television screen at a bar across the street, so that most universal of universal subjects initiated a conversation with Leighton (a Tottenham Hotspur fan) and his wife, Ashlyn. Eighteen months later, we shared an incredible road trip along the Garden Route of South Africa, jumping one of the world's highest bungee jumps at Bloukrans Bridge in Nature's Valley.

For many years, the late Bob Hoskins repeated a famous phrase in BT adverts: 'It's good to talk.' Meeting people and making new friends from different countries and cultures is another one of travel's gains. I had never met a Filipino before I went to the Philippines, but Filipino friends connect with me on social media. As British novelist, Amelia E. Barr, observed: 'The great difference between voyages rests not with the ships, but with the people you meet on them.'

How true that is.

## Chapter 12: Ruined Ruins and Caodaism

I enjoy visiting the faded monuments of past civilisations such as Machu Picchu, Chichen Itza, and Angkor Wat; they are fascinating archaeological marvels and awe-inspiring alien worlds. When I admire their cultural achievements, I contemplate the passing of time; these footprints of the ancient world are a reminder that we should all make the most of the time given to us. Time is the one constant that holds history together, but she is a dispassionate companion and makes a slow ruin of all men, eroding their legacies with casual indifference.

A visit to My Son is all about the impressive UNESCO World Heritage ruins. My Son's abandoned Hindu temples and tombs, constructed between the fourth and the fourteenth century AD, are the legacy of the kings of an ancient Champa kingdom. Dedicated to the worship of the Hindu god Shiva, they now present a vivid picture of spiritual and political life during a critical phase in Southeast Asia's history. My Son's tower-temples create a dramatic valley vista as they poke their heads above an emerald canopy to contest the longevity of the sky above. Located in what was once impassable terrain, the surrounding jungle, and two shielding mountain ranges, offer protection. The birth of the Wright brothers and the invention of the American B-52 changed all that, even contesting the destructive capacities of time.

My Son is Vietnam's claim to world heritage status. It is the micro-equivalent of Cambodia's Angkor Wat, Indonesia's Borobudur, Myanmar's fields of pagodas in Bagan and Thailand's Ayutthaya and Sukhothai kingdoms. Once the religious and political capital of the Champa Kingdom, only twenty of the original seventy temple structures remain. Some temples have been painstakingly restored to their partial former glory, while others are at the mercy of the encroaching jungle. The architecture has many surviving decorative details and delicate carvings influenced by Hinduism, with many Hindu deities memorialised in its stonework. It takes about an hour to explore the structures, and my guide provided a contextual background for the ancient national heroes and Champa royalty laid to rest on this site.

My Son is less than an hour's drive from Hoi An in central Quang Nam Province. The theme of American bombing returned, as many of the temples were shelled to rubble like the ill-fated structures in Hue's Forbidden City. The jungle protected them for hundreds of years until the area doubled as a strategic base for the Viet Cong soldiers; the US bombing raids found a new target. President Nixon approved aerial bombing campaigns and the B-52s did their work with calculated efficiency, dropping their payloads with devastating effect as a thousand years of history and culture was dismantled and reduced to dust in seconds. The craters of precision bombs surround the temples where NVA encampments were once located.

Tour operators in Hue and Hoi An offer organised trips to My Son at reasonable rates, but for that price they include unadvertised shopping stops and factory tours. I try to avoid organised tours for that very reason alone, but also because the companies follow a planned schedule, with multiple coaches arriving at precisely the same time at attractions, factories, restaurants, and toilets. At My Son, I watched an exasperated guide struggle with an impractically large group of animated Chinese tourists. He deserved everything he got. As his charges clambered carelessly over ruins to take hurried selfie portraits (rarely bothering to look at the structures with their own eyes), it was like watching a slow-motion version of the great wildebeest migration across Kenya's Masai Mara on a science and nature documentary.

When I arrived at the site, I was disappointed that it couldn't be explored unguided, but as the area remains extensively mined with unexploded US bombs still to be detected, it was only right that my guide should take charge and lead the way. Ominous signs declared the obvious (mines are dangerous) and my guide ensured my limbs remained where nature intended them to be. I remembered the advice and mandatory rules of *The Highway Code* and assiduously applied one of these: The Three Second Rule. There have been some serious restoration efforts in recent years, and the main sites are now free of bombs and wartime debris. The World Monuments Fund has assisted on-going conservation efforts, and international scholars and archaeologists have given the My Son site the recognition it deserves. To appreciate its former glory, I will return in a decade, but I suspect My Son will, regardless, remain relatively unknown outside Southeast Asia, despite its UNESCO World Heritage status.

I have visited the temples of numerous world religions, observing their spiritual traditions and symbols and learning the main arcs of their narratives and sacred histories. From Taoism to Buddhism, Sikhism to Zoroastrianism (and every other 'ism'), each religion presents nuances of worship or dress like tableaux of religious diversity. Some have been modest when constructing their temples, while others have been elaborate to the point of spectacular. The Cao Dai Temple of Tay Ninh Province falls into the latter category, so I didn't mind making a sixty-mile journey by public bus to see it.

The word 'Great' introduces the temple, and it is a fitting introduction to Caodaism.

Other distinct South-east Asian temples include northern Thailand's Wat Rong Khun (better known as 'The White Temple'), which is a contemporary but profoundly unconventional Buddhist temple in the city of Chiang Rai. Privately owned, national artist Chalermchai Kositpipat started the project in 1997, and he has continued to work on it ever since, despite the indifferent efforts of an earthquake in 2014 which caused structural damage. I travelled to Chiang Rai to visit this temple and ghoulish traffic cones marked my arrival. The temple draws tourists from all over the world to view its incredible details, which include a Predator statue (from the Arnold Schwarzenegger film) emerging from a lawn, and the dangling plaster heads of Freddie Krueger (*A Nightmare on Elm Street*) and Pinhead (*Hellraiser*) suspended from a holy tree in its gardens. Its murals feature paintings of superheroes, movie stars and cartoon characters, but first I had to pass a surreal and hellish sea of hands to cross a bridge into the higher realm (with a bizarre penis-foot guiding the way).

Near Pattaya, on Thailand's eastern Gulf coast, the Sanctuary of Truth is a wooden temple with four beautifully decorated wings dedicated to Thai, Khmer, Chinese and Indian religious iconography. The architectural detail is impressive and so is its location, as it commands a breathtaking view of the Gulf of Thailand. The features of these temples make them unique and memorable for the visitor, but the Cao Dai Temple takes it to another level due to the singularity of its faith and the whimsicality of its worshippers. Colourful costumes converge like a Dulux colour scheme as the divine all-seeing eye watches formal proceedings from above.

I was struck by the temple's kooky colours and strangely idiosyncratic design, which looks like a layered cake decorated at an unsupervised children's party. Once I stepped inside, I half expected to see cartoon characters chasing each other around or waving to tourists as they entered. Its décor resembles a child's fantasyland with a blue star-studded and vaulted ceiling, pink dragon-entwined pillars, and yellow and purple mythical beasts. In *The Quiet American*, Graham Greene describes the temple's interior as: 'Christ and Buddha looking down from the roof of a cathedral on a Walt Disney fantasia of the East.' With 'dragons and snakes in technicolor,' the temple is Walt Disney on acid. The Cao Dai religion is as layered as its place of worship as the converted believe all the world's major religions contain universal truths, with their faith a spiritual mashup of them all. Their greater purpose is to unite all religions into one future world religion, and I wish them good luck trying to sell that idea to the Islamic State.

Before I set off for the provincial city of Tay Ninh from Ho Chi Minh, I checked the times of service as I didn't want to miss the brightly coloured worshippers in their ceremonial gowns of blue, red and yellow. When I arrived, right on cue, the noon service was about to begin, but the worshippers tolerate foreign visitors and cameras without fuss or complaint, and they have even constructed a balcony inside the temple for tourists to view and photograph the ceremonies below. Cao Dai plagiarises several world religions and borrows saints and divinities, so it is an unusual but inventive repackaging of faiths. Their movement is growing in strength, with four hundred temples and an estimated 2.5 million worshippers worldwide.

A trip to Tay Ninh Province was an opportunity to observe one of the world's most remarkable and atypical religions.

## Chapter 13: Saigon in Ho Chi Minh

Vietnam's leading and most progressive city is a gateway for exploring southern sites of historical, cultural and natural interest, including the subterranean world of Cu Chi, the fertile Mekong Delta and the Cao Dai Temple in Tay Ninh Province. Ho Chi Minh City is Vietnam's coronary artery. Having auditioned for a leading role on the regional stage, it pumps life and vitality into the country's post-war recovery and economic development. A city of commerce and culture, it is the blueprint of success others try to imitate. Cambodia's Phnom Penh has studied the print, but Ho Chi Minh has built it. Western influences reach for the sky with steel and glass fingers, and Vietnam's southern powerhouse has demonstrated the drive and ambition to outspeed and outthink its neighbours in capitals such as Bangkok and Jakarta.

Formerly known as 'Saigon' (its name changed to Ho Chi Minh City in 1976), it reminded me of troubled countries such as Myanmar and India where periods of turmoil, or struggles for independence, have resulted in symbolic changes, such as the renaming of major cities. Myanmar's Rangoon became 'Yangon' and India's colonial Bombay converted to 'Mumbai' once the period of British rule ended. The difference is that in Ho Chi Minh City, Saigon is still very much alive and kicking, having survived some heavy-handed rebranding efforts. The code for the city airport is SGN and bus timetables and route maps continue to list 'Saigon.' The river that flows through the city is called the Saigon River, and hotel proprietors continue the trend with listings for the Sheraton Saigon, Sofitel Plaza Saigon, Movenpick Hotel Saigon, Saigon Riverside Hotel and the Metropole Saigon. Elderly locals steadfastly refuse to use the name Ho Chi Minh as a form of semantic rebuttal and protest; they had to flee the country when the Americans lost the war and thus refuse to acknowledge former North Vietnam's conquest.

My first introduction to Saigon was the opening chapter (*Waiting in Saigon*) of Francis Ford Coppola's now iconic *Apocalypse Now*. As US helicopters napalm jungle villages to The Doors' *The End*, the sound of rotating helicopter blades fades to the humming of a ceiling fan, and this stunning montage introduces the film's cynical protagonist and that famous line: 'Saigon. Shit, I'm still only in Saigon.' US veterans flock to the popular city bar and nightclub Apocalypse Now, where they can pretend to be Captain Willard and attempt to make 'reparations' for the past with forgiving local women (who come at a low cost). I sat down at a bar across the road from this club for an episode of People Watching, but it was like an awkward United Nations reunion full of tight-fitting skirts, bra tops, and belt-busting bellies.

Whether Ho Chi Minh City or Saigon, the city has evolved into a dynamic urban area where ancient pagodas compete for space with modern skyscrapers and designer malls, while the architectural styles are a fusion of American and Chinese influences. Some districts are as neat and organised as Singapore, while others could sit comfortably in the Old Quarter of India's capital. To fully appreciate the city and its environs, I committed several days to my itinerary, and some war movie downloads to my hard drive. The best way to explore Ho Chi Minh City is on foot, and the main tourist sites are grouped conveniently in District One, which is relatively compact and easy enough to navigate without the need for a sweat-soaked map. The area around Pham Ngu Lao Street is tourist-friendly with many middle range hotels and backpacker hostels to choose from, western-themed restaurants and a vibrant nightlife scene.

When the sun descends, the party vibe awakens. Roads get thinner as the night gets longer, with more and more primary-coloured plastic chairs claiming pavement inches to form a bottled-beer blockade. Criminality lurks with insidious intent down narrow, insalubrious alleyways, so I kept my wallet and my wits about me and remained with the crowds on the main streets. Cockroaches, preferring the cover of darkness, are rarely seen during the day; the unsavoury types who frequent District One are similar, preying on drunken tourists who are ripe for scamming. I was offered cocaine and amphetamines by a heavily pregnant stranger (she sat uninvited on my knee and pretended we were intimate) and, looking over my shoulder, a street prostitute whispered from the shadows of a back passage: 'You go boom boom?' I had drifted into a frontier boomtown of the American Old West, so I watched my step and made selective eye contact as I didn't want District One to become my very own Tombstone.

Ho Chi Minh City has many cultural and architectural highlights. The Saigon Notre-Dame Basilica, or Basilica of Our Lady of the Immaculate Conception, is an arresting piece of architecture created by the French colonialists and teleported - it would seem - from the Place de la Concorde in Paris. South-east Asian countries with a history of colonisation have benefitted from the legacy of foreign invasion: gifts of grand architecture are left behind like a parting sweet sorrow. The old Spanish town and settlement of Vigan in the Philippines, for example, is the attraction of choice for many tourists. In Ho Chi Minh City, the French kept on giving, and the Municipal Theatre (or Saigon Opera House) is another example of a beautiful, classical construction. I wouldn't ordinarily get excited about a post office, but the Saigon Central Post

Office (which was designed by Gustave Eiffel) is a period classic. Ho Chi Minh City Hall (or Hotel de Ville) is another ostentatious government building which has a magnificent facade when floodlit at night.

The Independence Palace (or Reunification Palace), by way of contrast, looks like another Cold War relic with parked tanks gloomily waiting on its lawns. The Museum of Vietnamese History offers insight on Vietnam without mentioning the war, while the Buddhist An Quang, Giac Lam, and Taoist Jade Emperor Pagoda offer peaceful retreats from testing streets. I wondered into French-built Binh Tay Market which is supposed to be a traditional local market, but all I could see was bobbing backpacks carrying Lonely Planets. The stallholders were loud, rude and aggressive and the expectation was clear: if you choose to enter the market, you must leave with something cheap and useless. Oddly, it's listed as an attraction for tourists in guidebooks, but the only positive I could take from it was motivation to take an elevator to the forty-eighth floor of the uber-modern Bitexco Financial Tower, which resembles a vertical CD rack. It is the only platform to offer 'incredible views' of Ho Chi Minh City which, when examined, are quite ordinary.

Once I had explored the highlights of Ho Chi Minh, I took day trips to Cu Chi, the Cao Dai Temple in Tay Ninh Province and the Mekong Delta to experience the very best of Vietnam's south-west. My journey into the delta area was like turning the pages of a geography textbook, as this region is an index of diverse topics and features swamplands, coconut palms, rice fields, fruit orchards, sugarcane groves and some mighty Mekong waterways. The Mekong Delta is shaped like a comma and is Vietnam's rice bowl, providing one-third of the nation's annual food crop. A journey through it took me back in time to Vietnam's traditional agricultural past, as I passed children riding on the backs of water buffalo with backdrops of seas of green dotted with conical hats. I had succeeded in finding vintage Vietnam.

With all those rivers, canals and streams in the south, it was like stumbling onto the set of Kevin Costner's *Water World* as an extra. The only way to explore this fertile region is by boat, and just about everything floats, including hotels and markets. I could even take to the white-sand beaches of Phu Quoc and hide away for days, weeks or years if I wanted to. Interpol would never have found me.

'Floating' and 'market' are words synonymous with Thailand, but the waterscapes of the Mekong Delta have fabulous floating marketplaces of their own at Cai Be and Cai Rang. But unlike Thailand, these markets remain focused on the locals' needs rather than tourist trinkets. Cai Rang is Thailand's famous Damnoen Saduak before rampant, unchecked tourism turned it into another stomping ground for tourist tat. Cai Rang reminded me of Amphawa in Thailand's Samut Songkram district, having retained its traditional identity and purpose with vegetables and fruits the exchange of choice, despite all those curious tourists. Phong Dien is the best pick regarding authenticity, and I have since worked out an equation for calculating a floating market's appeal: subtract the number of motorised craft from traditional rowing boats, and the higher the number, the more authentic the market.

At just under three hours by car or bus from Ho Chi Minh City, My Tho is the gateway market town into the Mekong Delta area, but it is a busy port with few attractions of note. Vinh Long is the entryway to its islands, so I passed through both to get downriver to see the region's incredible Delta vistas. I declined the offer of a private cruise on the Mekong River, as I had already experienced this from The Lao People's Democratic Republic end. Instead, I headed straight for the islands (taking a long-tail boat with me) to explore the waterways that connect northwards to Cambodia, Laos, Myanmar, China and Tibet. I sampled more fruit on the islands than I would have eaten in five lifetimes, and visited a jungle candy factory which is a traditional cottage industry in these parts. The Delta highlight was to explore the secondary canals of the Mekong by rowing boat, as this provided cultural contrast to the imposing modernisation of Ho Chi Minh.

My travels in Vietnam proved the Vietnamese are right: renewed from the ashes of its past, Vietnam is a country, not a war. And while it left me speechless at times, it also gave me a few stories to share.

## Part 2: More Khmer, Less Rouge

## The Kingdom of Cambodia

*Don't reject the crooked road and don't take the straight one; instead, take the one travelled by the ancestors.* (Cambodian proverb)

### Chapter 14: The Road Not Taken

In Robert Frost's autobiographical poem, *The Road Not Taken*, the American poet makes the decision, when faced with two diverging roads, to walk the one 'less travelled by.' When I journeyed across the cobblestoned continent of Europe, I walked in the footprints of the kindred spirits who went before me. Madrid, Paris, London and Rome are all wonderful cities, but they are a familiar road. I knew where cameras and potholes were waiting, where to expect a horizontal or vertical curve and the safe and legal speed limit at every junction. I rarely felt a sense of discovery or challenge, that sensation of awe and wonder, unless I took on quests of mythical proportions to find it. Of course, Europe does have golden fleeces of its own such as Dracula's Castle (Bran Castle) in Transylvania and the Chernobyl Nuclear Power Plant in the Ukraine, but Cambodia is one of those roads less travelled by and that, as Robert Frost discovered, 'has made all the difference.'

Cambodia, much like Vietnam, has a timeline punctuated by conflict and hardship. While Vietnam is in the final stages of its post-war recovery, Cambodia's traumas are still fresh and ooze into the bloody bandages of rehabilitation. Tourists no longer hesitate to book flights to Vietnam, but Cambodia's airports may as well have landmines for runway lights as international travellers continue to associate it with despot Pol Pot, political genocide, and the brutal Khmer Rouge regime. Modern-day Cambodia is more *Khmer* and less *Rouge*, as the green shoots of recovery are watered and fertilised by a flourishing tourism industry that has finally grasped the potential of its appeal to culturally covetous, international eyes. Thailand is a jewellery shop full of sparkling gold, silver, polished chrome and glass, but Cambodia is a diamond in the rough. Its brightest sparkle radiates from the north-west ruins of an ancient Khmer Kingdom which is Cambodia's Pink Star diamond: Angkor Wat.

The first time I travelled to Cambodia, I was conscious of stepping out of my travel and comfort zone. I understood the journey would be difficult, but at least it would be *different*. Located in the southern portion of the Indochinese Peninsula, Cambodia shares a border and a history of conflict with neighbouring Vietnam. Historically, the Vietnamese have invaded Cambodia militarily and economically, and as recently as 1979, the Vietnamese toppled the toxic dictatorship of the Khmer Rouge regime. A second and more covert operation followed and was fought on the less muddy but much murkier battlegrounds of Cambodia's fledgling economy, as Vietnamese firms flexed their financial muscles to gain a foothold before a controlling interest. Cambodia stands in the ashes of its past, while Vietnam has taken flight on mythical wings, launching itself from the shoulders of regional neighbours.

Vietnam seized the opportunities of a post-war reality by embracing foreign direct investment in manufacturing industries, and by developing the infrastructures to support sustained and rapid progress. With the widespread availability of electricity and modern communication technologies, it established itself as an attractive prospect for foreign markets. Cambodia, the younger sibling, tolerates a hand-me-down existence. As Vietnam continues to outperform its neighbours in the Human Development Index (used by international businesses to measure competitiveness), it will continue to reap the rewards of its progressive policies and outlook, as other countries claw at the scraps that fall from its table.

With past reputation linked intrinsically, and somewhat inevitably, to modern-day perceptions, Cambodia is further disenfranchised. Internationally, its reputation endures like epoxy resin as one of the world's most isolated, troubled and high-risk countries. Whenever I told friends or family that I was returning to Cambodia, I was swimming with sharks while bedecked in a novelty seal outfit. They just couldn't understand the appeal, perhaps thinking I was reckless and flying too close to the flame. People enjoy horror films and visiting fairgrounds because they offer the adrenaline rush of fear in safe and controlled environments. Beachside holidays are universal-rated, but destinations such as Cambodia come with a parental advisory warning, and that is part of their appeal. If you were to take away the intensity and the energy of an adrenaline rush, dangerous sports such as base jumping and bull running wouldn't exist. Places like Cambodia are the travel equivalent.

Almost everything I watched on television documentaries, or read in books, featured images and stories of war and genocide, so Cambodia was, initially, a country I hesitated to visit. With Thailand displaying its proud and attractive plumes on its western border, I found myself returning over several summers like a devoted mate, enticed by its showy vibrancy, tropical climate, and paradisiacal islands. Cambodia, however, can boast something Thailand will never have: an 'Eighth Wonder of the World.' Thailand has impressive historical spoils in Ayutthaya and the old kingdom of Sukhothai, but they are a featherweight in comparison to Cambodia's prize fighter: the UNESCO World Heritage of Angkor Wat (which is the largest religious monument in the world).

Having taken three separate trips to explore the country and get beneath its bruised and blood-spotted skin, I now regard Cambodia as one of Southeast Asia's most captivating and inspiring countries. Like anchovies or raw oysters, it is an acquired travel taste. It is often true that first impressions matter most, but in Cambodia's case, I would argue that the opposite is true. Had I bumped into Lemony Snicket in a Phnom Penh bar, I am sure he would have agreed with me:

> *I don't know if you've ever noticed this, but first impressions are often entirely wrong. You can look at a painting for the first time, for example, and not like it at all, but after looking at it a little longer you may find it very pleasing. The first time you try Gorgonzola cheese you may find it too strong, but when you are older you may want to eat nothing but Gorgonzola cheese.*

(The Bad Beginning)

Carpet-bombed by the US during the Vietnam war, ravaged by Pol Pot and his Khmer Rouge cadres in the 1970s, occupied by Vietnamese troops in the 1980s and engulfed by civil war in the early 1990s, Cambodia was a black hole of travel and tourism for decades (even for hardened backpackers). Attitudes are changing by degrees, as the country has opened its doors to global tourism, and its government has recognised the need for it to develop travel infrastructures like its neighbours have already done so, to reap the economic rewards of international curiosity. It is a land that is slowly healing from past traumas, but it does at least have one eye firmly fixed on a strife-free future. Like a sleeping giant that was once an ancient, regional superpower, other ASEAN nations should take note and perhaps be a little warier as a tentative step becomes an assured stride, which could impact on their visitor numbers.

Although a delayed entry to the party, Cambodia has found ambition as a forward-thinking country. Its Department of Tourism target of eight million annual arrivals by the year 2020 reflects this goal (4.5 million tourists visited in 2014, rising to 4.75 million in 2015 which almost doubled 2010's total in Cambodia's Tourism Statistics Summary). I witnessed the early effects of this aspirational target when two years passed between my first visit to Siem Reap in 2012, and my return in 2014. I was astonished by the pace of development in such a small town, as luxury hotels popped up at breakneck speed along the highways to and from Angkor Wat, often to the detriment of green spaces. The Cambodian government is quite serious about that target, and with Angkor Wat currently generating 20% of the country's annual GDP, who can blame them for milking a meadow overrun with cultural cash cows? Cambodian Prime Minister, Hun Sen, openly acknowledges the importance of foreign tourism to the future development of the country, commenting to local media in 2014 that tourism is one of the key sectors 'supporting the economy.'

With visa exemption agreements now in place between Cambodia and all ASEAN member states, exponential tourism and economic growth will be nurtured by escalating visitor numbers. There are serious preservation concerns about the adverse impact on protected Khmer heritage sites, as a disproportionate number of Cambodia's tourists head straight for Siem Reap to explore the ruins of Angkor Wat, often ignoring the nation's southern capital altogether. With the Tourist Visa on Arrival (TVOA) scheme encouraging inbound international travellers, visiting Cambodia has never been so stress-free and easy. It might be one of the least-developed countries in the region, but it has one of the fastest-developing economies.

The caveat of progress is that unchecked development can threaten the very thing you want to protect, like piranha surrounding a prize-fighting fish. When I visited the Giza Plateau to witness first-hand the stately gravitas of Egypt's Great Pyramid of Khufu, I had already marvelled at countless still and moving images of this limestone icon from my school days to adult years. Travel websites, television documentaries and the pages of travel guides and tourism brochures tempted me like payday loans. But what surprised me most about the pyramids was not the pyramids themselves or their four-thousand-year history, as you would expect, but the power of a carefully cropped image.

The sprawling city of Cairo, Africa's largest in terms of population density, has clawed its way to the feet of the Great Sphinx to bask and share in the commercial opportunities it presents. To say this lessened the impact this ancient archaeological site had on me, would be something of an understatement. There are plans to abate this intrusive, culturally insensitive development by the Egyptian government, but it's a case of too little too late. The horse has already bolted; the damage is irreversible. Some travel websites offer alternative, more truthful photographic representations of prominent hot spots, and their images sharply contrast with the global tourism industry's often misleading, carefully cropped and usually airbrushed depictions. They demonstrate - all too clearly - how the modern world has not respected the cultural space of significant world heritage.

I explored the pyramids on horseback, but the experience was New World rather than Old World. I wasn't trotting through antiquity at all: I was on the periphery of a crowded, galloping desert metropolis. As the wind picked up, litter and sand swirled in the air like a trash vortex, as roaring jet engines thrust and cut like rapiers through the clouds above. What was wrong with me? Had travel lost its allure? How can 'great' pyramids underwhelm? I returned my horse to its obnoxious, grasping owner before sampling some traditional Egyptian fare at a branch of Pizza Hut which was, quite incredibly, granted permission for an onsite restaurant boasting *Splendid Khafre Views!* To add insult to injury, the ground floor housed Colonel Harland Sander's secret formula for Kentucky Fried Chicken. I never imagined contemplating the ancient engineering prowess of the pharaohs through the greasy-fingered windows of a Pizza Hut, but there I sat, Margherita slice in hand.

That was some years ago, but it's a safe bet that a host of international chains have since joined their swelling ranks with golden arches and crowned mermaids. I enjoyed watching Karl Pilkington's almost identical reaction to the pyramids on the popular television series *An Idiot Abroad*, and I laughed out loud at his comic dismay. His first words upon seeing the pyramids conveyed the truth of their present state:

> *A lot of erm… shit. A lot of shit. You don't always see this, do you, you don't see that many buses there. It looks like it's stuck in a nice desert but it isn't, is it. It looks like a building site. You don't see that in the brochure, do you?*

Siem Reap is at risk and could find itself morphing into Anytown Asia as the touts and vendors move in, an exodus from Cambodia's rural villages, to stand shoulder-to-shoulder with the young party crowd with backpacks and a migration of sex workers from the capital. Pub Street was a sedated place on a Saturday night in 2012, but by 2014 it was more Club Street as the backpackers moved in and multiplied, and the whole area was awash with braided revellers, tattooed tourists and thumping playlists. It had, like so many other places in Southeast Asia, become yet another imitation of Bangkok's Khao San Road prototype, with a catwalk of baggy fishermen pants emblazoned with colourful but badly drawn elephants. I observed the conspicuous neon of expat watering holes, detected the oily scent of massage parlours and rolled my eyes at the exposed flesh of cocksure transgender prostitutes.

With Siem Reap securing economic status as Cambodia's wealthiest city, the criminal fringe has, not surprisingly, stepped into the inner circle. The Cambodian government would be wise to make the effort to protect its greatest, inherited asset. In 2012, I was seduced by the charms of this small town which, by 2014, was more postmodernist and less Oscar-Claude Monet. Paradoxically, the capital Phnom Penh is more like the small provincial town you would expect Siem Reap to be.

## Chapter 15: An Unexpected Journey

The first time I visited Cambodia was, oddly enough, the result of a chance encounter in the summer of 2012 at Ayutthaya Historical Park in Thailand. A friendly couple in their early twenties approached and asked me to take their photograph beside some temple ruins, and we shared our travel experiences and recommendations. They had just returned from a short trip to Angkor Wat where I had considered taking a flight myself, but I had been put off by the exorbitant prices of Bangkok Airways which represented poor value for money for a forty-minute flight across the border. There were few carriers at the time and only a limited number of scheduled daily flights, so I was at the mercy of the airlines and refused to surrender.

I was fated to meet those travellers, as they went on to explain how they had travelled to Cambodia for just forty-eight baht (the equivalent of one British pound). They had taken a train from Bangkok's Hualamphong Station all the way to the Cambodian border in Thailand's northeast, dissecting Isan Province to reach the chaotic border town of Aranyaprathet. When I returned to Bangkok that evening, I was exhausted by my day trip to Ayutthaya, but I was excited by the prospect of visiting Angkor Wat. Finding just enough energy reserves to do some late-night travel and visa research, I resolved to leave Thailand and enter the heart of darkness.

The very next morning, I jumped out of bed and into my clothes at the sound of the alarm clock, departing my hotel before the sun had a chance to rise or change my mind. With a light heart, weary eyes and a fuzzy head, I caught the early 5:55 am service from Hualamphong to Aranyaprathet. As I made my way to the MRT underground station at Asoke Interjection (the central point of Bangkok's transport crossroads), I passed a tapestry of human carnage from the previous dead of night as inebriated expats, sexpats and tourists sat awkwardly on the unsteady stools of roadside bars. With a day of regret and recovery ahead of them, I was going back in time to explore the greatest continuous empire in the history of Southeast Asia.

Arriving at Hualamphong Station with a flimsy and rather pathetic-looking 7-Eleven carrier bag (and a single change of clothes), I was dog-tired and hadn't even bothered to book a room for the night ahead in Siem Reap. I would worry about that small detail when my energy and necessity returned. Having located the correct ticketing booth for the journey (passing multiple signs in Sanskrit and not a single sign with any English), I purchased my ticket, bought some pastry treats with unfamiliar fillings, and boarded a train which looked every part the budget option. For the price, I didn't deserve a reserved seat, so reclined where I could with astonishment written all over the lines of my face. The couple I met in Ayutthaya had not exaggerated at all, and I could hear my budget laughing inside my wallet.

Travel in Southeast Asia, if you are prepared to put in the hours, can offer exceptional value for money - value, that is, when balanced against hours lost in transit. An American friend, preoccupied to the point of obsession with getting a 'good return,' booked tickets for a journey by bus from Bangkok to Kuala Lumpur which takes some thirty-one butt-busting hours (if the roads are clear). I value my time more than penny-pinching, so I booked a budget flight which delivered me to Malaysia's capital two hours later. By the time I had explored the city and was waiting to board my return flight, his bus slowly chugged its way into Puduraya Terminal.

My journey to the Cambodian border lasted six gruelling hours, and it came with complimentary seat changes. Lots of them. I regretted not paying another fifty pence for a reserved ticket, and I was embarrassed when farmers boarded with reservations and glanced at me with a mixture of sympathy and disdain. I had taken the concept of budget travel to its apex, and for no good reason. I convinced myself that as the seats were haemorrhoid-inducing, I had probably done myself an inadvertent medical favour. At least my unseated behind and I would remain firm friends as well as travel companions, and just like the comedy desperados Rik Mayall and Ade Edmondson in *Bottom*, we would survive the unfortunate circumstances we found ourselves trapped in.

When I arrived at Aranyaprathet, I wasted no time crossing over to Cambodia's mirror-opposite border town of Poipet, which is a notorious Helldorado for the scamming of unsuspecting travellers. I introduced myself to a British couple with giant backpacks, and they asked me what had happened to my own. We agreed to share a taxi into Siem Reap town centre for thirty dollars, but we had to obtain tourist permits first and, right on cue like a well-rehearsed stage production, a uniformed guard approached and asked us to present our visas. We explained that we were about to procure them, and he generously offered to get them on our behalf.

'Wait here,' he commanded before a dramatic pause, 'and I will come back.'

We all decided to trust this stranger (who did a passable impression of Arnold Schwarzenegger) as he took charge of our three passports and disappeared. We joked that he probably hired his uniform from a fancy-dress novelty shop, but when he didn't return for nearly half an hour, we considered the possibility that we may have fallen for a confidence trick. But he did return, a passport genie, and we handed over our American dollars with more gratitude than that whole-page green visa sticker deserved.

I have often wondered why so many countries in Southeast Asia insist on sticking such ridiculously large permits in tourist passports. Like a hostile takeover, Cambodia now occupies three full pages of my current passport, while other countries are quite content with a small and understated stamp. Are they deliberately trying to fill up as many pages as possible to keep us out, or delay our return with expensive renewals? I used to enjoy collecting stickers when I was a child, but Cambodian visas do not come even close to those Panini football collectibles I swapped with friends as a playground enthusiast. Some of the backpackers I met removed their visas once they had left Cambodia. I admired their creativity as they tried to free up more space, but such an attempt is ultimately a reckless act if you ever plan on returning. It is also illegal.

Cambodian immigration officials are trained to place official entry and exit stamps over the border of the visa sticker, thereby rendering the page useless if you do remove it. A backpacker shared his misfortune - with the amusement of hindsight - when he explained how he was caught out on a return visit to Cambodia. The immigration official flicked through the pages of his passport and noticed that an expired visa had been removed. Before being issued with a replacement, he was forced to write a letter of apology to the government of Cambodia for desecrating its sovereign property. Of course, you are not supposed to alter anything in a passport as tampering will render it invalid. His fate could have been worse, so a letter was the lesser of two evils.

With visas and a taxi fare negotiated with the border mafia, a stranger wearing the red of an Arsenal football shirt rushed toward me like a long-lost friend to proclaim my emotional state:

'You must be so happy! You've just signed our best player!'

I had no idea what he was talking about, but it wasn't difficult to deduce which football team I supported as I was covered in sponsorship logos like an advertising hoarding. Football shirts and shorts were part of my survival strategy in Southeast Asia, as the polyester mesh dries quicker than cotton, so when I packed for my two-year adventure in Southeast Asia, I folded twenty pairs of shorts with twenty matching shirts. Case closed. I had been busy travelling in Ayutthaya the previous day, so I had just enough time to check a few travel details for my trip to Siem Reap. Politely, I replied that I hadn't read the latest player transfer news, and with tremendous enthusiasm for a fan whose club had just lost their best player, he continued:

'You've just signed Robin van Persie for twenty-four million pounds!'

I hadn't signed anybody, but I accepted this news as a good omen for my hastily planned trip to Cambodia, and Robin van Persie's goals secured Manchester United the Premier League title the following season.

The couple I shared a ride with asked me which guesthouse or hostel I wanted to be dropped off at, and explaining that I hadn't booked one, doubts formed in their minds as they considered the possibility that I was on Interpol's Most Wanted list. With my friendliness and charm overcoming their anxiety and suspicion, they sympathetically suggested that I stay at their hostel (which set me back four dollars) and feeling somewhat liberated and extravagant, I remained a second night to see the very best of Angkor Wat.

Chance encounters on the road can lead to all kinds of discoveries, and even moments of unexpected kindness, so a little bit of friendliness and a warm smile are just as valuable as the currency in your pocket and the green visa sticker in your passport.

I experienced another Bob Hoskins moment on a road I hadn't even planned to take.

## Chapter 16: Khmer Kingdom to Khmer Rouge

What's in a name? *Say* Cambodia, *think* Vietnam war. *Say* Cambodia and a generation will *think* of *Apocalypse Now* and Marlon Brando's legendary portrayal of Walter E. Kurtz, a renegade colonel and self-appointed god of a mysterious jungle tribe, who journeys into the heart of darkness. For others, *say* Cambodia and they will *think* of the 1984 British drama *The Killing Fields*, evoking scenes of a country with a charred and chequered past as Oscar winner Haing S. Ngor (murdered in 1996, his death a suspected Khmer Rouge assassination) escapes a death camp to stumble upon the infamous killing fields of the regime (even slipping into a muddy cesspool filled with the thick stew of putrefying corpses).

A trip to Cambodia will, invariably, induce an element of dark tourism, and there are lessons still to be learnt from this country that should have been put to bed at the close of the Second World War. The recent history of the Khmer Rouge Communist Party and their infamous leader, Pol Pot, continue to cast a melancholic shadow over this ancient Khmer kingdom. A land with more landmines than smiles, Cambodia is one of recent history's most heavily bombed countries: the US carpet-bombed it from the air in an attempt to disrupt suspected Viet Cong activity along the Ho Chi Minh Trail.

On my third expedition, I visited The Cambodian Landmine Museum and Relief Facility, fifteen miles north of Siem Reap. Established in 1997 by former child soldier Aki Ra, I was troubled to learn that there are an estimated four to six million unexploded landmines haphazardly scattered across the Cambodian countryside, patiently waiting a few inches beneath the soil for their next unwitting victim. Aki Ra was himself responsible for planting thousands of these mines, but he has since removed thousands more, explaining that their purpose was to inflict appalling wounds on enemy combatants that would, in turn, create a financial burden of care, as well as being a potent symbol of fear and terror. Official figures show that on average, thirty to thirty-five people are injured or killed every month in Cambodia from direct contact with landmines, many of them being children. Cambodia might be the road less travelled, but unlike Little Red Riding Hood, I followed the advice I was given and resisted the urge to stray from the path.

Grandma's cottage in Cambodia comes in the form of a temple-shaped UNESCO World Heritage icon, with Ficus Strangulosa trees replacing a cross-dressing wolf. Annually, an estimated two million international tourists follow flight paths to Siem Reap Province for the express purpose of visiting crumbling temple complexes. Without them, most travellers to this region would fly straight over Cambodia to visit Vietnam in the east or Laos and

Thailand to the north and north-west. Cambodia's history of violence will, inevitably, continue to deter many visitors. It remains a poor and struggling third-world nation, marred by corruption and chronic crime, but that is what makes travelling to this country worthwhile as you must earn memories the hard way. It is a nation desperate to emerge from the shadows of a troubled and tragic past to share in the tourism and development spoils of a progressive ASEAN future.

I revisited and revised my first impressions of Cambodia with each return to the country. Lemony Snicket was right: I had acquired an insatiable appetite for Gorgonzola cheese. I met some of Cambodia's expats on their excursions to Bangkok, but they had more in common with malodorous varieties such as Limburger and Époisses de Bourgogne.

## Chapter 17: Wild Wild East: Phnom Penh

Pushing and shoving my way along the cluttered pavements of central Sukhumvit Road, a tourist thoroughfare in Bangkok, I stopped to bargain for a T-shirt with *Phnom Penh* on the chest and the slogan *A Sunny Place for Shady Characters* printed on the reverse. I was planning my first trip to the Cambodian capital and considered this a witty introduction. Much to my chagrin, the only size I could pull and forcibly stretch over my head and shoulders was an unflattering XXXL. When I joined friends for dinner and drinks at one of Bangkok's prime nightlife spots, known locally as Sois Eight and Eleven, the novelty quickly wore off as conversations were triggered with strangers I would have preferred not to have met. Hindsight is a contemptuous creature, encouraging the thirsty to drink water from a fire hydrant when there's a convenience shop across the street.

Sexpats are bastions of the phrase 'dirty old man,' and Thailand's Pattaya is the capital of Sexpat, with Phnom Penh its twin and second city. I found myself admiring the typical sexpat's capacity for self-delusion, as this strange breed of men sincerely believes its powers of seduction can reverse the laws of conventional attractiveness. And you can spot them a mile off too, like a trophy parade, except the 'cup' is made of flesh and bones and is usually youthful, good-looking and of Southeast-Asian origin. For as long as Southeast Asia exists, sexpats will never find a place on WWF's endangered species list and *Pretty Woman* will continue its profitable business in counterfeit DVD sales.

Before I moved to Thailand, I read Jerry Hopkins' *Bangkok Babylon*, which is a chapter-and-verse profile of twenty-five of the most colourful and unforgettable characters he met in Bangkok. He met his fair share, and certainly a greater number than I did as he lived in Bangkok for more than a decade. I could understand his inspiration for writing the book, as there is an abundance of willing subjects on Bangkok's streets and they are quite intent, it seems, on writing their uncensored obituaries. Whether I cared to listen or not, they shared and repeated their personal life stories, only pausing for more drinks which acted like full stops. The more stories of sex and excess shared, the more they sounded the same. They were stereotypes. Hackneyed. Some of them were from Hackney. I wondered whether they had all read the same poorly written guide to expat life in Southeast Asia, as their shared knowledge was an encyclopaedia of banality and emptiness.

Some of the lost and doomed expatriates I met had chosen the crooked road. With little hesitation or regret, they had relocated to Cambodia's capital to lead unashamedly debauched lifestyles, while deceiving themselves that they were kings of men because they could afford to live in a third world economy and date beautiful girls. I noticed a recurrent theme emerged as they extolled the many virtues of expat life, and yet the company they kept indicated otherwise as they detailed (with imitation sunglasses straddling receding hairlines) anarchic lifestyles featuring transient females and permanent bottles, which seemed to be attached to their hands like a sixth green or brown finger. Their lifestyles readily revealed their character, and when one of these dignitaries jovially announced that he had just married a Phnom Penh prostitute, his character arc was complete. Of course, he naturally preferred to describe her using the more neutral nouns 'bar' and 'girl,' but as Thais are quick to explain, this was very much a case of same, *same but different*. Engaging with the services of a sex worker doesn't necessarily result in sexual acts, as one of my highly principled colleagues paid a bar girl to shop with his girlfriend for two hours so that he could watch the Manchester derby. It was a win, win, win situation for all concerned.

Phnom Penh is the last displaced frontier town of America's Wild West. As infamous as Dodge City in Kansas and equally feared by lawmen, it is a mean city full of cowboys and outlaws where saloons brim with dancing girls doubling as sex workers. Mischief, mayhem, and murder are the orders of the day, and with street crime and more serious crimes on the rise, a growing number of international embassies are warning their citizens to exercise caution. Behind those messages of concern is a thinly veiled desire that they do not, in fact, go there at all.

A culture of chaos can be as exciting as a thunderstorm, and that is the appeal of Phnom Penh for many travellers. As the late Vivian Greene observed: 'Life isn't about waiting for the storm to pass. It's about learning to dance in the rain.' In Phnom Penh, a downpour is often a deluge, but I always carried my dancing shoes.

Along the riverside area, which is popular with tourists, I noticed suspicious motorbike gangs waiting to give opportunity a ride but unlike their Wild West ancestors, they prefer to steal passports instead of horses. Passports are golden tickets as they are precious to hardened criminals for a host of reasons, including identity theft which is the fastest-growing crime in an increasingly digital world. A passport can pass from its owner's hands to those of a petty street criminal, before finding itself fingered by organised gangs. Intoxicated western tourists are the surest of victims, and if there were ever a time for an intervention (aside from the divine type), it would be on the late-night streets of Phnom Penh. My country's embassy considered it necessary to state the obvious by reminding (but also complimenting) its citizens abroad that they are '…an attractive target for criminals.' I wouldn't disagree with that statement, but I would argue that it's true of any major city, but with armed robbery also on the rise in Phnom Penh, vigilance, and common sense are the precautions of choice.

## Chapter 18: Fusilli Flashbacks

I took a short break in Naples on my return to Europe after a two-year hiatus; I had desperate cravings for the cobblestones of European culture and Italy is as reliable as jalapenos and heartburn. I booked a room at the UNA Hotel on Piazza Garibaldi, opposite the Central Station, as I had warm-hearted memories of alfresco dining on the piazzas of Venice, Florence, Siena, and Rome. Piazza Garibaldi, much like the whole city of Naples, is Italy's troublesome and challenging southern relative. With flashbacks over fusilli pasta, the dirty streets of the capital of Campania morphed into the dusty roads of Cambodia. I was back in the Penh.

Naples has earned an enduring, and unfortunate, association with organised crime and the streets have a Third World grubbiness about them as they are littered with piles of foul-smelling trash. Sacred sites are spray-painted with the gibberish of urban renegades, and the average Neapolitan lives in fear of the notorious and controlling Camorra, which is the local mafia equivalent of the Cosa Nostra and a powerful crime syndicate. Trash tsars manage the city's waste management and landfill sites, but they tend to serve their own interests before those of the people. There isn't much money to be made from daily household waste, but industrial waste is an altogether lucrative prospect. Despite the protests that were sparked by the city's unsanitary conditions when locals set fire to the rubbish on their streets, the piles of garbage continued to stack, mount and rival the supremacy of Vesuvius. Urban legend claims the Camorra never sleeps, so you would think they could find the time to don some cleaning gloves and give the city a good ol' scrub down.

In metropolitan Naples, crime is as common as fresh-egg pasta and pickpockets are as plentiful as grated Parmigiano-Reggiano. The infamous Scippatori are a motorised gang of bag thieves but Neapolitan pickpockets, on the other hand, are an unseen menace much like an airborne disease. When a young woman broke into tears on a train to Sorrento, I wasn't at all surprised by the story she sobbed and shared with her over-enthusiastic carriage audience. I suspected they were only sympathetic to a point and were probably more relieved that she had been robbed instead of them. She explained that as she boarded the train, she was pushed and shoved by platform passengers before discovering (as the train left the station) that her purse and passport were missing from the zip pocket of her backpack.

Whether they deserve it or not, Italians have a reputation for their directness, which is often interpreted as rudeness. A middle-aged Italian woman, standing next to Naples' latest victim of pickpocketing, was unable to resist asking a question the rest of us had already deemed insensitive, unhelpful and entirely unnecessary: 'Why didn't you put your valuables somewhere safe *inside* your bag?' Compounded by the condescension of her tone, expression and those emphatic hand gestures Italians are fond of, I found some empathy for our young victim when she tried to defend herself by claiming that she hadn't noticed anyone suspicious-looking waiting on the platform. To support her claim, I didn't spot anyone wearing a black and white striped convict outfit, a black eye mask or carrying a swag bag with a large dollar sign either. In Naples, some passengers are perennial borders, and if you present them with an opportunity, they will undoubtedly snatch it.

As I waited at Napoli Station for another train to Herculaneum, I couldn't help but notice Italy's most conspicuous passenger sitting on a platform bench. He was more Snoop Dogg than Calvin Cordozar Broadus Jr., so my initial amusement quickly turned to suspicion. He had tried too hard to look like a moneyed teenager, and his demeanour suggested he had criminal intent. Besides, he was wearing sunglasses *inside* the terminal building, and that was all the evidence I needed. Booked and charged. He may have had a medical reason for wearing them, such as photophobia, but I suspected he wore them to mask watchful eyes. As a detective of sorts, when I get a hunch I am usually right, so I imagined Snoop Dogg was wearing a *Fun Lovin' Criminals* T-shirt under his jacket.

And I was right. As the train came to a stop, Snoop quickly removed his coat, wrapped it around his arm to conceal his light-fingered movements and joined the passenger scrum. Within seconds of the doors closing, a senior man regained the vigour of his youth and wrestled him off the train before it had even left the station. Snoop Dogg had evidently tried and failed to pinch his wallet, and I wondered whether he wore those sunglasses to conceal a blackened eye from another failed pickpocketing attempt. He was lucky he wasn't cuffed and chained like the dog he was.

Southeast Asia developed my knack for spotting a shady character in a blackout, and Phnom Penh is full of inky sketches.

## Chapter 19: Infernos and Black Paintings

Phnom Penh has its snoops and dogs, and while the capital is home to genuine God-fearing people, its bars and nightclubs are a rogue's gallery of Francisco Goya's *Black Paintings*. These cautionary tales in human form are as fascinating as rarely seen exotic animals, except for the fact that these are men who have put themselves behind bars of their making. For many of the expats I met in Bangkok, Southeast Asia was an opportunity to escape drudgery or reinvent their lives, but one thing they all had in common was that 'Cambodia' was a safe word.

Generally considered (in expat circles) as a final frontier, to consider relocating and permanently settling in Phnom Penh was tantamount to abandoning all hope of a conventional life. Gary Glitter chose Cambodia for a place of residence before being jailed, deported and banned from the country, and he is a good yardstick by which to measure some of the personality types that call Cambodia 'home.' In the western world, men will rarely admit - even to their closest friends - that they have engaged the services of a sex worker. In Cambodia, Vietnam, and Thailand, expats are more likely to marry and introduce them to their mothers. Conventionality may as well rest in pieces.

Severe poverty and gender inequality have created a thriving market for sexual slavery and the exploitation and trade of virgins (sold to the highest bidders like cattle at the market). The sale of virginity is just one of Cambodia's scandalous trades as the wealthy coerce the desperate, while impoverished mothers agree to the unthinkable: selling their daughters' innocence to the highest bidders. Some Asian men believe intercourse with a pure virgin can ward off illness and give them magical powers to delay the onset of old age, with thousands of virgins sold each year for this purpose. The market is overflowing, with a steady supply of impoverished families from the fields, and the police rarely enforce the rule of law. It is a buyers' market, and Cambodia is a source, transit and destination country for human trafficking and exploitation (child sex tourism is its darkest trade).

Like that reflex drivers get when they slow down to observe scenes of carnage at a roadside accident, Phnom Penh is a curious road trip to the outer realms of dark tourism. With killing fields containing the mass graves of genocide victims and former school classrooms turned into prison and torture cells, a stay in this city can be a disturbing experience. Dante Alighieri's *Inferno* describes a journey through the nine circles of hell, but that hasn't stopped millions of people from reading and enjoying his epic poem. You just wouldn't want to join him there. The history of Phnom Penh is as close to hell on earth as it gets, and without caution and sunscreen protection, there's a real risk of getting burned. But there is a silver lining to Phnom Penh, no matter how hard those mean-spirited monsoon clouds try to hide it.

Phnom Penh is all about the difference. *Cultural difference*. It is not like any city I have visited, though Naples did have some similarities, and there is something wonderfully refreshing about its imperfections. The difficulty of its haphazardness and the discomfort of its chaos makes it a unique challenge for travellers. It is a cultural obstacle course. When I spent a week visiting Dubai, it was like visiting a fully immersive Lego city built for adults. The designers have used their bricks with inspired creativity and the Burj Khalifa, the Dubai Mall, and the Burj Al Arab are all impressive constructions, but Dubai is an artificial place that is far too clean and polished for its good. Historic Munich was flattened by the bombs of World War Two, and what has been built in its stead is attractive on the eye and similarly spotless, but it failed to quicken my pulse or stimulate my travel appetites, aside from those famous German beers houses such as the Hofbrauhaus and Weisses Brauhaus. The opening line of Leo Tolstoy's *Anna Karenina* captures the essential difference between a Dubai or a Munich and a Phnom Penh: 'All happy families are alike; each unhappy family is unhappy in its own way.'

Historically, Phnom Penh was the epitome of an unhappy and broken family, and when brothers killed their brothers, it became the epicentre of an ideology of genocide, ignorance, hatred, and fear. But it is, at the very least, an unnervingly unique place to visit.

Phnom Penh matches the definition of that overused phrase 'compact capital' and it is saved, in part, by its riverside location as it sits at the confluence of three rivers: the Bassac, Tonle Sap, and the Mekong. Its name connotes an eastern exoticism it doesn't rightly deserve, and travellers can often be heard debating its correct pronunciation. I noticed significantly fewer tourists in the capital as its cultural highlights are, quite understandably, overshadowed by its northern frontrunner. Genocide, it would seem, is not on every traveller's bucket list. And without a developed tourism infrastructure in place, Phnom Penh is a compendium of hardships.

Roads and streets are inescapably dirty, and the air is full of construction dust as the wheels of motorbikes spin and kick it all back up for easy inhalation. Packs of stray dogs are ever watchful too, but at least they don't have motorbikes or hands to pinch and grab. They are more likely to *give* rather than take, so a rabies jab is a necessary precaution. Some tribal societies claim that the eating of earth and dirt - geophagy - promotes good health, and this city has an abundant supply. I was reminded of that fact when I watched a small boy crouch at a kerbside to scoop a plastic cupful of black and oily gutter water. Before I could intervene, he gulped it down and developed a lifelong immunity to poverty.

A visit to Phnom Penh is a multisensory experience as motorbikes roar past on roads and pavements, while the gentle sounds of chapei kluoks, a traditional wooden instrument, escape from heritage buildings to vie for aural space. Market stalls present exotic flowers in buckets splashed with animal blood, while the pungent stench of decapitated fish heads at the next stall reminds visitors that this is a city of contrasts. Old and new, wealthy and poor, charming but chaotic, Phnom Penh is vibrant, bustling and very much alive. There is no such thing as mundanity in this capital as spontaneity rules. All five senses are kept in a state of continuous high alert as Phnom Penh is an active travel experience, with Hoi An its cultural antonym. The more I use my senses, the more I absorb and remember, whereas a week lying prone on the beach will always feel like the same day on repeat.

Hostel and guesthouse windows often come with bars in Phnom Penh, and uninvited night guests, such as cockroaches and mosquitoes, customarily joined me for naps, but at least they hurried me out the door the next morning to travel and explore. An expat shared a story about an invited 'night guest' he picked up from a flophouse for a fixed price at the end of a drunken evening (I was wearing that *A Sunny Place for Shady Characters* T-shirt, so the situational absurdity was lost on him). He capped his debauchery and intoxication by making the beast with two backs with a stranger, and once his companion with a single purpose was dismissed, his needs satiated, he fell asleep in the flickering shadows like a crumpled banknote. When he awoke the next morning, he noticed his shorts were not where he remembered kicking them by the door; they had relocated directly beneath a barred window on the opposite side of the room. While he slept, a thief used a device to fish his shorts across the floor so they could steal his wallet. They must have been tipped off by that kind stranger as they took his cash, leaving his credit cards bound together with a rubber band on the window sill, fearful no doubt of being caught with such compelling evidence of their crime.

Why did he share that story? Why would *anybody* want to share that story? The sequel that followed was worse, like watching *Saw* and all its sequels in one sitting, as he boasted about having slept with at least a hundred prostitutes in Southeast Asia, Cambodia mostly, having never worn a condom.

Not even once. Perhaps he thought he deserved a trophy for coming first in the world's most dangerous sport.

While there is more to Phnom Penh than vice and the associated misery of its past, Tuol Sleng and the killing fields of Choeung Ek are the 'attractions' of choice for tourists wanting to see more of Cambodia than the ancient history of Angkor Wat. The city is home to the Royal Palace and Silver Pagoda, the National Museum, the Independence Monument and other notable historic sites, but the steady international investment is changing its cosmetic appearance. War and revolution have kept its development in check, but it could become the scarred face of almost any other modern South-east Asian city if it doesn't protect itself from the metropolitan acne of international brands, such as MacDonald's and Pizza Hut. What makes it distinct could soon be lost to progress, but it does at least survive as one of Southeast Asia's wildest frontiers.

Phnom Penh is another Marmite capital full of sleazy bars with bright neon and shady characters with charming smiles. It is an open-air museum of the unconventional, and it is as fascinating as it is shocking. Only in Phnom Penh could orchards and green meadows be turned into killing fields, a school into a prison of interrogation and torture and a playground gymnastics beam into murderous gallows. There are very few expat saints walking the streets of the capital, as the majority have been turned into sinners in the girlie bars and brothels. Phnom Penh is Wilder than West, and it may as well have a plate of noodles for a sheriff as the law is an ineffectual and invisible presence. I wouldn't want to live there myself, but it is one of Southeast Asia's unforgettable capitals.

# Chapter 20: The Killing Fields

A word cloud for Phnom Penh is likely to feature 'Khmer Rouge,' 'genocide,' 'torture,' 'murder' and 'mass graves,' so a trip to Cambodia's killing fields is about as far removed from the world of package holidays as it gets. Just ten miles south of the capital, Choeung Ek (its local name) is often added to itineraries as an afterthought, but for some travellers, it is the primary purpose of their visit and a field trip like no other. As I had already spent Christmas Eve at the Dachau Concentration Camp in Germany (as a visitor, not an inmate), convention no longer mattered as I welcomed in my thirty-eighth year at one of the unlikeliest settings for a birthday celebration.

As their name suggests, the killing fields of Cambodia are brutally unambiguous, but they're not covered in the blood splatter of a television crime scene investigation. Dexter Morgan was nowhere to be seen. I was flabbergasted when I overheard two Australian tourists express their disappointment that 'there isn't much to see.' Perhaps the dead should try harder. But what exactly had they expected to see? They were visiting the scene of one of the darkest episodes in the history of humanity, not the set of an Eli Roth slasher. The short flight I had taken from Bangkok to Phnom Penh established the mood for this encounter with dark tourism, the pilot navigating violent thunderstorms and heavy turbulence. As I fixed my eyes on towering cumulonimbus clouds with fingers crossed and everything else sweating, the weather was a suitable precursor to the horrors of a genocidal ideology as strong headwinds willed me back to Bangkok.

Visiting the killing fields of Choeung Ek is a macabre, sombre experience and a quiet reminder of humanity's capacity for evil which didn't come to an end with a cyanide capsule, a gunshot, and Hitler's alleged suicide. Much like my visit to Hiroshima in Japan and Auschwitz-Birkenau in Poland, I knew what I was letting myself in for when I re-entered the echoing realms of Cambodia's darker-than-most tourism industry. The tragic events that unfolded in these now-benign fields entered my consciousness when I was a boy of just ten years of age. My parents rented a VHS copy of the award-winning 1985 film *The Killing Fields*, which introduced the word 'genocide' to my adolescent lexicon. I remember being disturbed by brutal scenes of torture and execution, but it was just another film, surely, like all those American films about the Vietnam War. I was too young to understand or make any sense of what I was viewing.

Standing in the eerily quiet fields of a former longan orchard a quarter of a century later, I remembered my history teacher's impassioned delivery of a lesson about the rise and fall of the Nazis. Like an unpoetic impression of the late Robin Williams from *Dead Poets Society*, he explained with great animation (much like Hitler himself) how world nations joined together on a wave of global optimism in the aftermath of the Holocaust. Their pledge was pure as they vowed never to allow a history of genocide to repeat itself. *Never again!* But it did happen again, far away, and they allowed it to happen. Mr Sexton neglected to mention that fact as he stroked his wiry salt and pepper beard, presumably because 'Cambodia' and 'killing fields' were not to be found within the pages of his curriculum.

Before I visited the memorial site, I read insightful blogs on travel websites that warned their readers that Choeung Ek is not a place for the faint-hearted, or travellers of a 'sensitive disposition.' One writer summed up the totality of his experience by stating: 'It is a sad place.' Comedian Steve Martin should remind their editors that a day without sunshine is 'like, you know, night.' In many respects, the fields of Choeung Ek are the perfect spot for a picnic: the area is quiet, peaceful, has acres of countryside and reasonable toilet facilities, but I didn't need to be reminded not to pack a family and alfresco feast with summery salads and quiche. I knew what to expect as I had seen similar scenes or worse in Poland when confronted by piles of human hair and mobile incineration units. I did not want my experience and understanding of Cambodia to be bookended by ancient Khmer temples; I wanted to get a rounded sense of Cambodia, its people, and its recent history. I had taken the road travelled by the ancestors in Angkor, but this was the crooked one I was compelled to walk.

I have friends who enjoy annual holidays to the popular and pristine Sharm el-Sheikh resorts on Egypt's Red Sea coast. I have not been myself, but they tell me they enjoy sunbathing on long beaches, diving in clear waters and walking clean promenades neatly dotted with exotic palm trees. I try to encourage them to visit the celebrated, ancient attractions of Egypt's pyramids and temples along the Nile River Valley, but they rarely stray from the relaxed luxury of swimming pools and sundecks. They love Egypt, but they haven't been to *Egypt* at all, just a hotter, more distant suburb of Spain. Cairo is undeniably dusty, dirty and noisy, but it is also vibrant, exhilarating and exotic. There are of course different horses for different courses, but to my travel mind they are returning to a gallery of priceless exhibits and wearing a blindfold. The same applies to Cambodia, where rough should be taken with smooth, as glorious ancient kingdoms and gruesome killing fields exist in the same space.

Moving respectfully and sorrowfully past the graves at Cheoung Ek, I noticed every other visitor was doing the same, subconsciously imitating speed and movement like a kinematic equation for low spirits. On entry, I was given a complimentary audio guide with my admission ticket (seriously, it's ticketed) but struggled with the vintage 1980s headphones set when I tried to adjust and extend its arms to reach the ears of my oversized head. The audio guides serve a dual function, sharing valuable information about harrowing events and haunting survivor stories, while managing to keep everybody respectfully quiet. That, I suspected, was their greater purpose.

As I listened to the incongruously high-born voice of a Clarence House resident (because all British people speak like American stereotypes), the whole gamut of human emotion was on show around me, like an improvised mime. Horror, anger, and disbelief were etched onto grave-looking faces but for some visitors, it was all too much, and their salty sorrow streamed over their cheeks. Picture boards presented further visual evidence (should it be needed) of terrible suffering and indignity. Lives were brutally cut short by a regime which preferred to beat and hack its victims to death with axes, knives, hammers, hoes, cart axles, machetes and bamboo poles because bullets were a commodity too precious for executions (others faced death by slow starvation and forced labour in the fields). Executioners were fond of using the cut-price serrated edges of sugar palm branches to slit open their prisoners' throats, resulting in a silent death that was less likely to disturb their neighbours' peace or arouse curiosity. They hung speakers from trees to broadcast revolutionary songs, to mask the sounds of suffering and hide their heinous crimes. Many of the regime's victims were still alive when they were shoved into pits brimming with decomposing bodies, before being covered with chemical insecticide DDT to mask the stench and accelerate the process of decay.

A campaign slogan - adopted by the Khmer Rouge to justify the murder of babies and infants - reads like the kind of advice you might find in a gardening centre: 'When you dig up the grass, you must pull up the roots.' My audio guide explained how infants and babies had their heads smashed to pulp against Chankiri trees (also called Killing Trees) and hundreds of multi-coloured bands are pinned on them to commemorate the loss of so many young lives. The executioners barely registered the human forms of their victims as they grabbed them by their legs or feet, smashed their heads against the thick trunks of the trees and casually slung them into the open mouths of mass graves. A sign by one such tree used the euphemism 'beat' instead of 'killed,' displaying its capitalised message in both Khmer and English:

KILLING TREE AGAINST WHICH EXECUTIONERS BEAT
CHILDREN. It is the most unequivocal sentence I have ever read, despite its
attempt at semantic restraint. When the site was discovered, so too were the
traces of blood, children's hair and brain matter that lodged in the bark of these
trees as evidence of the regime's crimes.

There is a small, thought-provoking on-site museum with photographs
and information about the Khmer Rouge leadership and the ongoing trials of
surviving war criminals. The audio guide features the chilling recount of a
former guard and executioner named Him Huy and as the recording plays, his
monotone voice confirms and details the callous techniques employed by a
regime as evil as their Nazi predecessors. Having seized control of Cambodia in
1975, their period of rule was, fortunately, short-lived and came to a brutal end
four years later courtesy of a Vietnamese invasion supported by Cambodian
rebels.

The remains of close to nine thousand people were exhumed in 1980
from mass graves at this site, and a Buddhist Memorial Stupa contains more
than five thousand skulls. Pol Pot's bloody 'Year Zero' cleansing campaign
claimed the lives of some estimated two million 'undesirable' civilians
(accounting for 21% of the population at the time) in sites similar to this across
what was then called Democratic Kampuchea. But there was nothing remotely
democratic about a state controlled by the government of the Khmer Rouge.
Like the Nazis before them, they manufactured death on an industrial scale and
this, in part, accounts for the country's relatively small population (which
currently stands at 15.4 million).

Episodes of genocide have repeated throughout history, but the 1948
UN Convention on the Prevention of the Crime of Genocide aimed to prevent
recurrences of some of the most grievous acts committed by humanity against
his fellow man. Their goal was noble, but it was ultimately doomed to fail.
Dozens of genocidal campaigns followed in the footsteps of the Nazis in
Rwanda, Tibet, Indonesia, Libya, Yemen, Bosnia and Herzegovina, Sri Lanka,
Sudan, Burundi, Uganda, Bangladesh, Nigeria, Guatemala, Zanzibar, Brazil, and
Cambodia. Genocide has occurred for a diverse range of justifications on every
corner of the globe, in ancient and modern societies. Some are on-going in
North Korea, Darfur and Syria, but the Khmer Rouge's unflinching and
relentless capacity for brutality and cruelty places it alongside the Nazi Party.

With hollow sockets staring back at me through yellowed acrylic, I
couldn't help but contemplate the personalities those bones once housed and
the stories they could tell, if they had the chance. I noticed that some skulls

were fractured while others had their fragments piled in pieces, so it didn't take much to imagine the violence they suffered at the hands of their tormentors. I have been to many historical sites where tourists are encouraged to show respect through quietness, and I have often been dismayed by the ignorance of some, especially those in large tour groups who seem to think every destination is a variation on Disneyland. At Choeung Ek, nature itself was subdued into silence.

As I made my way across the peaceful grounds of the notorious killing fields, the sun shone in a cloudless sky to pour light into the hollows of mass graves while the voice in my headset explained the appalling conditions and terrible fates of the poor souls who perished at Choeung Ek. Tourists are encouraged by the Cambodian government to visit this historic site but to fully understand the scale of its human tragedy, a visit to Tuol Sleng Genocide Museum is essential. At Tuol Sleng, prisoners of the regime were interrogated (or executed) before their eventual transfer, murder and mass burial at the killing fields. I witnessed first-hand the fragments of human bones and clothing that persist in revealing their suffering and secrets, poking their way up through the soil after a generation of silence.

Some bones are routinely collected after torrential rainfall and placed in display cases by the mass graves. When I stumbled upon a complete lower jaw with teeth, I sat in the shade of a Chankiri tree for a moment of quiet reflection. Other visitors had done the same, equally overcome by their raw emotion, as they tried but failed to come to terms with such senselessness. Shakespeare explored the human condition in his plays, and his characters are often flawed creatures, but even he would have struggled to make any sense of this place or the thinking and motivations of the Khmer Rouge.

I was warned that Choeung Ek would leave me feeling 'sad,' but why had I visited? Why do so many tourists travel to this site from all over the world? I had a better understanding of modern Cambodia and the country's recent history of violence, but the killing fields also took me closer to an appreciation of the stoic resilience of the Cambodian people. Cambodia is recovering from the tragedy of its past and is pushing forward with renewed optimism and hope in the twenty-first century. I admire the Cambodians for their capacity for forgiveness and reconciliation; they are an inspiration for future generations as they raise a glass half full when the bottle has been broken and is held together with sticking tape. When I reflect on the problems of my life, they are trivial by comparison. I vowed to remember the victims of

Cheoung Ek whenever I faced future difficulties, aiming to overcome them by thinking and acting positively.

Tuol Sleng is a museum in central Phnom Penh that chronicles the history of Cambodian genocide, and as such, it is one of the attractions of abhorrence in the capital area. The Tuol Svay Prey High School, once a typical high school with the sound of children at play, was transformed into the stuff of every child's nightmare when it became the badly kept secret prison of Pol Pot's terrifying regime, acquiring the pseudonym 'S-21' and a perimeter covered in barbed wire. The torturers and executioners made full use of their killing space, as they converted a playground gymnastics beam into makeshift gallows to hang undesirable inmates.

Tuol Sleng was the final 'home' of an estimated thirty thousand political prisoners of the Khmer Rouge Communist Party and a place where regime victims were interrogated (with an emphasis on *terror*) and forced into a confession, starved to death or tortured before their late-night escorts to the killing fields of Choeung Ek. Hundreds of thousands were left to die in the rice fields, as they were considered an insignificant threat to the regime as they had very little education or understanding of politics. The political prisoners were regarded as dangerous, conspiratorial enemies and thus had to be crushed or expelled, with murder the most effective and permanent guarantee of silence.

When the Vietnamese army entered and liberated Phnom Penh in collaboration with Cambodian rebels, the regime members fled in haste but killed as many of the inmates as they could manage. It was a final act of spite, but significantly, they left behind a wealth of documentary evidence of their crimes which is now displayed in a converted museum of remembrance. The day I visited the site, I was fortunate to meet two former inmates as they interviewed for an anniversary programme for broadcast on Phnom Penh's cable television company (PPCTV). Chum Mey and Bou Meng are two of only twelve known survivors, and both have released books detailing their traumatic experiences and personal survival stories as prisoners of S-21. Bou Meng lost his wife and only child to the regime, and as the cameras rolled, I tried to comprehend how these two calm and enduring figures could have survived a past of such personal tragedy and horror, and still find forgiveness in their hearts. I wondered if there could ever be justice for such crimes.

With access to classrooms turned into makeshift prison and torture cells, it wasn't difficult to imagine the evils that occurred there; pictures of bloody corpses line the walls and traces of human blood continue to stain the floor. Upon abandonment of the prison, fourteen victims of the regime were found chained to metal bed frames with hideous mutilations, while pools of blood congealed beneath them. The close resemblance to Auschwitz-Birkenau in Poland was what struck me most, as piles of clothes and inmates' belongings are displayed behind glass next to torture devices and a gallery of ghosts. The regime didn't discriminate, and neither did the Nazis, as I saw photographs of young men, senior men, women, teenagers, children and infants as tender as five or six. With its white and terracotta floor tiles and dusty-black chalkboards, Tuol Sleng seemed like an appropriate setting to read and learn about one of the darkest chapters in the history of humanity.

The grounds and separate school buildings readily revealed the secrets of a ruthless regime, and marching in the footsteps of fear and helplessness, I reflected on all those lives so mindlessly extinguished. I considered it strange that like the Nazis, the Khmer Rouge obsessively documented their crimes for the rest of the world to hold them to account for, but it confirmed their strong beliefs and dedication to a communist ideology and a society free of social classes. There was just that small matter of having to murder anyone who disagreed (or might disagree) with them first, as they pursued their high revolutionary ideals.

It is a universal truth that travel broadens the mind, but my own had been wrenched apart and kicked about in bloody fields and playgrounds. Benjamin Disraeli proposed that travel 'teaches toleration,' and I can't think of a more suitable location to learn that lesson.

## Chapter 21: Temples and Tomb Raiders

I tried and failed to master the cack-handed controls and awkward gameplay of those *Tomb Raider* computer games. Unable to get to grips with a controller that was as confused as I was, Lara Croft couldn't get to grips with her environment of ledges, ladders, stairs, crags, cliffs, beams, walls, rock faces, crates and everything else the designers wanted me to climb on and fall off. I died the same death a million times as I mastered the technique of a tedious but challenging jump from one ledge to another, before eventually getting it right. It was a long game of patience, and I didn't have quite enough.

The only aspect of the *Tomb Raider* games that interested me were the cinematics and their beautifully rendered graphic landscapes. I wanted to immerse myself in mysterious worlds of pixels and crumbling temples overgrown by jungle, so I paused the game to look at picture postcards of places that did not exist. I didn't know it at the time, but the architecture of Cambodia's ancient Khmer Kingdom inspired some of their digital settings. I watched university friends play the game instead, but this usually resulted in very slow progress with Lara Croft using her knees instead of her feet to move about, with a commentary punctuated by smutty schoolboy remarks as the third-person perspective allowed compromising views of the ponytailed protagonist.

When I visited Angkor Wat for the first time in 2012, the landscape was familiar and came in high definition as I found myself immersed in the real-life world of *Tomb Raider*. It was easier to navigate using my legs and feet instead of hands and toggle buttons, and my patience was rewarded at long last as I didn't have to worry about being ripped to shreds by packs of stray digital dogs while I freely explored the jungle ruins. As I climbed over boulders, skimmed along ledges and ducked under beams at Angkor Wat, digital fiction evolved into real-life animation. It was the perfect cultural return on my cross-country adventure and a stupendous introduction to Cambodia.

The highlight of any journey to Cambodia will, undoubtedly, be Angkor Wat as it is one of the world's renowned travel and archaeological sites and an outdoor adventure playground for adults. The national flag of Cambodia carries an image of the main wat - with its six distinctive lotus bud prangs - on a striking background with a blue border and central red stripe. Angkor was the spiritual foundation of a powerful, wealthy and ancient civilisation which reached its cultural and political zenith in the eleventh century; it was one of the largest cities of the ancient world and boasted a proud history of a thousand years. It is now one of UNESCO's most famous

World Heritage sites. A single day was enough to visit the pyramids of Egypt, but I could have spent weeks exploring the enchanted landscapes of Angkor.

The name 'Angkor Wat' derives from the ancient Khmer words 'Angkor,' meaning 'city' or 'capital city,' and 'Wat' which means 'temple' or 'temple grounds.' The Angkor Wat temple complex was put together over a period of four hundred years as a symbol of stability and continuance, so it is fitting that it has found a new role in modern-day Cambodia as the stronghold of the country's tourism growth and commercial development. The site suffered the effects of war, conflict and neglect over the centuries, but Cambodian officials have endeavoured to protect and preserve its history with the welcome support of international experts.

Angkor Wat is one of the world's largest religious monument groups, showcasing miles of elaborate and perfectly preserved bas-relief carvings with spectacular scenes of vast armies preparing for war with their regional neighbours. It was a symbol of civilisation and regional dominance, and a structural statement of a nation's wealth and power. Historians claim that many of the temples served dual administrative and religious functions in a strictly hierarchical society, where religious belief and ceremony were integral to Khmer life. The cultural magnificence and artistic distinctiveness of the temples allow Angkor Wat to dine at the same table as the Pharaohs and Mughal emperors, as it's frequently mentioned in the same breath as the pyramids of Egypt and India's cultural axiom in Agra: The Taj Mahal.

The Khmer people were ahead of their time as they undertook massive engineering projects to open trade routes and expand their empire. In many respects, they were Southeast Asia's equivalent of the Roman Empire. And just like the Romans, they understood the value of roads and were the only nation in their region to build and connect their empire with seven thousand miles attributed to the kings of this kingdom. They were also partial to grand statements of grandeur, as they built more than a thousand temples in the Siem Reap area alone, with the majority dating from between 802 and 1431 when the Khmer Kingdom flourished. Close to two hundred of these temples remain standing, presenting different architectural nuances characteristic of different periods and Khmer kings.

The great Khmer Kingdom dominated Southeast Asia of the Middle Ages for six hundred of its one thousand years of existence, and it is now one of the ancient world's greatest archaeological mysteries. Why did the Khmer people suddenly pack their bags and abandon their spiritual and symbolic capital in the fifteenth century? Archaeologists have used modern technology to scan and map this medieval metropolis and have concluded, tentatively, that the catalyst for the kingdom's decline was not warring nations as all those bas-reliefs might suggest, but that essential element of all life, no matter how great or small: $H_2O$.

Frequent regional flooding resulted in the collapse and failure of the kingdom's critical irrigation systems which rendered the entire Angkor area a non-viable settlement for its people. The Khmer had humble beginnings as rice farmers, so the value of water wasn't taken for granted, but when they did lose it, they left their glorious kingdom to the mercy of nature and the fates of the gods. Angkor passed from glory to shadow as a lost jungle Atlantis, while the capital relocated south to Phnom Penh. Angkor Wat was never truly abandoned as the temple grounds have been a regular place of worship since the day of their construction. It was never deserted by faith, as Buddhist monks tended to its grounds and helped preserve it for future generations of worshippers and tourists.

When I visited the site in 2012, a friendly tuk-tuk driver approached me on the gravelled street outside my hostel and enquired whether I wanted to be taken to see the temples (it was a fair assumption to make). His name was Mean, which he explained means 'wealthy' in Cambodian, but he didn't look it as he wore a pair of heavily scuffed orange Crocs with more holes than their original designers intended. He didn't look very *mean* either. I had been in the country for two short hours, and I was already impressed by the kind consideration and generosity of the Cambodian people (except Mean wasn't offering a free ride). In most western countries, people prefer to live in boxes with tightly secured lids, but in Southeast Asia, they spend more time on the streets than they ever do in their homes. I have always been impressed by the ease of travel in this region as there is no need for advance bookings secured with credit cards; you can just turn up and go. Southeast Asia is the happy-go-lucky neighbourhood of the world.

Mean was a taxi driver by trade, but he didn't own a cab as such. He had a tuk-tuk, a motorised tricycle named after the sound of its engine and which is a traditional symbol of Southeast Asia. With tourists regarded as vertical stacks of mobile currency, logic naturally equates anything with wheels and a tourist on top to a profitable small business. I was a short-term venture, and Mean wanted to earn an honest wage, so we agreed that for fourteen American dollars, he would offer fourteen hours of his time, wheels and petrol and take me to all the popular tourist sites graced by the presence of Lara Croft. With the average annual wage in Cambodia being $950 or $2.6 a day,

Mean was earning the equivalent of a week's pay for a day's work. He was doing well by Cambodian standards and living up to his name.

Fourteen dollars tasted more like twenty-four, as it included a complimentary breakfast and as many bottles of iced water that I could manage to drink before the onset of water intoxication. Mrs Mean prepared a takeaway container of bai krob chanti (cinnamon cashew rice) with a flask of sweet iced coffee. Mean packed his cool box with a slab of ice and a dozen bottles of water, and this was appropriate, given that I can drink my share in tropical heat, especially at archaeological sites. I feared Mean would be red-faced in the red by the end of the day, and a little less than kind and friendly.

Southeast Asia is a mecca for backpackers and budget travellers for a good reason, and this arrangement suited us both. I was also relieved that Mean wanted payment in dollars rather than Cambodian riel, as the national currency is one of those worthless monies that you need a whole suitcase of to buy a banana. The notes are colourful with images of famous Cambodian icons (such as Angkor Wat), but they're not accepted or traded internationally, so I set aside the spares in my wallet as currency souvenirs. Getting up before the cockerels at 3:30 am the next morning was no easy feat, as my mobile phone danced to life on the opposite side of the room.

By habit, I place my phone's alarm out of reach as I can resist everything but temptation and snooze options. As I fingered in the dark for a switch on the lamp, something black with twitching probes scurried out of sight down the back of the bedside table. For four dollars a night, I had the pleasure of sharing a room with indescribable stains, damp sheets, and uninvited bed bugs. The scourge of mosquitoes that waited patiently on the ceiling throughout the day announced their presence at night as wings whirred and buzzed about my ears (while they searched for a safe landing strip to offload their diseases).

I don't mind mosquitoes (even though they are the deadliest creature on the planet) because they don't have fearsome teeth like sharks and lions, or the quick and unpredictable movements of cockroaches. If a mosquito is smart enough to calculate that the only part of my body that I haven't sprayed with DEET is my face, I consider it worthy of a drop or two of blood. I raised my glass to them; intelligence deserves a reward. A friend contracted dengue fever in Malaysia, which is a viral disease of the tropics transmitted by mosquitoes. He suffered intense fever and acute pains in his joints, and he partially lost his sight for a few days which, fortunately for him, returned. He was overweight like most westerners adapting to a carb-heavy diet of rice for breakfast, rice for lunch and rice for dinner, so he was delighted with the side effects of an unexpected weight-loss plan that any Weight Watchers follower could only dream of achieving. Every cloud has a silver lining, and he reduced the lining of his trousers.

Despite my cockroach phobia (katsaridaphobia, which developed into an obsession in Southeast Asia), if I don't see any signs of them when the lights are on, I'm willing to take my chances at night while I'm asleep in their preferred six-legged darkness. One of my former colleagues, who lived in an apartment close to mine, is the only person I have met who casually accepted their presence like a pet cat or dog. Roaches lived inside his toaster because it's a favourite family hideout as it's cosy and warm, and they can feed on freshly toasted breadcrumbs every day, without having to scurry an inch in search of food. In return, they are more than happy to share pathogens such as E. coli and salmonella.

I introduced my toaster inhabitants to the freezer every month, as that was the surest method I could think of for killing the adults and the eggs they laid inside. I accepted this was by no means a rational act as it was more likely to trigger a white-coat intervention, but desperate times require desperate measures. The alternative was to buy a new toaster every month, or never eat toast again.

Confirmation of my germinating fear came when I bought every airtight container I could get my hands on at the Bangkok branch of IKEA in Bangna District (their profits must have soared in April 2013). I was determined not to allow any cockroaches to get their spiky appendages on my cornflakes and rice, but I failed to protect the latter as weevil eggs would often hatch and hide inside. I noticed the adults when pouring rice into a pan, their dark bodies contrasting against the rice. Picking out as many as I could find with a teaspoon, I was confident that any weevils missed would otherwise boil to death.

I knew my fear of the roach bordered on the irrational, but I took some comfort from the fact that my fear can be traced to ancient Egypt. In their desperation, Egyptians fashioned spells to control them as they didn't have supermarkets or the convenience of insect sprays and repellents, instead imploring their ram-headed god Khnum to banish them from their kingdom. History was on my side, but the cockroaches weren't going anywhere, as they have been present on planet Earth for more than four hundred million years.

My friend of the roach, by contrast, was a kind and generous host as he even allowed them to share his bed. Cockroaches prefer a warm spot for a nap, and with his toaster already fully occupied, some had the audacity to cosy-up with him and bring the expression 'as snug as a bug in a rug' to life. He casually described the sensation of his bed guests moving about for space, and how he pulled back the sheets one morning to find some baby cockroaches curled up in the hairs of his chest. He explained that 'they don't bother me at all' and I couldn't decide whether I should hold him in great esteem, or never speak to him again. When he invited me over for dinner, I hoped and prayed toasted bread was not on the menu. I can understand why pet owners allow their cats or dogs to sleep at the end of their beds, but cockroaches and bed sheets are like scientists mixing with religious leaders.

At Thailand's Khao Yai National Park, I got closer to nature than I ever intended. My safari guide wished me a good night's sleep, dropped me off at my jungle lodge and disappeared, but I was deeply disturbed when I switched on the porch lights to startle an intrusion of cockroaches that darted every which way for cover. When I dropped off my backpack earlier that first day, the room was dusty and basic but tidy enough. There's not much point in paying for a fancy hotel room if you are going to return late, sleep and rise at the break of dawn. As cockroaches move under cover of darkness, I hadn't noticed them inside food cupboards or under the mattress. But when I entered the bathroom to collect the items placed there for convenience, a nonchalant cockroach reclined on the bristles of my toothbrush.

Seized by a fight or flight instinct, I grabbed up my backpack and possessions and darted toward the exit, leaving my toothbrush behind. The cockroaches could eat the bristles for all I cared, as I was never going to use it again, and they were welcome to my bed for the night as there was no chance that I was going to find peace and sleep in my idyllically infested lodgings; that small patch of Khao Yai was more *Tireland* than Thailand. Isolated and alone, there was nothing for me to do except sit outside and wait for the dawn and salvation to arrive.

With the only light coming from a cloudy moon, I had a long and testing night ahead of me, and as I sat there minding my own business, I was disturbed by the occasional late-night cockroach rambling home without apology. I was tempted to wish each intruder a good night's rest in the bed I had paid for, but I was fearful they might reply with hissed thanks and tip me over the edge of reason. After two hours of restlessness, I was saved from my misfortunate when a passing park ranger spotted me in his headlights. He took pity and offered to take me to what he promised was a 'roach-free hotel' with modern facilities, possibly fearful of a bad review on the Holy Book of Travels:

TripAdvisor. The manager had an available room and must have thought I was crazy, as the only word I repeated amid delirium was 'cockroaches.'

I have stayed in some nightmarish hostels and hotels in Asia and Africa, and I can tolerate most things, including excrement wiped over a toilet wall or someone else's used and discarded condom, draped over the edge of a bin next to the bedside cabinet. If it doesn't move or climb all over my face in the middle of the night, I'll turn a blind eye to most things and not complain.

Mean was waiting downstairs in the dark, and he gently revved his tuk-tuk engine to let me know he was there. I decided against taking a shower as it probably didn't work and besides, I would soon be showering in my sweat. I appreciated Mean's efforts and punctuality, as I wouldn't have gotten up so early for a stranger and if I had, I would have demanded more than fourteen dollars for doing so. Mean greeted me with a warm but practised smile as we shared perfunctory morning greetings (or was it still night?), but he couldn't pronounce my name no matter how many times he tried, so I settled on being called 'Gallon.' Fortunately for him, I am not one of those precious types that insist on the full and correct pronunciation of their name (my Thai students struggled with 'Griffiths' so we settled on 'G'). As my relationship with Mean had a shelf life that expired the same day, it didn't matter what he cared to call me.

With a cough and a heavy smoker's splutter, Mean's tuk-tuk broke the morning's silence like a motorised cockerel as its *tsjoek, tsjoek, tsjoek* woke the dawn. We set out to discover the mysteries of the Khmer Kingdom (at least I did) and take revenge on a thousand cockerels as we announced a new day before they even had the chance to wake, stir and aggravate their neighbours.

As we left sleepy Siem Reap for the highway connection to Angkor Wat, hundreds of tuk-tuks carried identical yawning tourists, like returning spacecraft to a cultural mothership. I was witnessing a bizarre abduction, and I was one of the abductees. It occurred to me that career pathways in Siem Reap are quite limited and present three choices: stand all day in muddy rice fields and develop early curvature of the spine; stand all day behind a reception desk at a hotel or hostel and develop curvature of the mind; or sit and sleep all day in a tuk-tuk and pass the time with tuk-tuk friends. Mean chose the smartest option; had I been born a Cambodian, I would have joined him.

Mean stopped at a checkpoint so I could purchase the Angkor Archaeological Park Pass, which represents exceptional value for money as it permits access to all the Angkor temples and monuments in the Siem Reap area (one day=20US\$, three days=40US\$, seven days=60US\$). I always carry a handful of passport photographs in my wallet, and I was glad that I did so as the officials refuse entry to the park without one. Angry tourists berated their drivers as early morning tempers got the better of them, but I could understand their disappointment as they were going to miss the Angkorian sunrise. I paid for a one-day pass as fourteen hours seemed like enough time for a rubble workout, and Mean dropped me off at the site just after 4 am. With my breakfast box in hand, a flask of iced coffee and a litre of water, I joined a dense crowd and patiently waited for the day to break over Angkor Wat.

Angkor Wat is the largest Khmer temple and the most-visited Khmer site. It is protected by a moat and outer wall that stretches for two miles, and this seemed like a good spot to eat my rice breakfast. I was surrounded by tired and sleepy faces that may have been regretting getting up so early to stare at a black sky that was the same as the one above their gardens back home in London or Los Angeles. We were all waiting for the sunrise to theatrically reveal the splendours of Angkor Wat, but it was more of a cloudrise than a sunrise, and I had seen better displays from my apartment balcony in Bangkok. Nature was not in an obliging mood.

The Angkorian temples are spread over a vast area of some 248 square miles, and Angkor Wat is the principal attraction that draws tourists to Cambodia (Lara Croft raised its international profile). Some temple sites are saturated by tourists and dripping sweat, especially Ta Prohm, popularly referred to as the 'Tomb Raider Temple' as this is the complex where Angelina Jolie shot scenes for the first film in the series: *Lara Croft: Tomb Raider*. When I returned to the kingdom for a second, longer stay two years later, I probed beyond the obvious to find less-visited temples and search for a less-touristic experience closer to the scenes in those computer games of my university youth.

I considered taking a hot air balloon over Angkor Wat as there would be fewer tourists floating in the sky. I was warned that the experience is expensive for what it is and misleading too, as the tourism authorities haven't granted any of the balloon companies permission to fly over the actual temples. UNESCO prohibits the companies from doing so as they present a landing risk to the ruins which, in their defence, are damaged enough already. The balloon companies fly *near* Angkor Wat but not *over* Angkor Wat. I say tomato; you say to*mah*to. My camera didn't have a mega-superzoom lens, so I decided the experience would be a lot of hot air and abandoned it. When I took a balloon flight over the ancient Bagan temples in Myanmar, the company had UNESCO permission and the experience provided a unique opportunity to view the temples and plains like the birds and the gods. I had a similar experience in Egypt over the Valley of the Kings, albeit with a partial crash landing in a field of sugarcane. At Angkor Wat, I settled on using my feet.

While little statuary remains at the main temple of Angkor Wat (which lends the area its name), the gallery of bas-reliefs is a masterpiece in ancient storytelling, depicting detailed narrative scenes from Hindu mythology and history, connecting the present with the past by giving the sprawling compound a sense of context and personality. The bas-reliefs are as extensive as they are impressive, forming a corridor narrative around the circumference of the central wat with some of the first depictions of Thai people represented as Siamese mercenaries. Some visitors completely miss this age-old art gallery as they work their way through the sites like a shopping list, but I found it paid dividends to explore carefully and to take as much time as possible inside - as well as outside - the main and lesser temple buildings.

Archaeologists consider Angkor Wat the pinnacle of Khmer art as its blocks of sandstone are a vast canvas of political propaganda depicting the power and wealth of ruling King Suryavarman II, who commissioned it as a funerary temple in the early twelfth century. As a temple dedicated to the Hindu god Vishnu, it features carvings of beautiful goddesses and magical creatures, and the wealth of the empire was poured into its construction in an area four times the size of Vatican City (it took forty years to complete). King Suryavarman wanted to eclipse everything that had come before it, and he achieved his goal. There is a small reflecting pool at the front of the main prasat structure with a view of the temple's iconic Khmer towers, which stand shoulder-to-shoulder with the trees that cloaked this area for centuries until missionaries discovered its secrets while exploring the Cambodian jungle that surrounds it to this day.

From Angkor Wat, and just a short distance north-west, is the less-visited Buddhist temple that I regard as the most visually striking of them all: The Bayon Temple in central Angkor Thom. It featured in a wide shot in the first *Tomb Raider* film, but most tourists are seemingly unaware of this fact so rush straight to the less-than-subtle Tomb Raider Temple. The distinguishing features of the Bayon Temple (commissioned upon completion of Angkor Wat) are the huge, smiling faces carved into the towers which keep watch at every compass point. A common misconception is that the faces represent Gautama Buddha, in various meditative states, but they are in fact impressions of King Jayavarman VII (the Khmer king who commissioned it). They are a statement of his power and authority as he majestically surveys his kingdom from every conceivable angle, though he now keeps a strict watch over tourists. Originally, there were two hundred sculpted faces with a set of four faces expressing different emotions on each tower.

King Jayavarman VII was a religious reformer who wanted to remove the power base of the old religion (Hinduism), so switched the national faith to Buddhism in the twelfth century. Consequently, Angkor Wat was initially a Hindu temple before it transformed into a Buddhist one, and King Jayavarman's legacy endures in the present day as Buddhism remains the state religion. During his reign, the greatest construction effort of the medieval world took place, with many of the temples that tourists admire today sanctioned by this king (even more impressive when you consider the simple tools at their disposal).

The Bayon Temple layout is close-packed in comparison to Angkor Wat, so it was easier to appreciate its micro aspects, which include a gallery of majestic bas-reliefs with thousands of carved figures depicting over three hundred legendary and historical scenes, as well as gloating victories over neighbouring Vietnam. The Bayon reliefs are impressive because they offer a complete picture of Khmer life, which includes scenes of ordinary people engaged in activities such as cooking, gambling, cockfighting and fishing. King Jayavarman left behind a document carved in stone that would reveal the secrets of his kingdom to future archaeologists. I enjoyed exploring this small temple as narrow pathways revealed hidden steps to higher levels, and I didn't have to climb along ledges or jump onto elevated platforms like digital or cinematic Lara Croft.

The Angkor area pays quiet tribute to ancient Egypt in the shape of Baksei Charnkrong, which is a rare pyramid-shaped temple. Mean didn't recognise the name or the location on the map that came with my pass, but I could see it was just a short distance from the South Gate on the main road to the Bayon Temple. When I noticed a structure emerging from the tops of the trees, I asked him to pull over so I could explore on foot. I was the only tourist in the area, and as I climbed the steps to the uppermost level of the pyramid, I was immediately hit with a sensation of vertigo, so climbed back down with all the composure of a blindfolded geriatric.

From there I visited the Terrace of the Leper King beside the Terrace of the Elephants, and on the first appearance, it doesn't promise much, but small wooden signs point to a narrow pathway hidden from sight but filled with some of the region's most impressive bas-relief displays. I completely missed these bas-reliefs on my first trip to Angkor Wat as I had been distracted by pangs of hunger and desires for cold beer, which helped me forget to find them. When I returned to the UK, I read a book about the history of Angkor Wat which waxed lyrical about how splendid they all are. I took that as a challenge to seek them out on my return to the kingdom.

On my second visit to Angkor Thom, I was better informed and prepared: I carried a small rucksack packed with bottled water and heat-resistant snacks to keep my energy levels above dying. Hard experience taught me the preciousness of toilet paper, which seems to be as rare as painite gemstones in some Asian countries (I resorted to using a stranger's sanitary towels when nature called in a tribal village in the mountains of Vietnam). I have also learnt that hunger and empty-handedness can result in a game of Russian roulette with my bowels. There are plenty of vendors selling cans of Coke and Angkor Beer at temple sites, but the Angkor Thom area is one of the few to have a row of stalls serving the most basic of 'meals.' To eat meat or not to eat meat? The answer was obvious. I could only assume the stray and ragged dogs loitering by the food stalls had sampled the leftovers; they could have auditioned as extras in *Day of the Dead*. I continued walking, and my stomach didn't dare to grumble.

Ta Keo is in walking distance of the Bayon Temple. Shaped like a temple-mountain, a climb to the top offers leafy views of bucolic Cambodia with the sounds of nature replacing the incessant chattering of tourists. Too many cooks may spoil the broth, but too many tourists ruin the view, like trying to watch a football match to the tune of fifty thousand vuvuzelas. The Baphuon Temple is another temple-mountain requiring yet another steep climb to the top, but all that scaling and scrambling over sandstone in high humidity took its toll on my knees and ankles, and I finally understood the logic of a three or six-day archaeological pass. The city gates are worth stopping for rather than just driving through, with the South Gate the most picturesque as it features images of Khmer deities with demons furiously pulling mythical nagas across the bridge entry point (it could be the first ever attempt at a tug-of-war). Each statue carries a different countenance as they guard the old-world entrance to Angkor Thom, protected by a moat full of nature's carelessly discarded debris.

Preah Khan is close to Ta Prohm, and I was glad that I visited this before setting foot inside the latter. Otherwise, its impact would have been lost to its rival's exceptionality. In its halcyon days, its central shrine was decorated with sixty tonnes of gold plating, and I could see the markings where plates were once affixed. Banteay Kdei sits diagonally across from Ta Prohm and features similar scenes of nature's tussle with the Angkor ruins. For a spectacular sunset, I asked Mean to drive me to the area of Srah Srang that overlooks the royal baths so I could climb Bakheng Hill, which offers a splendid view of Angkor Wat poking its head through the canopy of the trees. I arrived early only to discover that scores of tourists had the same idea, as we all staked claim to square inches as if the lives of our loved ones depended on it. There is a temple at the top (Phnom Bakheng) and the walkway to reach it follows a circular route around the hill by foot, or on the back of an obliging elephant. The view was worth the wait and effort to see it.

For a temple with a difference, I visited the Banteay Samre Temple (which translates to 'Pink Lady' or 'Temple of Women') which is a journey of some nineteen miles and forty-five minutes from the main sites at Angkor Thom. The temple, like Angkor Wat, is protected by a moat within an outer wall and some of the inscriptions on the arches are so well preserved, they could have been inscribed there yesterday. With scenes from the Indian epic *The Ramayana*, the carvings are quite possibly the region's most intricate. It is worth making the effort to see distant temples as the pastoral scenes along the road are breathtaking, and as I passed one temple after another, I got a sense of the scale of the Khmer Kingdom that wouldn't have been possible had I visited the tourist highlights near Angkor Thom. I stopped beside a Khmer lake to photograph fishers on their boats and pulled over at Pre Rup, another temple-mountain, which features intricate false doors on its upper level as well as an incredible view of the unspoilt countryside. The element of roadside surprise was the highlight of this excursion which was punctuated by rice fields and vibrant village life.

Ta Prohm is the temple of popular culture, and it is impossible to miss its atmospheric ruins, no matter how unreliable a visitor's sense of direction might be, since every local assumes this is the only temple a foreigner would want to visit. It is also impossible to escape cries of 'This way to Tomb Raider Temple!' and I didn't want to miss it, as there were valid reasons for a film crew to fly across the world to use it as a prebuilt set. I was looking forward to this temple more than most, but the tourist buses huddled outside suggested an early morning or late afternoon visit would be more enjoyable and less crowded, with tourists ensconced in the air-conditioned comforts of their hotels. I delayed my gratification and stopped to listen to a band of musicians playing traditional music (they were all victims of landmines), returning later that evening hoping to find it as deserted as Lara Craft had found it.

Ta Prohm is the ultimate Indiana Jones fantasy and the architectural embodiment of the ancient world with delicately carved reliefs sprouting lichen, moss, and creeping plants. Its features and atmosphere are so unusual, almost otherworldly, that it could easily double as the set of some Hollywood fantasy production such as *The Hobbit* or *The Lord of the Rings*. Having been left to ruin and the muscular clutches of the living jungle, it is ironic that it's one of the most popular temples in this area. The temple is small but once inside, the narrow corridors with their twists and turns create a labyrinth of exploration and photographic potential. I was so enrapt by this temple on my first viewing in 2012 that I knew I would return to admire its bold trees protruding indifferently from ancient rooftops. Time makes ruins of us all, but Ta Prohm has benefitted from its ruined state as the jungle and temple enjoy a strange symbiosis.

Ta Prohm initially functioned as a Mahayana Buddhist monastery and university. Unlike many of the Angkorian-era temples, it has been left in the condition it was found with its unique features earning it UNESCO World Heritage status in 1992. There is a serious restoration effort underway which aims to intervene before nature destroys this valuable site, and I had a close look at some of this work on my return visit in 2014. I was pleased to see the reconstruction of collapsed outer walls, but there are less-than-gentle plans to push nature back completely by removing some of those iconic tree formations before any more temple structures collapse under their weight. The two species which predominate are the larger silk-cotton tree (Ceiba Pentandra) and the smaller strangler fig (Ficus Gibbosa), which resembles a spider's web as sections intersect and trap the vulnerable ruins. These trees are the unique and distinguishing feature of Ta Prohm, so the archaeologists find themselves between a rock and a hard place.

Exploring Ta Prohm can be a somewhat frustrating experience, as the tour groups descend on the ruins to queue for group photographs at popular spots such as the 'Tomb Raider Tree,' named after a scene from the film in which Angelina Jolie stands above an ancient doorway covered by a giant strangler fig. Quieter areas of interest include the many towers, courtyards and narrow corridors where I could discover hidden gems, such as bas-reliefs, beneath the masking foliage. Many of the corridors appear to be impassable as piles of carved stone clog their interiors, but that didn't deter me as I got into character like Lara Croft and crouched and climbed when necessary. Nature successfully reclaimed its place at this temple and the roots of the trees are like alien fingers, slowly pulling up the foundations of the buildings which they gently push into ruin. If I had to choose just one ancient site to visit in Cambodia, Ta Prohm would be it.

Angkor Wat is a time capsule of Cambodia's ancient history, but it is also one of the main pillars supporting and promoting the country's future economic development. The Khmer kings left behind a legacy of continuance, just as they had envisaged, and the Angkor area, a road once travelled by the ancestors, now welcomes millions of international tourists to Cambodia.

## Chapter 22: A Mushroom in the Dark

Siem Reap Province is a prosperous region and its capital - Siem Reap Town - has gone from sleepy hollow to boomtown blowout. It lives up to the bold and historical claims of its name, which translates to 'Siamese defeated' - a reference to the Khmer Empire's victory over a neighbouring Thai army in the seventeenth century. Located in Cambodia's north-west, it is the cultural gateway for tourists visiting the country and its hotels and hostels mushroom in the darkest lanes and narrowest passageways. It is reaping the reward of close association with Angkor Wat, and the designated Pub Street area shows how far the provincial government will bend to accommodate and embrace its tourism industry. It is a small town proud of its newfound global stature, but this pride has historical foundations.

Travellers visit Siem Reap for its easy convenience and proximity to Angkor Wat, not for the town of Siem Reap itself, where I encountered more westerners than local people on its streets. Siem Reap is a resort town for middle-aged tourists who prefer to stay in upmarket hotels, and a cultural fairground for the backpackers who spill out of burgeoning hostels. I didn't expect to find anything remotely resembling real and authentic Cambodia, but it does at least try to cling onto a small-town atmosphere and charm. Its grip has loosened somewhat in recent years, and an international mentality is replacing a provincial outlook.

A short stay is a relaxed and carefree affair, at least away from Pub Street, which is Cambodia's micro version of Las Vegas with its food, beverages, sweets, treats, bugs, brews, music, lights, crafts and souvenirs. I will never forget the night I played musical tables at Banana Leaf when cockroaches and rats forced me to relocate further inside, but the dining options are superb, and some parts of the core are easy on the eye with their mix of Chinese style alongside the colonial architecture of the Old French Quarter. There are numerous local and tourist markets to spend away a shipping container's worth of Cambodian riel, but the labyrinthine Old Market is the most appealing as it sells traditional and authentic souvenirs such as natural soaps, gems, silk bags, clothing, statues and carvings. The Angkor National Museum is a short distance from the downtown area and is home to a wealth of rescued Khmer artefacts. The museum's exhibits completed my understanding of Khmer daily life and history and provided some context for all those temples I spent days exploring over two separate trips.

The various restaurants at the centre of town offer recovery and recuperation from energy-sapping temples, and they are a culinary discovery, as it was in Siem Reap that I tried my first Khmer red curry at a traditional Cambodian restaurant. It is like the Thai red curry (but not as spicy) and is usually served in a coconut sauce with sweet potato and carrots at special occasions such as weddings, family gatherings and religious holidays. The French legacy permeates even traditional Cambodian restaurant menus, as a Khmer curry often comes with a basket of freshly baked bread. As I waited patiently for my food to arrive at a table placed directly over a drain, something caused my lower leg to itch: a friendly cockroach pulled itself up my laces, climbed onto my trainer and was halfway up my sock. My reaction was wholly instinctive, as I jumped up and down in considerable distress and screamed expletives. With said cockroach safely ejected, I noticed the well-to-do elderly couple - sitting to my immediate right - with faces full of horrified contempt for the ill-bred yob beside them. I offered a posh apology and my best impression of Hugh Grant, hoping the roach would later return to haunt them at their table.

Cambodian cooking uses a distinctive herbal paste (or 'kroeung') which is the base ingredient of quite a few national dishes. It embellishes the taste with its exotic flavours and the distinct herbal aromas of garlic, galangal, lemon grass, turmeric, zest of kaffir lime and shallots, but two dishes I am unlikely to attempt at home are the Cambodian 'ant salad' or 'red tree ants with beef and holy basil.' With my Dutch courage fuelled by one or two Angkor Beers (a modest estimate), I was unable to resist such tempting offerings.

When in Rome, eat tree ants.

My dishes were brought to the table bespeckled with the stains of former careless diners, and the stir-fried red tree ants were larger than I expected them to be (some were an inch long) and sat motionless on green leaves, looking as surprised as I was. I half expected the waitress to carry an ant hill to my table for me to stab at with my fork as they tried to escape their fate but the ants were, for my convenience, dead crispy. I had already eaten every bug imaginable either raw or fried in Thailand and China, so this was the equivalent of choosing a pear over an apple. The ants are supposed to compliment the beef with their sour flavour, but the chillies overpowered everything. When offered a complimentary bowl of ant larvae, I didn't dare to touch or eat it. I doubt Jamie Oliver will ever include such a recipe in one of his cookbooks, as I can't imagine his readers following these instructions:

*1. Add 3 tbsp. of oil and a fistful of red tree ants to the pan*

*2. Spring onions, finely sliced*

*3. Red Asian shallots, finely sliced*

*4. Lemongrass stems, white part only, finely sliced and stir!*

I tried to find a restaurant in Phnom Penh and Siem Reap that served stir-fried tarantulas, but they evaded me and remained in their underground jungle burrows. They are popular with tourists and are served with a spicy dip so you can snap their legs off like Doritos tortilla crisps. They are a speciality snack in the town of Skuon, but that was too far to travel for a crispy treat. I was more likely to find them in the villages of Siem Reap where they are bred in holes or foraged like wild mushrooms, before meeting a well-oiled fate with a sprinkling of crushed garlic, sugar, and salt. The habit of spider-munching is believed to have been born out of desperation during the period of Khmer Rouge rule when people starved in the countryside and substituted rice for spiders. I asked Mean if he had ever tasted one and he replied enthusiastically, and quite predictably, with: 'Yes, like chicken!' Even jungle spiders taste like chicken. There are claims that the average person 'eats' at least four spiders in their sleep, probably more, so I'd already had my fill without knowing it.

Pub Street is full of pubs and bars, and it is the beating heart of Siem Reap's nightlife scene, so when the sun sets, temple-goers fill the street to sit and watch the passing people and recover from their cultural toils (alcohol usually does the trick). *Angkor What?* was the first bar to open its doors to tourists in 1998, but a host of venues and clubs have since emerged to compete and claim their share of the tourist spoils. Side streets and alleys off Pub Street offered an escape from the noise when I wasn't in the mood for a party. Le Malraux, on Sivutha Street, celebrates Cambodia's French past in the best way possible by serving gourmet fusion food in a beautiful art deco building, and the menu includes confit of duck legs and salmon carpaccio. I found this restaurant quite by chance and enjoyed some of the best dishes I have eaten in Southeast Asia.

Before leaving the town, I wanted an alternative to visiting temples and found it in the War Museum of Cambodia, the Butterfly Centre at Banteay Srey, the Prek Toal Bird Sanctuary and a cultural performance at the Apsara Theatre. Sometimes dinner, drinks, and a relaxing foot massage were the most satisfying pursuits after a strenuous day hiking through temples and clambering over boulders. I could sense when my feet were preparing to protest, and you should never underestimate the importance of doing nothing at all. When I stop and sit still, I reflect on some of the amazing experiences I have been fortunate to enjoy. Life should come with a pause as well as a reset option.

A trip to Siem Reap, combined with a visit to capital Phnom Penh, will complete most cultural journeys to Cambodia. With three separate visits, I could appreciate the country's cultural highlights as well as its genocidal lowlights, and I was only a train or flight away across the border in Thailand. Tourists rarely associate Cambodia with beach holidays, but it does have white-sand beaches of its own in Sihanoukville and several undeveloped tropical islands that are a poignant reminder of what tropical paradise looks like before overdevelopment sets in with parasols and jet skis. Koh Rong is a short ferry ride from Sihanoukville, and this tropical island has picturesque and pristine beaches to choose from, while Mondulkiri Province offers an insight into Cambodia's natural beauty away from all those killing fields and historical ruins, with thickly forested mountains, powerful waterfalls and the rolling hills of the west.

There is more to Cambodia than temples and tragedy, and over the course of three separate visits, I managed to take the crooked road, the straight road and the one travelled by the ancestors.

I also found myself wanting to eat nothing but Gorgonzola cheese.

## Part 3: Burmese Days

## The Republic of the Union of Myanmar

*This is Burma, and it is quite unlike any land you know about.* (Rudyard Kipling)

### Chapter 23: Myanmar, the Golden Land

Rudyard Kipling's *Letters from the East* (1898) gave what is now modern-day Myanmar the kind of mythical endorsement you might find in a travel guide or travel agent's brochure when he claimed the country is: '…quite unlike any land you know about.' Kipling's fairy-tale words had the effect of making Burma of the late nineteenth century sound like something you might find if you walked through wardrobe doors in C. S. Lewis' *The Chronicles of Narnia*, and that is part of its appeal for curious, twenty-first-century travellers.

With Myanmar's doors thrown open and international tourists warmly welcomed like gifts at a wedding, all it takes is a little bit of courage to step into a parallel universe full of secrets and discoveries, in a golden land that even has its own White Witch. But it hasn't always been that way, or that easy. Between the years 1962 and 2011, Myanmar was crippled by decades of controversy with its 48.7 million population having suffered one of the world's most vilified and oppressive military governments. The ruling generals rebuffed accusations of human rights abuses, and the country they governed with an iron fist was condemned internationally, and thus positioned as a pariah state. Even within its regional circles, Myanmar was persona non grata.

Kipling would have been disappointed to learn that it has taken more than a hundred years for the rest of the world to heed his words of enticement, but Myanmar is a country defined by a history of instability and regional violence which are strong deterrents, even for the foolhardiest of travellers. Myanmar barely registered a sound or visual trace on travel radars for more than half a century, fading from memory and maps to take its unwanted place among the world's forgotten territories such as Tajikistan in Central Asia, or the Transcontinental Presidential Republic of Azerbaijan, which rests between Eastern Europe and Western Asia. Travellers were unsure whether they should call the country 'Burma' or 'Myanmar' which is a moot point when really, it shouldn't be.

But that is all about to change, as Myanmar is back on the electromagnetic spectrum with a blip, a ping, and a steady pulse. A process of gradual liberalisation unfolded from 2010, and in early 2016, that process came full circle when democracy, a civilian government, and a new president - Htin

Kyaw - ousted the military junta. History was made and a child named Optimism was born with the election of Myanmar's first civilian president in free and fair polls. The people could genuinely hope for a better future.

Whenever I told friends I was travelling to or had recently returned from a trip to Myanmar, their response was predictable: 'Where's that? I've never heard of that country.' When I explained that I meant Burma, they usually shadowed their first reaction with, 'Oh... *Burma*. Why did you go there?' Considering all the negative press of military dictatorship, civil war, human rights violations and the embryonic state of its tourism and travel infrastructures, it was a fair question. Some travel restrictions were lifted in 2012 following the suspension of European Union sanctions although, tellingly, the arms embargo and the ban on equipment with potential use for internal repression, was retained. I wanted the challenge of travelling in a country with so many security issues, John Rambo was reluctant to enter it. Secretive places are luring, and Myanmar is one of those genuinely off-the-beaten-track destinations. It is a Third World country when measured by political rights, civil liberties, the freedom of its press and the repression of its people.

In Amsterdam, the hour I spent inside the Anne Frank House - learning about the Dutch resistance to the Nazi occupation of the Netherlands - was far more interesting and memorable than all the art museums I sauntered through in detached silence, or romantic seventeenth-century canals. The Secret Annex where Anne, her family, the van Pels and Fritz Pfeffer hid from their Nazi persecutors for more than two years was a threshold I would never have crossed, had the Franks remained undiscovered. It was a moment of mixed emotions when I crouched to pass through a secret doorway behind a moveable bookcase, to enter cramped rooms and narrow corridors where the Franks and their companions pretended they didn't exist, before being sent to their fates in the concentration camps. It was a short but fascinating entry in the page-turner of dark tourism; Myanmar, by contrast, has a whole chapter's worth of entries, but it is beginning to balance light against black-letter print.

The international community imposed heavy trade sanctions on Myanmar for more than half a century, and the extent of this global isolation was evident when Myanmar was one of only three countries in the world denied the right to sell and taste Coca-Cola (along with Cuba and North Korea). If the Coca-Cola Company can't get access to a country, tourists have no chance at all. In many respects, Myanmar is the same country Kipling visited in 1898 as it was frozen in time due to its forced separation from the rest of the world. With a more progressive open-door policy in the second decade of the twenty-first century, times are changing, and headway is being made as canned drinks now come with a fizz. Backpackers migrate across the border Myanmar shares with Thailand to share its secrets with the rest of the world which, in turn, has created a chain reaction of interest.

Myanmar is Southeast Asia's curio of choice for open-minded and venturesome travellers who want to escape the cliché of beach holidays and well-trodden tourist trails. Thailand is the region's default setting, and when Swiss adventurer Ella Maillart summarised the general appeals of travel, she also captured why Myanmar is the latest El Dorado for backpackers: 'You do not travel if you are afraid of the unknown; you travel for the unknown.' Myanmar remains relatively mysterious to the Western world as it is the last country in Southeast Asia to be touched by globalisation. It is the travel and cultural antithesis of neighbouring Thailand, as Myanmar offers the traveller an opportunity to lace boots and push boundaries in an untamed land. They've just got to decide first whether they want to call the country 'Burma' or 'Myanmar' and stick with their choice.

The names 'Burma' and 'Myanmar' are used interchangeably, but they are unmistakably political. Officially The Republic of the Union of Myanmar, most travellers shorten this sovereign Buddhist state's name to the more manageable 'Myanmar.' The former ruling military junta initiated this change from Burma to Myanmar in 1989 when thousands lost their lives in the suppression of a popular uprising. Rangoon became 'Yangon,' but despite these rebranding efforts, 'Burma' and 'Rangoon' remain fixed in travel lexicons and I often find myself switching between the two in conversations with fellow travellers. The pro-democracy movement preferred traditional 'Burma,' rejecting the military government's renaming of the country as it never accepted the legitimacy of its right to rule, though their concerns focused more on human than naming rights.

The change from 'Burma' to 'Myanmar' has been recognised by the United Nations, but not by the United States or the United Kingdom; the decision of the latter nations to persist with 'Burma' was rooted in a desire to show political disapproval of the country's then noxious regime. It was a semantic rebuttal of a government that claimed legitimacy and a right to governance, despite its rejection of democracy and its democratic processes. A trip to Myanmar would have been unthinkable at the time, and the modern-day equivalent is a holiday to Yemen or Syria. When US President Barack Obama visited Myanmar in November 2014, he sat on the political fence of diplomatic courtesy when he referred to the country as both Burma and Myanmar, interpreted at the time as a symbolic shift in Myanmar's positioning on the global stage. The political pariah found a friend, democracy was finding a voice and international sanctions were steadily reversing.

As part of developing Southeast Asia, Myanmar is bordered by Bangladesh, India, China, Laos and Thailand with this cross-fertilisation of influences creating an ethnically diverse nation. It is a cultural melting pot with more than a hundred different ethnic groups vying for cultural and religious space, in a country that is finally warming to the presence of an outside world. Myanmar is the size of Germany and Italy combined, but unlike those European countries, travellers were not allowed free passage once they entered (despite their visas). The authoritarian government strictly controlled where the tourists' feet could wander and for a good reason too, as some regions were in a state of perpetual civil war with the government, while the violent clashes between Buddhists and Muslims formed the letters and column inches of damning global newsprint. Myanmar is the world's second largest producer of opium and as the beating heart of Southeast Asia's infamous Golden Triangle, some regions are defiantly lawless. Heroin is Myanmar's White Witch, and she comes with a sprinkling of genocidal dust in a country where restrictions on movement remain in place.

The infamous Golden Triangle of Southeast Asia is a mist-shrouded, mountainous and somewhat inaccessible area shared by Myanmar, Thailand, and Laos with close to 400,000 square miles forming a tropical shield for the region's opium producers and their jungle laboratories. The CIA gave this area its name in the 1920s as opium cultivation was (and still is for some) a highly lucrative industry. Thailand has since curtailed the activities of its domestic poppy growers by naming it an illegal crop in 1959 and offering incentives and subsidies to its farmers, but the industry flourishes across the border. The poppy fields are rooted out on the Thai side, but that hasn't stopped trucks packed with opium and methamphetamines from being trafficked into Thailand every day. Myanmar leads the criminal way and is second only to Afghanistan which is the country at the heart of the corresponding Golden Crescent in Central Asia. Afghanistan is the current global leader and factory house that fuels the worldwide heroin trade, but Southeast Asia once held that hazy status.

I explored the safer Thai side of the Golden Triangle first - one of Thailand's least developed areas - and the city of Chiang Rai is the golden gateway to this northern corner. Thailand's former opium regions are the stronghold of the Lanna culture and one of the few unspoilt landscapes that haven't yet ceded to the demands of global tourism. Its stunning natural landscapes (it was once called 'The Land of a Million Rice Fields') are the main draw, and they were my primary motivation for spending five days in the north. Chiang Rai is the northernmost large city in Thailand (often overlooked for touristic Chiang Mai) and the perfect platform from which to take excursions to explore the remotest nooks and crannies of this province, including that corner with three sides and an atomic number of seventy-nine.

The Golden Triangle is popular with tourists who want to shake off the shackles of conventional life by setting foot on the very same soil as drug kingpins and their loyal henchmen. It is one of those dark and dangerous places that are, in fact, perfectly safe to visit (it is the principal duty of the guides to ensure their tourists venture nowhere near the ganglands). Golden Triangle day trips to the Mekong River deliver anxious and excited tourists to its confluence with Ruak River and a vantage point with a view of the intersection of all three countries. There's a Hall of Opium which is an excellent museum that painstakingly documents the five-thousand-year history of this illegal - but still thriving - triangular interest.

Trips to opium museums in a gangsters' paradise lean toward the darker shades of tourism, much like a walk in Cambodia's killing fields, but the Golden Triangle is a unique form of drugs tourism as the area has become an unlikely attraction. The Tourism Authority of Thailand displays helpful brown signs to point the way to this crime-zone-of-unprecedented-proportions, with the Golden Triangle having acquired the dubious status of a prized cultural asset. The local tourism industry has cashed in on this unexpected windfall with Golden Triangle hotels, bars, restaurants and even a Golden Triangle Casino. There's a Golden Triangle Public Toilet too where the overhydrated can get instant golden relief, with a small charge for tissue paper and soap.

I hired a Kawasaki Versys 650cc in Chiang Rai and blazed a trail to the watery border of Myanmar with John Denver's *Take Me Home Country Roads* stuck in my head like a persistent earworm. My two-wheeled adventure lasted just under three hours, but it revealed the unexplored and incredible biodiversity of Thailand's mountainous north. To paraphrase T. S. Eliot, it was the journey to the Golden Triangle - not the arrival itself - that mattered most and left a lasting impression. On the Laos side, I was able to stretch my legs and rest my hands from their rigor-mortis grip in the Golden Triangle Park. It sounds like a lovely place for a family stroll and picnic, except for the fact that it was full of stalls with vendors selling unboxed sex toys, flavoured passion fruit lubricants and pornographic DVDs with titles as colourful as their front covers, such as *A Fistful of Frida*.

Travellers don't often get the chance to witness heroin-themed tourist traps, but with the opium warlords weeded out on the Thai side, the only dangers to tourists these days are food poisoning, sunburn, and dehydration. The area has a newfound, sanitised respectability, so I wasn't surprised to be offered a cappuccino instead of a needle and heroin hit-kit. Strategically placed signs remind visitors they are standing in the Golden Triangle, but they should have put up a few *Danger! High Voltage* signs for good measure. As I tipped the frothy dregs of a cinnamon-heavy cappuccino into my mouth, I had a Phuc-free flashback to my time at Vietnam's Cu Chi Tunnels as I watched over-enthusiastic tourists haggle for poorly made, tacky souvenir dolls of hill tribe people like they had just found the panacea for all incurable ills. I finally understood why Thailand's northern farmers abandoned their poppy fields, as they now cultivate a far more reliable, speciality crop.

My friend Charlie, an expat colleague, is a case in point. I was dumbfounded by his sheer folly when he explained that he had spent several hours on a public bus from Chiang Mai, all the way north to the Mekong waterline. He was determined to take a golden selfie standing next to a splintered sign declaring that he had reached: 'The Northernmost Point in Thailand.' The sum of his experience was to tick a travel box and boast of having stood on a pile of hazardous soil in the Golden Triangle. He uploaded his phototrophy to Facebook, bought a T-shirt and boarded the next returning bus to Chiang Mai. That gruelling trip was a journey of several uncomfortable hours across 340 miles of Northern Thailand; it accounted for a whole day of his life and a third of his time in Thailand's north, so I wondered what he had hoped to achieve by going there. Travel kudos, probably: been there, done that, got the T-shirt.

On his return to Bangkok, Charlie was full of the pride that comes with mileage. I was drowned in a stream of consciousness as he detailed all the angles of his travel triangle from Chiang Mai to Chiang Rai (where he spent less than an hour at the famous white temple of Wat Rong Khun, before moving on to the Golden Triangle) with a final stop at Mae Hong Son. He spent more time busing to the latter than actual time spent *in it*, which is a terrible shame as Mae Hong Son Province has the mountain ranges of the Thai Highlands for adornment, tropical rainforests and hill tribe communities to rival those in Vietnam's Sapa District. Louis L'Amour, the American author, was referring to travellers like Charlie when he reflected: 'Too often I would hear men boast of the miles covered that day, rarely of what they had seen.'

Had Charlie spent more time in the Golden Triangle and resisted his scattergun approach to sightseeing, he could have purchased a visa for ten dollars and crossed the river from Thailand's Mae Sai to Myanmar's frontier town of Tachilek in the Shan State. A further journey downriver from Chiang Khong would have delivered him to Huay Xai in Laos, from which an hour's drive would have taken him to the ancient city of Souvanna Khomkham. He could have visited three countries for the price of one, had he known, but stupid is as stupid does: he sat on a bus.

The tourism signpost for the Golden Triangle is a familiar landmark for the intrepid. Charlie had photographic proof of his intrepidness and further evidence (should it be needed) printed on his T-shirt which boasted: 'I've been to the Golden Triangle!' I wasn't so easily impressed myself, as I have visited genuinely dangerous places such as the lawless townships of Cape Town and the notorious Tondo slums of the Filipino capital: places which can be counted among the world's deadliest neighbourhoods as they are hideouts for criminal gangs and gun crime and casual murder are rife.

Filipino friends were genuinely surprised (and slightly concerned) when I visited the Tondo slum neighbourhoods. Some still live in Manila and its environs, but they never dared to set foot in, or anywhere near, the district of Tondo. I didn't feel the need to buy a T-shirt to confirm that I had been there, and besides, there weren't any for sale. I couldn't resist the opportunity to visit the real-life setting of *Trash*, and as I was staying in neighbouring Binondo, I decided to go for a walk on the wild side.

Tourists enjoy the vicarious thrill that comes from proximity to danger, and the Golden Triangle is an unusual destination they can pin to their travel maps, but it's the equivalent of playing a game of Russian roulette when you've emptied the chamber yourself and you know there's absolutely no risk of harm or death. I took to the countryside trails of northern Thailand and crossed the river to explore as much of the eerily quiet Myanmar section of the Golden Triangle as my petrol tank allowed. As I passed derelict agricultural buildings made of broken-down pallets and fenced off by thorny shrubs, I imagined they doubled as production sets for scenes in *Breaking Bad* as such idyllic pastoral settings would be the perfect foil for the Golden Triangle's illicit economy. Perhaps Walter White was cooking up an almost-pure batch of his blue product inside.

Curiosity killed the cat, as the proverb warns, but cats have nine lives so I imagined a wrong turn would result in a shallow grave if I stumbled upon the jungle jackpot of a methamphetamine factory. The camera that swung from my neck foreshadowed a possible fate. Passing unsmiling, shotgun-toting farmers (who could have been crime lords, but they were probably just farmers), I didn't want to end my days smoking on the muzzle end of a barrel held by the angry eyes of a Heisenberg wannabe. Imagination was everything as the reality of my cross-country experience was trees, fields, farmers, the occasional shed abandoned to nature and more trees, fields and farmers. India's Golden Triangle, by comparison, is a more rewarding experience as it is a cultural journey through historical Delhi, Agra and Jaipur with a lot more to offer than said trees, fields, and farmers.

Change comes at a slow pace in Myanmar, and the country has a habit of returning to what sells: heroin. The opium trade drives the country's economy, and it has acquired a reputation for the superior quality of its refined tropical snowballs; consequently, it demands high export rates for this unofficial national product. The irony of the country's modern tourism slogan seems to be lost on the authorities: 'Welcome to Myanmar, the Golden Land!' Aside from this reputation and historical association with hard drugs, Myanmar has been marred by internal conflict, military coup d'état, rebellions and civil war since attaining its independence from the United Kingdom in 1948.

It will take some time for Myanmar to shake off a legacy of troubles as other countries, such as Vietnam and Cambodia, have discovered.

## Chapter 24: The Voice of a Nation

It would be very remiss of me to sidestep the hotbed of Myanmar's politics to skip straight to its attractions, distractions and 'things to do.' The next three chapters will, unapologetically, focus on the darker side of the country's transition to democracy and liberalisation, before finding balance with balloon flights and UNESCO World Heritage. Myanmar is a country shaped and defined by its politics and political religion especially, so they are inescapable topics.

Following the reforms of 2011 and 2012, Myanmar's younger generation enjoyed newfound political freedoms and optimism. But there was just one caveat: the changes were, and continue to be, somewhat superficial as the new civilian government is infiltrated by a strong military presence. The appearance of change is often enough to appease even the greatest of doubters; the leopard's spots are still visible and even though its retractile claws are hidden out of sight behind soft fur, it retains a powerful bite. But after decades of international sanctions and isolation, relations have gone from cold war to gentle thaw and Myanmar is no longer an international exile. It has been brought in from the cold, albeit with some reluctance and resistance. The awkward pariah that deterred foreign visitors with arcane bureaucracy, now displays welcoming and open-hearted billboard messages. The painfully slow process of global rehabilitation is well underway, and while Myanmar remains Southeast Asia's poorest country, the green shoots of recovery have sprung at last and a warm summer is expected to follow a long winter of discontent. At least that's the hope.

A national icon and distinguished heroine, Aung San Suu Kyi, the leading and influential pro-democracy and opposition politician placed under house arrest for fifteen years by the former military junta, urged travellers to defer their travel plans to Myanmar as an act of external protest and support for her pro-democracy campaigns. With the country critically destabilised at the time, and with international embassies similarly compelling travellers to stay away from Myanmar, they probably didn't need that much encouragement to board flights somewhere less volatile. The Land of Smiles was beaming.

Because of modern and progressive reforms, Aung San Suu Kyi's stance softened, and as Chairperson of the National League for Democracy, she actively encouraged international inbound tourism, regarding it as an economically vital means for sustaining the country's growth and future development. Tourism doubled as a political opportunity to present the country to global eyes and invite economic investment, while addressing its historically austere image. Closed doors are a powerful symbol that invariably create speculation, suspicion, and myth. There is no better way to dispel it than to invite your neighbours over for an open-house viewing, showing them your finest interior features and getting to know them a little bit better, even if that means having to pretend to like them. That's how international diplomacy works.

Aung San Suu Kyi was a thorn in the military government's side for decades, and she has attracted worldwide interest and support for her politics and policies for positive change. She was a catalyst for reform and continued her father's work as Aung San was assassinated in 1947, months before Burma attained its independence from the British when it became a democracy founded on the model of a parliamentary system. Aung San Suu Kyi's father was Deputy Chairman of the Executive Council of Burma, but his influence was short-lived as his political rivals assassinated him. The apple, however, didn't fall far from the tree. Aung San's daughter, almost single-handedly, tasked herself with reversing the military socialist era and returning the country to a democratic state.

Aung San Suu Kyi welcomed the overseas sanctions imposed on her country, despite the adverse effects these had on the population at the time, as pressure helps to bring about change and she didn't want the ruling military regime to get too comfortable in the seats they never earned the right to sit in. She was placed under house arrest as an alternative to assassination, and her story is as remarkable as it is inspiring; she has since been recognised and bestowed with numerous international awards and honours, which include the Nobel Peace Prize (1991) for her non-violent struggle for democracy and human rights in Myanmar. Sylvester Stallone picked up the baton in 2008 and earned some unexpected accolades of his own.

Sylvester Stallone's 2008 *Rambo* hardly helped to assuage Myanmar's problematic reputation and uneasy relationship with the outside world, but it did at least turn a spotlight on some of the country's pressing and troubling issues. The fictional plight of the death-proof hero may be far-fetched, but it takes place in a world based on facts with art closely imitating life. With real-life episodes of systematic violence, humanitarian crises and persistent violations of human rights, Myanmar has been an ever-present source of concern for United Nations officials. There have even been claims that the former military government was complicit in ethnic cleansing campaigns, with anti-Muslim violence having been genocidal in its scale. International onlookers feared Myanmar was readying itself to repeat Cambodia's dark legacy, though it is hoped that the new government will push for a more unified ethnic map and a ceasefire in religious hostilities. The words of the epic poet Homer capture Myanmar at its political crossroads: 'I know not what the future holds, but I know who holds the future.'

The plot of *Rambo* follows serial protagonist John Rambo's (a retired US Army Special Forces soldier) attempt to rescue a group of misguided missionaries kidnapped by a brutal military regime - the Tatmadaw (which is the official name of Myanmar's armed forces) - led by a ruthless and sadistic military officer named Major Pa Tee Tint. With scenes of ritual slaughter, as whole villages are rocketed to ruin and helpless villagers are forced to run across mine-infested marshes for shits and giggles, the portrayal looks like a rather blatant exercise in American propaganda. The film was written, directed by and starred Sylvester Stallone so it would be easy to dismiss it as ninety minutes of bloody but politically exploitative entertainment. Myanmar's opposition youth group Generation Wave did, however, copy and distribute the film as anti-Tatmadaw propaganda, so Stallone found himself a new generation of fans and is now a real-life hero as well as a fictional one.

*Rambo* is ultra-violent and borders on farce as its protagonist single-handedly wipes out an entire armed regime with every conceivable weapon (from a survival knife to a submachine gun/tank), but if one man can do all of this, why can't the people join ranks and make a stand for themselves? That's right, because that man is none other than John Rambo. Unsurprisingly, the film was not received well upon its theatrical release so the military authorities immediately banned it which - of course - had the unintended (but predictable) effect of making it the most popular film in the country at the time. The black-market demand for counterfeit copies of the DVD prompted the government to threaten and order vendors not to distribute the film, but bootleg copies were available everywhere.

Much like Vietnam and Cambodia, Myanmar shares a history of internal conflict and tragedy. For decades, there have been widespread reports of the ethnic cleansing of minority groups, such as the Karen people who dwell in the hills bordering the mountainous eastern region and Irrawaddy Delta, primarily in the Kayin State. The film's reception by the Karen Freedom Fighters was positive, with some frontline fighters reporting that it gave them a great boost of morale, even adopting its dialogue as rallying points and battle cries, such as Rambo's action hero one-liner: 'Live for nothing, or die for something!' They were probably hoping John Rambo would borrow a Schwarzenegger catchphrase and some of his weapons to join their fight: 'I'll be back!' In a Telegraph interview, Stallone responded to the news of the film's reception in Myanmar with: 'That, to me, is one of the proudest moments I've ever had in film.' To be fair, he's probably not had too many of those moments so he should embrace the fervour while it lasts.

World authorities have estimated that more than 500,000 people have been killed in Myanmar in the last thirty years alone, with ethnic minority villages burned to the ground and innocent people summarily executed. Scores of refugees praised Stallone's bloody unmasking of an oppressive and ruthless regime (the Karen and Rohingya people), and rather than claiming it to be the sensationalist work of a special effects team, they considered it a realistic portrayal of their suffering and fate. They found a voice in an unexpected medium and were buoyed by the response of a worldwide audience which is paying attention to their plight in a country where a veil of secrecy is thrown over subjects such as accepted ethnicity and religious hegemony.

Newfound political freedoms and autonomy of thought have, however, given birth to a new freedom in Myanmar: the freedom to hate.

## Chapter 25: The Buddhist Face of Terror

Like its neighbours in Vietnam and Cambodia, Myanmar is predominantly Buddhist in faith with this main religion comprising 89% of the country's population. By contrast, Myanmar's Muslims account for just 4% and they are a disparate minority, spread thinly in pocket communities such as those of Malay, Indian or Chinese descent. The Rohingya Muslim ethnic minority group has mixed ancestry; residing predominantly in the north-western state of Rakhine, it has a population shy of a million. The Rohingya's historical uprisings, and campaigns to create an Islamic state within Western Myanmar is the source of their present-day hardships and suffering, as they face strict discipline and severe punishments.

The Rohingya have been labelled by the United Nations and news commentators as the world's most oppressed people as they have been stripped of all their rights, including rights of citizenship, and have endured systematic campaigns of hate, discrimination and marginalisation. They had survived in a political and racial system resembling the conditions of apartheid which divided South Africa when its National Party governed between 1948 and 1994. The former military government remains accused of violations of Rohingya human rights, with ex-president Thein Sein having gone on record to claim that there are no Rohingya Muslims remaining in the country, which sounds like the ominous outcome of a successfully executed campaign of genocide and expulsion. But why has no one helped them? Why has the world turned its back again?

Surprisingly, even Aung San Suu Kyi has remained tight-lipped on this subject (which international commentators have roundly debated). National flags can reveal so much about a country's sense of self or indeed its failings; Myanmar's tricolour flag has three equal horizontal stripes with yellow sitting over a layer of green and red, plus a central five-pointed star which represents a consolidated union. The yellow line symbolises solidarity among all ethnic groups, so Myanmar can be said to have failed spectacularly on that count, while the green represents peace and tranquillity in a country where conflict and civil war have prevailed. The only hope for Myanmar comes from the red stripe of its flag which stands for courage and decisiveness, two qualities it will need in abundance if it is to recover the spirit of a broken past.

As the Rohingya fled from persecution and ethnic purging, boarding dangerously overcrowded boats that were not even sea-worthy, the outside world was forced to take note as breaking news stories flashed on television screens. The word 'Rohingya' entered the global consciousness, despite the fact that these people have suffered in a vacuum of silence for more than a quarter of a century. As ships were turned away by neighbouring Thailand and Malaysia in 2015 (their governments felt no shame admitting they did not want them on their shores), it seems Myanmar's tentative steps toward democracy have created a slipstream of detestation and a radically firmer stance against minority groups. The Rohingya have borne the heavy brunt of racial tensions as they are not recognised as a distinct ethnic group but as illegal immigrants, daring to intrude on Myanmar's cultural tapestry. Myanmar's dominant colours do not mix or run, and the Rohingya Muslims are not of the preferred palette. They are the domestic enemy.

Living in Thailand as an expat, I developed a broad understanding of Buddhism and Buddhist teachings and precepts, so I was surprised to learn that a Buddhist group - calling itself the '969 Movement' - could exist across the border in Myanmar. There have been claims that the 969 movement promotes Islamophobia and actively provokes and morally justifies anti-Muslim bloodshed, when the principle of non-violence is central to Buddhism and the promise not to kill is the first moral precept introduced during monastic training. *Time* magazine was bold enough to feature a head-and-shoulders portrait of the group's unofficial spiritual leader - Buddhist monk Ashin Wirathu - on the front cover of its July 2013 edition with the controversial headline: 'The Buddhist Face of Terror.'

A wave of hyperbolic clickbait headlines have appeared in mainstream publications including 'Saffron Terror,' 'The Mad Monks of Myanmar,' 'The Buddhist Bin Laden' and 'Burma's Brutal Buddhists' and yet, bizarrely, the Buddhist perspective on the concept of peace is that through spiritual inner peace, a state of world peace can be achieved. There is something rotten in the state of Buddhist Myanmar.

The 969 Movement is a nationalistic crusade whose supporters are vehemently opposed to what they regard as Islam's expansion into Buddhist Myanmar. News agencies captured images of rallying monks on camera, carrying placards with antagonistic messages and incendiary rhetoric: 'The World is not only for Muslims.' With a clever nod to numerology to credit their cause, the first digit represents the nine special attributes of Lord Buddha, the second his six core teachings (loosely interpreted) and the final number the nine attributes of monkhood (very lightly applied). But it is a numerology of hate, not faith.

As a means for showing my public support for Manchester United Football Club, I place stickers of the club logo on the rear or passenger door windows of my car, but in Myanmar, anything made of glass is likely to carry a 969 sticker from shop windows to the wing mirrors of motorbikes and betel nut carts. They are a craze that has swept the nation like Pokémon or Merlin Premier League collections, with fanatical patriotism verging on collective racism as a hive mind has zeroed in on a single, common and vulnerable enemy. When a Muslim girl accidently collided with a monk while riding her bicycle, a ridiculous overreaction saw a Buddhist mob attack mosques and burn more than seventy homes in Oakkan, a town sixty miles north of the former capital, Yangon. A girl's breaking error resulted in one reported death, nine serious injuries and dozens of homeless, displaced families.

The rainbow flag is a universal symbol of lesbian, gay, bisexual and transgender pride but 969 is a Buddhist pride movement that goes beyond celebrating its faith. Instead, it seeks to crush and remove another, with its outspoken leader bizarrely nicknaming himself 'the Burmese Bin Laden' and figurehead of this war on Islam, as he regularly broadcasts anti-Muslim sentiments on social media such as Facebook and YouTube. Accused of inciting racial hatred and extremist brainwashing through rabble-rousing rants, growing ranks of devotees have empowered his position and toughened his stance. He served nine years of a twenty-five-year prison sentence for spearheading attacks on Muslim communities, but his early release in 2012 enabled him to continue his crusade. He is undeterred by prison bars, and he hasn't learnt his lesson as his country hasn't yet learnt *his*. When he addressed an audience in 2014, he wore saffron robes and spoke with a voice that was steady, gentle and calm, yet his vitriolic denouncement of the world's Muslim population delivered a sweeping statement with a subliminal focus closer to home: 'Muslims are fundamentally bad. Mohammed allows them to kill any creature. Islam is a religion of thieves; they do not want peace.'

A radical Buddhist, Wirathu could audition for a leading role in a production of Macbeth. He looks like the innocent flower, but there is no mistaking the fact that he's a militant and divisive serpent hissing beneath its cloaking petals. Mixing Buddhism with radicalism has had the same effect as ammonia with bleach, with Wirathu's corrosive speeches producing toxic reactions like a chloramine vapour. As the country stumbled toward democracy, Wirathu returned it to the Dark Ages by preaching to newly robed neophytes and promoting racial stereotypes, paranoia, rumours and misinformation while claiming Myanmar is, metaphorically, '...being raped in every town.' He also believes Myanmar is being violated in the literal sense, as he has warned the people of his faith to be vigilant against the Muslim threat as

Muslim men '...target innocent young Burmese girls and rape them.' He has urged Myanmar's Buddhists to boycott Muslim businesses, to restrict property ownership, and deny them employment opportunities in a coordinated effort to push them to the farthest margins of society, and drive them out of the country amid a machete madness.

Wirathu believes separatism is the only pathway to a peaceful Myanmar, so he concludes, in one broadcast, that: 'Buddhists and Muslims have to live separately.' With their nod to Nazi ideology and the Nuremberg Laws of 1935, he naturally endorses his country's anti-miscegenation laws which restrict interracial marriage between Muslims and Buddhists. There are parallels with the events of the Kristallnacht (Night of Broken Glass) which are as ominous as they are obvious. On a November night in 1938, the Nazis accelerated the removal of the Jewish population from their communities when they coordinated attacks and burned their synagogues and businesses to the ground; it was a symbolic act that demonstrated how undesirable their presence had become in the German Reich, and a historic event that foreshadowed the terrible fate awaiting Europe's Jews in the gas chambers and crematoria of the Nazi concentration camps.

The Nazis used derogatory terms to describe the Jews such as 'Untermensch' (subhuman, or racially inferior) and 'Judenschwein' (Jewish pig). Wirathu's words are a long-delayed echo as he has gone on record to label Myanmar's Rohingya Muslims as 'unwanted parasites,' 'snakes' and 'mad dogs.' In an interview with the *New York Times* in June 2013, he asserted: 'If we are weak, our land will be Muslim.' I doubt whether Wirathu believes this 'threat' is real when nine out of every ten people in his country are practising Buddhists. The numbers don't add up, and neither do his arguments. But like the Nazis, his words are nasty.

The north-west Rakhine state was a Muslim stronghold before tensions between Rohingya Muslims and Rakhine Buddhists resulted in the religious riots of 2012, which claimed the lives of hundreds of Muslims and the displacement of thousands more, as their villages were looted and torched. These conflicts spilt further south with at least forty people killed in the central city of Meiktila (mostly Muslim), while thousands were again forced to flee as their mosques, shops and houses reduced to ash and rubble. The displaced were rounded up and retained in coastline internment camps with the close company of disease and malnutrition, away from prying eyes and behind barb-wire barricades, while others led an exodus to neighbouring Bangladesh or sympathetic Muslim states. History, it seems, has been played on repeat. The situation became so volatile that international aid agencies faced expulsion from the Rakhine state.

When Karl Marx observed that 'History repeats itself, first as tragedy, second as farce,' he may well have been predicting a future in which holy men are labelled as 'terrorists' and religious devotees display stickers of hate to honour their faith. Southeast Asia has a habit of breaking the pane of the conventional.

The Rohingya Muslims choosing to remain in Myanmar are caught in a desperate poverty trap: they are damned if they do and damned if they don't get out. They have not yet been forced to wear the equivalent of a yellow badge to mark them out in public places, but anything is possible as the 969 Movement has already demonstrated a commitment to symbolic gestures with novelty stickers. I saw 969 stickers for sale in a Yangon street market, but I resisted the urge for a dark souvenir as neutrality is always the safest passage through a foreign country. The stickers are brightly-coloured with distinct numerals, and they wouldn't look out of place in a child's sticker collection, but they are an ethnic animus.

I experienced the effects of the Baader-Meinhof phenomenon when I noticed the stickers everywhere I looked. The recency effect of my brain's cognitive focus - and its prejudice to search for patterns - took control and guided my eyes to stickers on shop windows, taxi windshields, food carts, street signs and lamp posts like some bizarre, but inescapable, blitz marketing campaign. Wirathu's speeches were available for sale on DVD in shops and market stalls; newspaper vendors waved them in their hands to passers-by with their front covers crying out for attention as Wirathu competed for space with the 969 logos. Supporters can buy the stickers online in sheets of six and have them delivered to their front doors. For the Muslim population still living in Myanmar, they are a symbol of fear, suppression and genocide, like the Nazi swastika was for the Jewish people.

I walked past the Ma Soe Yein Monastery in Mandalay, with its riverside location, in Myanmar's second-largest city and last royal capital. I didn't feel comfortable enough to enter as my intrusion and camera may not have been welcome with all the intense media scrutiny, but it is Wirathu's holy headquarters where he preaches and presides over the movement of a supposedly non-violent faith whose image, his words, have globally tainted. Buddha believed in the teachings of tolerance and equality, so preaching and inciting religious hatred through the rhetoric of speeches and the eye-catching colours of sticker campaigns, is a warped reversal of the Buddhist faith. The

Bible warned of the destructive powers of ignorance in Hosea 4:6 when the prophet spoke of ignorant men just like Ashin Wirathu: 'My people are destroyed for lack of knowledge...' and '...seeing thou hast forgotten the law of thy God, I will also forget thy children.' He should borrow a history book to learn about the fate of the Nazis and re-read the sacred scriptures of the Tipitaka.

It has been estimated that a million migrants have illegally crossed the border from Myanmar into Thailand, and I met some of the Karen migrants when I visited Chiang Mai in Northern Thailand. Rather than celebrating their release from persecution, I was disappointed to discover their predicament as refugees allowed the unscrupulous to exploit their desperate circumstances. They were forced to live in a touristic folk village, which the owner charged tourists an admission fee to enter. It was to all intents and purposes a human zoo as tourists gawped at the Karen women's long necks, a cultural attempt at pronounced sexual dimorphism, as they posed for tribal selfies. I was unconvinced their circumstances had improved that much, but at least they had their lives and a refracted sense of freedom.

Modern slavery and human trafficking are transnational businesses in Southeast Asia and factions of Thailand's fishing industry share Gordon Gekko's sinful mantra: 'Greed is good!' Thailand's fishing nets have benefitted the most from trafficked Rohingya Muslims by taking advantage of their vulnerable statelessness and selling them into slavery. Once aboard a fishing vessel, Rohingya captives can spend years out at sea suffering inhumane conditions and forced labour as they serve the interests of global demands for seafood stocks. They are a better catch than fish for traffickers, and their ready supply guarantees bulging nets. Fishing boats are converted and refitted to carry this lucrative new export line to stockpiled camps of Rohingya Muslims in Thailand, where in 2015 the mass graves of trafficked refugees were exhumed. This arrangement has been mutually beneficial, as Myanmar has offloaded thousands of its undesirables and Thailand has been more than happy to oblige and count its profits, with corruption and complicity linked to senior officers in Thailand's military government.

I met some of Myanmar's more fortunate refugees who crossed the border to find work at elephant camps in Thailand's Kanchanaburi and Ayutthaya provinces. One of the international volunteers explained that some of the mahouts (who care for and ride the elephants) escaped Myanmar's political subjugation by taking pathways through the border mountains and jungles to start new lives in Thailand. I worked closely with Kyaw, who didn't speak a word of English, so I was only able to communicate with him through gesture and universal hand signals as I helped him tend to the needs of the camp's elephants. There was a darkness in his eyes that defied the tropics, and I noticed he rarely ever smiled; the camp was probably as much a sanctuary for the refugees as it was for the elephants.

Myanmar is changing for the better, but it is a slow-moving and complicated process. The country's travel and tourism potential could transform global perceptions, with inbound incomes reducing the need to rely on opium production to keep it afloat. I enjoyed my Burmese days as I walked in the footsteps of literary greats such as Orwell and Kipling in one of the world's former socialist and one-party states. Myanmar remains an unstable, deeply divided and cash-starved nation, but the tourism hot spots are insulated from the troubles with tourists cocooned in the comfort of luxury resorts with swimming pools and golf courses. Holidaymakers are often oblivious to the suffering of the poor and the persecuted they leave behind; people who are unable to afford an airline ticket to a happier existence.

It seems that for every progressive step forward, Myanmar has been hell-bent on taking two steps in reverse. If its troubles remain unresolved by the new civilian government, the doors to Narnia may close once more. Myanmar desperately needs the revenue that comes from mass tourism as a firm foundation for the future cannot be built with poppy seeds alone.

## Chapter 26: Saffron Revolutions

Myanmar is a cup of freshly brewed Kopi Luwak. An elite product for the cash-rich and the world's most expensive coffee, twenty years ago it would have been mocked as it is, essentially, a cup of litter-box leftovers. Now everyone wants a taste of fashionable Kopi Luwak, which is made from civet droppings once the coffee berries have 'fermented' in the animal's digestive tract and have been extracted and processed for a 'unique taste.' I tried this quirky crappuccino on Bali Island in Indonesia, but it tasted - as I expected - like any other ordinary coffee, except for the artificially inflated price. I observed the delightfully disgusting production process with interest (the extraction of berries from dried excrement), before swallowing the liquid-brown discharge with each sip accompanied by images of squatting civet cats.

In New York City, a cup of Kopi Luwak can cost as much as a hundred dollars which surely proves human intelligence isn't superior to that of other animals. If there were ever such a thing as a coffee bucket list, Indonesia's Kopi Luwak would almost certainly be at the very top of it. An unusual twist on the familiar bean-based beverage, for connoisseurs it is the universal elixir of choice. The civet cats must be laughing, but Myanmar is like Kopi Luwak because it is different, exotic and is becoming fashionable.

The language of Myanmar's landscape has shifted in recent years with 'exotic' replacing 'dangerous,' and 'difficult' becoming 'desirable.' Seasoned travellers have tasted every brand available on supermarket shelves and are desperate to try something they've never sampled before. Myanmar was once a forbidden fruit, but tourists are queuing up to take a bite. Myanmar is playing catch-up, and it will take years of investment and development in its infrastructure to support its burgeoning tourism industry so like the coffee, hotel rooms come at premium rates as demand exceeds supply. It is ironic that it was the monks of Myanmar who projected the country onto the international consciousness, staging the largest street protests in over two decades against Myanmar's military leaders in 2007. Hundreds of monks marched through Yangon to defy and oppose a government's anti-democratic tactics and protect the people their faith represents. International observers applauded the actions of those selfless, noble monks, but time can alter perceptions quickly, and the 969 Movement has since slashed them into pieces.

*Time* magazine referred to the monks as 'The Fighting Monks of Burma' on the front cover of its September 2007 edition and even championed the spirit of their resistance as saffron robes splashed across global newsprint. Another media outlet coined the term 'Saffron Revolution,' which highlighted the central role Myanmar's Buddhist monks played in a series of economic and political protests and demonstrations which took place over the months of August, September, and October. As images of military police clashing mercilessly with holy men circulated the world, Myanmar's reputation as a combustible and dangerously anarchic country was confirmed. If monks can be tear-gassed, battered with clubs and arrested, why would tourists want to take their chances? Shocking images such as these could have set tourism and development ambitions back several decades, but they were, instead, a preface to reform.

The monks found sympathy and support from a worldwide audience for their bravery, and they set a heroic example (despite the risk of bloody crackdowns) when they defied a corrupt government's anti-democratic measures which had squeezed the life out of the population, with even basic food items priced out of reach. Aung San Suu Kyi reminded her people that fear is 'a habit,' but the pattern broke when thousands of monks marched peacefully through the streets of Yangon in a protest supported by thousands more, accompanied by a symbolic voice that demanded democracy and a rebooting of Myanmar. With many thousands killed in similar circumstances in 1988, the risks were certainly high, so it came as no surprise when the trigger-happy military leaders reacted with predictable violence against the unarmed protesters, even raiding monasteries and detaining the monks arrested.

Despite the state control and strict censorship of Myanmar's media, protesters could capture military brutality on video cameras and mobile phones, and these images were shared with the outside world which watched the mask of the regime slip as it revealed its cruelty and predilection for bloodshed. It tried to hide from plain view by disconnecting internet and mobile phone networks, but the damage was already done as damning images went viral and sparked worldwide outrage and condemnation. Myanmar was threatened by the international community with further economic sanctions, but as it had already had its fifty lashes, adding another five to that sentence was an insufficient deterrent. It was numbed to external pressures, and a regime capable of killing monks set new precedents for ruthlessness and dictatorship. When I first visited the country in 2013 for a weekend in the former capital Yangon, the winds had already changed as the political landscape had shifted tentatively toward democracy, ushered in with the aftermath of the Saffron Revolution.

Having read and studied all of George Orwell's novels while at university, I was unable to relate to *Burmese Days* on any level, and yet in modern-day Myanmar, Orwell could be a national hero as his novel is available for sale at every market stall. I enjoyed reading Orwell's stories, even some of his more obscure essays, but the politics of *Burmese Days* went over my head as a student with a narrow view of the world which, for all I knew then, could have been flat. I bought a bootleg copy of *Burmese Days* on a street corner in Yangon, and I have read it again with an appreciation that comes from visiting the country and understanding its colonial past. The pieces finally came together; I just had to travel thousands of miles to find them.

Orwell was a police officer in the Indian Imperial Police and served five years on duty between 1922 and 1927 when Burma was established as part of the British Empire and annexed to India. He used the book as a vehicle for criticising British rule from his unique position as a participant-observer. When Myanmar gained its independence, however, it struggled to fill the vacuum of control the British left behind, and it has since endured a bitter-sweet period of political turmoil and upheaval.

Despite the peaks and troughs of progression and setback, Myanmar retains some notable travel eccentricities, especially for the first-time visitor. It is inevitable that travel perceptions of Myanmar will be skewed by news media coverage, so expectations and visitor numbers remain relatively low compared to the region's tourism superpowers. Travellers I met on the road admitted they visited Myanmar to put a final tick on their Southeast Asia travel list; others crossed the border from holidays in Thailand or Laos because it was convenient and flights were low-priced. I took advantage of this travel apathy myself, as I wanted to visit the UNESCO World Heritage sites of Bagan before the tour groups descended to spawn and follow flags with matching headsets. The plethora of hastily drafted guide books and websites have sparked international interest into a raging fire, and travellers find themselves flying against their expectations to land in Myanmar instead of Thailand.

With the transfer of political powers, Myanmar has emerged as Southeast Asia's newbie on the scene, and it continues to break its annual visitor records. Myanmar welcomed two million travellers to the country in 2013 and a further three million in 2014, having surpassed the million mark in 2012 for the first time. Due to this tourism boom, some hotels increased their prices by as much as 350%, and I was advised to make advance bookings myself. There is a severe shortage of hotels, and this pressing issue will take years to address and a lot of hasty and imperfect construction efforts. The Tourism Master Plan of 2013-2020 set a 2015 target for inbound tourism of five million tourist arrivals, which is an increase of 60% in two years.

There are hopes this objective will be outmatched by an ambitious 2020 target closer to eight million arrivals, boosted no doubt by the introduction of the e-visa launched in September 2014. The problem of hotel shortages is going to get a lot worse before it gets any better, but Myanmar has the potential to become Southeast Asia's tourism supernova. But first, it needs to manage the words and the actions of its monks, let its Muslims live in peace and rewrite its disastrous PR campaign of the last half decade.

In Bangkok, I made frequent trips to the embassies of neighbouring countries. At the Vietnam Embassy, I never had to queue outside on Wireless Road (Soi Wittayu) and my visa applications were processed in minutes. Myanmar's rush in popularity was apparent when I stood outside its embassy and observed a queue that formed inside, but stretched all the way along Sathorn Nua Road. Unlike Cambodia, Laos and Thailand, the practical Tourist Visa on Arrival Scheme has not yet been fully embraced by Myanmar (except for business travellers, who bring obvious benefits), but it is possible to avoid the queues by paying for the more expensive online e-visa service which costs fifty American dollars. It seemed perfectly natural for me to shuffle along in a line for hours, as it is a skill I inherited from my ancestors and a British pastime for which we could all win Olympic medals. I took my place, lost a few hours of my life, and saved a few dollars in the process.

The United Kingdom has not been forgiven for its years of rule from 1824 to 1948, as it is one of the few remaining countries still exempt from e-visa eligibility. I had no choice other than to join the lengthy queues and read a trilogy or two. Those fortunate enough to have been born in one of the visa-exempt countries (there are only six of these at present: Brunei, Cambodia, Indonesia, Laos, the Philippines and Vietnam) could avoid the queues and additional bureaucracy. Filling out the requisite visa forms did, however, provide some light relief. I am still wondering why it was necessary to record personal information such as the colour of my hair and eyes, my complexion, and height, but if that is what it takes to get a visa from the government of Myanmar, I'll share my favourite colour and childhood story.

Designated 'restricted areas' remain in place throughout the country, so my visa didn't give me carte blanche to access Myanmar, and for some established areas of conflict, I would have to request special permission from the authorities, but I had no desire to bring a travel guide to a gun fight. When I checked with the British Foreign Office, I was advised against all but essential travel to the Rakhine State because of on-going religious tensions between Buddhists and Muslims, and I was told to avoid the Kachin State in the north due to the high risk of armed conflict. I was more than willing to comply with these travel warnings as I had entered Myanmar to see pagodas, not machine guns.

My visa allowed me the opportunity to witness a country take its first tentative steps on the long road to recovery, and I could appreciate the privileges and freedoms I often take for granted in Europe. With widespread internet connectivity, I could remain in contact with the rest of the world, though the networks crawled and were reliably unreliable - a technical issue and not political (I couldn't rely on a regular supply of electricity). New press freedoms had facilitated rapid growth in news publications when all stories were previously submitted to and scrutinised by the regime, so it was unusual to see newspaper stalls selling dailies like a scene from an old black and white film. I never lost sight of the fact that my experience of Myanmar was comparable to an invite to a cultural banquet at Macbeth's castle. The castle has a 'pleasant seat' with a 'delicate air,' but the terrible night that followed was full of fierce storms, strange screams of death and a gloomy, long-delayed dawn. For all the gentle courtesies, Myanmar was Macbeth's castle in a far more exotic location than Inverness. I watched my step and bolted my hostel door.

In Thailand, 'exotic' is taken to its extreme form as I got used to seeing men wearing skirts (and bras) as the transgender population is estimated at 0.5% of the total population, but in Myanmar, menfolk prefer to wear the traditional longyi which is a wraparound skirt. Women tend to secure it at the side, which is useful for visitors to know when they've had one Dagon Beer too many and they're uncertain of their companion's late-night gender. It is completely acceptable for a foreigner to wear one, and I was reminded to wear a longyi whenever I visited temples as my Manchester United shorts were deemed *too short* for Buddha's sensitive eyes (perhaps he's a Liverpool fan). They are not a bad souvenir either, but it was unlikely a longyi would form part of my attire back home in England if I wanted to live and see the next day, and the last thing I ever wanted to do in Myanmar was to wrap another layer around myself in stifling heat.

Having travelled India, a country with a long historical relationship with Myanmar and a strong cultural influence, I was quite used to seeing the longyi, and I had also grown accustomed to being greeted by smiles full of unsightly, red-stained teeth. Had I not been to India first, it would have been like wandering onto the set of a sequel to *The Lost Boys* or a new *Twilight* film. Chewing the highly addictive betel nut is a national pastime in Myanmar and India, and the bloody evidence stains pavements and public buildings. I never asked the locals to smile for the camera, and I resisted walking within reach of the phlegmy trajectory of their chewing and spitting habits. I also thought it prudent to wear a necklace of garlic and carry a wooden stake, just in case.

Cash is king in Myanmar, so I brought plenty of it with me as there are very few currency withdrawal machines. They are not too keen on credit cards either, which they regard with the suspicion of a magician's trick; they still need to see the colour of the money as mobile chip and pin machines are an alien technology. The only places prepared to accept credit cards are hotels of the five-star variety, or the more exclusive shops and restaurants. Attitudes are slowly changing, but it will take time and with reported crime against foreigners surprisingly rare in Myanmar (if the authorities are to be believed), I could have piled my cash in a wheelbarrow and pushed it about in front of me. It is possible to exchange currency at the airport, but I wanted to avoid the local legal tender as kyat (pronounced 'chat') is another valueless money like the Cambodian riel, with one dollar converting to nearly nine hundred kyats when I last visited in 2014. I had no desire to build up my biceps by carrying paperweights, so I brought dollars into the country as they are the second but preferred currency.

There is an amusing nationwide obsession with crisp and flat notes. Should a shopkeeper detect the slightest crease, stain or mark on a note, they won't hesitate to return it; Myanmar is a country full of currency martinets. When exchanging baht to dollars in Bangkok, I explained to the teller that I needed the cash for Myanmar, and she opened a separate drawer with tightly compressed notes. She pre-empted my next request, and I placed my pristine dollars inside a thick book and wrapped it tightly with an elastic band. The things we do for the love of travel!

Contrary to popular belief, Thailand does not have a monopoly on water-throwing festivals. The festival of Songkran is famous throughout the world as the Thais make a great occasion of the New Year celebrations, but they aren't the only ones to do so. In the same month of April, Myanmar welcomes the New Year with the Festival of Thingyan (which also lasts four days), and the ritual of throwing water has the same literal and symbolic meaning for the people of Myanmar as it does for Thais: the washing away of sin and misfortune. In similar scenes of frenzy and joy, Myanmar comes to a dramatic stop and Thingyan is a welcome break from long spells of turmoil and gloom. I first experienced Songkran festival joys when relocating to Thailand in April 2013, and I enjoyed reverting to childhood days with a neon-coloured water gun, playing and pranking on the streets of Bangkok. I had a symbolic restart, just like my hosts.

Thailand, Malaysia, Vietnam, Indonesia and the Philippines are all renowned for their incredible white-sand beaches and postcard palm trees, but Myanmar has its understated share of tropical soils and spoils. The Inle Lake has received international acclaim for its natural and scenic beauty and is now one of Myanmar's increasingly popular tourism sites. The difference between Myanmar and its regional neighbours is that until recent changes in the government's stance on travel restrictions, it was mostly undiscovered by tourists and unspoilt by development, though that could all change as a new era of welcome is ushered in. I discovered what Thailand, Malaysia, Vietnam, Indonesia and the Philippines once looked like before their thriving tourism industries took hold, for better or worse.

## Chapter 27: Yangon vs. Nay Pyi Taw

When the Romans invaded Britain, they built a bridge over the River Thames and established a small town named Londinium. It has remained the country's capital for two thousand years of continuance and extraordinary history, albeit with some minor grapheme changes. Southeast Asia, on the other hand, is the land of roving capitals and travellers often - but wrongly - assume Yangon is still Myanmar's capital city, which of course makes perfect sense since it is the country's largest urban centre with an estimated population of five million people. Yangon lost its capital status in November 2005, when the military junta announced its relocation to purpose-built Nay Pyi Taw and ordered its government workers to up sticks overnight to the country's central dry zone. If they wanted to retain their comfortable positions, privileged salaries and lifestyles, they would follow the money trail.

Myanmar's former secretive government made every effort to keep its new development off the national radar, and with news media agencies state-controlled, they began their work in earnest in 2002. A decade has passed since its official unveiling, but the world is still none the wiser regarding the reasons for this dramatic and controversial change, which may have been brought about by astrological alliances, though political anxiety seems a more likely motivation. The latest capital incumbent is a mouthful north of Yangon, and it is the butt of a common joke in the former capital. With the government's penchant for renaming the country and its cities at whim, the people patiently waited for it to rename its new capital with a felicitous title such as Ghost Capital, as it has everything from golf courses to Vegas-inspired hotels, except for that one essential element of all capital cities: people.

The new capital's name translates to the singular 'Seat of the King' which, unwittingly, predicted its plural failings. Government officials could sleep easier at night, as they didn't have to worry about political protests and popular uprisings on their pristine streets. But with only 2% of Myanmar's population choosing to live in Nay Pyi Taw, to all intents and purposes Yangon remains the country's stubborn powerhouse, robbed of prestige, while Nay Pyi Taw has become an Orwellian curiosity. Yangon no longer boasts the title but is does carry a significant portion of the population, the cultural icons the tourists come to admire and an abundance of the rich colonial heritage of Myanmar's past. In a battle of new versus old, Yangon winds hands down.

The regime relocated their capital to secluded Nay Pyi Taw in a multi-billion-dollar undertaking, rather than following logic and practicality by moving to an already-established urban centre. It was an unintended and symbolic statement of their loosening grip on power, and a tail-between-the-legs retreat from Yangon. The experiment failed spectacularly, as Nay Pyi Taw is now an incongruous blot on Myanmar's landscape and if the country's people still can't find a reason to relocate their lives when a decade has passed, tourists should take note as there isn't much of interest to see. The city planners were over-optimistic as they built a hotel zone (which is more of a dead zone) and Nay Pyi Taw's only attraction for my brief visit was its reversal of convention. When I passed through the city (which sits halfway between Myanmar and Yangon), I had no desire to extend my stay as its structural artifice and grand posturing reminded me of the soulless, ostentations cities of the Arabian and the Persian Gulf. At six times the size of New York City, it is a towering statement of insensitivity and emptiness as the former government - which hardly spent a kyat on healthcare for its people - could find the billions it needed to create this vanity project in the sand.

In the film, *Field of Dreams*, an Iowa corn farmer named Ray hears a voice that tells him: 'If you build it, he will come.' He interprets this as an instruction to build a baseball diamond in his corn fields, and the message of the film is clear: if you believe in the impossible, the incredible can come true. They tried but failed in Nay Pyi Taw, but at least they have a reliable supply of electricity, high-speed internet connections, shopping malls, traffic-jam-busting twenty-lane super highways, neatly manicured roundabouts and residential neighbourhoods that wouldn't look out of place in postcard-perfect Wisteria Lane. The similarities don't end there, though, as both are facades and life is far from ideal behind twitching floral curtains.

Nay Pyi Taw could double as a film set for one of those last-man-on-earth dystopias about the post-apocalypse. The advantages are obvious for directors, as they wouldn't have to ask for permission to close off the streets as the city's one million city inhabitants (again, if official figures can be trusted) are rarely seen, so there wouldn't be any budget demands for post-production effects editing either. International audiences have joined the locals by laughing from afar at this bizarre capital, and the BBC's popular *Top Gear* programme chose Myanmar for one of its country specials. Nay Pyi Taw proved a ripe subject for the playground humour and antics of the show's presenters, as they staged drag races on the capital's deserted thoroughfares and griped about the morning rush hour when the only vehicles on the road were their own.

With an unwieldy scale estimated at some three thousand square miles, it is impossible to navigate Nay Pyi Taw on foot or detect the pulse of a city centre. Probably intentional by design, it prevents large groups from gathering as they did for the Egyptian Revolution in Cairo's Tahrir Square and the Tiananmen Square protests of 1989 in Beijing. In a 2007 edition of the magazine *Himal Southasian*, Indian journalist Siddharth Varadarajan described the calculated layout of Nay Pyi Taw as a form of 'dictatorship by cartography.' The government's glistening emblem of a New Myanmar was a coating of paint, hastily applied to old and peeling surfaces covered with nail holes and scuff marks. Yangon has had the last laugh as it is a bustling and traditional Asian city full of street life and cultural variety. And people.

In addition to Yangon's fabulous golden pagodas, I could get closer to nature at the Yangon Zoological Gardens and take a day trip from the urban chaos to Hlawga National Park. To get a sense of the city's faded, colonial past, I walked the compact core and remembered to avoid the many distractions on its streets as I looked upwards to admire the imposing but crumbling facades of British colonial legacy. The National Museum of Myanmar showcases the country's art, history and culture, and there are beautiful lakes with boarded walkways and a giant reclining Buddha at Chauk Htat Gyi Pagoda. Many of the region's faiths find representation in the city with mosques standing shoulder-to-shoulder with Baptist churches and Buddhist temples, but religious tensions continue to simmer with some beliefs tolerated more than others as they co-exist on a layer of ice that is getting thinner by the day.

I had a brief but bizarre encounter with a 969 enthusiast outside a Yangon mosque on a quiet side street away from the city centre. When I visited Turkey's historic city of Istanbul in 2009, I developed a sense of the rules and etiquette for visiting mosques as the city showcases more than three thousand grand relics from the days of the Ottoman Empire, with their minarets puncturing the clouds at every turn. Returning to established routines in Yangon, I removed my sunglasses and bright yellow Nike Mercurial trainers, remained respectfully silent, turned my camera to its silent mode and disabled the flash as I took photographs of intricate inner details (which is entirely permissible, so long as periods of ritual worship are not interrupted). I followed all the rules, and the local Muslim community didn't seem to have any issue with my presence, so I crossed the street to photograph the mosque's distinctive architecture, constructed from contrasting blocks of striking black and white marble.

As I adjusted the lens, my camera knocked to the right as an aggressive stranger stood in front of me to deliberately obstruct my view. He was determined to stop me photographing the mosque, and as he growled in a foreign tongue, his oily whiskers danced to the ill-omened tune of his lips. I had lost myself in a bubble of contented clicking, so I failed to notice the pack of intimidating men that had gathered around me in the shade. When I sidestepped my troublesome adversary, he tried to sideswipe my camera a second time, and I sensed other footsteps were inching closer. With my fight or flight response activated, my nervous system warned me that it would be wise to offer a false smile, put my camera away and retreat to the main streets, as I was a stranger in an intolerant land and some of the locals were even stranger. I didn't realise it at the time, but anti-Muslim tensions were about to boil over into a nationwide epidemic of mosque-burning and bloodshed, so I could only conclude, with hindsight, that my act of photographing an undesirable building had caused offence to anti-Muslim activists.

Yangon isn't a party town in the mould of a Bangkok or Siem Reap, as there is no such thing in Myanmar, where the only parties are political. Some parts of the city do come to life at night, but I had to search long and hard to find them, such as Nineteenth Street in the Chinatown area. I grabbed hold of a grubby plastic chair and joined the enthusiastic local drinkers as they devoured glass after glass of intoxicating Dagon Beer. The less time I spent sweating on dirty-damp sheets in my hostel, the better my mood, as the walls reverberated with the sounds of insects crawling behind cheaply woven bamboo panels. I prayed in the darkness that they weren't curious cockroaches, while the Dagon did its work and put me into a mild coma. The quality of the street food in the Chinatown area meant that it was surprisingly edible, so I joined the locals for servings of their national dish: mohinga. Mohinga is an earthy bowl of rice noodle and fish soup in a hot and sour broth, with lemongrass and as much chilli as my charred taste buds could tolerate.

I heard a lot of kissing sounds as I sucked and slurped from a steaming bowl, and peering over its chipped and discoloured rim, I traced the origin of the sound to groups of men stooping over nursery tables and realised - with some relief - that none of it was for my benefit. To call a waiter, drinkers make the sound you might make to get the attention of a cat, and I wondered how many foreign ears had found that cat-call offensive, or confirmation of their irresistible charm and beauty. I was their exotic pet for the evening, so they allowed me to join them at a table as we shared glasses of Dagon Beer, awkward smiles but not a single word to allow us to converse meaningfully. I was careful not to let my guard fall drunkenly to the floor, as I was the only unfamiliar face on the block and there was absolutely no chance I would be able to keep up with their drinking competitions (they were serious connoisseurs of the brown bottle).

It is impossible to overlook Yangon's two prized pagodas, even with the early morning symptoms of beer or wine flu, as they announce their sunny presence on the city skyline from every angle. Shwedagon Zedi Daw carries an enormous gilded stupa and is also known as the Great Dagon Pagoda or, more literally, the Golden Pagoda. Built 2,600 years ago, it is a famous icon of the city as it regularly features on the front covers of guide books, but it is also a symbol of national identity as it marks the historic centre of the political activity of Myanmar's independence movement. It is the city's cultural and spiritual highlight, so I spent several hours admiring and photographing the pagoda's details and vibrant temple life. I wondered whether the beer I was becoming rather fond of drinking was named after this pagoda. If it had been, it was a fitting tribute.

The modern city of Yangon crowds about the feet of Shwedagon, but the pagoda stands tall and proud at the top of Singuttara Hill like a spiritual fortress, where it remains the most sacred and impressive site in all of Buddhist Myanmar (strands of Buddha's hair are enshrined inside). The pagoda stands at a staggering 110 metres in height, and a host of white stupas encircle the central stupa with its decoration of hundreds of gold plates and exactly 4,531 diamonds (somebody counted, apparently). It was remarkable when viewed up close or from afar, and once I had ascended the hill and made my way to the platform inside, I was impressed by its sheer scale as temples and statues congregate to form a holy shield around the pagoda core. The grounds were full of worshippers and admirers holding cameras, and it provided an authentic glimpse into the spirituality of the people as monks washed statues of Buddha, while devotees offered flowers or meditated quietly.

The Sule Pagoda, while an attractive religious site, doesn't have the fortune of a pleasant hilltop location. It is impressive nonetheless, if second only to Shwedagon. It stands in the centre of the city like a counterfeit Arc de Triomphe, and it was from this setting the British began their grid planning and remodelling of the city to western proportions. The pagoda is octagonal in shape and is another prominent city landmark which claims to have strands of the Buddha's hair inside (there seems to have been enough of him to go around all Southeast Asia's temples and pagodas). My visit was brief, but it was still worth making the effort to see it. The pagoda is close to some nearby attractions which include the Independence Pillar in Maha Bandoola Park, the Immanuel Church, Bengale Sunni Jamesh Mosque, the imposing City Hall of Myanmar and the High Court Buildings with their distinctive, colonial-era architecture. All that glittered in Yangon was cultural and travel gold.

An artificial lake it may be, but city spaces such as Kandawgyi Lake are precious escapes from the traffic, noise, and pollution of Asian cities. The boarded walkways provided a pleasant retreat as I passed pensive monks transfixed by the reflections of glittering Shwedagon in its calm waters, and floating Karaweik Hall, which looks like a giant golden barge but it's a palace cum Chinese restaurant. With my senses revitalised, I negotiated a taxi to another green space at the Taukkyan War Cemetery in the village of Taukkyan. An hour's drive north of central Yangon, the journey was rewarded with peaceful, landscaped gardens created for the Allied soldiers of the British Commonwealth who gave their lives when they engaged in conflict in Myanmar during the Second World War. It is the final resting place of some 6,374 Commonwealth soldiers, and while visiting graveyards is not a common holiday pastime, I took this opportunity to learn about Myanmar's bit-part role in one of the twentieth century's greatest conflicts.

## Chapter 28: Tinkling Temple Town: Bagan

A dazzling flame for migrating moths, the old kingdom and crumbling temple town of Bagan is the country's primary draw for heritage tourists. When the famous Venetian explorer Marco Polo visited the royal city in the thirteenth century, he defined it for his readers as 'one of the finest sights in the world.' Bagan was once the seat of a powerful, ancient kingdom ruled by King Anawrahta, who managed to unify his country under the banner of Theravada Buddhism. And just like the ancient Khmer heritage of Cambodia's Angkor Wat region (which had a tourism head start on its westerly neighbour), it is one of the celebrated and significant archaeological sites in Southeast Asia, and the most striking pagoda panorama in the world. The side effect of generations of closed-door secrecy was to push Bagan into the arms of obscurity and the realms of forgotten tourism; it was more elusive to travellers than the fabled Lost City of Atlantis. The Great Pyramids of Egypt. *Check.* Machu Picchu. *Check.* Petra. *Check.* Bagan? Cue tumbleweed.

In *The Travels of Marco Polo*, Bagan is described as 'a gilded city alive with tinkling bells and the swishing sounds of monks' robes.' Hundreds of years may have passed, but it is still very much alive to the sounds of tourists with their clicking cameras and excited chatter. Of the many thousands of temples that once adorned the plains of Bagan, approximately two hundred remain standing, which should be enough to satisfy the needs of serious temple enthusiasts for weeks on end, while tourists compelled to see everything will continue to suffer from visual agnosia. The golden temples had the effect of cultural awe and wonder on Marco Polo which translated into descriptions of beautiful stone 'covered with gold a finger thick so that the tower appears to be of solid gold.' The gold is mostly gone, and the stucco has been peeled away by nature, but the temples that survived the ravages of time have aged gracefully, standing in all shapes and sizes and different states of preservation and disrepair.

The dusty temple town of Bagan is the heritage equal of all those renowned UNESCO World Heritage sites but until only recently, access was limited by the country's insular government, which put restrictions and arcane bureaucracy before progress and development. It might be a small town regarding physical space, but it undoubtedly has city ambitions, having forced its way out of retirement like a heavy-weight fighter to compete with Cambodia's Siem Reap. Bagan has been pinned firmly in place on the must-see map of the ancient world. Word-of-mouth recommendations have created global awareness without the need for advertising campaigns, as travellers recounted tales of fields of pagodas bathed in the kindly glow of spectacular sunrises and sunsets. There is no place like it in the world and that is why archaeologists, architects, artists, seismologists, historians and English teachers flock to the site to study its secrets in a peace broken only by tourists.

Old Bagan is a mysterious empire's final footnote in history, and its ruins are the place markers of a period of great prosperity and glory, as the kings of Bagan had total control over a vast area that is now contemporary Myanmar. And just like the kings of Angkor, at the height of their powers between the eleventh and thirteenth centuries, they protected their legacy so it endured beyond their years, as they too were rather fond of building temples and pagodas with thousands of them dotted across their empire. Historical and modern Bagan is a cultural timeline folded in half, with the glories of a former kingdom co-existing in perfect unison with an emerging tourism industry. Bagan's golden age was abruptly ended by a Mongol invasion and sacking of the city in the thirteenth century, while a welcome incursion of foreign tourists has aided recent recovery efforts. The most significant battle Bagan has yet to win, however, is recognition from UNESCO that it deserves World Heritage status. Myanmar's Ministry of Hotels and Tourism first applied for this gold-standard prestige in 1996, but their claim remains uncertified due to the neglect and mismanagement of this ancient site. Bagan's authorities have had their wrists slapped for a series of unforgivably shoddy 'preservation' efforts, which conservationists regard as a form of historical and architectural treason.

Like the urgent decoration of a house to get a quick sale, beautification projects were launched by the former government using industrial materials and modern building techniques (they went as far as altering some of the original temple designs). The devastating earthquake of 1975 is partly responsible for this mismatch of old and new, as it caused widespread damage to Bagan's already-crumbling structures and prompted government officials to order rapid and ill-conceived reconstruction efforts to restore cultural dignity to the province. Myanmar's Humpty Dumpty would be put back together again; cowboy builders heard the call and galloped across Bagan's plains clutching trowels and bags of wet cement. Bizarrely, they whitewashed ancient murals with lime and added a few new constructions of their own for good measure (including a viewing tower, which is a horrible blot on the landscape). The government handed a first crayon set to a classroom of infants and left them unsupervised.

UNESCO has a global reputation to uphold and protect, but the organisation is at least providing some local guidance and much-needed training. UNESCO fears that any cultural status it bestows on Bagan could trigger an avalanche in visitor numbers when the site doesn't have the infrastructure to support and protect its already-threatened heritage. Many of Bagan's temples have limited security and protection; had I felt a tomb-raiding inclination, I could have carved out an ancient mural to sit alongside my fragment of the Berlin Wall and piece of the Great Pyramid of Egypt. I resisted the urge.

When visiting Yangon in late 2013, I didn't have enough time to explore the heritage of the north, so I returned in 2014 with a compact travel bag packed with time and temple notes, but without a chisel. Having read extensively about the history of a region I previously knew nothing about, I charged my camera batteries, hired an E-Bike (which I hoped the owner fully charged) and set off to explore dozens of the temples, pagodas, shrines, stupas and overgrown ruins dropped all over Bagan. It is the densest concentration of Buddhist temples and pagodas in the world, and while some have been allowed to fall into ruin, others have been restored to their former glories or restored so earnestly, they could pass for new builds (such as the Ananda Temple).

The Ananda Temple is the most revered building in the Bagan area and the 'surviving' masterpiece of Mon architecture (the Mon people were one of the earliest ethnic groups to reside in Southeast Asia). The touchy-feely love-in with Ananda has, structurally, gone too far with the plastering and whitewashing of walls and the regilding of its towers. The temple is a brilliant white, so I had to wear two pairs of sunglasses to protect my eyes. It is also quite modern-looking compared to its dusty peers, so I could have been forgiven for pulling over to order a classic burger with fries. The Ananda Temple is a reconstruction of the original, as most of its original features cracked and peeled away. I prefer my ruins ruined, but there are exceptions to the rule.

I was thoroughly impressed when I stood in front of the reconstructed Globe Theatre on the banks of the River Thames in London, as the original was destroyed by fire in 1613 before it was rebuilt and demolished by a wave of puritanism. Using historical records for a blueprint and authentic period materials such as English oak, this timber-framed building is a faithful replica of Shakespeare's playhouse and is the only building in the capital permitted a thatched roof since the Great Fire of 1666. Had the original theatre still existed and the British government rubber-stamped a rebuild, historians would have broken through security gates to protest on Downing Street. Not so in Bagan.

I didn't want to take the scattergun approach to sightseeing. Fearing I would miss my mark, I planned before leaving my hotel room to avoid being overwhelmed by the scale of Bagan's archaeological zone, or ignorantly scooting past its finest features. All Buddhist temples are sacred, but there is a limit to my respectfulness and the number of times I am prepared to bend over and take off my trainers and socks. I was selective with temples and shoe removal like parents trying to choose the very best schools for their children, having developed some terrible habits in Thailand where sightseeing is synonymous with religious buildings. I wore flip flops for ease of removal, but I occasionally stood on a temple's threshold and used my camera to zoom in on all the lovely details inside.

Bagan has a division of 'New' and 'Old' sections, and the provincial government has recognised the power of its appeal and the seismic commercial opportunities it presents. Ambitious plans for the city's growth and development have already been set in motion, as Bagan has emerged from its past to become one of the country's major income generators. Old Bagan remains a relatively quiet tourist town but a large area of former farmland, which borders the archaeological zone, has been sectioned off to create a modern hotel zone with international chains muscling into space on the minting plains of Bagan. Its future is all too easy to predict, with the overzealous development of Siem Reap running on parallel tracks but with a different running number. Bagan is lagging the leader and would be wise to take advantage of its placing to look ahead and evaluate where a lap of development should become a red-flag stop. The authorities can't do much about the lapping waters of the Irrawaddy, which has already washed away half of Old Bagan's temples, but they would be wise to curb some of their commercial enthusiasms.

The local people are quite used to welcoming their foreign guests with casual aplomb, but behind the smiles, they are acutely aware that their visitors provide a significant proportion of the region's wealth and the money in their purses. My trip to Bagan began as I meant for it to go on, and quite unlike so many of Southeast Asia's airports, Bagan's Nyaung-U Airport is a short drive from the principal tourist areas, and so was my hotel on Anawrahta Road which I timed at five minutes by airport taxi. At Subang Airport in Kuala Lumpur, the late-night transfer to my hostel lasted more than an hour, and the driver struggled to stay awake. As he nodded off to sleep with every third blink of his one remaining eye, our roles reversed as I was forced into a state of full alertness as I periodically tapped him on the shoulder, while he filled the air with the guttural belches of an elephant seal. I suspected he was drunk on cheap beer and fatigue and hadn't planned on making a cross-city pickup from the airport. Bagan, by contrast, is a meticulously planned city with the onus being on comfort and convenience with the tourist dollar protected, and probably more sacred, than all those temples and pagodas.

Before I arrived in Bagan, I took the shortest flight of my life (which lasted just under twenty-five minutes) from Mandalay and probably spent more time taxiing on the runway than I did in the air. It is possible to book international flights directly into Bagan, but most visitors to the north usually take in Mandalay first, before embarking on a cultural pilgrimage south to the ancient city which will be determined by three essential factors: budget, patience or a preference for sadomasochism. I chose the quickest option so booked an economy flight with Air Mandalay in what looked like a toy aeroplane, complete with turboprop propellers. Air Mandalay is, in fact, a Yangon-based airline so quite unlike the advertising slogan, this airline doesn't do what it says on the tin.

Despite the existence of an established rail connection (I could have taken a ferry, a public bus or a taxi), having spoken to fellow travellers in both Mandalay and Yangon about the overnight rail services to Bagan, their message was as unanimous as it was unequivocal. Myanmar's rail network is in a state of disrepair - journeys are painfully slow, overcrowded, numbingly uncomfortable and a real test of human frailty and endurance. I didn't fancy imitating Jesus in the wilderness, so a short flight was a temptation too much for me.

Myanmar's train services have a reputation for cancellation and delay, so a journey from Mandalay to Bagan, which is advertised to take seven hours, could take ten hours or more to complete. A traveller shared her regret about how she was totally exhausted when she finally arrived at Bagan and wished she had spent a few dollars more on a flight. She experienced arctic-cold in her sleeper cabin and shivered the whole way south, having spent the previous two weeks on Thailand's southern beaches where the days are scalding and the nights offer the small relief of being hot. It was an easy decision to make as I didn't want to repeat her mistake: I booked a budget flight.

At the arrivals hall, I paid for my Bagan Archaeological Zone pass which was a snip at ten dollars and valid for five days. Positive karma does not come readily to those who cheat a developing country out of a few dollars, and as officials check passes at the temples with the better views, the last thing I wanted was to be turned away from the Sunset Pagoda (Shwesandaw Pagoda) as the sun was readying itself to set. Others had taken the chance, and luck deserted them while karma paid them back in spades, as they were unable to enjoy views of pagodas that looked like giant pineapples silhouetted against the setting sun.

The obvious highlight of any trip to Bagan will be all those stunning temples with pagoda views, and the best way to get about the dusty plains is on the soft seat of an E-Bike. The Old Bagan area is vast at twenty-six square miles, but the main roads are in excellent condition to meet tourist needs and expectations. As I whizzed about with the wind in my face and a few flies in my mouth, I could relax and enjoy the scene as Bagan's drivers are the safest and most considerate I have encountered in Southeast Asia. They manage to keep a safe distance, pass slowly and give a gentle honk of the horn to let you know they are there. Away from the main roads, it's all about the dirt tracks which are great fun for the adventurous and getting lost is part of the experience. I never felt or feared that I would get lost in the real sense of the word, as the temples provide some obvious markers, but for those with a poor sense of direction, there are plenty of signposts as a precaution.

There are several transport options to choose from, which include private or guided group tours in air-conditioned taxis, coaches or minivans. I didn't want to be chauffeured around Old Bagan to someone else's agenda, bombarded by historical facts about each temple with unnecessarily long-winded explanations of what each of Buddha's gestures might mean, or the mythical stories that inspired ancient mural paintings. I rarely remembered anything that was shared by travel guides in Southeast Asia as I was usually out of earshot (which was my fault, not theirs), or their English was so pitiable I mistook it for an ancient language that was as dead as my interest. I often found myself wandering off mentally as well as physically, or distracted by the function wheel of my Canon camera, editing photographs in-camera as the opening paragraph of a guide's explanation turned into a complex historical narrative.

Attempting to explore Bagan on foot would be the summit of all imprudent undertakings, as some of the temples are set great distances apart. It is possible to hire a horse and cart which would seem to be the rural ideal, but this is a slow alternative and just one step above the walking option. Selfies with the horse may well have impressed friends back home, but I didn't want to have to wait a month before I could sit down comfortably. A popular alternative is to hire a bicycle and peddle around at leisure, but for the trifling sum involved, I spent my days in the pleasurable company of Bagan E-Bikes.

For just eight dollars a day, these battery-powered bicycles helped me navigate the plains at a moderate speed, and they were far more comfortable than the peddle option in Bagan's penetrating heat. They are safe, relatively noiseless, and they are also kind to the environment. The municipal authorities have banned foreigners from riding motorbikes, so E-Bikes are the next best thing. Bagan takes good care of its tourists, so their convenience is the political modus operandi; E-Bikes can be hired from hostels, cafes, shops and restaurants with ease. I wasn't asked to provide personal documentation (or complete any paperwork) as I loaned them with minimal fuss and waved goodbye to their owners, before setting off to the sands of history.

I must admit that I was, initially, hesitant and suspicious, fearing the batteries would fail me when I got lost in some uncharted, isolated area. The idea of hauling a heavy bike across hot sand prompted me to do some preliminary research. Owners display laminated cards on the fronts of the bikes with their personal identification and telephone numbers, which was handy when I returned from a temple to be greeted by dozens of them, with some the same colour and model as my own. I took a photo of my bike's ID card on my mobile phone so if I ran out of current, I could at least give the owner a call so they could send a replacement (if they could find me). Most owners claim a bike's battery charge will last a full day, but I needed a replacement every single day. Once I had mastered the basic controls, Bagan was all mine to explore at leisure. I resisted wandering off to distant locations in the evenings, fearful that should my battery lose its charge, I would have a long wait for a replacement to arrive. If I ventured too far out into Myanmar's wilderness, I might never be found again (but a forensic team might find my skeletal remains).

When riding on the dirt tracks, I was prepared to fall off a few times, and I didn't fail to live up to my clumsy expectations as I fell from an embankment and earned myself a few cuts and grazes. I blamed the temples as they were a terrible distraction, and I narrow focused my efforts by dipping in and out of Bagan's more significant sites, admiring external architectural details or shaded internal frescoes, murals and statues of Buddha. I could write the next volume of *War and Peace* as there are so many temples and pagodas to visit, but that is the business of historians and archaeologists. Most tourists spend two or three days sightseeing Bagan, and that is more than enough time to do it justice as the law of diminishing returns applies, and it is better to leave before the wanderlust is lost.

Temples which stood out include the Ananda, which is curiously modern but considered the holiest temple on the plains. Bupaya is a golden, dome-shaped temple by the river and Dhammayangyi was commissioned by a king who assassinated his father and wanted to atone for his sins. Dhammayazika has beautiful, pentagonal terraces; Gawdawpalin has Indian stylistic influences while Htilominlo is a grand statement in scale. Shwegugyi is one of the most intact temples to have stood the test of time; Shwesandaw is the favourite sunset temple, while Thatbyinnu is the tallest pagoda. Shwezigon Pagoda, located further away in Nyaung U-town, would not look out of place in Yangon. To broaden my understanding of the history of the region and to view ancient artefacts recovered by archaeologists, I visited the Bagan Archaeological Museum, and for a panoramic view of the temples, I took to the sky in a hot air balloon.

My warmest memory of Bagan is not all those temples as you would expect, but the freedom those E-Bikes allowed me and the sense of adventure they created as I explored the landscapes of Southeast Asia's forgotten history. As persistent sweat clung to my shirt and an attentive sun kissed my face, I agreed with Ernest Hemingway when he observed: 'It is by riding a bicycle that you learn the contours of a country best.' I may have cheated slightly with battery assistance, but I found Bagan's contours on my own, without having to flick through the pages of a guidebook or listening to the humdrum of a local guide.

Marco Polo was right: it is one of the finest sights in the world.

## Chapter 29: Travels with Charlie

When John Steinbeck wrote his intimate travelogue *Travels with Charley: In Search of America*, he described a road trip with his faithful canine companion. When I journeyed to Bagan, I was relieved that my 'friend' Charlie wasn't sitting by my side. I managed to keep my return to Myanmar a state secret - we had already travelled to Yangon together - and I was determined not to socially or culturally mix with Charlie ever again. I enjoy time away with close friends, but shared holidays are the quickest way to lose them as expectations rarely meet in the middle. Some people like to relax on the beach with an easy read while others prefer cultural crusades, visiting every temple within a fifty-mile radius. Charlie falls into the second category and with his obsessive-completest mentality, had he joined me in Bagan he would have compelled me to inspect every nook and cranny of every temple and pagoda, before rushing off to the next thing to do on an exhaustive list he would have spent the night compiling by candlelight. If there's a needle in a haystack waiting to be discovered, Charlie will almost certainly find it.

Travelling with friends is a marriage of movement and shared discovery, which can result in renewed vows or the bitterest divorce. Despite my reservations, I travelled with Charlie to Yangon following a friendship-testing weekend in the countryside town of Kanchanaburi in Western Thailand. I found his quirks of character and his travel eccentricities entertaining in small doses in Bangkok, but when magnified by proximity and long hours spent together, they became a great source of irritation, and the friendship was doomed not to last. Enthusiasm can be infectious for only so long, and as Charlie yapped at everything he saw like a new-born puppy, I found myself wanting to repeat that scene in Steinbeck's *Of Mice and Men* when one of the ranch hands shoots Candy's dog to put it out of its misery. If I had to endure another weekend with Charlie, I would have turned the gun on myself. In Mark Twain's *Tom Sawyer Abroad*, one of his characters observes: 'I have found out that there ain't no surer way to find out whether you like people or hate them than to travel with them.' I found out the hard way and repeated the mistake.

I met Charlie in Bangkok, and we quickly became 'expat friends' (a friendship of convenience) over tales of travel and stale beer. He was full of unusual but ultimately useless trivia, and his habit of precisely recalling how goals were scored in football matches - decades before he was born - was amusing. He would tell me how many seconds the ball was in flight before it hit the back of the net and the exact angle of its trajectory. He was very odd, that was for sure, but at least he wasn't dull. He also had a habit of walking out on bar and restaurant bills for no good reason at all. When he visited the Sky on 57 rooftop bar at the exclusive Marina Bay Sands Hotel in Singapore, he complained that it was too expensive for his budget as his bill for four cocktails came in at just under one hundred dollars with service charges. So, what did Charlie do? He left without paying, and let someone else pick up the tab. I do not suffer fools lightly, but in Southeast Asia, I found myself socialising with a plentiful supply of them. My social pool had reduced to a trickle.

When we travelled together to Kanchanaburi, I tried to cure Charlie of his kleptomania (when he visited The Iron Fairies bar in Bangkok, he stole their iron fairies) when he insisted we shouldn't pay for the perfectly acceptable meal and drinks we enjoyed on our very first evening. The restaurant was expensive by Thai standards, but it was all about the location as it jutted out and over the waters of the River Kwai, right next to the famous bridge of the same name. The restaurant's exit was an athletic climb over several banks of steep steps, but Charlie was determined to attempt his mission impossible without a mission, despite the stacked odds against him. I put him out of his misery with swift and decisive action, calling the waitress over to pay the bill. Charlie begrudgingly counted out his smallest twenty-baht notes to cover his exact share of the bill, and not a baht more. He was getting petty when he could afford to pay, and he was behaving like I had just stolen his life's savings.

We left the restaurant - without a police or citizen's arrest - and began our long walk back to our 'floating hostel.' It was the cheapest dosshouse Charlie could find online, with a location on the fringes of the town (possibly the next town), and as Kanchanaburi doesn't have taxi services like the capital, our only late-night transport option was to use our four feet. A weekend with Charlie was becoming a relay of strange, and with our bellies gorged with giant river prawns, barbequed meats and enough rice to fill a small barge, Charlie spotted a group of sporty Thai men playing an active game of five-a-side football and asked if we could join in. They were built like miniature Olympians and blessed by the vigour of youth, but they also had the skills to play competitive football beyond a car park kickabout. They also had sobriety on their side. Charlie and I looked like two gasping, badly-drawn boys grasping onto the last vestiges of youth.

Playing football on a full stomach, topped with churning natural acids and Chang Beer, is an egg-and-spoon race disaster but Charlie was not to be deterred in the small hours. I started out in midfield, but as opposition players ghosted past me with ease, I was swiftly dumped on my backside and put in front of a makeshift goal, and told to stay there and not move. I found my natural, preferred position. They soon realised their mistake as they had seriously over-estimated my ability to stand still. Sitting on an oven-baked tarmac, I prepared myself for the ultimate humiliation as I waited to be converted into a goal post. I wore a full Manchester United football strip, but I was a pub-team player; Charlie was a Premier League superstar as he covered every inch of weed and concrete in sweat. He removed his T-shirt as all the Thai players were bare-chested and he was desperate to assimilate, but I kept my shirt on as I was fearful the captain would order me to wear a sports bra if I took it off. After an hour of standing and sitting in front of the goal (I barely moved), Charlie eventually wore himself out like a toddler before bedtime. As we made our second attempt at a return to our hostel, Charlie's body odours destroyed crops and all living creatures within a ten-mile radius of Kanchanaburi Province.

Charlie booked a hostel described as 'a floating river bungalow' which sounds idyllic and desirable enough, but the five-pounds-a-night-reality meant the floors consisted of sponge, and as I crossed the room, my feet sank at least an inch deep. I was afraid of falling asleep, as my additional body weight could have pushed the bed through the floor to drown me slowly in the river. The windows had no glass as they were formed of wire meshing pulled over wooden frames, and they were an open invitation in mosquito season. The shower water was pumped directly from the river where I returned the undigested leftovers of those giant prawns I had eaten, and the toilet wasn't even a flushing toilet to boot. The hostel owner placed a barrel of water next to it so every time nature called (and she often screamed in Southeast Asia), I could scoop up some liquid and hope its weight was enough to force my foul waste down the pipe. There was science in there somewhere, along with the effluent.

The River Kwai is a scenic and historic Second World War site, so every scoop felt like an affront to nature and history's tragic heroes. Charlie booked a room next to mine, but the walls were wafer thin so we could have saved money and shared. He wouldn't stop talking as night became day, and the last thing I remembered that first night before falling asleep or awake was: 'I bet SpongeBob SquarePants has stayed in these spongy rooms!' Charlie chuckled at his joke and annoyed me for two whole days in Kanchanaburi, but it was the second weekend in Yangon that proved too much for our short-lived friendship.

The trip to Yangon was all Charlie's idea, so he booked the flights and hostel and arranged and collected our visas in Bangkok. All I had to do was turn up at the airport. Our trip didn't get off to a flying start, as Charlie arrived at the airport as our budget AirAsia flight was ready to depart. We charged like the Light Brigade through immigration and security, but at least we didn't have to locate our seats on the plane as they were the only ones unoccupied. Pulling on an apologetic mask for the delay 'we' had caused, I was privately grateful that Charlie was seated a dozen rows ahead. As he couldn't chew off my ear, he repeatedly called the flight attendants to order items from the in-flight catalogue which included AirAsia stationery, toy mascots, and a model aircraft. He waved down the aisle to get my attention and held his aviation trophies above his head with the pride and exhilaration of a father at the birth of his first child. I gave him a thumb up, turned to the stranger sitting to my left and whispered: 'I don't know him.'

Once we had landed and passed through immigration at the Yangon end, Charlie noticed a poster of the Kyaiktiyo Pagoda in the Mon State, a granite boulder covered in gold leaf on Mount Kyaiktiyo, which is, ultimately, a rock. Yangon no longer mattered to Charlie as Kyaiktiyo Pagoda was his latest obsession and go-go-go, see-see-see. When the taxi driver explained that it would take at least ten hours to drive to the rock from Yangon (he didn't much fancy the journey either), I hoped that would be all the cold water I needed, but Charlie asked him how much it would cost for a return trip. We were yet to arrive in Yangon, and he was already planning a detour somewhere else.

I wasn't prepared to allow myself to be confined in sweat and salt deposits for twenty hours, so I reminded him we were in Yangon to see *Yangon*, not a rock. Cue expletives. Charlie reluctantly agreed that we should stay put, but I found myself being dragged and pushed to a succession of the most random of sites and caught up in someone else's travel tornado. The moment he produced a shopping list of attractions, I finally understood: we are incompatible travellers cut from entirely different cloth.

Charlie's mantra was quantity *always* before quality, so when he visited any major city in Southeast Asia, he would wander off to small towns and provinces nobody has ever heard of, including the local people. Travellers who want to look at everything see nothing at all, and like a demented dictionary, the only word Charlie seemed capable of uttering was 'Amazing!' with a thick Birmingham inflexion. Everything was *amazing*. Charlie was incapable of mastering the adjectival phrase; he was a single-word crusader and a punishing tormentor. A neat row of pigeons, perched on an electric cable in Yangon, was equal in status to UNESCO World Heritage. Two days travelling with Charlie is enough to turn a Buddhist monk apoplectic, but I had at least learnt an essential travel lesson: choose your travel companions carefully, or else go solo.

# Chapter 30: Ballooning over Bagan

Ballooning over the historical plains of Bagan is one of those singular and ultimate travel experiences. It was comparable to crossing the Sea of Sand on horseback to reach Java Island's Mount Bromo in Indonesia or standing on Table Mountain to take in the views of Cape Town and distant Robben Island, where Nelson Mandela was incarcerated for twenty-seven years. I suffer from acrophobia which derives from the Greek words 'acron' (meaning heights) and 'phobos' (meaning fear), but I have faced my fear head-on by skydiving, taking flying lessons and piloting a Cessna 152, jumping from one of the world's highest bungee platforms (with a freefall of two hundred metres) and hot air ballooning over Egypt and Myanmar. I never allowed fear to become a barrier to adventure, but it sometimes erupted at the most inopportune moments.

Like the time when I took a wobbly hike along the active crater rim of Mount Bromo and its ashen mouth greeted me by spewing out a cloud of thick and eggy sulphuric gas (which reduced my visibility to within a few feet in all directions). The view into Bromo's volcanic and ghostly core was clear enough and reminded me that a single misstep (there were no guide or safety ropes) could result in an impromptu impersonation of the creature Gollum falling into the frothing cauldron of Mount Doom. My fear of heights returned and snatched away the last of the tottering resolve in my legs, which quivered as I got down on all fours like a dog in a thunderstorm. Mount Bromo presents one of the natural world's ultimate combinations of beauty and danger, but I was thrilled when my feet returned to the sandy safety of terra firma.

Hot air ballooning is the oldest form of human flight technology, and it continues to hold a romance for travellers and adventurers. Adventure travel usually comes with risk, and hot air balloons are as unpredictable as the wind patterns they rely on, as they often land where they're not supposed to. Bagan's balloon companies have a spotless safety record, and despite the steeply prohibitive cost of a sunrise escapade, there are always plenty of willing participants with demand for this once-in-a-lifetime activity consistently set to high. Viewing the temples and pagodas from a graceful floating basket is incomparable, and the service providers know it. I listened to online advice and booked ahead to avoid disappointment, and I got an unexpected two-for-one bucket list bonus.

When I took to the skies over the western bank of the Nile River and Egypt's Valley of the Kings in 2008, the experience failed to meet my expectations. The views were limited to the fertile farming areas of the Nile Delta area and the imposing Mortuary Temple of Queen Hatshepsut, with its three collonaded terraces set against the mountains. It was my first balloon ride, so I enjoyed the thrill of being in the air, but the fault of expectation was my own as the providers delivered what they promised, with a balloon path over the Valley of the Kings revealing arid landscapes and the specks of tomb entrances. Everything of interest was below ground and the experience was enjoyable enough, though the highlight shouldn't have been an awkward landing in a field of sugarcane as locals rushed out to sing and dance with over-priced souvenirs their preferred encore.

In Egypt, I left with the impression that profits come before safety, as correct and rigidly enforced safety measures always lead to greater costs. There was a distinct lack of professionalism in everything from the rushed booking to the balloon's clumsy return to earth. I wasn't at all surprised when I turned on the news to discover that nineteen tourists - having used the same balloon company I had chosen - fell to their deaths when their balloon caught fire in 2013. Hot air balloons have been flying over the Luxor area since Victorian times when surveyors mapped the area from the sky above, so I assumed a certain level of expertise inheritance for the current providers of this service. My flight was a steal at £45 until I arrived at the frenzied launch field which was a high-yielding cash crop of balloon baskets crammed full of eager-faced tourists. The balloons defied physics, and I was surprised they could take off with all that western weight of soft flesh and dense bone. I had no choice but to have sex with my clothes on, as I was pressed head-to-toe against an elderly French lady in a lasting and sweaty embrace, our foreplay limited to a brief exchange of 'Bonjour!'

Bagan might be a Third World country and a cash-starved nation, but I was charged £250 for my balloon adventure. The return on my memory investment was a punctual and unhurried experience, and I didn't have to fall to my death to make a landing. Balloon experiences in Egypt mostly come at an economy price and without frills, but in Myanmar, the only option is the premier business class which comes with a post-sunrise champagne breakfast of freshly baked croissants, banana bread and an assortment of sliced and exotic fruit. It took Herculean efforts to rise in time for a 4:30 am hotel pickup, but I was pleasantly surprised when a restored vintage passenger bus pulled over and opened its creaking doors, instead of one of those modern, white and air-conditioned tourist minivans. Balloons over Bagan is the established, recommended company that owns a fleet of Canadian-built relics from the Second World War, formerly used for the transportation of soldiers. When it proved too expensive to ship wooden buses back to Canada, they were abandoned to local entrepreneurs and cleverly converted into tourist transports.

With the crumbling crust of a night's interrupted sleep still gathered at the corners of my mouth and eyes, and with my brain still resting on a pillow stained yellow by someone else's saliva, I clambered aboard and announced my arrival by bashing my head on a rusted handrail. I pretended it didn't hurt as thoughts turned to tetanus shots, before noticing that I was the only passenger wearing flip flops, wafer-thin cotton shorts, and a nylon counterfeit football shirt. I had packed little else and looked like an over-sized toddler; the only thing I cared about - more than a fashion faux pas - was keeping fresh.

I underestimated the bone-chilling cold of daybreak, while my group was evidently better informed and prepared as they sat insulated within layers of smugness, socks, gloves, hats, jeans, light fleeces and winter coats. I stood out for all the wrong reasons, like Prince Harry in a Nazi uniform at a fancy-dress party. Glancing casually about the bus and trying to conceal my shivering self-consciousness, I noticed sympathetic expressions with detectable traces of condescension, with my ill-chosen apparel the unspoken focus. I half expected that Italian woman, the one on the train from Naples to Sorrento, to pipe up with an unhelpful remark. To my profound relief and distraction, I wasn't the only passenger to make this early morning miscalculation as an Eastern European woman boarded the bus in polka-dot beachwear. Her refrigerated nipples introduced themselves through her bikini top before she had a chance to tell us her name was Arina.

Upon our arrival at the launch site, we were offered coffee and shortbread biscuits, but I couldn't hold either as I was gripped by a shaking frenzy. The balloon captain was a Frenchman, and he introduced himself as Gerard before reassuring us that we were in very safe hands. He suggested we gather together to share our body heat as they readied the balloons for take-off, and I took this opportunity to step a little closer to Arina. Gerard asked the balloon party a question to keep us awake or entertained:

'Does anyone know who manned the first hot air balloon?'

He was quite advanced in his years, so I was tempted to reply:

'Was it you?'

My well-wrapped balloon group was frozen in silence and the left-over fatigue of the previous day, so we all stared at Gerard as it was too early for an aviation quiz.

'Well, well, well,' he continued (like Rene from '*Allo, 'Allo!*), 'that flight was piloted in Paris in November 1783 by none other than… Jean-Francois Pilatre de Rozier and Francois Laurent d'Arlandes!'

Silence.

Unimpressed by our collective resistance to his national pride and impersonation of the late Gorden Kaye, he offered explanations of optimal weather conditions and balloon safety rules. Gerard gave me a complimentary baseball cap which I accepted with more enthusiasm than it deserved, as it allowed me to warm the crown inches of my head. As we waited in the dark, I found myself inching closer and closer to the basket as they fired it full of hot air. I was the first in my group to fall into the balloon basket (there is no graceful way to enter one) as I wanted to be as close to the burner flame as my eyebrows and common sense allowed.

Quite unlike the companies in Cambodia's Siem Reap area, Bagan's balloon companies have permission to fly over the archaeological zone, so there is no false advertising in their claims of birds-eye temple and pagoda views. My first expedition was a disappointment of epic proportions, as I spent close to an hour drifting over a farmer's field next to the planned hotel zone, with a view only interrupted by the intermittent vomiting of an American tourist who was, thankfully, not in my portion of the basket. The farmer didn't have grounds for complaint, as his sesame crop was watered by an unlikely source. Gerard was apologetic, but all he could do was fire more heat from the burners into the balloon which had a yo-yo effect, but without any headwinds, we were going nowhere and not even fast. When he explained the region's crops and detailed preferred farming methods, he was thinking on his airborne feet and over-compensating the tragicomedy of our circumstances. We were not alone as other balloon groups were performing a parade of uppers and downers, with one landing on the roof of a farmer's cottage.

As the rippling silk of the balloon was carefully packed away by the crew and the basket hoisted onto a truck, our captain made an urgent phone call (I knew it was serious as he spoke only in French) as his balloon group reassembled in a circle of despondency. Gerard re-joined us, apologised for our disappointing experience and offered complimentary flights the next morning. I was surprised by this generosity of spirit, but with additional firms fighting for a share of a market Balloons over Bagan once held a monopoly over, they couldn't risk a basketful of negative reviews. Getting up for a second attempt at 4:30 am was a punishing trial I didn't want to repeat, but the winds were high enough to push the balloon across the plains, and the views were as spectacular as they had promised them to be. As Gerard pointed out all the temples I had visited or viewed from the seat of my E-Bike, my eyes were distracted by the sparkling brilliance of the Irrawaddy River and the distant Delta region, so I vowed to take to the waters later that day for a sunset float along Myanmar's historical lifeline.

The source of the Irrawaddy River flows from the Himalayas through Myanmar's northern border, all the way south where it empties into the ever-thirsty Andaman Sea. It is the country's largest body of water, and it is emerging as one of Southeast Asia's unlikely river cruise destinations. The name of the river has been translated by scholars as a 'blessing' to the people of Myanmar: its water floods their land to create fertile soils for crops, providing drinking water to sustain life and a rich fishing source. The river is integral to local life as the people choose to live beside it, wash and swim in it and travel and trade on its currents. I managed to negotiate a river tour with a friendly local fisherman - for three dollars an hour - as I wanted a view of Bagan's famous sunsets without the crowds.

I followed logic the previous evening when I witnessed the sunset from the Sunset Pagoda, but it was more of a sunset scramble as hundreds of tourists climbed to the pagoda's upper terraces to jostle for space and push away any charm or romance the experience could have held. A woman standing to my left was so green about the gills she could swim, having enjoyed one too many bottles of Beer Mandalay or eaten something that violently disagreed with her. As she bowed her head to relocate the contents of her stomach into a clear sandwich bag, I tried to focus my eyes on the sunset. But when Sick Lady tied her sick bag in a knot and left it on the floor, I was terrified that passing tourists might burst its contents all over my lower legs like a poorly applied fake tan. An overweight tourist standing to my right was sweating profusely, and every time he took a photograph, his arms extended, touched my own and shared their warm fluids. I needed a break from the maddening crowds.

The Irrawaddy River promised solace from vomit and sweat, but the pier wasn't easy to find. I knew I was heading in the right direction as strangers approached with the same five-worded question: 'You want boat trip, sir?' Some steps lead down to the riverbank below Buphaya Paya, which is an enormous, bulbous-shaped golden dome and reportedly the oldest pagoda in the region. As a shiny replica of the original which fell into the river during the 1975 earthquake, I would argue that it lost that claim to be the oldest pagoda the year I was born. If we rebuilt the RMS Titanic to its original White Star Line design in the Harland and Wolff shipyard in Belfast, would we pretend the original wasn't on the bed of the North Atlantic Ocean? I wasn't prepared to debate this with the monks gathered about in prayer, so I followed a narrow pathway past a small river village with stalls selling local dishes fished from the Irrawaddy, and a thousand neatly stacked cans of Coke. The Coca-Cola Company has reached a new and thirsty post-sanctions market in Myanmar, opening its first production facility for sixty years in 2013. Cuba and North Korea continue their wait for carbonated soft drinks.

I approached a busy boatman - tidying away fishing nets - who had already set up a table and chairs on the stern. With a bottle and a plastic cup in hand, I hoped that my Red Mountain Estate Wine would be more than a palatable local vinegar. As the sun reflected off the sparkling water and the sides of my glass, I toasted passing boats, and the people settled on the embankment as pagodas glistened in the last rays of the day's light. I was in 'emperor mode' again, and as my boatman steered me down the Irrawaddy, scenes of river life played out like a cultural performance at the water's edge as river communities bathed in the river and went about the daily rituals of their lives. Shelducks, lounging in the shallows, took flight and silhouetted against the sunset while gold panners crouched at the water's edge in the sand and silt, with evidentially more to be found in the Irrawaddy's waters than fish.

I didn't spot too many local people living in Old Bagan as the tourist hotels have squeezed them out like juice from an orange, but I discovered where they relocated to and got a glimpse of Bagan that was truly old.

## Chapter 31: The Mysteries of Mandalay

Modern Mandalay is a former ancient capital and royal city and the second largest urban area in Myanmar. It rests on the east bank of the Irrawaddy River, and its only striking landmark feature is Mandalay Hill which is a natural watchtower from which visitors can view sunrises and sunsets over pancake-flat plains. The city's holy hill has a crown of glistening temples and pagodas which include Su Taung Pyi, the wish-granting pagoda, where most tourists probably wish they were someplace else like Bagan. At its feet, two huge white lions stand on sentry duty as spiritual walkers are politely forced to remove their shoes before they climb to the top, barefoot on the damp and dried stains of monkey urine. The rest of Mandalay is quite unremarkable at first glance, and it certainly wouldn't win any beauty contests as it's a hot, dusty, chaotic and noisy place. But it is alive with people and a multisensory energy that is typical of Southeast Asia's streets, where sitting on the kerb late at night is preferable to a soft and cosy indoor couch (though they sometimes drag their couches outdoors).

I planned my second trip to Myanmar primarily to see Bagan, but I did not need a whole week to explore pagoda ruins. With variety the spice of travel life in Southeast Asia, I decided to head north first on a voyage of discovery to unearth the mysteries of Mandalay, as my knowledge of the city came from travellers' soundbites as they waxed lyrical about a distant metropolis full of historical charm, wonder, and romance. Rudyard Kipling wrote a poem about the city and its sunshine, palm trees and 'tinkly temple bells,' but the Mandalay he knew lies beneath bricks and cement. I am always cautious when I listen to other travellers' recommendations as one man's treasure is often another man's trash, like all that junk I sold on eBay. Beauty will always remain in the eye of the beholder, but as I lived in Bangkok and found plenty to admire in its unplanned urban sprawl, I was prepared to give Mandalay a chance and take it as I found it.

Mandalay held an exotic fascination until the moment I arrived and realised that it looks like every other poorly constructed city in Southeast Asia. In Pablo Neruda's poem *Ode to a Naked Beauty*, he describes the appeal of his lover and her naked beauty with: 'As if you were on fire from within. The moon lives in the lining of your skin.' When I arrived in Mandalay, my heart was chaste, and my eyes were pure as I desperately hoped Neruda's description matched the gridded ugliness and lacklustre concrete that has formed over Mandalay to screen its cultural treasures. It was certainly on fire from above, but I sensed I would have to peel back a few layers to find the moon. The city's beauty and charms are masked from view, and that explains why so many travellers use it as a hub of convenience for day trips. I didn't want to judge a book by its torn and greasy-fingered cover, so I probed a little deeper to find what it didn't want to reveal readily.

With the spirit of exploration and a lot of perseverance in the heat, Mandalay reveals its secrets in the form of mosques, churches, backstreet craft workshops, local markets and everyday street life. Like most foreign visitors, I took the pilgrimage route to the top of Mandalay Hill by foot and left my counterfeit Nike trainers to chance at the entrance, climbing 230 metres of betel nut and monkey-stained stairs to reach the summit. I was shaded by a canopy of makeshift roofs and the leaves of obliging trees, as I climbed and dripped sweat over 1,729 concrete steps. The city panoramas and the rundown shrines were hardly worth the effort or the burn in my knees, but as Mandalay is short on visitor attractions, I had time to spare. Walking in the footsteps of Buddha, legend claims he visited Mandalay Hill and prophesied that a great city would be founded below in the next thousand years (or thereabouts). There is a standing statue of the Buddha pointing towards the modern city below to illustrate this historic moment, but I wasn't convinced that Mandalay lives up to his definition of 'great.'

I was surprised to encounter only a handful of tourists on my way up (the taxi ride option - with air conditioning - is the preferred route). Passing the occasional vendor selling cans of Coca-Cola and poorly made tourist trinkets, I had Mandalay Hill to myself. I was half expecting to find the place overrun with monkeys and tourists like so many other similar sites in Southeast Asia, so I was quietly pleased that there were neither. At the summit, I was mildly impressed by the Su Taung Pyi Pagoda as its richly coloured shrines and glass mosaic pillars are quite spectacular in the sunlight, albeit for a few brief seconds. Lazy tourists, short of time and effort, packed the upper terraces and swung their selfie sticks in every which way. Having recovered some of my energy and taken a few photographs of my own, I retraced my steps to the lions watching over my trainers with thoughts dominated by a more pressing prophecy: a cold glass of Myanmar Beer. I came, I climbed, and I quenched my thirst, but I didn't see anything of great interest.

Temples that don't require a vertical hike to heaven to enjoy them include the Mahamuni Pagoda - a pilgrimage site - which is older than Mandalay town itself and was one of Kipling's personal favourites. For the people of Mandalay, this is their most sacred temple and place of worship, so I wondered if Mandalay Hill is a clever decoy for the tourists, allowing the locals to worship at Mahamuni without tour buses and camera flashes. I spent an hour inside the temple complex but didn't see a single western tourist, joining the locals (with my longyi wrapped about me) whether they liked it or not. The temple's ancient sculptures are a robber's loot, stolen from the kings of Cambodia, so they lost the moral high ground and needed to make far more merit than I did.

The pièce de résistance is a deified four-metre bronze image of the Buddha on which devotees generously rub sheets of gold leaf, consequently making him chubbier than he already is. Only men are allowed access to the inner confines of the temple, so I joined them for a daily session of deity rubbing. Having arrived in the early morning hours, I could witness a crowd gather for the ceremony and ritual washing of Buddha's face, which is as surreal as a Monty Python sketch. The ritual is more of a wash, style, and blow dry as it went on for longer than my legs could remain comfortably crossed, with ornate containers and platters placed in front of the Buddha for his inspection and blessing. I respectfully suppressed the urge to laugh out loud when a monk wrapped a gold cloth around his neck like a giant bib and brushed his teeth with handfuls of rice, before washing the residue from his mouth with water from a gold can. Buddha is a messy eater.

I found Kuthodaw Paya at the foot of Mandalay Hill, which is famous for housing the world's largest book as it contains 729 slabs of marble placed inside 729 separate white stupas, with each 'page' containing the holy script of the Buddhist Tipitaka. The pagoda is a remodelling of the Shwezigon Pagoda in Bagan, and its gilded dome looks like the purest form of gold when contrasted against the surrounding white stupas. Nearby Sandamuni Paya is similar in appearance and boasts the world's largest iron image of the Buddha, so size matters in Mandalay. For a few lines of dark tourism, I located the Ma Soe Yein Monastery where Ashin Wirathu prefers to preach nationalistic hate instead of peace, but I declined to enter as I didn't want to disturb his latest YouTube rant.

The Shwenandaw Monastery is one of the most impressive structures to be found in Mandalay, built almost entirely of teak with intricate carvings. It is one of the city's prized historical and religious buildings as it survived destruction in its former location inside Mandalay Palace. Everything else burned to the ground, except this building made entirely of wood, perhaps providing compelling evidence of divine intervention. I took a break from the sun inside and found an excellent collection of ten Jataka panels depicting past life stories of the Buddha, while young monks studied quietly under the shade of monastery trees.

The view of Mandalay Palace - from Mandalay Hill - is more impressive than a visit to the palace itself. Built between 1857 and 1859 as part of King Mindon's founding of the new royal capital city of Mandalay, it has been partially restored to its former glory, allowing visitors to walk its grounds which are surrounded by a moat and punctuated by old Burmese palace architecture. When the British arrived in 1885, King Mindon was conquered and banished with his royal family to India. The Second World War had a long reach, as the palace felt the touch of bombs in 1945 and what remains of it today is used as a military installation. There is a museum in the western section of the palace displaying the regalia of the former kings of Myanmar, and as I needed a break from the busy roads outside, I welcomed a retreat into a quieter space. I found a roadside restaurant on my exit, but what the food lacked in taste was compensated by quantity (Charlie would have loved it), as I was brought bowl after plating of god-knows-what which is a very popular dish in Southeast Asia. When I pleaded, 'Please, no more,' the waitress did the exact opposite, and a swarm of flies gathered on the rim of every untouched bowl.

There are numerous day trip options available from Mandalay, including another former capital at Amarapura where I could visit Maha Ganayon Monastery, Kyauktawgyi Pagoda and the picturesque teakwood U Bein Bridge that spans Taungthaman Lake. At Sagaing, I climbed another hill and visited another pagoda (Kaunghmudaw Pagoda) and from Mingun, I was able to visit more ruins and the Hsinbyume, Settawya, Pondaw and Mingun pagodas (as well as the gigantic Mingun Bell, which weighs ninety tonnes and claims to be the largest ringing bell in the world). After three days of boomeranging to pagodas, monasteries, and historical ruins, the cultural law of diminishing returns produced the effect of sight without seeing. Preferring afternoon retreats to my hostel and its 'rooftop restaurant' (where I was able to devour millions of complimentary peanuts and enjoy effortless views of sunsets over satellite dishes), I had come to the end of my Burmese days. It was time to turn the next travel page.

I wanted to get closer to nature, so logic compelled me to board a flight to a mythical land that boasted having a million elephants: The Lao People's Democratic Republic.

## Part 4: Land of a Million Elephants

## The Lao People's Democratic Republic

*When you've heard it, you must see it; when you've seen it make a judgement with your heart.* (Laotian Proverb)

### Chapter 32: Hydroelectric Elephants

Once a forgotten country cast in the same mould as Myanmar, developing Laos is one of Southeast Asia's most authentic and unspoilt nations, which is hardly surprising when you consider that until as recently as 1988, tourists were barred from entry by a secretive Communist Party. Pronounced with a silent *s*, historically Laos was The Kingdom of a Million Elephants, but in the twenty-first century, legend had become myth and travel hyperbole as I failed to see a single wild pachyderm, a pile of dung evidence or their elongated, oval footprints when I journeyed south to north and back again. Which is a terrible shame for Laos' emerging economy when eco-friendly writing paper, fashioned from elephant excrement, is a strangely popular memento of Southeast Asia (where else can shit become a souvenir?).

A single adult elephant can push out - on average - 50kgs of fibrous waste each day which, I was reliably informed, is enough mucky mass to produce 115 sheets of fragranced paper. The pulp and paper industry has found a genuinely greenish-brown solution to recycling; if Laos were still home to a million toilet-trained elephants, it would be a superpower of the global stationery business.

The origins of the country's nickname can be traced back to Laotian history of the fourteenth century when conqueror Fa Ngum founded a unified territory named Lan Xang Hom Khao (which translates to 'The Kingdom of a Million Elephants'). Time and tide wait for no man, with 'land' replacing 'kingdom' in 1975 after the dissolution of the constitutional monarchy; when the communists came to power, they renamed the country 'The Lao People's Democratic Republic.' That preceding bold claim was a statement of military power and prowess, as an army boasting a million elephants would have been considered invincible by its regional foes, with those Goliaths in grey the equivalent of modern-day tanks on Asia's historic battlefields. A Laos army would have looked something like that scene from the third *The Lord of the Rings* film (*The Return of the King*) when a battalion of monstrous oliphaunts sweep across the Pelennor Fields to smash the Rohirrim warriors to pieces.

The reservoirs and dams feeding Laos' hydroelectricity industry are its twenty-first-century mechanical elephants. Hydroelectric power is a significant and developing resource in Laos, which is itself becoming a powerful regional player and, potentially, the battery pack for power-hungry Southeast Asia. Having negotiated supplies to Thailand, Vietnam, and China, the power of its current currency could return it to trumpeting, halcyon days; Laos even launched a stock exchange - Lao Securities Exchange - in 2011. Despite this apparent economic progress, Laos remains one of the poorest countries in Southeast Asia with inadequate infrastructure and an unskilled workforce, but an electric shock has jump-started its heart, and a steady rhythm has returned after decades of cardiac arrest. There is only a small hope that those mythical elephants will ever return to their former numbers, but I was still mindful of one Laotian proverb: 'Although he who walks behind an elephant may feel very secure, he is likely to get splattered with elephant dung.' If I chanced upon an elephant, I would stand behind the man *standing behind* the elephant.

Laos' relentless logging industry - and resultant deforestation - slashed elephant numbers and destroyed their natural habitats (an estimated 40% of the country remains covered by closed-canopy forests). Elephants are an integral cog in the logging machine, so they have been forced to dig their own graves with their numbers having diminished to fewer than a thousand and falling, including domesticated elephants. If their present mortality rate continues, Laos' living icon - with its important symbolic connotations - could be lost forever. With unabating demand for timber resources (Laos exported 1.4 million cubic metres of timber to China alone in 2013), logging has accelerated rapid forest degradation. Additional triggers include land converted to plantations and cash crops, the development of industrial infrastructures (such as roads, hydroelectric dams, and artificial reservoirs) and the expansion of urban settlements. With designated 'protected areas' and safeguarding initiatives, Laos' surviving elephants may yet fend off the seeming inevitability of extinction, which would be a high price to pay for picnic tables.

The growth of ecotourism projects in Laos, supported by the National Tourism Administration, offer further hope of salvation as they provide alternative employment and improve working/living conditions for the elephants, as tourists are lighter loads than cumbersome logs. The income they generate covers the cost of expensive medicines and the 200-600 pounds of food they eat - on average - every day (elephants can spend up to 12-18 hours a day feeding). Animal rights activists are correct to complain when animals are used for the purpose of sport and entertainment, but when the alternative (as one sanctuary volunteer informed me) is to be force-fed amphetamines so they can be overworked to carry dangerously heavy loads up impossibly steep terrain, the situation seems a little less about the rock and the hard place. I visited an Elephant Village in Laos and non-profit sanctuaries across Thailand (which function as a welfare-state-of-sorts for retired and ailing elephants), where I discovered first-hand what truly magnificent creatures they are and witnessed some incredible conservation efforts aiming to secure the Asian elephant a future without precarity.

Laos is a mountainous and landlocked country (it is, in fact, Southeast Asia's only landlocked country). It shares borders with Myanmar and Thailand (to the west and south-west), Vietnam to the east, Cambodia to the south-east and China to the north. It is no longer isolated from the outside world as padlocked doors have opened to reveal smiling faces and waving hands, which beckon travellers with their guidebooks and cameras to a tropic landscape with a million secrets. Laos is often regarded as the vanilla country of Southeast Asia, a footnote on travel itineraries, when squirrelled away in its northern region is one of the world's most enticing and magical cities: Luang Prabang.

A trip to Laos is a journey into the past, as it retains its centuries-old traditions and a genuinely laid-back attitude and lifestyle that has all but disappeared from the rest of the subcontinent. Even the capital - Vientiane - holds all the old-fashioned charm of a relaxed riverfront town. Buddhist precepts help to give the country a sixties chilled-out ambience, but despite this, Laos continues to be overlooked because its neighbours are better-dressed. It is an utterly beguiling destination with an under-the-radar vibe, and tourists who cross the border from Thailand to extend their visas surprise themselves by staying longer than they planned to. Laos' reward is instant and obvious: nothing quite beats that Neil Armstrong feeling of visiting places where few Western boots have trodden before.

Laos has a few eccentricities too, and as one of the world's few surviving communist states, it loosely adheres to a Marxist ideology which is hard to ignore with all those omnipresent red stars on uniforms and state buildings. The national symbol, the gilded stupa of spellbinding Pha That Luang, has, however, replaced the hammer and sickle, even on the state seal. Laos is one of the world's poorest countries with 80% of its population working in agriculture, having been set back decades by a protracted and bloody civil war (1962-1975) and two Indochina wars, during which it played the unenviable role of piggy-in-the-middle. It was more of a roasted and part-charred porker, as it was bombed extensively by the US to disrupt the supply of arms along the Ho Chi Minh Trail, with an estimated 30% of those weapons failing to detonate on impact.

Like Cambodia, Laos struggles to this day with the aftermath of unexploded ordnance and a quick search on Google Images will reveal a pockmarked land resembling a cut of Swiss cheese - an indispensable reminder to younger generations of the dangers that lie beneath. For good measure, they could do with a few more *Mind Your Step* signs dotted here and there across the countryside.

'The Land of a Million Bombs' is a more fitting moniker for Laos' post-war reality. It has earned the unfortunate distinction of being the world's and history's most heavily bombed country per capita (especially along the northeastern border with Vietnam, and Xieng Khouang Province in particular, as this was where the Laos communist headquarters were situated). To put this in perspective, try to imagine this: more bombs dropped on Laos than all the mainlands of Europe during the Second World War, and yet the country is similar in size to Great Britain. Some 260 million US cluster bombs (that's a whopping 2.5 million tonnes of munitions) were dropped all over the green canopy of Laos, courtesy of 580,000 bombing raids. To make matters worse, whenever US aircraft failed to drop their deadly payloads on Vietnamese targets, they conveniently dropped them all over Xieng Khouang Province as they returned, dejected, to military bases.

Waste not, want not.

A team of monkeys sitting in a laboratory somewhere has worked out that this was the equivalent of dropping seven bombs for every man, woman and child (still) living in the country. Or, more incredible still, releasing a planeload of bombs every eight minutes, every hour of the day, for a continuous period of nine years. Perhaps it was those bombs that were the real-life Army of the Dead that wiped out all those elephants. It is quite incredible to think that anything but the mountains survived the onslaught or reduction to a smoking crater, its people condemned to the pages of history like the inhabitants of Pompeii (the population currently stands at less than seven million). Even notable Phou Bia, the highest mountain in Laos, remains inaccessible to tourists and mountaineers as it is dusted with a layer of ordnance.

Keeping with the theme of strange souvenirs and resourceful recycling, I bought spoons made from a deactivated US bomb at a tourist market in Luang Prabang. Strolling past the usual handicraft suspects of silk cushion covers and tissue boxes, sold on repeat, I stopped at a makeshift stall (an old towel spread out on the ground) with bracelets for sale, earrings, and spoons with unusual colouration. Leaning in for closer inspection, I noticed a small handwritten sign in broken English which read:

> *These bracelets were bombs. We make bracelets. Not war. Our bracelets are made from aluminium which was part of a plane or bomb dropped on our province during the Secret War. After the war, someone taught us what to do with the bombs that destroyed our lives. From bombs, we made spoons and recently we began to form bombs into beautiful bracelets. We bring new meaning to the bombs which help us escape poverty. Thank you so much for your support! The villages of Ban Naphia.*

Laos is the world's capital of scrap metal, and Ban Naphia is a tourist hot spot and another example of the global appeal of dark tourism. I chuckled when I spotted unintentionally jocose tourism signs displaying the village's unofficial title: *War Spoon Village*. The people of Laos are unable to farm vast expanses of their land for fear of unexploded ordnance (UXO) because when they plough the soil, they never know if they're going to unearth a dormant device. An alternative source of income is the scrap metal industry, so thousands set off from their homes every day with homemade metal detectors in one hand, and crossed fingers on the other. Local entrepreneurs and artisan families were shrewd enough to realise that if tourists are prepared to pay hard-earned money for elephant dung transformed into writing paper, why not melt down the deactivated UXO and make it into… spoons! And so, a new industry was born, which also helped to reverse and part-erase a terrible legacy. With the support of a Swiss NGO and an American designer, they broadened their product range with UXO bracelets, earrings, keychains, and chopsticks. The industry has exploded, and their products should carry origin labels that read: *Dropped and Made in Laos.*

As I made my way across the country by taxi, tuk-tuk, bus and bike, I saw more bomb casings than elephants and tourists, and I never failed to be surprised by the ingenious and extraordinary ways the Laos people have recycled weapons of mass destruction into creative new forms. Deactivated bombs are commonly reimagined and improvised as foundations to support houses (or props to protect against flooding), with smaller shells turned into planter boxes, water containers, cups, and even cowbells. A broad smile flashed across my face when I crossed a bridge and noticed canoes fabricated from the fuel tanks of former American bombers. In Laos, there is life after bombs. It is, however, the deadliest form of recycling with large missiles, rockets, grenades, artillery munitions, mortars, landmines and cluster munitions the profitable target of enthusiastic recyclers, many of whom are children.

There are an estimated three hundred causalities from UXO explosions every year, and when I visited the COPE Centre in Vientiane (the Cooperative Orthotic and Prosthetic Enterprise), which offers rehabilitation services across the whole of the country to the afflicted, the dangers and consequences of this deadly industry were all too explicit. Recycling is far from being a noble pursuit when it costs people their limbs and lives. With my UXO spoons in hand, Southeast Asia once again proved itself adept at reversing logic and overturning convention.

The two red stripes on the Laos national flag are appropriately symbolic of all the blood that was shed during internal struggles for freedom. The white circle on the blue line is a literal representation of the moon over the Mekong River and unity under a communist banner, which sounds more akin to propaganda. The blue connotes the country's wealth, but that is either wishful thinking, a nod to the country's distant and tusked past or an accurate prediction of hydroelectric potential. Accusations of genocide have blighted the international standing of Laos' neighbours, and the Laotian government is no stranger to controversy itself, having been tarred by similar denunciations as well as religious freedom and human rights violations against the ethnic Hmong minority group. But as the country remained relatively obscure to the eyes and ears of the outside world, its transgressions have mostly gone unnoticed, like the beating of a hollow drum.

Laos is Southeast Asia viewed through rose-tinted spectacles except when you take them off, the tincture remains. Like the wallflower at the party, her reticence is likely to be overlooked as brazen, uninhibited and cosmetically enhanced appearances offer immediate distraction and reward. The Lao People's Democratic Republic finds it impossible to compete with the self-possessed charms of neighbouring Thailand, which is free of cluster bombs and continues to draw the lion's share of visitors to the region. Competition for the tourist pound is fierce, and it's snowballing in the heatwave, now that Myanmar has grasped its newfound political and social freedoms with unimagined assuredness. I was relieved to learn that they sensibly accept US dollars and Thai baht in preference to their domestic currency (the Laotian kip) as one British pound in 2013 converted to over twelve thousand kips. I could put my textbooks away, as there was no longer any need for me to study for a

Cambridge Mathematics Degree to buy a bowl of noodle soup, and I didn't have to iron my notes flat and crease-free for fussy currency inspectors either.

Laos' untouched wilderness (the part that hasn't yet been hacksawed flat) is a reminder of the natural riches its noisy neighbours have already surrendered to overdevelopment and aggressive westernisation policies. Laos concerns itself with short-term gains rather than long-term problems; it exists *in* and *for* the moment and is carefree like a hippy on the one hand, and as unthinking as a match in a forest on the other. The devastating effects of the logging industry are evidence of this, as sustainability remains a buzz word, not practicality. Laos' neighbouring countries may steal all the travel headlines, but the tide is turning as tourism is Laos' fastest growing industry; it has found a tentative foothold on international travel charts and is no longer a mere afterthought or convenient border run for visa chasers.

As a Bangkok resident, I would on occasion stand on my balcony with a heavy heart and wonder where the real Thailand had disappeared to, as the undeniably modern cityscape of Bangkok makes a passable impression of Lower Manhattan with high-rise office buildings, apartment blocks and condominiums all fighting for space in an overcrowded and muggy metropolis. When I walked to the BTS Skytrain (an elevated, rapid transit system), I passed McDonald's, Pizza Hut, Chester's Grill, Dunkin Doughnuts and Domino's Pizza, which are all housed in an enormous Tesco Lotus superstore. The only item missing from the transcultural ensemble were those ubiquitous yellow cabs (although they have just about every other colour imaginable). Even the historic 'River of Kings' - the Chao Phraya - is choked by the hands of modern development as new edifices erupt like smallpox along besieged and befouled banks.

By contrast, the mighty Mekong River that bisects Laos - it was once entirely inaccessible - can be cruised gracefully and leisurely, and it is even possible to sail its waters for hours without seeing a single sign of the digital age. For a glimpse into *Asia then* rather than *Asia now*, this requires a leap of faith into one of Southeast Asia's few surviving frontiers. Laos - for the time being at least - remains the Asia of yesteryear and a travel step worth taking, even if it doesn't have any conventional beaches of its own. It does have 'beaches' of a different kind as the Mekong River in Southern Laos holds a secret it seems reluctant to share: Si Phan Don, an archipelago of islands whose name translates to 'The Four Thousand Islands.'

Unlike the elephants, there are four thousand islands. Travellers can explore the raw naturalness of the south close to the border with Cambodia, spot rare Irrawaddy dolphins or admire Khone Phapheng, Southeast Asia's largest waterfall. The pace of life is slower than a speeding microorganism, and cows, goats and pigs outnumber the backpackers. The time to visit is during the dry season when the water level of the Mekong recedes to reveal those four thousand islands and islets, some of which are permanently inhabited. The relaxed rural atmosphere is the star attraction with hammocks swinging between island trees with views of rice paddies, sugarcane and coconut farms. It reminded me of my time travelling the waterways of Vietnam's Delta Region.

Most international visitors fly straight to northern Luang Prabang Province to find love at first sight, rarely venturing beyond the cultural core of its Lilliputian capital which is dwarfed by the Phou Thao and Phou Nang mountains. And this is quite understandable, as Luang Prabang is the jewel in Laos' crown, proudly showcasing all those European, colonial touches as a badge of honour (impressively, the whole town is listed as a UNESCO World Heritage site). The Plain of Jars is an equally remarkable heritage site and megalithic archaeological landscape in the Phonsavan area, while the religious oddity of Xieng Khuan Buddha Park is just a short excursion from the capital. The region's oldest human fossil was discovered in Tam Pa Ling cave in Northern Laos in 2009, and the country shares illicit - but whispered - interests with its neighbours as the world's third largest producer of opium. Business is booming as Laos makes the most of its Golden Triangle, cross-border connections.

Laos has more in common with Vietnam than bombs and the rugged peaks of the Annamite Mountains, which provide a natural and rather useful buffer zone against tension and conflict. It is home to similarly diverse and colourful hill tribe populations, and like the Vietnamese, the legacy of French Indochina endures. Café culture floods the air and fills the nostrils with the smells of freshly baked baguettes and slow-roasted coffee beans which escape cluttered roadside cafes (Laos' leading and legal agricultural export is coffee). There was no requirement for me to wear a beret or a black and white striped jumper to enjoy the Euro ambience at Café Croissant d'Or; I simply added a float of cream and a teaspoon of Cointreau to my coffee and stirred.

Laissez les bons temps rouler!

Unexploded ordnance and poor infrastructure continue to pose a challenge to tourism, but Laos is steadily finding its feet as an upswing in upmarket accommodation offers an alternative to existing backpacker hostels, and an opportunity to broaden its visitor demographic, with the onus on wealthy tourists and the luxury market. With Vietnam, Cambodia and Myanmar having already recognised the need to broaden their appeal beyond a backpacker niche, Laos is at the back of the queue, but at least it's standing in the right one. Thailand was the first country in Southeast Asia to grasp the fact that backpackers don't like to spend their money, so its tourism market went through a structural refocus to attract high-spenders, rebranding itself as a luxury destination like Singapore and Hong Kong. Thailand wanted to shake off its rite-of-passage image as a backpacking mecca, replacing tattered guidebooks with glossy credit cards. Laos is playing catch-up, and one of its greatest success stories and in-demand exports is the nation's favourite - Beerlaos - which is brewed by the Danish giant Carlsberg. If there was ever a destination worthier of the manufacturer's slogan, it's Laos:

*That calls for a Carlsberg!*

## Chapter 33: The Francophonic Capital

Vientiane is a cosmopolitan and compact capital, and yet it is the largest urban area in Laos with a population shy of one million inhabitants. For a principal city, the vibe is surprisingly friendly and relaxed as the languorous waters of the Mekong River flow past its southern boundary which - I discovered - is the perfect spot for a promenade perambulation. There is a distinctly European flavour, most pointedly French, in faded and crumbling colonial architecture which only enhances its charm and appeal, as the city stares southwards with covetous senses across a border of water into Northern Thailand.

Vientiane is, quite possibly, the tiniest capital city I have ever set foot in, and it differs from other South-east Asian cities due to its colonial street planning (much like the French Quarter in Hanoi) with broad, leafy boulevards and graceful but imposing mansions. This pocket-sized capital could, however, be used as an advert for third-rate project management as ancient ruins and gleaming stupas intermingle haphazardly with sloppily constructed new builds, while the heritage of French Indochina looks on with raised eyebrows. It is certainly a quirky place full of interest and unusual sights, but its attractions are not immediately obvious in all that dust and dirt as they are in Luang Prabang. With a steady eye and willing legs, its treasures slowly reveal themselves.

The city is at risk of becoming yet another Backpacker Ville as the tourist demographic for Laos is predominantly bearded, braided and tattooed. The 2014 Statistical Report on Tourism in Laos revealed that the highest frequency visitor has an age between twenty and twenty-nine, and backpacks are landing in ever-greater numbers each year. The secret is out, and the proof of the pudding is in the eating: Laos had just 14,400 tourist arrivals in 1990 and 4,158,719 in 2014. International flights land at Wattay International Airport with a significant number of those visitors - especially the ones wearing Thai fishermen's pants and coral necklaces - immediately heading north to Vang Vieng. Vang Vieng is the most tourist-oriented town in the country and its former backpacker central (before the Laos government cracked down on the chaos and revelry in 2012). Rubber tubing and kayaking on the Nam Song River were once the main attractions, but international eyes are finding refocus on the natural wonders of this province.

Vientiane used to be the primary gateway into Laos but is superseded by Luang Prabang. The visitors it attracts tend to rush on through like a supermarket sweep, often spending a single day or night in the city. A longer stay can be rewarding as Vientiane offers an excellent selection of local Laos and western restaurants and cafes, so the ambience is serene and soothing like a visit to Vietnam's Hoi An (albeit less pleasing on the eye). Nam Phou or Fountain Square is an excellent spot for alfresco dining, but the most popular area for tourists and locals alike is the riverside, which offers a delightful sunset-over-the-Mekong digestif. To indulge in people watching, I found Vientiane's only Belgian beer bar (Chokdee Café) where I sat, idly observed and guessed strangers' personal life stories as they passed by.

Getting to and from, and up and down in Laos was less relaxing. I booked international and domestic flights with the government-owned national carrier (Lao Airlines) which has a historically poor safety record and reputation. Of course, I had no knowledge of this and was blissful in my ignorance, until a friend in Bangkok kindly informed me of the facts a few days before my departure. He travelled to Laos himself and described getting there like a white-knuckle ride through turbulence, with steep descents that defied physics, and rough landings that were comparable to skating over cobbles. Challenging weather conditions are an aviation issue for the entire region as Malaysia Airlines flight MH370 reminded the world in March 2014, but Lao Airlines has a history punctuated by serial mishaps.

As recently as October 2013, one of the airliner's domestic flights (ATR-72) plunged into the Mekong during a severe storm with forty-four passengers and five crew members. I have heard the aviation myth that the best time to travel with an airline is after one of their planes has crashed, and as this tragic event occurred just eight weeks before my flight into the country with the same airline, I was nervously optimistic for a safe landing. My fears found exacerbation from the newly acquired knowledge that Lao Airlines used to operate a fleet of Chinese and Russian castoffs (Yakolevs, Harbins and Antonovs) and suffered a spate of five crashes between 1990 and 2003. And while it was with great relief that I learnt that it had upgraded its fleet with airworthier models, as my flight persistently rattled and rolled through intolerant clouds, I found myself sitting bolt upright for the entire journey. I finally understood what Sir Alex Ferguson had meant by his famous catchphrase: 'Squeaky bum time.' Some nationalities clap their hands or cheer loudly when a flight lands safely, and this act reminds me of the dangers of air travel, but there I sat in seat 5A, the only passenger full of rapturous applause as wheels touched down on sticky tarmac.

Vientiane is in a state of flux and transition, with its authorities busily overseeing a propitious period of sustained economic growth. As it continues to broaden its horizons beyond a provincial outlook, it is inevitable that the charming air of this backwater capital will dissipate, as it pushes its doors open further to accommodate the next wave of foreign investment. I had already seen the outcome of unchecked ambition when I visited Siem Reap in Cambodia. Without those million elephants it once claimed to possess, Laos will find it hard to resist the inexorable invasion of fast food outlets and coffee shop chains that have already wrapped their links in a stranglehold around the rest of the planet. It has already suffered an occupation of sorts, as Thai investors have exported their dullsville, concrete egg-carton style architecture to fill in the gaps between temples and colonial mansions. Modern Vientiane still has charisma, but it doesn't benefit from the same UNESCO protection as Luang Prabang, and that is why its northern rival has usurped it and reclaimed cultural dominance. Perhaps Luang Prabang never forgave its southern counterpart for taking its 'capital' crown when King Setthathirat moved the capital to Vientiane in 1560. And just like the Cambodian capital Phnom Penh, visitors are invariably drawn north to Laos' second city and cultural star attraction.

I was pleasantly surprised when I arrived at my four-star hotel - the Salana Boutique - as it looked exactly like the photographs I scrolled over on the internet (which is a rare find in Southeast Asia) and came at the discounted price of a budget-oriented hostel. It won the 'World Luxury Hotel' award in 2012 (if that golden plaque mounted in the reception area is to be believed, much like all those ever-present and proudly framed 'Certificate of Excellence' awards from TripAdvisor) so a pleasant night's sleep, without complimentary cockroaches, was guaranteed. The yin of my flight balanced against the yang of my lodgings, and for the first time in an extended period on the roads of Southeast Asia, I had a perfect night's sleep and didn't have to resort to breakfasting on a box of Pringle crisps. When I entered the bright and airy breakfast room the next morning with modest-to-low expectations, I was one of the Israelites in the Exodus presented with a roomful of manna from heaven.

As a former French protectorate, I figured there would be more on offer than rice, but as I was totally unfamiliar with the cuisine of Laos, I didn't realise that Laos bread is, in fact, made entirely of rice. Having eaten curry for breakfast in India (and for lunch and dinner), I opted for a bowl of khao piak sen, which is a Laos noodle soup made with rice noodles and served for breakfast, lunch and dinner. I was in Rome again, so I did as the Romans do: I ate noodles and lots of rice. The sweet breakfast baguette comes with a generous filling of condensed milk, but I prefer a spoonful in my coffee, so instead opted for a helping of freshly baked croissants with noodles (mornings presented culinary confusions).

When my first breakfasting puzzle was nearly complete, a waiter approached my table with a face full of obsequiousness and not enough space for his eyes, to politely ask me if I was enjoying my stay at the hotel and whether I had made any plans for the day ahead.

'Wonderful, thanks. No plans yet,' I replied, 'nothing at all.'

That was my inferred, 'please go away and leave me alone' request, but the less than considerate hard-sell-over-breakfast began, which was entirely my fault as I had failed to follow one of my survival rules in Southeast Asia: I hadn't been quite rude enough. And so, he continued:

'Would you like some recommendations for day trips? We have a driver and air-conditioned vehicle, and we can offer tours tailored to suit your personal interests.'

My interests were singular: breakfast.

While chewing on a buttery croissant, I remembered American travel writer Paul Theroux's observation that tourists often don't know where they've been to, and travellers don't know where they're going to, so I declined his offer by shaking my head so vigorously, it brought on a mild concussion. Travel has also taught me that sometimes the best plan is not to have a plan at all. I had plenty of time to unearth Vientiane's cultural treasures (which didn't include live munitions for a change), and I wasn't in any rush to see them either. Vientiane was having a positive effect on me so I exited the lobby, paused in the shade to look at my guidebook's front cover, and approached a sleeping tuk-tuk driver draped over his passenger seats. I asked him if he would kindly take me to the golden temple of Pha That Luang, the national symbol of Laos, and pointed at the cover of my guidebook as a pictorial translation. If it was important enough to feature as the cover image, it was the logical place to start.

You might be wondering why I asked the driver if he would take me to my destination, instead of climbing aboard and assuming that he would take me anywhere I requested, but that's not how the taxi and tuk-tuk system works in this region. They are not obliged to take their passengers anywhere; if his need to sleep was greater than my need to sightsee, I might have had to walk.

Pha That Luang (also called 'The Great Stupa') is Laos' most sacred monument, and it is hard to miss it as it glistens in the sun like a religious Belisha beacon. Pyramidal in shape, it is surrounded by thirty smaller stupas which resemble castle crenellations, and my tuk-tuk driver was proud to inform me that it is one of the finest examples of Buddhist architecture in the world. Having to take his word for it, I blushed upon the discovery that his English language development was beyond the level of picture books. Pha That Luang is more fortress than temple with its gleaming, gilded central stupa a challenge to the bright blue of the sky above (its golden spire reaches forty-five metres high). Pha That Luang has been restored and remodelled so many times, practically nothing of the original remains, having suffered collateral damage in both national and international conflicts. It also suffered the indignity of looting by foreign invaders, but that's what happens when you're showy with your wealth. I couldn't argue with the entrance fee which was only 5,000 kip (or 37p), but it is hardly worth the effort charging tourists and running an admissions desk for such an insignificant sum. It does, however, make Vientiane one of the top value-for-money capitals in the world, as the government practically gives the country's culture away.

I couldn't spend my cash no matter how hard I tried. In fact, whenever I got any change back in kip, my wedge of multiple currencies only got thicker. But that, of course, is one of Southeast Asia's greatest attractions (aside from all those temples and beaches). I will never forget my budget-zapping trip to Venice, which managed to flush me out in a single day as an amateur poker player in Vegas; I even had to resort to eating a sad-looking slice of pizza Margherita as a combined breakfast, lunch and dinner package. In the words of Amy Winehouse: 'What kind of fuckery is this?' In Stockholm, I lost my thirst for adult drinks when I stopped at a British bar and ordered an imperial pint of cider, to be charged £10 in exchange for 568 millilitres. It was liquid extortion. Money goes much further in Southeast Asia, which meant I could travel for as long as I wanted to without worry about budgets.

There is a statue of King Setthathirat in the Saysettha Gardens near the front gate of Pha That Luang, adorned with crisping flowers and gifts of sticky rice or Red Fruits Fanta, where worshippers gather to pray at his feet. He commissioned the construction of Pha That Luang in 1560 when he relocated the country's capital to the south, with the temple a structural symbol of the newfound power and stature of Vientiane. Once I had explored the inner courtyard (which only took a few minutes as there is not much to see, aside from five hundred kilos of gold leaf and more statues of Buddha), I visited the lesser-known temples of Wat Luang Nua and Wat Luang Tai which share its grounds and more interesting details, such as the statue of a reclining Buddha.

It didn't take long for me to appreciate that the Vientiane experience is not about city sightseeing, but the atmosphere, cafes, bars, and restaurants.

There is no hop on, hop off bus service ploughing tourist routes here as there aren't any tourist routes to be turned over. The city does have interesting sites to explore - and no shortage of Buddhist temples and shrines - and the majority are in walking or cycling distance of the city centre and the Patuxai Victory Monument. Vientiane's most celebrated temple is Wat Ho Phra Keo, which was once home to the Emerald Buddha before it was returned to Thailand's temple of the same name (different spelling) in Bangkok: Wat Phra Kaew. The temple is a stunning construction set amidst attractive gardens and a gallery of eighteenth-century bronze statues of the Buddha, but they are not all presented so considerately in the capital.

Vientiane and Luang Prabang have an equal blessing in the multiplicity of temples they house, but the difference is all in the setting: in Vientiane, temples are surrounded by clouds of construction dust and the sounds of pneumatic drills. Wat Sisaket has an unusual feature for a Buddhist temple (which conveniently distracts attention from said dust and drills), having thousands of small niches in the outer wall with each one containing a small Buddha image. There are - per officials - 6,840 Buddha images inside the temple's grounds which find embellishment from fading murals illustrating the story of the Buddha's life. The temple would not look out of place in the Grand Palace of Bangkok, or among the stunning temple vistas of Luang Prabang with its striking design of decorated pillars and a five-tiered roof. I applied the less-is-definitely-more mantra to my temple trudges in the capital and capped it at three.

Wat Si Muang, Wat Ong Theu, Wat Mixay, Wat Chan, Wat Inpeng and Wat Haysoke are temples I visited on my return to Vientiane. With limited information in the English language and none at all in my guide book, my eyes glazed over all that gold as they looked without seeing. By contrast, Luang Prabang's temples readily share information about their history, traditions and purpose, thereby offering meaningful context for foreign visitors.

On Vientiane's riverfront, the Chao Anouvong Park is an attractive green space and a popular spot for a tai chi workout with its lovely view of the elegant Presidential Palace on one side, and the Mekong River the other. An enormous and majestic bronze statue of King Chao Anouvong was erected in 2010 to mark the city's 450th anniversary, with one arm extended southwards to offer a greeting hand to Thai neighbours. There is a love-in of sorts going on between the governments of Thailand and Laos as a series of Thai-Lao Friendship bridges have been built; it seems there's no greater foundation for a friendship than mutual economic benefit.

I stumbled upon the Patuxai Victory Monument quite by chance (bottled water was a more pressing concern), and it was immediately familiar as it is a schizophrenic remodelling of the Arc de Triomphe, with architect Jean François Thérèse Chalgrin's design interspersed with images of Hindu gods and traditional Laotian aesthetics. It is a distinctive city landmark and one of the few spots for a view of the city, though the best views are of the monument itself, as the surrounding area features all those egg-carton monstrosities. I climbed the stairs to the upper level for sunset views over concrete blocks and passed a shaded tourist market on my way down, but at least I could kill two birds with the one stone as I found a stall selling bottles of lukewarm water with suspiciously broken seals.

The creation story of this monument is probably more interesting than the monument itself, as it was funded by donations from the US government for the building of a new city airport. The local authorities created a 'Gateway of Triumph' instead as they wanted to celebrate their status as an independent state liberated from the French (their need to gloat was greater). It also commemorates Laos' wartime dead (those who lost their lives in the pursuit of that goal) and is, quite appropriately, nicknamed 'The Vertical Runway.' It seems the irony of imitating an iconic French monument has been lost in translation.

The Laos National Museum promised much but delivered dryness, so I rushed through its poorly presented exhibits which include a set of dinosaur bones displayed next to a single jar from the Plain of Jars. There were no helpful labels or explanations of what I was looking at; it was a jumble sale of dusty artefacts. I was the only visitor in a museum without rhyme or reason, but I did take a glance at the clumsy presentation about Laos' history of war and occupation before making a quick retreat of my own. At least it was nearly free to enter.

I took a similarly sedate trip to the Laos Brewery Company for a factory tour, hoping it would be like the Guinness Storehouse in Dublin or the best of the brewery bunch: The Brussels Beer and Brewery Tour. I was, yet again, the only misguided visitor of the day as the factory sits to the side of an empty road in the middle of nowhere, about eight miles south-east of Vientiane (even my tuk-tuk driver struggled to find it). Entering a sparse foyer, I was greeted by a wordy sign which stated: 'Lao Brewery Company Limited is to express the warm welcome to everyone passing by and interested to see and visit the factory.' I was confident that I was the *only* person likely to be passing by that day, and the fact that there was no staff present and available to give me an actual tour, was confirmation. I guess they don't care too much about the tour profits since the Beerlaos Company owns 99% of the domestic market share.

By contrast, the COPE Visitor Centre was one of the unlikely highlights of my two separate trips to Vientiane. It is the epitome of the kindness of strangers and reminded me of Cambodia's Landmine Museum in Siem Reap Province, another non-profit organisation that is worth supporting with donations as they aid the victims of unexploded ordnance. Outside the main entrance, there's a commemorative sculpture by local artist Anousone Vong Aphay, of a mother holding her child's hand with her free hand raised to the sky. Crafted from 500kg of UXO, it is a dedication to the memory of those who suffered injury or lost their lives or loved ones to UXO. With graphic displays of human suffering, I felt guilty about those souvenir spoons I purchased in Luang Prabang and decided it was time to make a generous donation and earn some merit.

I spent two hours learning about the ongoing efforts to remove UXO from the Laos landscape and educate younger generations of the very real dangers of its presence, watching a short documentary on a television screen encased in a pyramid of prosthetic legs. UXO defines modern-day Laos and is very much a part of the national psyche, both conscious and unconscious. The charity is self-sufficient, and their staff is dedicated, creative and resourceful, fashioning wheelchairs from bicycle parts and all manner of scrap metal (except, of course, UXO). The victims they support are often innocent children, and COPE provides them with care and prosthetics, mobility assistance and the rehabilitation their families can't afford to pay for, so they can go about the business of their daily lives and overcome terrible injuries.

I read a tragic story about four children who died while making a fire in 2012, not realising that an unexploded US bomb was buried inches beneath the soil where they built it. As they warmed their hands, they inadvertently readied a bomb for detonation. Other stories told of the deaths of ordinary men and women tending to their gardens, fishing in muddy rivers or searching for scrap metal. Some of the displays were powerful and brought the statistics to brutal life, including the suspended casing of a cluster bomb (now banned in most countries) with hundreds of small 'bombies' or 'bomblets' spilling out in suspended animation. It was quite unnerving to stand beneath it and consider all that potential (and, I hoped, deactivated) carnage. Cluster bombs were the armament of choice for the US Air Force as they contain multiple explosive submunitions, fall like a monsoon rain and can saturate an area the size of several football fields in seconds. They are like landmines as they are indiscriminately fatal to anyone who crosses their path, even decades after the original conflict has ended. And with an estimated eighty million of them patiently waiting to claim a victim in Laos, COPE will need all the support it can get.

I spent my evenings in Vientiane strolling the main riverside road of Fa Ngum in the gentle Mekong breeze, dining on traditional local dishes and sipping from bottles of icebox-chilled Beerlaos. There is a daily night market on the promenade which caters more for the townspeople than the tourists, and continuing westwards, I passed a cavalcade of cuisine as enticing street food stalls with comfortable, cushioned seating and brilliant views of the sunset, vied for my attention and custom. I grazed like a starved and thirsty herbivore, tasting unfamiliar smells and discovering Laos' delicious delights to the saliva-inducing sound of an orchestra of sizzling woks. It was the perfect instrumental background.

Food is presented in small bowls like mini tasting dishes, so I could sample everything from sticky rice (khao niaw) in a small woven basket to green papaya salad - tam mak houng - with flakes of hot chilli, sour lime, salt, fish sauce and sugar. As I migrated from stall to stall, I could have been sampling food for a microbiological examination as noodles, sausages, soups and stews passed between my lips. I had heard of the concept of 'food tourism,' but I now understand what that means; Vientiane turned me into a veritable foodie. Travel is as much about trying the local food and drink as it is about visiting temples and laying on white-sand beaches.

Quite often in Vientiane, turning a corner resulted in a pleasant surprise, like stumbling upon the black stupa of That Dam which sits in the middle of a busy roundabout, surrounded by guesthouses and restaurants, or a shop on the outskirts of the city dedicated to selling Santa Claus outfits. On my return to Vientiane, I had a less-than-pleasant surprise on arrival, as some of my yang had worn off as I accidentally booked a hotel in Vang Vieng. I thought it prudent to switch from Beerlaos to soft drinks before the next leg of my journey, which included a walk in the footsteps of the dead and inebriated.

# Chapter 34: Bucket-Hugging Zombies

Vang Vieng, a former party town, is a few hours north of Vientiane by road or rail and is tucked into the rocky wilderness of Vientiane Province. Bugged by negative press, Vang Vieng is a tourist town on the backpacker circuit of Southeast Asia, but it does at least offer a break from the temples of the capital and Luang Prabang as it presents a delicious, rural banquet of karstic landscapes and iridescent rice fields. Now that the Laos government is re-establishing the province's rustic appeal, nature-based activities are back on the menu as an alternative to buckets of Tiger Whisky and Red Bull.

Resembling Luang Prabang in setting only, the town straddles a river (the Nam Song) and is surrounded by mountains, but a transformation took place when a single backpacker arrived, shared its rubbery secrets and multiplied like bacteria in a petri dish. It is one of the world's most unlikely locations for a party town, where tales of death and drowning were part of its charm and allure. And it was here that the rule book on cultural sensitivity was torn to shreds and thrown into the river. Every modern convenience is taken care of as money talks loudest in the Third World, so the main street is full of bars, internet cafes, guest houses, restaurants, tour agencies and dripping tourists, much like Pham Ngu Lao Street in Ho Chi Minh City.

The backpackers were, initially, a welcome infestation in peaceful and traditional farming/fishing communities as they came armed with cash that wasn't their own, and they were too tanked-up to care how they spent it. Local opportunists were an obliging and accommodating lot, all too eager to relieve their foreign guests of their currency burdens. However, as the partying got out of control (to the extent that it prompted the Laos government to act), those same locals were less than thrilled when their once-sleepy village became universal shorthand for drugs, hedonism, and death by reckless stupidity. With revellers able to gulp down magic mushroom shakes, take bites from opium-topped pizzas and cleanse palates with buckets of whisky if they wanted to, the word got out, and the contamination was complete. Paradise went for a walk, and Milton turned in his grave.

Luang Prabang, by contrast, is the cultural blueprint of Laos the government is eager to share with the outside world. I can understand the pubertal appeal of Vang Vieng but having visited so many places like this (I did, after all, live in Thailand, which is the birthplace of the Full Moon Party), I now regard them as a somewhat tired cliché of Southeast Asia (though that may well have more to do with my age and outlook). For travellers seeking a rite of passage experience, there was probably no better place to play out all those adolescent fantasies than Vang Vieng. When scores of deaths by tubing misadventure (or harmless fun and games, like the aptly named 'Slide of Death') propelled Vang Vieng and Laos onto global news wires for all the wrong reasons, the game was up.

The town proved the downright obvious that a cocktail of teenagers, alcohol, rubber tubes, rocks and river water are a deadly concoction. These are the type of damaging headlines the country's tourism authority is keen to bury in its past. The cost in human tragedy has been inexcusable, and in 2011 alone, twenty-seven tender-aged tourists were reported to have lost their lives by either drowning while under the influence or from smashing their heads on razor-sharp rocks (despite warning signs telling them not to jump into shallow waters).

Local villagers prefer not to swim in the river as they believe evil spirits dwell in its waters; they must have regarded all the party people as a horde of affable zombies as they stumbled about in ragged clothes and neon body paint. The merrymaking, inevitably, had to come to an end as the music was turned down or else switched off permanently. Every dog has its day, and the half-naked bucket-huggers have had theirs, though they've probably relocated their partying elsewhere and are now someone else's problem. The walking dead can always return to their spiritual homes and a Full Moon welcome on one of Thailand's besieged party islands on the Gulf or Andaman coasts.

It is a strange coincidence that the river got its name from legend when the body of King Phra Nha Phao of Phai Naam was spotted floating in its waters. Hundreds of years later, the bodies were still coming. The idyllic peace of this region was deflated and collapsed entirely when a local farmer and visionary - Thanongsi Sorangkoun - had the idea of pumping up some of his tractor wheel inner tubes. It was intended as an act of kindness to his volunteers, allowing them to relax and unwind on calm waters after a day's hard graft in the fields. It caught on like a blazing and uncontrollable wildfire, with every guesthouse and tour company eager to capitalise on the latest craze and backpacker obsession - flotation devices - and an unlikely legend was born.

As dreadlocks moved in to become deadlocks, the town expanded, and inner tubes were as precious as a parking spot in Manhattan or Raphael's *Head of a Muse*. Understanding that backpackers and beer bars go together like thrush and itching, a bar scene hurriedly knocked together with loud speakers, swings, slides and zip lines. And drugs, lots of drugs, in a country where all drug use is illegal (and where, in 2010, four men received death sentences on drug-trafficking charges). The tourism industry in this region experienced an unprecedented growth spurt, and because it was unchecked and unregulated, a blind eye turned, and cultural genocide was guaranteed.

It was also inevitable that the scene would eventually burn itself out as the death toll rose and international embassies started asking awkward and pointed questions, forcing the Laos authorities to act and send a task force to investigate and begin the shutdown. Echoing Thailand, the leader of the task force (Boualy Milattanapheng) explained how the tourism authorities were looking for a new 'face' (presumably one without paint) to visit the region and restore its credentials as a haven for ecotourism. The tubing industry still exists, but it is strictly regulated, and they've even introduced curfews and life jackets. The 'happy shakes' and 'special sandwiches' have all gone, along with the tales of lurid excess. Visitors are now more likely to go caving, hiking, mountain biking, climbing, ballooning or kayaking than rubber tubing. Those still interested in a spot of recreational tubing and drug-taking have missed the party and can no longer drink and float; the Darwin Awards should find a new exhibition space.

In 1975, Italian economic historian Carlo Cipolla wrote a humorous but thought-provoking treatise on the power of stupidity: *The Basic Laws of Human Stupidity*. He describes 'stupid people' as an unstructured yet powerful group, and argues that when individuals suffer due to the actions of others, it is not due to malicious actions but *stupid actions*, which all sounds rather familiar. Vang Vieng could have been a case study, and he was of course right when he observed: 'Always and inevitably everyone underestimates the number of stupid individuals in circulation.' I have always found them rather easy to identify, as they usually wear 'I went tubing in Vang Vieng' or 'I've been to the Golden Triangle!' shirts.

You may have detected a modicum of prejudice against backpackers in this chapter, but let me clarify: this is true only of those backpackers in Southeast Asia for whom the pursuit of drunken excitement is their raison d'être. They wouldn't dare jump into a river when blind drunk back home, knowing there's not a single hospital for miles around, yet in places like Vang Vieng, it is all they can think of doing, like short-tailed, thickset lemmings on a headlong rush to destruction. It is a scene like all those easy rider motorcyclists with bandaged legs and exhaust pipe burns on their calves. I have witnessed the behaviour of some of the world's worst tourists in this region, but Darwinism seems to be restoring the natural balance.

British historian Thomas Fuller hit the nail on the head when he observed: 'If an ass goes travelling, he'll not come home a horse.' Paradise is returning to Vang Vieng Province, and the zombies are all but dead.

# Chapter 35: Luang Prabang Province

Luang Prabang is an ancient town, a former royal capital and the centre of Buddhist teaching in northern Laos. It is the country's premier tourism destination and a humble showstopper, with markedly middle-class leanings reflected in an artificial economic bubble, within which prices are overblown in most cafés, bars, restaurants and accommodations. With its palm-lined riverfronts and pearly frangipanis, a glittering canopy of golden stupas and hundreds of saffron-robed monks collecting daily alms with their novices, it effortlessly combines its elements to create a postcard-perfect image of Southeast Asia which is increasingly difficult to find.

Luang Prabang's superlative magnetism is a phenomenon that attracts travellers from all over the world to admire and appraise its extensive natural wonders, so I didn't mind paying a few extra kip for the pleasure. It is the most attractive town in Southeast Asia by a country mile, where east meets west to settle down and sup. British explorer and travel writer Freya Stark was right when she observed: 'To awaken quite alone in a strange town is one of the pleasantest sensations in the world.' Luang Prabang is, without a doubt, one of the most agreeable places in the world to arouse.

Despite its growing popularity and immeasurable loveliness, Luang Prabang modestly reclines against the banks of the Mekong River, content with its status as a UNESCO World Heritage listing, but careful not to sing its praises too loudly. The charm of the town was once a close-kept secret, whispered in the dark corridors of hostels and protected by the intrepid who discovered its untouched splendours and a scenic seat on a pristine peninsula formed by the Nam Khan and Mekong rivers. It can resist and defy the forces of global tourism, preferring the hospitality of homestays over impersonal high-rises, and has found the perfect equilibrium between tradition and progress as its UNESCO status (awarded in 1995) helps to preserve its rich heritage, shielding it from the advances of modern development. Restoration efforts have been gentle and respectful with many crumbling, colonial buildings restored to their former glory, or finding a new lease of life altogether when transformed into charming guesthouses or restaurants. The town's cultural core is a dedication to its tourist visitors, with a clearly defined trail leading to all the royal palaces and temples of note. Everywhere of interest can be reached by foot, but the leisurely and preferred way to get about town is on the soft seat of a bicycle, and these are complimentary at most hotels and homestays.

As my Lao Airlines flight began its slow descent to Luang Prabang International Airport, I opened the window shutter to take in the magnificent views of the Phou Thao and Phou Nang mountains (which encircle the town like protective arms). Luang Prabang is the best of bygone Europe in Southeast Asia; a seamless fusion of Laos' traditional Buddhist architecture and timber houses with the European colonial styles of the nineteenth and twentieth centuries. Legend claims that Buddha smiled with contentment when he visited the town to rest his legs for a day, even prophesying that it would one day be a rich and powerful city. He predicted the same for Mandalay but missed the mark completely, so I guess the law of averages dictated that he'd get it right eventually.

That wealth he predicted lands hourly at the airport in the form of the tourist pound, while its power rests on its international reputation and acclaim, attracting visitors from all corners of the globe and even supplanting the southern capital. Laos won the 'World's Best Tourism Destination' award in 2013 (courtesy of the European Council on Tourism and Trade), but Luang Prabang was the city that announced the country to the world. It received the Top City Gold Award after being voted the world's top tourist destination by Wanderlust (a UK-based travel magazine) from 2006 to 2008, and again from 2010 to 2012. Some visitors, not surprisingly, never venture beyond the borders of Luang Prabang Province, but Laos is a richly coloured diamond with each side emitting a different hue.

Luang Prabang understands its appeal to international travellers, and even the hardest of travel hearts would struggle not to warm to the place. It knows how to serve its visitors' needs, and has consequently become the public face of the country's tourism industry as well as a rural cash cow. The international cuisine is reliably first-rate, and most nationalities find inclusion on restaurant menus. The café scene is bustling, and at night the main roads transform into a thriving night market where hill tribe artisans mix with tourists, selling all manner of products from pungent spices and handmade handicrafts, to delicate silks and UXO spoons. I wasn't prepared for the cold December nights as I had gotten used to Bangkok, which has just one season and annual setting. Having packed only shorts, T-shirts, and flip flops, I shivered in the cold and could see the condensation on my breath. That market was a godsend, allowing me to top up my winter woollies. I recalled those frozen Eastern European nipples I met on a frosty Myanmar morning in Bagan and realised I hadn't learnt my lesson from another past mistake.

When the northern nights turned cold (and they were reliably chilly), I made my way to the only Belgian restaurant in town - The House - for bowls of hot stoofvlees (a classic Belgian stew of beef and pan-fried onions, slowly cooked with French mustard, herbs, and dark Leffe beer) and mugs of mulled wine with cinnamon sticks. If they had an open log fire, I could have been convinced that I had entered a portal into one of Europe's warmest places. Most restaurants offer complimentary movie nights as 'rest' is a popular item on any Luang Prabang menu. While ambling awkwardly to the small cottage I rented by the banks of the Nam Khan River, I seriously contemplated staying in Luang Prabang Province forever and forfeiting my apartment in Bangkok.

A bucket of ice was poured all over those warm and romantic notions when I made the erroneous decision one evening to stop for a massage at a low-cost local spa, as I was ever-protective of my kip, dollars, and baht. The spa owner was evidently protective of his budget too, as the heating was turned off (if it had ever been turned on), and I shivered through my massage like a nervous Chihuahua and wondered if the entire population of Laos had walked over my grave. My masseuse took an eternity to notice my obvious discomfort, before sympathetically understating:

'You ok?'

I was close to a hypothermic death as open window shutters welcomed the cold. 'Cheap' comes at a price in Southeast Asia.

You can spend a single day in Luang Prabang or stay for a month, sedately soaking up the French café ambience by the riverside, while enjoying glass after glass of refreshing Namkhong Beer. Luang life has a leisurely pace, and a trip to this charming town will be exactly that, as it gently lulls its visitors into a somnambulant state. The population is small at fifty thousand and includes twelve distinct ethnic minority groups. The town's rules are relatively straightforward and reasonable enough to observe without complaint while serving the dual function of spelling out - in no uncertain terms - the type of visitor they don't want to encourage or grace their quiet streets:

*1. Cover your body.*

*2. No bare chests.*

*3. No bikini tops.*

*4. Respect the morning alms-giving ceremonies.*

Luang Prabang attracts a different category of traveller to Vang Vieng, so anyone desperate for a Full Moon party experience should consider a flight to one of Thailand's southern islands instead. There is a curfew on local businesses which must close at 11:30 pm, allowing locals and tourists alike to get home before a blackout at midnight. I noticed an apologetic sign hanging over a bar that read: 'We would certainly love to be able to sell you more drinks, but it's the law!' The people of Laos prefer an early night so they can rise before dawn and give alms to monks in return for merit. If any visitor is in doubt, there are signs to drive that message home: 'Be quiet on public streets after 10 pm!' There is absolutely no chance the party crowd will ever invade this sleepy hollow.

Luang Prabang is packed full of beautiful temples, and Wat Xieng Thong is the best of the bunch with its stunning exterior artwork and intricate details. It is called the 'Golden Tree Monastery' due to its effulgent 'tree of life' mosaic, and there are many exquisite carvings to view in this grand temple complex which was once the coronation site for Laotian kings. I visited former royal palaces and a plethora of delightful Buddhist temples, where I could observe religious ceremonies and the monks in their distinctive burnt-sienna robes. There is a sizeable community of Buddhist monks in central Luang Prabang and morning alms-giving ceremonies (the tak bat tradition) are a great opportunity for tourists to observe local customs, so long as they remember to keep a respectful distance, as this is a spiritual ritual and not a holy catwalk. I wandered into a monastery at Wat Sensoukaram as I couldn't resist taking a photograph of the novice monks' robes hanging out to dry on a washing line. It is not something you see every day, and I was curious to check whether their mothers had stitched name tags in the linings.

I enjoyed climbing to the top of Mount Phousi which is a favourite spot for watching the sunrise or sunset, as it offers a spectacular natural platform from which to view the town's temples against a striking mountain panorama. It is a distinctive and dominant landmark on the skyline, and a great opportunity for a strenuous workout as I had to climb hundreds of taxing steps to reach the summit. My common sense didn't fail me on this occasion, as I packed a bottle of water as there's nowhere to hide from the sun. My climb of Mount Phousi was a painful parody of that popular scene in *Rocky* when Sylvester Stallone runs up the stairs of the Philadelphia Museum of Art; my arrival was less triumphalism and more a case of drenched and desperate relief to have survived the climb.

On my return to the base, I passed shrines and Buddha footprints tucked behind protruding boulders, and I was mindful of snakes when one fell from a makeshift thatched roof and landed inches behind me (it could have landed neatly around my shoulders). I do not share Indiana Jones' phobia, so I watched it find its way to shelter while others screamed and ran, missing the fantastic views of the Old Town and the Mekong River, which itself snakes around Luang Prabang like a protective coil. I couldn't think of a better way to celebrate the climb than to find a bar on Sisavangvong Road, where I gulped down a glass of snake whisky poured from a bottle with a whole snake's body poked neatly inside.

There was only one aspect of my stay in the town that I did not enjoy, and that was crossing the Old Bridge to my riverside bungalow. It certainly lived up to its name, as it was a rickety mess with a barely boarded walkway for pedestrians (some of the planks were completely loose and shifted underfoot) with an unintended aerial view of the Nam Khan River. Every time I crossed, I was a tightrope walker passing over a frayed rope, but the only alternative was to cross the Bamboo Bridge which was all twisted out of shape and partly submerged in the river. I should have read a few more pages of the Buddhist *Book of Protection*, or made some merit. Instead, all I could do was hope and pray that the donation I made in Vientiane still held spiritual currency and would retire me safely to bed.

Southeast Asia has a considerable number of interesting, multicultural towns with UNESCO World Heritage status. Charming Vigan is a well-preserved Spanish colonial town on the island of Luzon in the Philippines, and having spent a week in Metropolitan Manila before my arrival in Ilocos Sur Province, it gave me a cultural nosebleed. In West Malaysia, Malacca and George Town sharply contrast with the capital, Kuala Lumpur, where I saw the bad and the ugly but precious little of the good in a city which brands itself as 'exciting,' 'surprising' and 'enticing.' With so many grey and congested cities with boxy buildings and potholed pavements, we should count our travel blessings that places such as Luang Prabang exist.

## Chapter 36: A Plain of Jars

I had never heard of the Plain of Jars until a friend showed me a picture (which he found in a travel magazine) of what looked like a giant's prized collection of earthenware. Glossy, photoshopped images failed to overawe me, and its flatly bland name is hardly a unique selling proposition, with a trip to a plain full of jars sounding as uneventful as a Sunday afternoon outing to a Homebase or IKEA superstore. But if I could manage to squeeze in a stop off at the party town of Vang Vieng, I would have been guilty of intercultural ignorance had I not taken a detour from Luang Prabang to Laos' megalithic, archaeological landscape. I had the time and the inclination; I just didn't know how to get there.

Like deep sea anglerfish, every country in Southeast Asia has at least one ancient attraction to entice and allure tourists. If that interest carries the stamp of UNESCO World Heritage approval, its tourism development and latent economic potential is all but assured (it will also find itself bumped up the world's sightseeing rankings). Each tourism authority wants a slice of the Angkor Wat pie. The Plain of Jars is the closest Laos comes to having its share, so I wasn't at all surprised when my guide told me that the Laos government has applied for UNESCO World Heritage status. It is eager to place its planters and pots on maps of the ancient world and the travel section shelves of international bookshops.

There is nothing plain about the Plain of Jars. It is a unique and enigmatic site with hundreds of giant stone urns scattered across hundreds of square miles of upland valleys and lowland foothills, close to the town of Phonsavan in Xieng Khouang Province. It is, quite possibly, the most mysterious of Southeast Asia's ancient sites as nobody knows for sure which civilisation created its peculiar clusters. This curious circumstance found acute exacerbation from the country's self-imposed isolation from the outside world for most of its recent history. There are loose estimates that the Plain of Jars dates back to the Iron Age, somewhere between 500 BC and 200 AD. Recent history has played a more dynamic and turbulent role in a patchy narrative, when they could have been erased from the pages of history altogether as Phonsavan's remote northeastern setting, close to the border with Vietnam, placed it directly in the flight path of US bombing raids. And like central Vietnam's ancient My Son ruins, it survived the war but was left with the open wounds of blunt force traumas.

The Phonsavan plains (especially the ones sprouting perennial crops of antique jars) are partially clear of dangerous UXO and, not for the first time during my travels in Southeast Asia, I was warned not to stray from the main tourist pathways if I wanted to keep my limbs attached. Access routes have red-and-white marker stones to guide visitors, and I found myself observing these modern additions more carefully than the main attraction. I watched a handful of Chinese tourists march nonchalantly into unmarked danger zones in search of must-have pottery selfies, while I kept my distance, camera ready, hoping the *Highway Code* would be updated to provide a safe stopping distance for stupidity.

I found myself completely awestruck when standing face-to-stone with this ancient oddity and intellectual odyssey for determined archaeologists and historians who dispute, to this day, the original function of the jars. Were they used, as some claim, merely for the storage of vast quantities of rice wine or as funerary containers for storing the dead? What the archaeologists know for certain is that they are carved from sandstone and granite and are thought to be 'about' two thousand years old, but that is the extent of certainty. I tried some home-brewed rice wine on a farm in Luang Prabang Province, so I could understand why - if that was indeed their function - the jars might have been used to store it. It is delicious. The pre-history inhabitants of Laos must have had one hell of a thirst on them, and I wondered whether the plains are the origin site of the modern-day pub crawl.

They reminded me of the Rapa Nui people's giant monolithic statues on Easter Island. The moai have baffled modern scientists who have tried, but failed, to solve the mystery of how an ancient and primitive people were able to move such colossal sentinels in stone from quarry sites to distant points across a volcanic island (without the benefit of wheels, large animals or modern tower cranes).

Tour providers (those operating in the tourist towns) try to charge extortionate rates to take cash-rich travellers to see Phonsavan's plains. I hired a local and recommended driver named Somdy (who quadrupled as a guide, reservation specialist, and lifesaver) and had complete freedom of choice, fewer constraints on my time and even fewer demands on my wallet. The journey to the plains took several bumpy hours from Luang Prabang, along winding roads and through charming mountain towns, but it can take up to eleven hours by public bus. I enjoyed listening to the novelty of old magnetic cassette tapes as Somdy shared his favourite South-east Asian pop songs, which I knew would be more interesting than the made-up or half-guessed exposition he was likely to give me upon our arrival at the jars.

Phonsavan is the capital of Xiang Khouang Province, so I decided I would stay overnight in a homestay before embarking on the next chapter of my Laos expedition. Somdy advised me not even to try to book ahead, as there's no such thing as an internet booking (that's if you can get a connection), and few country folks speak any English, so he kindly offered to make all the necessary arrangements on my behalf. For just five dollars a night, I wasn't complaining and besides, I was quite prepared to live without a western-style toilet. I had become so adept at the squatting position that if it were to become an Olympic sport, I would probably win gold for my bronze.

There are three main sites to visit at the plains - imaginatively titled *Site 1, 2* and *3* - and most tours include all three in a combination package. They have been cleared of unexploded ordnance to allow almost-safe access and encourage regional inbound tourism. The remains of broken and misplaced jars are a visual reminder of the consequences of a misstep, as these are hapless victims of the imprecision of casual bombing campaigns. There are in fact ninety sites spread across this province (with twelve open to tourists), so the notion of it being a singular 'plain' is somewhat misleading. You could argue that once you've seen one cluster of jars, you've seen them all. A single jar was found with decoration - a bas-relief carving at Site 1 - while the rest are unadorned. I needed a full day to see the very best of the pots and crocks and most tours are single day options, but there are extension packages for those with a predilection for all things cylindrical and sticky repositories.

I must admit that the excitement wore off rather quickly, and I was glad of my research which helped to trigger my imagination and justified the fourteen hours I spent in the back of Somdy's *taak-see*. At least the area is still mercifully undeveloped, so there isn't a single branch of KFC or Pizza Hut like the ones stacked beside the ancient pyramids of Egypt. The symbolic soul of Colonel Sanders has yet to be convinced to invest in Phonsavan, but I would have walked across minefields for a box of his extra-crispy chicken nuggets and an ice-cold Coke.

Somdy asked me if I wanted to take an additional trip to a site called Phakeo - a two-day trekking experience - but I didn't want to take my chances with all those bombs and sandstone jars are, ultimately, sandstone jars, and not worth risking life and limb for (or more blisters on super blisters). They are unusual subjects to photograph, and they were worthy of the deviation as was all the countryside scenery, fresh air and walks across fields of wheat and gentle streams. When I later reviewed my photographs in Luang Prabang, I couldn't believe how many repeat shots I had taken and would have to edit and delete (most went the way of the trash can icon). If my camera had been stolen or lost, its new owner might have wondered if its previous holder was a deviant with a penchant for pottery.

I had hoped that some thoughtful hill tribe people might kindly wander in front of my lens to add some much-needed cultural colour to all those black and muted jars, but they had chosen to stay at home (there were few tourists to buy their trinkets). Had this been Sapa Town in Vietnam, the jars would have been outnumbered by ten to one. Before leaving the site, I paused for a final consideration and a dozen more photographs. The twilight hours lend the plains a haunting quality as the jars sit in a sinister silence, an army of blackened figures defending and defiantly holding their secrets (if nothing else) from inquisitive generations to come.

Phonsavan sits in an eerie silence of its own as modern tourism has barely scratched the surface of the town's dirt roads and if the Plain of Jars continues to retain its mysteries and relative obscurity, the global brands of the fast food and service industry must keep on waiting. I was spoilt by Luang Prabang's café, bar and dining scenes, but couldn't find a single place to eat or drink on Phonsavan's dusty streets. My homestay included an evening meal as an add-on for a good reason, so I crossed my legs to form a makeshift table for my over-flowing bowl of piping hot noodles, and slurped in the company of strangers. A visit to Stonehenge was long overdue, so I added that to a future to-see list when I returned to the UK.

*One Buddha, two Buddha, three Buddha, four.*

The Xieng Khuan Buddha Park is an anomalous attraction on the Thai-Laos border near Vientiane; what marks it out as a place of interest is the sheer number of Buddhist images concentrated in a small space. It is a 'park' of sorts, but not a park for family outings, sunny picnics or for breaking bread to feed the ducks; it is a pocket park with an unusual collection of religious statuary, surrounded by village farms and rice fields. As a sculpture park with a difference, it reminded me of Nek Chand Saini's secret rock garden in Chandigarh, Northern India, as it too is the artistic expression and vision of a single man. It is not far from the capital (about fifteen miles), so I was able to negotiate a fair fare with a tuk-tuk driver. I had no desire to throw my lot in with a company of strangers and besides, I wanted to visit the first Thai-Laos Friendship Bridge which I was convinced wouldn't be on too many sightseeing lists.

The bridge has been the subject of much criticism with some observers suggesting the word 'friendship' should be replaced by 'trafficking.' On a single day in February 2015, customs officials seized over 300,000 counterfeit products, so they have a valid point to make. Aristotle believed in three different types of friendship: utility, association by pleasure and virtuous friendship. In *Nicomachean Ethics*, he described the first category as shallow in form and thus 'easily dissolved,' using the example of trade and the transfer of the ownership of goods between opposing people for mutual benefit and gain. Counterfeiting is big business in Southeast Asia, and almost anything can be counterfeited, from medicines to cigarettes. I finally understood the black-market appeal of building four Thai-Laos Friendship Bridges.

I visited the Xieng Khuan Buddha Park in the early morning hours, and avoided all the tour groups before they set off from Vientiane in the mid-afternoon with their exasperated, flag-toting guides. It often felt as if China was following me everywhere I went in Southeast Asia, and not wanting to start my day by sharing a ride with backseat breakfasters, watching others crunch and chew through the sinewy joints and toes of cold chicken feet, I opted to go Han Solo. I developed a rare form of podophobia in Southeast Asia: chicken feet.

I accidentally ordered a plate of chicken feet at a roadside food cart in Bangkok when I recognised the Thai word for chicken (gai) on a greasy laminate. It is hard to get it wrong with chicken, and that's why there are so many chicken chains such as Chester's Grill, Nando's and Kentucky Fried. When the vendor placed the inedible into my hands, instinctively I gave the plate straight back. From that day forth, whenever I came across dishes I either didn't recognise or simply couldn't eat, they were all servings of *What the Fuck?* Chicken feet are a popular bar snack in Southeast Asia in preference to the salted peanut, but I neither had the courage nor the craving to try them. American magician and film actor, Channing Pollock, claimed: 'No man in the world has more courage than the man who can stop after eating one peanut.' I would safely bet that he never set foot on either East or South-east Asian soil.

A wooden sign signalled my arrival at the park using the shorthand of 'Buddha Park' for the tourists and 'Xieng Khuan' for the locals which, translated, means 'Spirit City.' It made perfect sense as soon as I walked through the entrance gate, as the park contains over two hundred statues interpreting Buddhist and Hindu folklore, including an enormous and impressive reclining Buddha which is 390 feet in length. Its creator (a priest-shaman named Bunleua Sulilat) had an eye for the unorthodox when he started working on this project in 1958, and it is now one of Vientiane's popular day trips. Ambitiously, Sulilat wanted to integrate Hinduism and Buddhism into a single religion, so the sculptures are a fusion of the iconography of each faith with Buddha, Vishnu, and Shiva all jostling for spiritual elbow room.

Some statues are quite menacing in their countenance and defy convention, while a combination of exposure to the elements and roadside pollution has touched them with antiquity when they are in fact just a few decades old. Xieng Khuan Buddha Park has similarities with the Park of the Monsters (Parco dei Mostri) in the Garden of Bomarzo in the northern region of Lazio, Italy. Commissioned in 1552 by Prince Pier Francesco Orsini, it was created as an expression of grief and was designed to shock its visitors. Sulilat's version combines serene statues of the Buddha with frightening mythical creatures standing over piles of human skulls, but they are PG in comparison to the 'hell gardens' of Thailand, where I entered the wretched bowels of Buddhist Naraka. I was surprised to discover that such a place as a Buddhist hell garden could exist, with statues graphically depicting torturous impalements or wild dogs viciously ripping the flesh from terrified, naked and adulterous sinners.

Having done some research, I set off by public bus from Bangkok's Eastern Terminal to the Wang Saen Suk Hell Garden, the largest garden of its kind in Thailand. It is hidden away in the backstreets of the small coastal town of Bang Saen, a weekend resort for Thais and an hour's drive south-east of the capital. Whoever commissioned this unorthodox collection of blood and guts must have been a dedicated gorehound and fan of b-horror movies. The temple grounds present a disturbing diorama of human suffering: a Buddhist version of hell in the form of cement-and-plaster statues with all manner of blood and exposed entrails. It is a brutally brilliant sight to behold, and my eyes could barely register what they were seeing. Tobe Hooper, John Carpenter, and George A. Romero could have found inspiration from this place. I didn't know whether to be afraid or to laugh out loud, as they have gone so far to stress their point (If you sin, you will be punished!) that it looks like the spoof production set of a splatter movie gone wrong. If the statues are not a strong enough deterrent for potential sinners, ominous signs have been written by five-year-olds (with a reasonable grasp of punctuation in a country that doesn't punctuate its own language) to reinforce the message:

*Ones who make merit go to the heaven; ones who do bad go to the*
*hell, plunging themselves into the hot copper pans and being stabbed*
*by the hell-keeper with the spears every day.*

The enormous, emaciated and eye-catching figures of Nai Ngean and Nang Thong - two hungry ghosts with skeletal forms and elongated tongues - detachedly observe the suffering of all the unclothed and tortured souls gathered about their feet. I was impressed by some of the imaginative punishments which make Christian depictions of hell look like a holiday camp. Signs in the English language explain how each horrific punishment connects to an individual sin, but I had difficulty taking any of it seriously, or accepting that Wang Saen Suk is a site for religious worship. Places like this are, culturally, without rival, as they tear up the pages of convention and throw them into a bubbling cauldron of blood and guts. Confirmation came from Thai families, for whom a Buddhist hell garden was the perfect spot for an afternoon picnic - with spicy bamboo rice rolls and fried broccoli balls - when Bang Saen's beaches were only a short walk away. The early Netherlandish painter - Hieronymus Bosch - would have loved to have joined them with an easel and brush, as he too was fond of fantastic imagery and illustrations of religious concepts and narratives.

I spent a leisurely hour exploring Xieng Khuan Buddha Park's unusual and fascinating statuary arrangements. Some statues are oriented symbolically toward the east because the Buddha's enlightenment occurred while he was sitting and facing eastwards beneath the Bodhi Tree of Enlightenment. There are exceptions, as a few of the statues face westwards to capture the moment before the Buddha's parinibbana when, at his request, he laid on his right side beneath two Sal trees with his head pointing north but facing westwards. The tallest structure in the park resembles a giant demon-pumpkin, which I could climb and explore and joyfully return to childhood days (except there was no such thing as playground safety or supervision). Entering the demon's mouth, I climbed to the accompaniment of a terrible symphony of hungry mosquitoes, before proceeding into a symbolic hell that was also literal in all that humidity. The final stop was an aerial view of the statues which are clustered together like Phonsavan's jars (albeit in a far more peaceful patch of Laos's countryside which straddles the Mekong River).

When I returned to my tuk-tuk, the driver was predictably fast asleep. I didn't know his name and he cared less about mine, so it was an awkward moment when I woke him up by tapping his unwashed toes. I didn't want to risk a deep-sleep situation, and his toes were a safe gamble when south of the border it is considered an insult and highly invasive to touch a person's head. I understand Thai etiquette and customs reasonably well from lived-in experience, so I could only hope that Laotians are not as sensitive about their lower digits. In Southeast Asia, there is no stigma associated with sleeping in public places, while this is uncommon and frowned upon in the West. Southeast Asians can sleep almost anywhere, and it is even acceptable to catch a few winks on the job; Lord Sugar would have ample opportunities to use his famous two-word catchphrase, but it is not a sackable offence in this part of the world. It's the accepted norm.

When you feel tired, sleep.

Thai colleagues would nod off to sleep at their desks when I planned lessons or marked test papers in a shared faculty office; loud snoring was an accepted component in the office soundscape like vacuum cleaners and copier machines. My workspace was sandwiched between two Thais whose simultaneous snoring came with stereo sound. If there were ever an international competition for sleeping in the most unusual places, Southeast Asia would win first prize.

Scientists have studied the reasons why humans have been drawn to water since time immemorial, but I fell fast asleep before reaching their conclusions. I was ready for a boat trip on *that* river, and my impulse found motivation in popular culture, not genetics. I wanted my very own *Apocalypse Now* moment, to drift slowly and quietly upriver as palm trees waved beckoningly in the gentle winds. But unlike Captain Willard, I was prepared to get out of the boat.

## Chapter 37: Mekong Miscellany

Known regionally as the Mae Nam Khong, the Mekong River is an icon of Southeast Asia like the Amazon in South America. It is the subcontinent's seventh-longest river (the twelfth longest in the world), and its name connotes all the chemical-free exoticism of the tropics. When I visited Laos, I was excited to explore the waters of one of the world's greatest rivers which empty out into the South China Sea. I couldn't wait to climb aboard a slow boat for one of travel's greatest cultural journeys, but I am unable to disassociate the river from Francis Ford Coppola's *Apocalypse Now*, and haunting images of Captain Willard sailing up its hushed waters as he tries to locate Colonel Kurtz's Cambodian compound and retreat. Those scenes were filmed in the province of Laguna in the Philippines, so when I found myself island-hopping in that country, I deliberately sought out the Bumbungan River of Pagsanjan to sail and swim in its famous falls and pass the very embankment where Coppola created the set for Kurtz's compound. I found a commitment to a pointless cause like Captain Willard, while proving my credentials as a film buff.

Historically, the Mekong River was the spiritual lifeblood of the region, an artery that supplied precious food and water supplies to the settlements living on the banks of a trade route stretching nearly three thousand miles from its source on the Tibetan plateau into south-west China, Myanmar, Cambodia, Thailand, and Laos. In Laos, it is referred to as the 'Mother of Waters' which indicates its nurturing role and the veneration the Mekong still holds for the country's people. As I sailed the course of her waters on a converted rice barge, I stopped to visit Buddhist temples and mix with different ethnic minority communities, observing and photographing their traditions such as farming, fishing, weaving, mining, and logging. This part of the world can resist the sabre-toothed advances of modernity, so a journey on the Mekong leaves an unforgettable impression of a developing country's history and culture. I was ever-watchful of riverside stirrings, but I failed to see a single wild elephant.

First impressions can be unimpressive, as signs of industrial activity conflict with romantic notions of the river, but once cut adrift of the larger towns and their inherent hustle and hassle, the Mekong of my memory and imagination came back into plain view. Local operators offer river tours and a range of packages, which include single-day excursions to week-long voyages, stopping off at key points of interest such as the Ban Xang Hai Whisky Village. The village is nondescript - even by Southeast Asia's standards - so I wondered further in for incredible views of the countryside and the surrounding mountain plains. The Buddhist temples at the centre of the village were quiet and undisturbed, offering a more authentic glimpse into the spirituality of the people compared to Luang Prabang's well-established tourist trail. Whisky is the chief attraction, and while the villagers have a long tradition of producing stoneware jars, whisky production is a well-paid business. I sampled a few glasses of lào-láo made from fermented sticky rice and purchased a bottle for the folks back home. When I returned to the boat, there were a few more hairs on my chest.

The highlight of any boat trip on the Mekong is escaping the world as we know it; the longer I sailed, the further I travelled through the centuries with the only signs of human life the stilts that propped up home-grown houses camouflaged by dense foliage. As the waters lapped against the stern to create strange whirlpools, the spirit of travel was evoked all around me. I found nature in its unbesmirched form; a primaeval world had returned. And to think they thought Colonel Kurtz was crazy to relocate and settle in a place like this.


Having been to a Buddha park, a Buddha cave was a variation on a theme. The Pak Ou Buddha Caves sit inside limestone cliffs beside the Mekong River, and they are an important religious site with a history dating back thousands of years. The caves are fifteen miles north of central Luang Prabang and positioned at the confluence of the Mekong and Nam Ou rivers, surrounded by rugged cliffs, dramatic scenery, and a looming limestone peak. All nooks and crannies are filled with a total of four thousand Buddha icons which have, in turn, created a tourism hot spot with boats descending on a small station like scouting ants returning to the nest. The number of tourists outnumbers the statues, as they squeeze through a narrow stairway entrance to the first cave (Tham Ting) which is the only one worth visiting. I made the mistake of taking the route up a punishing staircase, carved into the rock face, to reach an upper level and second cave. There was no natural or artificial lighting inside, so I had to follow in the footsteps of another traveller, stalking and stumbling in the dark as he flashed his phone in strangers' faces. It was an utterly underwhelming experience as there was no reward for my hard work, just a fresh coat of sweat over the layer that had dried out on the boat.

The Tham Ting and Tham Phoum caves are sacred sites as they have been a repository for damaged and displaced images of the Buddha for centuries. Many were crafted by ancient hands and are replete with cobwebs and dust, while some have suffered fire damage, have missing heads or limbs or are full of termite holes. We all need a clear-out occasionally, but the Pak Ou

Caves are a rare case of spiritual recycling. As the images of the Buddha amassed over the years, the caves became a sacred pilgrimage site for the Laos people, and a means for gaining exceptional merit as they paid their respects to semi-abandoned Buddhas in a difficult-to-reach location. The caves were never intended as a tourist attraction, so the merit-makers must navigate the river and hordes of day-trippers if they want to honour them.

It didn't matter to me that Laos doesn't have any conventional beaches of its own as the country has an abundance of green delights and national parks. At Phou Khao Khouay, I was able to go trekking with a guide, kayaking, and cycling to a stunning backdrop of waterfalls, dense southern jungle, bamboo groves, sandstone plateaus, and rocky mountain slopes. The Kuang Si and Tad Sae waterfalls are a short distance from Luang Prabang and are spectacular sites of natural beauty, where I could dip my toes in the falls and admire breathtaking cascades.

The Living Land Company is a small community enterprise and organic farm in the village of Ban Phong Van, near Luang Prabang Town. I had never given much thought to how rice gets onto my table, and this was an alternative way to spend a few hours, learning about organic farming methods and the secret world of the cereal grain. It is a traditional rice farm where I could experience the life of a farmer, meet village inhabitants and plant rice.

There are twelve traditional steps for farming rice, and I was taken through them all, ploughing the earth barefoot in the mud with Suki, the water buffalo. When we stopped for lunch, one of the village elders fashioned a frog and bird from thin strips of bamboo and presented them as a gift. I have since added a coil of string, and they now hang on my international Christmas tree which has at least one decoration from every country I have visited (in Southeast Asia, they were recycled from glass, card, cans, colourful buttons, and bamboo). When I returned to Luang Prabang Town, I had a newfound appreciation of all the back-breaking work that goes into producing a single bowl of rice, and the villagers introduced me to the pleasures of an eastern alcoholic beverage: mijui (or rice wine). Plentiful cupfuls, I was quick to discover, are the perfect tonic for a day bent over double and knee-deep in buffalo shit.

French novelist Gustave Flaubert must have been referring to experiences such as these when he observed: 'Travel makes one modest. You see what a tiny place you occupy in the world.' As a backache got the better of me, I straightened up and glanced around at all the mountains crowned by mist, and quietly considered my place in the universe. I found a sense of spiritual connectedness with the natural world I had never felt before; Laos turned me into a veritable hippy, and I was far out, man.

Travellers' reviews of Laos tend to be superlative and now that I have seen the country with my own eyes, I can make a judgement from the heart. I wallowed like Suki in the unique sense of calm the country brings, its natural charms and world heritage, as I swallowed ice-cold Beerlao, home-made whisky and rice wine.

Laos was refreshing and intoxicating in equal measures.

# Part 5: A Precocious Peacock

## The Kingdom of Thailand

*If you see anybody wearing camouflage holding a machete, don't be scared. They sell coconuts.* (Bobby Lee)

### Chapter 38: Smiles and Dental Veneers

The Kingdom of Thailand sits at the heart of the Indochinese Peninsula like a floral centrepiece, sharing land borders with Myanmar, Laos, Cambodia and West Malaysia. The Andaman Sea and the Gulf of Thailand - an inlet of the South China Sea - provide extensive sandy coastlines and float dreamy equatorial islands. I will never forget the moment I first set foot on Thai terra firma: tropical heat and high humidity greeted and held me in a soupy embrace when I departed the air-conditioned comfort of Suvarnabhumi International Airport. The late morning sun was burning at its brightest, and the glare forced my eyes into a tight squint as startled irises adapted to the intensity. A layer of condensation formed over my glasses to complete the blinding, and as I wiped lenses clear of their foggy filter, I wished I had the foresight to pack a pair of novelty glasses with movable wipers. As my vision returned, the world reversed against its axis of rotation; I was taking my first steps in a land where the rulebook of western conventions is unpublished, and for the first time in my travel life, I was standing *outside* the box.

My arrival in Bangkok - in the summer of 2006 - marked my first trip to Southeast Asia and the sowing of the seeds of eventual relocation. The world I had known and journeyed was a coin flipped on its head to present a face unfamiliar; I left the churches, cobblestones and clichés of Europe behind me for a brave new world where the superabundance and force of convention on one continent created the effect of enantiodromia in another. You say *thank you*, we say *krap*. Thailand is the world in a reverse spin, a place where tourists can visit the murderers and rapists of Bang Kwang Central Prison (can dark tourism get any darker than that?) or take a gentle stroll in the peaceful grounds of the Chai Mae Tuptim Shrine, more commonly known as Bangkok's Penis Shrine. 'Penis' and 'shrine' are two words you would never imagine combining in a sentence, but the name fits, and this holy place wears it like a well-sized condom, displaying hundreds of phallic shapes crafted from stone or wood and some are decorated with neat, colourful sashes. Who needs a plain of jars when you can have a garden full of smartly dressed pillicocks? I wondered what staunchly Catholic parents would make of my Facebook updates as I smiled with arms around Mr Happy, John Thomas and Russel the love muscle.

'Only in Thailand' was a phrase I found myself repeating whenever I encountered (which was quite often) cultural strangeness or the downright unconventional, which always managed to put a smile on my face or a spring in my step. It reminded me of American writer Henry Miller's observation: 'One's destination is never a place but rather, a new way of looking at things.' I witnessed scenes I would have preferred not to have seen, including two transgender bar 'girls' performing fellatio on a Lemmy lookalike (the late, wart-faced singer of Motorhead) who sat at a table directly behind my own in a near-empty Bangkok bar. I should have thrown some salt over my shoulder before bolting the hell out of there, but I was at least beginning to understand why The Kingdom of Thailand is nicknamed 'The Land of Smiles.' Bizarre, indecent at times, but quite unforgettable.

Deep-throating, bikini-waxed men wearing lipstick, high heels and miniskirts are disconcerting enough, but the fright I experienced late one evening (when I left Bangkok's main Sukhumvit Road to turn down a quieter side street) could have finished me off. Crawling in the darkness, with awkward and unnatural movement, was the supernatural monster from the Japanese-American horror film *The Grudge*. As street lights crackled and flickered (possibly the result of my overactive imagination), I froze mid-step as my hypothalamus sensed the threat and signalled my pituitary gland to make a fight or flight response. I reversed and retreated to the safety of the main road, my heart thumping against my chest in a desperate attempt to break free and flee.

From out of the cover of darkness writhed a beggar, clutching a tattered plastic cup, the blackened stump where a hand had once been, and the botched amputation of a lower appendage that was a cauliflower of carelessly folded, stapled flesh. His clothes announced his poverty in the form of dirty grey rags, while his matted black hair masked his face and shame as he pulled himself along the pavement, his remaining arm outstretched as strangers nonchalantly stepped over him. With a trilby hat and dark sunglasses, he could have auditioned for the leading role in *The Invisible Man*. I dropped a twenty-baht note in his cup and hoped for better karma as I made a second attempt at a return to my hotel.

I encountered Bangkok's invisible man seven years later, crawling along the pavement outside On Nut Market near my apartment in the Klong Toey District, and I wondered if it had taken him all that time to crawl there from Asoke. There is no such thing as a welfare state in Southeast Asia, so it's a case of survival of the amputated. The UK benefits system is taken for granted, but for some of Thailand's poorest, it is an unattainable social nirvana as they succumb to the mercy of the street gangs who put them to work on the pavements as beggars. It's a hard-knock life and entirely 'their own fault' as karma has put them there; they should have sinned less in their former lives or perhaps visited a hell garden to heed the warnings.

Thailand is not a country in which to suffer serious illness or injury, as there is no National Health Service either. If you can't afford the medical care, you'll be returned to the Dark Ages to reset your bones with a splint and string. It is an unequal society, and because my school had private medical insurance for its overseas staff, whenever I had a cough or a scratch, a crowd of doctors gathered intently around me. They never listened to me when I tried to explain my symptoms as they were too busy filling out paperwork; all they cared about was sending me home with a wheelbarrow of unnecessary but costly medicines. How was a rabies post-exposure vaccination going to help me recover from a sprained ankle? Prevention, it seemed, was better than cure.

I was determined to avoid death or a serious accident while living in Thailand, having read about the body snatchers of Bangkok - notorious gangs of fearless collectors who flock to morbid crash sites and major fires to compete for corpses or the nearly dead. Dead is best, however, as fresh corpses can be wrapped up in white cloth before being packed in mustard-coloured coffins for quick and profitable cremations. The one country in the world where you don't want to drop down dead as a foreigner is Thailand, where you are likely to be shoved in the back of a van or battered pickup truck and carted off to a nearby hospital forensic lab. The competition for corpses is stiff, and the dead are silent partners in this thriving business, even the dismembered and decapitated, the haemorrhaging or the drowned who are fished from the rivers and canals like gory prizes. For a city of its size and pretensions, the Thai capital has seriously inadequate emergency services, so it's a race to the death for rival snatching groups whose members have brawled on the streets and, quite poetically, have put each other in the capital's hospitals and morgues.

Thailand is the global expert on breaking convention and doing things differently. It is a country, after all, in which a Thai subject can be sentenced to a forty-year prison term for insulting the late king's favourite dog, having ill-advisedly posted pictures on Facebook which appeared to mock the monarch and for 'liking' a doctored photograph. Tongdaeng, King Bhumibol Adulyadej's beloved pooch and a former stray, had more animal rights than the Thai people have human ones. The king published an affectionate 84-page biography about her - imaginatively titled *The Story of Tongdaeng* - in which he lovingly praised her loyalty and obedience (hint, hint, people of Thailand, hint, hint!). The first edition of the book was a sell-out, with all 100,000 copies of the puppy parable snapped up by the king's eager, loyal and obedient subjects, and it has been reprinted many times over to meet demand, outselling international bestsellers such as *Harry Potter*. Tongdaeng and her puppies even featured on special-edition Thai postage stamps in 2006.

A silver screen animation about Tongdaeng's life followed and was released in the same month as a new *Star Wars* film (December 2015), its director and producers supremely confident of box office success (at least in Thailand). Tongdaeng was a powerful, potent symbol and was used to illustrate the king's vision of how the Thai people should behave. Louis Althusser, the French Marxist philosopher, must be doing cartwheels in his grave as I am sure his concept of Ideological State Apparatuses never included an animated, anthropomorphic dog. Tongdaeng's demise was ill-timed, as she died just days after that controversial insult arrest. They say there is no such thing as bad publicity, so I can only imagine Tongdaeng is barking her way to the Bank of Doggie Heaven as the film shot straight in at number two in Thailand's box office rankings upon its theatrical release.

In the words of King Bhumibol Adulyadej himself: 'Tongdaeng is a respectful dog with proper manners; she is humble and knows protocol.' I think I can imagine how Amy Winehouse would have responded to such a claim about an over-pampered celebrity dog, but the canine offender in question (a factory worker named Thanakorn Siripaiboon) should have known better and followed strict protocol himself. Instead, and quite unwisely, he put his head into a noose of his making and fell afoul of Thailand's strict lèse-majesté laws. These laws make it a crime to criticise, defame or insult members of the Thai royal family. With fifteen-year sentences applicable to each transgression and, depending on the interpretation of the offence and the law and whether the judge got out of the right side of bed, all three counts can be combined and applied to a single sentence in a case of sedition. He must have been barking mad to insult his king and stand between the dragon and his wrath.

Jimmy Carr, the British stand-up and foul-mouthed comedian, wouldn't have lasted five minutes without bars had he been born a Thai. He is fond of mocking the monarchy and has made cutting remarks about Her Majesty the Queen, including this outburst: 'The thing I hate most of all about Christmas is the Queen's speech. I still watch it every year, though, cock-in-hand, awaiting that elusive tit-slip.' Had he made a similar remark about a member of the Thai royal family, the authorities would have skipped the arcane bureaucracy and formalities of a lèse-majesté charge. There would be no laughter in court, but I am sure there would be a few smiles on show in the public gallery as Jimmy was drawn by horse to a place of public execution, to be suspended from a rope to the point of death, before being emasculated, disembowelled, beheaded and quartered.

The dangers of social media and the powers of the state shouldn't be underestimated when visiting The Land of Smiles, a country which can sometimes experience a sense of humour failure as well as electrical cut outs. The thick blue stripe that runs diagonally across the centre of Thailand's tricolour flag acts as a gentle reminder and a visual deterrent, representing a monarchy that will not tolerate affronts to its dignity or the king's semi-divine status. The two thinner red stripes represent the nation, while the two white stripes signify religion and the purity of the dominant Buddhist faith. The three concepts of nation, religion, and monarchy unite the Thai people under one banner, but the monarchy is the glue that holds it all together. I was careful not to offend sensitive sensibilities, so I watched my step and closed my mouth, smiling like the *Mona Lisa* in all the right places. Perhaps that explains why Thailand is The Land of Smiles: Thais are so afraid of offending the monarchy, they hide their fears behind the mask of a smile.

Franz Lehar's romantic operetta of the same name - *Das Land des Lächelns* - refers to the Chinese custom of smiling no matter what happens in life. When a Chinese prince loses the love of his Austrian wife when she leaves him and returns to her homeland, he respects the rule of his custom and forces a smile. Primatologist Signe Preuschoft, an internationally respected expert on apes, has traced the act of smiling over thirty million years of evolution, and has classified one category of smile as a 'fear grin.' The concept of 'fear grinning' stems from apes and monkeys as they instinctively expose their barely clenched teeth to signal to predators that they are harmless, and therefore should not be perceived as a threat, even grinning through that terrifying and crunching moment when they become another animal's woodland lunch. Nervous laughter is a similar expression of awkward embarrassment, alarm, discomfort or confusion, and we all do it from time to time. The conclusion is obvious: never take a Thai smile at face value.

When first-time visitors return home from holidays in Thailand, they often comment on the kind Thai people they met and how very friendly they all are. The Thais are like the Cheshire Cat in Lewis Carroll's *Alice's Adventures in*

*Wonderland*, so when holidaymakers find themselves greeted by a warm smile, they naturally interpret that expression as a sign of welcome, openness, and friendliness. Smiles are contagious, so when someone smiles at you, it is an instinctive reaction to smile back at them. The Thai people are famous for smiling and so is the *Mona Lisa*, but are they really 'smiling' as we know it?

Leonardo da Vinci's *Mona Lisa* is the art world's most famous painting, and critics attribute her popularity to the secrets of her enigmatic smile. The portrait sits behind bullet-proof glass at the Musée du Louvre in Paris to protect Mona from art assassins and the millions of tourists and culture vultures that flock to see her every year. The Thais are just as enticing and beguiling, and their much-prized tourism industry figures are proof positive, with twenty-six million foreign arrivals in 2015 and a record thirty million estimated for 2016. There is a volume of research on the science of smiling and Thailand is the perfect case study; the Thai smile has even been categorised into thirteen distinct types of emotional expression. To get to the root of a Thai smile, you should look beyond dental veneers.

Before I made the country my home in 2013, I did some research and bought a book by Tom Tuohy with the title *Watching the Thais* which poses a critical question: Why does a Thai smile at you after crashing into the back of your car? I wanted to understand Thai culture below the surface of holiday beach waters, as I would be working and living among the people and wanted to negotiate our differences with as little cultural cack-handedness as possible. For Thais, a smile can iron out life's creases, and it maintains social harmony as it diffuses potentially negative energies. Foreign visitors often interpret a single meaning, as smiling in western countries is not a functional but a mostly spontaneous reaction. I discovered that attempting to solve the mystery of the Thai smile is the equivalent of trying to complete a Calcudoku or Sudoku puzzle wearing a blindfold.

In another revealing book titled *Working with the Thais*, co-authors Henry Holmes and Suchada Tangtongtavy have classified the Thai smile into thirteen types, with a formula for deciphering each one, matching each facial expression to a separate connotation. It is an interesting read, but in an everyday, practical situation, if I was to stare intently at a street vendor while he used a machete to cut open a coconut, he might be tempted to cut off the top of my head and put a straw in there too.

A cultural curiosity - and a rigid social custom - is the Thai national anthem, which plays on every TV and radio station at 8 am and 6 pm sharp, without fail or fault (unless there is a power outage). Public, private and international schools begin the day with the anthem, and every Thai child knows the words by heart, regardless of their age, filling their lungs with the pride of the nation as they repeat the lyrics like stadium soloists. Before the first note sounds, students line up in military formation on school yards and ceremoniously raise the national flag on prominently placed flag poles. The anthem blasts out of speakers at BTS Skytrain and MRT underground stations in the capital, and this is the perfect time to jump the queue and get a prime seat, as Thais automatically stop dead in their tracks in respectful stillness, until the final note of the song plays out. The first time I experienced this strange phenomenon, it reminded me of the opening scene of M. Night Shyamalan's science-fiction thriller *The Happening*, when an airborne neurotoxin has the dramatic effect of making the people of New York City abruptly stand to a stop before committing mass suicide.

I witnessed an awkward parody of that scene - without the suicide - every day I lived in Thailand and I was astounded by the loyalty and absolute obedience of the Thai people. I never quite got used to the anthem, even when broadcast on repeat at banks, shopping malls, bus and railway stations, hospitals, police stations, government buildings, parks and any other space deemed 'public.' In most developed countries, including my own, fans at football grounds struggle to maintain a minute's silence when mourning the dead and often shout obscenities, but Thais are programmed from birth to show respect for their national anthem which is a conduit of devotion to king and country. They don't have much of a choice either: it is the law.

While rarely enforced, there is a rule in the Thai constitution which states that failure to observe and respect the national anthem is tantamount to showing open contempt for the king, which can result in arrest and lock-up time. When given the option of standing still for sixty seconds with my students, or facing years in a Dickensian-Thai prison, it was an easy choice to make. I got used to sweating profusely in the morning sun which yellowed my shirt collars, and I was given the rather unfortunate nickname 'Mr Sweaty' by unsympathetic colleagues. Sweat dripped from my ears and brows and its salt content corroded the frames of my glasses. Foreigners would be wise to respect the anthem, even if it means having to wait for the next bus or train.

Another significant anthem is *The King's Song* (or Royal Anthem) which, as you would expect, is played at state functions and whenever a member of the Thai royal family is present at a public event. I attended the finals of the PTT Thailand Open in 2013, and the only daughter of the Thai crown prince, Princess Sirivannavari Nariratana, was the royal guest of honour.

She is a fashionista of sorts with celebrity credentials, having produced runway shows in Paris, and she stood out like a porcupine at a nudist colony as she opened the tournament wearing black platform boots and blue-sequin hot pants. She certainly got my attention - and the crowd's - so I joined in with my new friends and neighbours, standing to both the national anthem and *The King's Song* in quick succession. I was in the presence of Thai royalty, so I did not dare to disobey for fear of a public lynching.

*The King's Song* plays in cinemas before the start of every main feature and everybody - Thais, tourists, and expats alike - are expected to stand as a symbolic gesture of respect for the king. An on-screen message - in both Thai and English - instructs cinema-goers to stand, and this is a tradition torn from the pages of British history books. The ritual has origins in the early twentieth century when silent clips of King George V were accompanied by the national anthem of Great Britain: *God Save the King.* During the First World War, the anthem was part of a carefully orchestrated propaganda campaign used to whip up national sentiments to support the war effort, until it became a defunct practice in the 1960s. Thailand picked up the baton a decade later, and the general rule of thumb is if you can hear it, sing along (and put down the packets of sweets and boxes of popcorn).

Thais can get a bit touchy if they think a foreigner is not showing due respect for the dignity and divinity of their king. It is a beautiful song, set against a montage of fawning images of the late King Bhumibol Adulyadej from childhood to old age, surrounded by humble and devoted subjects (usually the rural poor) showing their heartfelt appreciation for his tireless efforts to improve the conditions of their lives. Life imitates art, as the Thais bow their heads toward the screen to join in with the collective show of appreciation and respect. But there are a few exceptions to the rule.

When a Thai man - who stood up for sitting down - was arrested in 2008 as one of two high-profile cases, Thailand's draconian laws were exposed to international scrutiny. The pressure for Thais to conform to social rules is king-sized, so when non-conformist and political activist Chotisak Onsoong bucked the trend, an angry observer filed a lèse majesté complaint against him which the police upheld with a formal charge. In the case of Rachapin Chancharoen, several cinema-goers made a collective complaint about her decision not to stand for the king. She escaped a fifteen-year prison sentence, but the authorities declared her insane and sent her to a psychiatric hospital instead. She was crazy for not standing. Make no mistake, some of Thailand's laws are among the harshest in the world and Big Brother is watching. It is always 1984 in Thailand, and just like George Orwell's fictional nation of Oceania, rebellion is swiftly quashed. Some wrongdoers were fortunate to be pardoned by the late king, but since anyone can file a lèse majesté charge, the line between freedom and incarceration is thin. Love thy Thai neighbour, and pretend to honour his king.

I was fascinated by the adulation lavished upon Adulyadej when I first visited Thailand, with super-sized portrait images of the world's longest-reigning monarch (he kept the throne warm for seventy years) adorning buildings and billboards with bold banners proclaiming: 'Long Live the King!' Tongdaeng sat by his feet and was a regular feature of palace photography. The king's omnipresence was the success of an intense - nationwide - blitzing campaign, so no matter where I looked, there he was. Like Mona Lisa in France, his eyes seemed to follow every step I took in Thailand. When I landed at the airport, portraits of the king and his queen were the first Thai faces to greet me, and they are framed and displayed like family pictures in homes and businesses. If the Thai king had been a product or service for sale, there would have been complaints about subliminal advertising. The psychological effects of image bombardment have resulted in behavioural and emotional control, unwavering affection, admiration, loyalty, and obedience. King Bhumibol is a curriculum subject as school textbooks lionise his near-century service to the nation, with each generation receiving the same carefully crafted and unconscious message during their formative years.

My first journey to Thailand coincided with the sixtieth-anniversary celebrations of the veteran king's accession to the throne. His diamond jubilee represented an opportunity to participate in a rare celebration of the divine right of kings - a doctrine which is rooted in medieval thinking but is still practised in a digital, scientific age. Exploring the capital, I quickly deduced that yellow is a favourite colour in Thailand as people wore yellow shoes, socks, scarves, skirts, shorts, shirts and, I presumed, underwear. I bought a yellow sweatshirt with an attractive emblem containing Buddhist iconography and ancient royal symbols. I didn't know it at the time, but I was wearing the king's insignia and colours; I was a loyalist and made a thousand foreign friends as my tourist attire attracted a host of strangers' smiles (with hindsight, those smiles may have been contemptuous).

King Bhumibol Adulyadej was born on a Monday so yellow was his auspicious colour (in Thai and Khmer traditions, an astrological ruling assigns a different colour to each day of the week). The determination of the colour depends on the shade of the God who protects the day, with Mondays protected by the yellow hues of Chandra. Thais could offset Monday morning blues by wearing cheerfully bright yellow togs, an informal homage to their king. He had a royal flag too (a plain yellow flag with a royal cypher), and this could be seen fluttering alongside the ubiquitous colours of the national flag. Queen Sirikit's flag is blue - she was born on a Friday - and this usually accompanied the king's colour.

Flags and royal merchandise are big business in Thailand as much as they are in the United Kingdom, with devoted shops supplying the high demand as Thais are keen to show their allegiance to the sovereignty of the king and state. And who can blame them, given the nature of some of Thailand's archaic laws? There are, in total, seventeen royal flags - a suitably high number for a country in which flying the flag is a characteristic feature of society and culture. The national flag flutters over taxis, boats, tuk-tuks and mobile roadside stalls.

To understand the Thais, you must penetrate two layers of disguise: smiles and masks.

## Chapter 39: Behind the Khon Mask

The Thai people are intensely proud of their history so they tend to display old flags as symbols, including a white elephant in regalia on a field of red, which harkens back to the days when Thailand was regionally powerful as the Kingdom of Siam. Thai history books claim that Thailand resisted invasion and colonisation and was never conquered, but that is *his story* and a small matter of interpretation, as I would beg to differ. To separate historical fact from the myth-making of national pride, you only need to look as far back as the Second World War when the Japanese invaded Thailand in December 1941 to build their ambitious Thai-Burma Railway project. If an armed intruder broke into my house, I wouldn't stand in his way either; when the Thais stepped aside and let the Japanese get on with their dark deeds, they certainly behaved like a conquered nation. They are likely to take the point of view that the Japanese occupation was a temporarily permitted alliance, an astute political duping and outmanoeuvring, as they secretly helped the Allies overthrow their troublesome guests.

Thai parents prefer to teach their children the myth instead of fact, perceiving their forebears as highly skilful negotiators who used cunning to repel foreign invaders. They cannot deny that Chinese communities and swathes of backpackers have colonised the capital, as Bangkok's Chinatown district and the Khao San Road area of Banglamphu are compelling evidence that they have. The annals of history reveal that from the sixteenth to the nineteenth centuries Siam and Burma fought a series of wars, with victories and losses on both sides. But when the Kingdom of Ayutthaya surrendered - a Siamese kingdom which existed between 1351 and 1767 - it became a vassal state of Burma and triggered the fall of Siam. I visited the ruins of historic Ayutthaya in 2012 which was not only invaded, it was ruthlessly sacked and almost destroyed by the Burmese.

The red stripes on Thailand's national flag represent the blood spilt by loyal Thais who sacrificed their lives to maintain their country's freedom and independence, but they did on occasion fail to protect it. They still struggle to let go of their prejudice or find forgiveness in their hearts, as the Burmese burned their temples to the ground and smashed the heads from sacred statues. It is something of a grudge war these days, as the Thai ethnocentric media and a nationalistic school system remind Thai children that the Burmese are malevolent invaders and their traditional enemy, while novels and films position their ancestors as heroic historical figures. Which explains, but doesn't justify, why Thailand turned its back on the thousands of Rohingya Muslims abandoned at sea by traffickers in 2015, when it engaged in a game of human ping pong with Indonesia and Malaysia, as they all made their excuses and turned them away.

Thailand has been much-criticised for being an openly xenophobic country, with accusations that the darker the skin, the greater the prejudice. Much like its regional neighbours, the prevailing attitude to those with a darker complexion is that their skin colour is undesirable, as it equates to unskilled outdoor labour and the lower social classes. The whiter in tone a Thai's skin, the more beautiful and desirable they become, while their social status likewise elevates. This attitude to skin colour is perpetuated by Thai media and advertising agencies as the models on their books are whiter than white. They dazzle. The north-eastern province of Isan is home to Thailand's poorest and most uneducated people, with the majority working and living off the land. Bangkok's city slickers are said to consider them as an inferior breed because of their darker skin tone, a prejudice compounded by the nickname 'kwai' - which means 'buffalo' - as the animal is regarded as a slow and stupid creature. By contrast, the whiter a Thai's skin, the more educated and financially successful they are deemed to be, with an assumption that they work indoors in an office or bank, thereby pigeonholing them alongside the nouveau riche elite. Insecurities with skin colour interweave with class prejudices in Thailand.

Skin whitening, lightening, and bleaching products are a highly profitable branch of the Thai cosmetics industry, but one Thai cosmetics firm overstepped the mark and was forced to withdraw its controversial advert for skin-whitening pills called *Snowz*. It was heavily criticised on social media, and branded racist by critics for its rather blunt slogan: 'Whiteness makes you win.' The world's neo-Nazi organisations could adopt that logo as a rallying call. A slogan which suggests people with dark skin are losers, and somewhere at the bottom of the evolutionary chain, is hardly going to win any LIA awards for advertising. Thailand's superfluity of whitening products should instead be nominated for comedy awards, as some of their users provided me with moments of unexpected (and unintended) amusement as I commuted to work on the BTS Skytrain, with hastily applied 'whiteovers' the Thai reversal of the poorly applied fake tan. They looked like mime artists wearing theatrical makeup, with brilliant-white faces contrasting against black hair, brown arms and necks.

Thai men and women will go to extreme lengths to protect a pale complexion, having invested their savings in whitening pills, drinks, creams, and lotions which all promise to fast-forward them to the whiter end of the white spectrum, like whitening for whole bodies instead of teeth. The sun is a fearful adversary from which they take shelter and arm themselves with umbrellas, rushing in and out of department stalls like vampires on a shopping spree. It should come as no surprise that black people are not too popular in Thailand, where it is assumed they all come from Africa; the Thai school I worked at had close to two hundred teaching staff, and with half that number recruited from overseas, there wasn't a single black face among them.

I was disappointed when one of my students commented that Nelson Mandela had 'dirty skin' during a lesson dedicated to his life (following his death in December 2013). A language-learning poster that was designed to extend students' vocabulary presented a white face described as 'beautiful' and a black face labelled 'ugly.' To drive that message home, beneath the dark face a caption stated: 'This man is ugly.' Xenophobic attitudes extend beyond dark skin as the Russian expansion into Thailand has not gone unnoticed, with protests in Phuket and banners demanding: 'Russians get out!' White westerners are 'farangs' and it is oft-debated in expat circles whether this is a racist term or not, depending on the user and the situational context of use. When I travelled to lesser-known towns or villages, I would hear calls of 'farang' which I interpreted as a pleasant surprise to see me there, rather than an ill-intentioned racial slur. I guess I'll never know.

The breaking of sandstone statues by Burmese invaders, hundreds of years ago, was terrible sacrilege but so too, apparently, is ill-considered graffiti. In 2007, a Swiss man with little common sense (but plenty of daring) received a ten-year sentence at the age of fifty-seven for spray-painting over and defacing portraits of the late king. What was he thinking, smoking or drinking? Oliver Jufer confessed to drunkenly spraying black paint over five posters of the king, and he arrived in court for sentencing with his ankles shackled, presumably still a menace to Thai society, sobriety and posters. His original sentence - for twenty years - was halved by Judge Pitsanu Tanbuakli, who showed some mercy despite summing up the case as 'the most serious crime.' He was guilty, as charged, of lèse majesté and his story illustrates the fact that foreigners are just as susceptible to charges, trials and incarceration as Thais. Same, same but different. Had he used white paint, he may well have been crowned.

I was always mindful not to contravene the strict Thai Criminal Code or the cultural minefield of crimes against social etiquette, but I laughed out loud from the other side of the world when the story, and international condemnation, broke about poor little Tongdaeng. Had I still been living in Thailand, I would have set my face to its disgruntled mode in a show of public disapproval. Dogs deserve justice! Travel guides wax lyrical about a land full of smiles and eulogise over fun-loving locals, but this is a white lie repackaged as the perfect pearly smile. Appearance is everything in Thailand, especially when it comes to tourism, as the economy has been dependent on this high-yielding industry for decades. An anxious Tourism Authority of Thailand launched a new slogan in 2014 (*Amazing Thailand. It begins with the people.*) following months of politicking and social unrest and falling arrivals and tourism revenues. Thailand is an amazing country, but it has its faults, which become more apparent over the period of a two-year stay instead of two weeks prone at the beach with cocktails in hand.

'Sanook,' which means 'fun,' is the guiding principle of Thai social life which is why it often features in the names of Thai and tourist watering holes. They are also rather fond of 'sabai' which translates to 'happiness,' 'relaxation' and 'wellness' which accounts for why so many massage spas have names such as Sabai Massage, Baan Sabai Massage or Sabai Thai Massage (ad infinitum). Of course, some holidaymakers like to mix their 'happiness' with their 'fun' in massage parlours such as Dream Heaven Massage in Bangkok which, unashamedly, advertises a special 'Lady of the Night Massage' on an enormous blue sign outside its doors. I guess 'Prostitute Massage' lacks subtlety, so they dropped the more neutral noun 'lady' in there instead.

Thailand and its capital confound the senses - especially common sense - on every street corner as failure to stand for the king's song can carry a fifteen-year prison term, yet it is perfectly acceptable to advertise prostitute massages. Pussy ping pong shows, dancing go-go bars and fish bowls (venues where the girls stand behind glass viewing screens to be selected like crabs and crustaceans at a seafood restaurant) are also fair game. And this, after all, is a country in which prostitution is supposedly illegal. Double standards treble in Thailand, where they test western workers for syphilis on entry to the country, but not their in-house sex workers.

Relocating to Thailand allowed me to get to know my hosts better, and I could peel back the social veneer to witness the violence and turmoil of the anti-government protests of 2013-2014, which were not an aberration but a political and historical norm. When Thais get angry, their emotions are quick to turn to fury. Having witnessed their ritual passivity for so many years, I was genuinely shocked when ordinary Thai people started to shoot and grenade each other on the streets of the capital in broad daylight. Civil war loomed, states of emergency were declared, the capital was shut down by anti-government protesters, and martial law imposed on the people. When translated, the national anthem boldly claims that Thais 'are not cowards' and will 'sacrifice every drop of their blood' to protect their nation, especially when it needs protection from the perceived corruption of unpopular politicians with a shared surname: the Shinawatra family.

I had the sense and sensitivity to not engage Thai friends or colleagues in a conversation about politics, as it is a charged subject. I witnessed that famous Thai smile turn to a scowl when ten people lost their lives and six hundred suffered injuries during shootings, bombings and vicious street fighting as rival factions warred on the streets of the capital. It was an ambitious and audacious plan to shut down the capital city, and they succeeded for a while. The anti-government protesters used the national anthem to support the legitimacy of their claims and actions, but the musical score that accompanies the fierce words of the song is an oddly cheerful ditty. Even after a thousand enforced performances, the only line I can remember (and phonetically parrot) sounds like 'rats are monkeys.' I don't think there are any rats or monkeys to be found in the Thai national anthem which, incidentally, was composed by a Russian man named Peter Feit. The Thais were never going to allow the small obstacle of truth to stand in the way of national pride so, hey presto, they changed his name to Phra Jenduriyang.

Delving a little deeper in the south will expose the ugly and smoke-stained truth hidden behind expensive surface veneers, as this is where one of Southeast Asia's longest-running conflicts smoulders on between Islamic insurgents and Buddhist state security forces. It is Thailand's conveniently forgotten war, but it is an ongoing war of attrition that has cost thousands of lives, yet most visitors to the country are oblivious to this as the tourist beaches and cultural hot spots are insulated to the north. In the south, the Malay Muslims have long been enraged by their cultural, political and spiritual alienation in a predominantly Buddhist nation. When tourists book their family holidays to Thailand, they would perhaps hesitate to do so if they knew domestic terrorists had planted improvised explosive devices in southern toy shops. They are yet to align themselves with Islamist terrorist organisations such as al-Qaeda, but there is a real and present danger that they are ripe for recruitment by transnational militant groups, such as Islamic State.

These incidents are, of course, rarely reported outside Thailand where the concept of 'face' - and saving face in particular - is all that matters. 'Face' is the backbone of Thai social interaction and it is the sense of self, respect and self-worth a Thai person feels; international perceptions of Thailand as a nation do, therefore, constitute a sense of uber-face (hence the re-writing of history in school textbooks). And this explains why Thailand's expanding middle class is obsessed with western culture and technical gadgetry, whitened faces and cornrow-perfect teeth. Thais naturally prefer to save face than lose it, so if you ask a Thai person if you are heading in the right direction to a temple or museum, they will point in the direction you are facing and nod their head in the affirmative, even if they have no idea what you asked them. Beheadings and bombings are not your typical holiday headlines or face-makers, so they are shunted to the backs of the back pages or, better still, not published at all. A high death toll, with a low international profile, equals the perfect imbalance. Behind the traditional khon masks of Thailand there's a devil's smile with bloody lips, and if you keep your eyes and ears open long enough, you'll be able to see it.

To lose one's temper in public is a terrible loss of face, as Thais consider emotional honesty both embarrassing and counterproductive. The keys to safe and successful passage through Thailand are patience, humour and a cool heart (jai yen), which means never losing your temper or raising your voice. When I was denied re-entrance to Thailand on my return from a trip to Myanmar, I remained calm in my composure, politely stood my ground and waited until a supervisor approached so I could explain my case with a broad and warm-hearted smile. I had a multiple-entry visa, so I was, by Thailand's immigration law, allowed to come and go as I pleased.

The immigration official I had the misfortune to deal with, asked me what business I had in Thailand so I explained that I was a teacher and named my school. He insisted on seeing my work permit (which I had never been asked to present before), so he was either new to the role or was having a bad day and wanted to take it out on me. The error was all his, as there is no legal requirement to show a work permit on a multiple-entry visa. He was never going to admit his mistake, as that would be a significant loss of face in front of a foreigner and his senior colleague, so I explained to his supervisor that I was a silly foreigner - that the fault was all mine - as I misplaced my work permit beneath a pile of paperwork in my apartment. He reluctantly waved me through, and I learnt how to be a duck in Thailand as I was calm on the surface but paddling like hell beneath.

There is something delightfully risqué about travelling in a country where standing on a coin or a note - with an image of the king's face - is a grave insult to the monarch and his people. If I dropped a note, I let the wind take it and *The Grudge* creature find it. I had grown stiff with the ramrod of convention while travelling in the Western Hemisphere but all my senses and joints were reawakened and reinvigorated by Thailand; I was an osteoarthritis patient on steroids when I entered The Land of Smiles for the very first time. Thailand epitomises the spirit of this book as it is an equal serving of sublime and ridiculous. Only in Thailand can sports enthusiasts play nightly bouts of Pussy Ping Pong, which includes the regular ball and bat, but a somewhat unconventional opponent: a vagina. Yes, a vagina. The girls shoot sticky balls from their lady bits (hence the rather literal naming of this pastime) as delighted onlookers knock them back, with mouths sealed-tight to avoid a nasty splatter catch. In Thailand, these types of sex show are passé, but for first-time visitors, they are as culturally shocking as the sudden electrical discharge of a lightning strike.

I knew I had developed a resistance to Thailand when I stood at a urinal, sandwiched between two high-heeled ladyboys, and didn't bat an eyelid. The setting reminded me of the promotional poster for *Ted* featuring Mark Wahlberg standing at a public urinal next to his cuddly teddy bear - eponymous hero Ted - who has a bottle of beer in one hand and a furry appendage in the other.

An extreme example it might be, but walking the streets of any Thai town or city is an obstacle course of Krypton Factor proportions. Pavements become stepper machines when walkers are forced to step up and step down, step over potholes, avoid loose tiles, and the ever-present menace of motorcycle taxis as the pavements are their unofficial lanes. It could be worse, as the elevated design is quite deliberate, preventing Bangkok's lawless drivers from turning footpaths into passing lanes or makeshift, citywide parking strips. Thailand is no country for old men, wheel or pushchairs and there is no such thing as a ramp as common sense rarely prevails. The pavement design is supposed to assist pedestrians during monsoon flooding, but it's a nightmare for hip and knee joints. Even the designers of the BTS Skytrain system neglected to include lifts and escalators at all its stations, which was a costly oversight.

The name of the Thai capital is the longest city name on the planet, so this does, in part, prepare the visitor for what to expect from a visit to Thailand. It is not an ordinary nation. The Welsh must be envious of Bangkok's full name, which is a marathon of a tongue-twister and a short-term memory test: *Krung Thep Mahanakhon Amon Rattanakosin Mahinthara Ayuthaya Mahadilok Phop Noppharat Ratchathani Burirom Udomratchaniwet Mahasathan Amon Piman Awatan Sathit Sakkathattiya Witsanukam Prasit.* Try writing that on a standard-sized envelope! If matters weren't already complicated enough, the official Thai Buddhist calendar begins with the death of the Buddha some 543 years before the start of the Christian calendar, so when my flight left London Heathrow on the 31st March 2013, I landed in Thailand on the 1st April 2556.

A holiday in Thailand can be a multisensory trip on LSD, except its powerful effects are real, not hallucinogenic. As my taxi driver considered the longest route to get me to my hotel on my first visit, my sense of smell was the first to recover from the jet lag as it experienced a unique and utterly unforgettable eau de toilette: Bangkok. Guidebook images prepare visitors for the aromas of lemongrass and jasmine flowers, scented burning wood and freshly chopped coriander, but it was the unmistakable smell of clogged klongs (canals) that I will carry with me to the grave. 'Pong' is a popular nickname in Thailand, but it could be used to describe the capital and every other sizeable city in this kingdom, which tend to be as noisome as they are noisy.

Thailand's capital is a river city and was - historically at least - crisscrossed by so many canals that it was dubbed the 'Venice of the East,' which is stretching a point of comparison to its absolute limit. Most of those canals have since been filled in with cement or excrement, and some of the survivors are in such a sorry state that their waters have turned black like a sea container oil spill (but you'll still see naked children swimming and rollicking in the shallows). Once you've had your first sniff of *that Bangkok smell*, it stays with you forever like a misstep in the swamps of the Bog of Eternal Stench in Jim Henson's *Labyrinth*. Ludo, the giant ginger beast that rescues Sarah from a group of mischievous goblins, was right when he complained that it: 'Smells… bad!' You get used to it after about six months, and nose blindness is guaranteed. The whole city is a dose of smelling salts, and while it is true that it revived my wanderlust, it also found ample opportunity to remind me of my fearful archenemy: the common cockroach.

Bangkok is the capital of cockroaches (some have human forms), and they are *everywhere*. A friend managed to establish eye contact with one when leaning into an ATM to read the display, only to notice something twitching in the dark and staring right back. Marlon Brando's famous line from *Apocalypse Now* comes to mind: 'The horror! The Horror!' When I exited the Hotel BelAire to take my first tentative steps on this subcontinent, an early monsoon downpour filled the sewers and pushed a Biblical plague of cockroaches up and over the tops of the drains, like a scene from the trenches of World War One. My hairy, clammy legs must have resembled a Noah's Ark for undesirable insects, as they tried and failed to clamber aboard my flip flops. Long-term exposure developed into a nervous tic, so whenever I stood still or sat down in a public place to rest or eat, I skimmed and scanned my environment for black, oval-shaped bodies with spiny legs and twitching antennae. The Indian Railways Network was the foundation of my fear, but it was Thailand that put the walls and a roof on top. In Bangkok, you can't live with cockroaches, and you certainly can't live without them.

My journey across Southeast Asia was rooted in the Thai capital which was the perfectly imperfect introduction. It was simply overwhelming and three days were enough to compel me to travel elsewhere. From the capital, I ventured north to Chiang Mai, and from there I went south to the resort town of Hua Hin where I stared out to sea for hours, watching the waves while hoping to avoid a repeat of the 2004 Indian Ocean earthquake and tsunami. A further five years had passed before I returned to the Kingdom of Unconventional in the summers of 2011 and 2012. I was getting hooked on a drug, and my limbic system was loving it, driving my appetite to return and repeat those first joys of awe and wonder, in a topsy-turvy world where every day presented strange new discoveries about the country and myself. Some discoveries were unwanted, which included a late-night horror show when a beautiful woman (she could have been a catwalk model) took a seat next to mine in a busy bar and introduced herself by hitching up her skirt to show me her flaccid penis. Who needs introductory etiquette when you can cut to the chase like that? I finished my drink and left. *Alone.*

I used to agree that the first joy of travelling to a new country is unrepeatable and that cultural and literary historian Paul Fussell was right when he observed: 'The wise traveller learns not to repeat success but tries new places all the time.' I have revisited European cities such as Paris, Amsterdam, and Edinburgh and left wishing I had tried somewhere new. Returning to Thailand had the opposite effect on me: every time I revisited, I made new discoveries and friends and felt more at home in a foreign land which was designed to make me feel uncomfortable. When I sat down to eat at Pantaree, one of my favourite cheap-eat restaurants on the Sukhumvit Road, I imagined one distant day - in a far-flung and fuzzy future - relocating my life and work to Bangkok. It must have been the Chang and Singha effect. I had no desire to uproot and live my life anywhere else, as I was perfectly content with my home in Kent (though I had briefly contemplated a financial smash-and-grab in Dubai), but there I was, a full-fledged resident with all the necessary paperwork, living in one of the world's most exciting cities. The travel bug was bored of biting my shins so swallowed me whole and wriggling. I was breaking bread at a different table on which convention preferred spoons over knives.

I tried and failed to learn Thai as it is an awkwardly tonal language, so an incorrectly pronounced tone can completely change a word's meaning. The Thai language has five tones - low, mid, high, falling and rising - and the distinct tone must be enunciated correctly for the intended meaning of the word to be understood. I was tone-deaf. Learning Thai was, to all intents and purposes, like trying to read and understand the meaning behind a Thai smile. The word 'kao,' for example, is a girl's name, rice, the number nine, knee, to come in, or news, depending on which tone you use within a given context. When I asked a taxi driver to take me to Ayutthaya, a former capital and historic city, I had to pronounce the name a dozen times to register a response. Fumbling with a linguistic combination lock, I tried in vain to guess the correct sequence of numbers. When I used a rising tone for the final syllable, he finally understood what I meant. Eureka! And then he refused to take me, suggesting I take a train from Bangkok's Hualamphong Station.

I will keep with the Laotian fondness for proverbs by letting the cat out of the bag and harnessing the Asian elephant in the room: there is simply no city in all Southeast Asia quite like Bangkok. It might be the head of a strutting, precocious peacock, but it is also the beating heart of an apex predator in the world of international tourism. Thailand is an incredibly diverse nation full of mythical beaches, tropical islands, the ruins of former kingdoms and modern, urban risings. A realm of endless wonders, it boasts spectacular natural, cultural and historical attractions. I have travelled Thailand more than any other country, including the country of my birth, and I have explored both the traditional tourist trails like everyone else, and areas of interest away from the beaten track. And like a trusty boomerang, I find myself returning to soft, jasmine-scented hands.

If ever there was a country more deserving of the word 'discombobulating' in its national description, it has to be Thailand. They should use it in their tourism slogans.

## Chapter 40: The Big Mango

Bigger, better, Bangkok. The Big Mango. A City of Angels (and a few demons), the Thai capital is the largest urban centre in Southeast Asia. It will never be able to contend for international beauty contests, but it is a fascinating city with a distinct personality. Like the Roman god, Janus, Bangkok has two faces. Vice and virtue co-exist in the same neighbourhoods, while tradition stands firm against encroaching modernity. Bangkok's fine-dining scene is trending with Michelin-starred chefs, but it is the world-class street food that excites (and occasionally bewilders) intrepid diners as they search for food-on-the-go in an on-the-go capital. New York is 'the city that never sleeps' but Bangkok is the city that *never* slept. Its tropical energy is exciting, irresistible and unabating; it wouldn't grind to a paralysed halt if snowstorms blanketed its eastern seaboard.

As the capital of a land that smiles, no other city in the world has managed to put so many grins on my face or laughs in my belly. When I visited the Snake Farm (the Queen Saovabha Memorial Institute and Thai Red Cross Institute), I closed a cubicle door to be presented with a laminate giving instruction on how to sit on a western-style toilet. The left-hand side carried the image of a cartoon figure standing unsteadily on a toilet seat, readying himself for the nightmare of all splashbacks, while a bold caption declared the obvious: 'Incorrect!' To his right sat a comfortably seated figure going about his business with a knowing smiling. It tickled every inch of me but to be fair to the Thais, the first time I used a squat toilet was a body-and-mind disaster as I had no idea what to do with my shorts, where to place my feet or which way to face by backside. Compounding my confusion and positional distress, an inch of water flooded the floor, and the source was a dripping hosepipe which is the Thai alternative to toilet paper - the dreaded 'bum gun.'

Thailand has embraced the western-style toilet like a long-lost relative, slowly phasing out the squatting variety which, it must be said, is the embodiment of progress in porcelain form. Despite having western toilets plumbed into place in hotels, bars and restaurants, papery piles of faecal leftovers greeted me in overflowing and foul-smelling waste bins. I shuddered as I entered humid chambers of unpleasantness, closed my eyes and held my breath. With Thailand's septic tank sewage systems and woefully inadequate treatment facilities, it simply can't cope with tissue paper, so the Thais are expected (and tourists are encouraged) to wipe and bin. Some bars cannot deal with toilet tissue *or* faeces, as well-known Cheap Charlie's, an expat bar on Sukhumvit Soi 11, displays a prominent sign politely reminding its patrons how to use their facilities: 'Only pee. DO NOT SHIT!' The 'shit' is underlined to emphasise the point, should the capital letters be ignored. When I returned from my first outing to Southeast Asia, I vowed never to take my toilet for granted again.

As Bangkok's full title suggests (though most Thais shorten it to Krung Thep), size matters in the nation's capital which boasts the largest weekend market in the world - Chatuchak, or Jatujak or J.J Market - with fifteen thousand stalls set over thirty-five acres, selling everything from puppies to pewter glasses. As a megalopolis in Central Thailand, Bangkok effortlessly fuses eastern and western cultures in one enormous melting pot which is appropriate, given it is the hottest city in the world. Thailand's eggs have all been placed in the one basket as the capital is the country's only sizeable city (and most populous), with eight million inhabitants living within the core, and a further fourteen million swelling their ranks in the surrounding Bangkok Metropolitan Region.

With 35% of the country's population living within spitting distance of the capital, Bangkok dwarfs every other major urban centre in Thailand for importance. While London must compete with Manchester and Birmingham, Beijing with Shanghai and Seoul with Busan, Bangkok is without rival. With the influx of multinational corporations following the Asian investment boom of the 1980s and 1990s, Thailand found status as one of the four dominant Tiger Cub Economies of Southeast Asia (which includes Malaysia, Indonesia, and the Philippines) when it embraced the potential of industrialisation and export-driven economic development. Thailand is a healthy cub because its progress is still in its infancy, as it follows in the shadows and footsteps of the Four Asian Tigers: Hong Kong, Singapore, South Korea and Taiwan.

First impressions of the capital are unremarkable, as it stretches out in all directions, a seemingly impassable confusion of concrete with the grey infrastructure of the BTS Skytrain snaking its way past condominium high-rises, shopping malls, and ramshackle slums near the city's main port. First impressions are not to be trusted as this city has so much to offer its visitors, with a spectacular temple and Emerald Buddha at Wat Phra Kaew and a gigantic, golden and reclining Buddha with mother-of-pearl-feet at Wat Pho. Boat trips by day or night take in the castaneous waters of the Chao Phraya River, the primary waterway of Thailand, which offers cultural views of Wat Arun, elegant Chinese pagodas and the enormous white chedi of Wat Prayoon. But what impressed me most was the city's soaring skyline, which must be one of the densest concentrations of skyscrapers in the world. They are a statement of intent and a fitting symbol of the country's tigerish ambitions. Their aesthetics are often pleasing on the eye too as luxurious, multi-purpose skyscrapers compete for elegant design and status, with MahaNakhon the latest addition to the towering collection in 2016, presenting a pixelated facade and having usurped the Baiyoke Tower as the tallest building in Thailand.

Bangkok is an extraordinary and demanding city of excess, and there's no such thing as order or predictability. A major regional force in finance and business, it is synonymous with sex tourism. It is one of the most-visited cities in the world, famous for its vibrant street life and cultural landmarks, and it's an exciting and multifaceted capital with something for every visitor to enjoy (whether shopping for clothes in designer malls, or flesh in the red light districts). Bangkok and Boredom have never met, and neither will they since, in the words of James Hetfield of Metallica, boredom 'sets into the boring mind,' not the place. Culturally, its potential is never-ending and as a tourist on holiday, I followed all the guidebook trails with stops at the Grand Palace, Wat Pho, and Wat Arun. The lovely Jim Thompson House, near central Siam, is a museum dedicated to the life of its former owner (successful US-born Thai entrepreneur James H.W. Thompson) who has been credited with reviving the now-flourishing Thai silk industry.

For more times than I can remember, I have taken friends to visit Jim Thompson's east-meets-west house, but it is still one of my favourite spots in the city as it's a garden-enclosed compound and oasis that sits on the bank of the Saen Saeb Canal. The house, comprised of six traditional teakwood buildings relocated from Ayutthaya and Baan Khrua, has been a museum and treasure trove of South-east Asian art and antiques since Jim Thompson's disappearance on holiday in western Malaysia in March 1967. He went for a walk in the Cameron Highlands and never returned. Following months of intense media speculation about his fate (theories ranged from death by tiger to kidnap by communists), he became a mythical figure and joined Bangkok's pantheon of legends. His lifestyle reads like the pages of an F. Scott Fitzgerald novel, and his former home and possessions are frozen in time to commemorate this lost Silk King of Thailand. It is a beautiful house with impressive collections of Chinese ceramics, Thai statues and artwork, but what caught my interest and imagination was the high-step room-separator at the entrance to Thompson's bedroom. The guide explained that bugs and pests remain at bay, and evil spirits - that visit the sleeping to paralyse them with terror - are denied entry. I shuddered as terrifying images of the black-haired, pale-faced creature from *The Grudge* filled my head, and I considered adding a spirit-separator to the threshold of my own bedroom.

Belief in the presence of spirits or ghosts is as much a part of Thai culture as Buddhism, with the legends of folklore having passed on from one generation to the next. Thai spirits are known as 'phi,' and they are a popular subject of Thai soap operas, films, and comics as there are so many ghostly characters to choose from, like a catalogue of the freakish. There is a Phi Kong Koi, a forest vampire with one leg, and Phi Pop, a malevolent female spirit with a penchant for chewing on human entrails. Thais do not take their spirits lightly, as an unhappy entity can bring great misfortune. Not all spirits have evil intent - some are benevolent. To ensure the happiness and wellbeing of a phi, dedicated 'spirit houses' are erected on the lands of every Thai home, place of business, restaurant, market, hotel, forest, and beach, to house and appease the spirit of the land that was disturbed by the construction of a new building on old ground (the 'phra phum'). In return, the guardian spirits offer protection and shelter.

Spirit houses are culturally ubiquitous in rural and urban Thailand. They are prominently raised on platforms and feature miniature Thai houses or temples, with daily offerings coming in the form of incense and flowers or food and drink (which includes packets of crisps and fizzy drinks). It was fascinating to watch the Thais interact with their spirit houses as they washed and tidied them, left offerings or prayed. Whenever a Thai passes a spirit house, they pause briefly to *wai*, the Thai greeting and show of respect when palms are pressed together near the chest before a gentle bow. Spirit houses are festooned with jasmine garlands (phuang malai) which are good luck charms in Thailand.

Close to the Memorial Bridge over the Chao Phraya River, Pak Khlong Talat existed as Bangkok's primary flower market and business bloomed in a spiritually symbolic area that was always open, until the Bangkok Metropolitan Administration closed it down as part of its clean-up campaign. It supplied the city's insatiable need to make floral offerings which can be seen hanging from the prows of long-tail boats and the rear-view mirrors of taxis, buses, and tuk-tuks. The Thais are a superstitious lot as they believe Mae Yanang - the goddess of travel - protects them from harm when they honour her with garlands (the cultural equivalent of carrying a St Christopher pendant). Pak Khlong Talat offered an authentic glimpse into Thai culture and tradition, and I enjoyed walking the streets of this market which was a veritable feast for the senses and a rainbow of red roses, green chillies, purple orchids and yellow chrysanthemums.

Thai children are encouraged - from an early age - to show a cool heart (jai yen) as evil spirits are drawn to hot hearts (jai rohn), which possibly accounts for the impeccable behaviour of my former students. When we studied *A Christmas Carol*, they gripped their books tightly and sat with open mouths as the ghosts of Christmas past, present and future revealed themselves to Scrooge. Mae Nak Phra Khanong is a well-known ghost story and a favourite of Thai cinema since the 1950s, with remakes and variations on the theme, which include a romantic tragedy and a comedy horror. My students introduced me to the story and the animated way they delighted to share it, suggested they believed the events were real, not imagined.

The story has origins in the nineteenth century and features a Thai wife named Mae Nak and her husband, Mak, who live beside the Phra Khanong canal in eastern Bangkok. Mae Nak's husband is conscripted for military service, leaving his pregnant wife behind who dies during childbirth. When Mak returns home injured, he is greeted by his wife and their new-born child. His neighbours try to intervene and warn him, but meet grisly ends, until Mak discovers the ghostly truth for himself when his wife prepares a meal, drops a lime through a crack in the floor and absentmindedly extends her arm to retrieve it. Having discovered that he's been living with the ghosts of his wife and child, Mak flees in terror with Mae Nak in hot pursuit, and suspecting the local people aided her husband's escape, she vows to take a terrible revenge on the neighbourhood.

The line between fiction and reality in Thailand is sometimes drawn in invisible ink, as Mae Nak has her very own shrine in the district of Phra Khanong, close to the site where she and her family are said to have 'lived.' I visited the memorial out of curiosity, as it was only a short walk from my apartment in neighbouring On Nut district. The longer I lived in the Thai capital, the more deeply I probed its mysteries and curiosities which, it must be said, are far removed from package tours and holidays. The shrine is close to Wat Mahabut, a community temple where Mak is said to have hidden, which has few tourist visitors in a city of 887 Buddhist temples. The temple is modest in design and has no claim to historical legend, but it is notorious for its female ghost as Mae Nak is a household name in Thailand (the temple is known as 'Wat Mae Nak Phra Khanong,' or 'Temple of Mother Nak of Phra Khanong' to the local community). And, stranger still, regarding her as a benefactor, they built a shrine in her honour on the temple's grounds. Her portrait hangs over an altar covered in garlands and candles, and her statue has a layer of delicate gold leafing.

Visitors come to the shrine to pay their respects with prayer and offerings, hoping for blessings and good fortune in return. Young Thai men, wishing to avoid the draft in Thailand's selective military conscription, hope Mae Nak will offer them salvation. We all appreciate thoughtful gifts when they are given to us, but Mae Nak receives more than her fair share as the shrine is full of cosmetics and colourful Thai costumes for Mae, and toys, nappies and bottles of milk for her dead baby. The shrine is a house of the dead, and Mae even has her own television set which is always switched on (even the dead get bored and watch Thai soap operas). The Grand Palace is Bangkok's star attraction with fabulous clusters of decorative temples, but I preferred the hour I spent at the Mae Nak shrine which, like the flower market, is about as authentic as the capital experience gets.

The 'Penis Shrine' (Chao Mae Tuptim) is another one of Bangkok's many hidden gems. A forest of phallic, blush-inducing offerings, it is a shrine to fertility goddess Chao Mae Tuptim - from whom the shrine gets its official name - and it has an unlikely setting: the quiet corner of a hotel car park. It wasn't easy to find, but with a nod in the right direction from one of the security guards at the Swissotel, I was presented with an outlandish panorama featuring a thousand one-eyed monsters. Its collection comes in all shapes and sizes, and while the majority are modest, handmade wooden carvings, some are erected at six feet and others are made of concrete with balls for penis feet. They reminded me of the monsters in the British post-apocalyptic horror *The Day of the Triffids*, whose triffid plants (which look like giant asparagus shoots) walk the earth on their roots to stalk and kill their human prey. Adorned with garlands, incense sticks and with baht and satang coins tossed about their 'feet,' Thai women visit the shrine to implore the goddess of fertility to grant them increased fecundity. It is quite typical of Bangkok that 'penis,' 'shrine' and 'car park' can feature in the same sentence; it is cultural comedy on the one hand and cultural gold on the other. The Japanese have a penis shrine of their own (the Kanayama Shrine in Kawasaki), and the city hosts an annual penis festival (the Kanamara Matsuri) and a parade of comically large phalluses. Surprisingly for Bangkok, its penis shrine is understated and often overlooked.

Ban Baat, the 'Monk's Bowl Village,' was tricky to find but is, again, Bangkok at its authentic best. The morning alms ceremony is an incredible cultural sight to witness in predominantly Buddhist Southeast Asia, with barefoot monks wandering their local communities to receive offerings of food. My commute to work started with a short walk to the BTS Skytrain at On Nut, crossing a Tesco Lotus car park where dozens of senior men and women went about their early morning tai chi workouts. Right on cue, every morning at 7 am, a local monk interrupted their routine as bagged foods overfilled his metal bowl or 'bat.' With a quarter of a million monks and novices collecting alms in Thailand alone, that's a lot of bowls to supply. Traditionally crafted by hand, the factory floor meets the demands of an industrialised nation with the onus on 'cheaply made.'

King Rama I established three monk bowl villages in Bangkok in the eighteenth century, but history and its artisans are in decline and have all but vanished, except for a single alleyway in the Ban Baat community. The sound of hammers on steel guided me to my destination and a tradition that has shrunk to one extended family. I met friendly Amorn Kuldinksamphan, a leading welder, who explained the symbolic process of joining eight separate strips of metal (representing Buddha's Eightfold Path) into one robust and impervious form, which is hammered into shape, fused with melted copper wire, and polished and lacquered in the village. Tourists are welcome to purchase a bowl, and I keep one myself as a souvenir of my visit.

Suan Pakkard Palace showcases postcard Thailand with five traditional Thai-style pavilions. Hidden out of sight by the modern edifices of Sri Ayutthaya Road, it has few tourist visitors due to its remote location. It is worth the effort to find it as the Lacquer Pavilion (which has a history of 450 years) is visually striking, with gold murals set against a black lacquer background. When I returned to view the museum's collection of Ban Chiang pottery eight years later, I was disappointed to see the concrete insensitivity of the Airport Rail Link which passes directly overhead the pavilion.

Everything flows and nothing stands still for long in Bangkok, and every time I returned to the city, new condominiums or supermalls had sprung up to replace longstanding residential neighbourhoods. The traditions of bygone Thailand have slowly eroded in the capital, and that is why I enjoyed visiting palaces and teak houses which are relatively safe from demolition. Another wonderful find near the area of Silom - the M.R. Kukrit's Heritage Home - is a house museum like Jim Thompson's as it presents five teak houses belonging to former Prime Minister M. R. Kukrit Pramoj (the collection is dedicated to his memory). Tradition just about survives (if you know where to look for it) as the Thai capital is an insatiable beast, feeding on concrete, steel girders, electrical cabling and diesel exhaust emissions.

Bangkok is a user-friendly city of convenience which is odd, given that its planners contrived for the opposite as they threw their Lego pieces into place in the dark. Modern and excellent infrastructure makes it easy to navigate, with an MRT underground and a BTS Skytrain transporting Bangkokians and tourists to all the major and some of the minor districts. It took some time to map the neighbourhoods of Bangkok to memory, but the city can be broken down into eight distinct areas connected by concrete corridors: Sukhumvit, Lumpinee, Silom and the Riverside, Siam Square (with Pratunam and Ploenchit), Chinatown (and Phahurat), Banglamphu, Ko Ratanakosin (and Thonburi) and Thewet (with Dusit). If I wanted a taste of culture and history, I would make my way to Ko Ratanakosin, the former royal centre; for bar-hopping and elegant, contemporary dining, Sukhumvit suited my needs. For sporting interests, I adopted the Port Football Club as my second Thai team with trips to the PAT stadium in the district of Klong Toey. It was on this ground that I discovered the passion of football at the grassroots level as the stadium has a 12,000 capacity, basic facilities and a ticket usually cost 100 baht (£2). I did not have to part with my life savings for membership, and there is no such thing as an executive box.

By contrast, Jakarta, the Indonesian capital, held no interest for me at all, and it lived up to its nickname - The Big Durian - which is the world's smelliest fruit (most hotels in Bangkok ban durian and fine guests for trying to sneak it in). On first impressions, Jakarta looks like the Thai capital with its crowded, hectic sprawl, construction cranes and horrendous traffic and pollution, but there was next to nothing of interest to do. My desperation drove me to the tea plantations of the Puncak Pass, where I watched the workers pick tea for hours. If I had a thousand lives to live, I wouldn't return to Jakarta for love nor money. Bandar Seri Begawan, the capital and largest city of the Sultanate of Brunei, is an obscure place to visit, but I had a day in the capital courtesy of one of the most indirect flights I have ever taken, which flew me beyond my destination to which I had to return on a connecting flight. I had four hours of numb buttocks to look forward to in the airport's waiting lounge when I noticed an advert for a two-hour transit tour of the capital. I signed up immediately, paid for a transit visa and sat back as I was guided to the capital's points of cultural interest.

The Sultan Omar Ali Saifuddin Mosque surpasses the mosques of Istanbul for grand design, with Italian marble arches, crystal chandeliers and a dome of pure gold. It was closed to visitors, but I appreciated its flashy exterior from across a lagoon with a ceremonial boat. After five minutes of pointing and clicking, my guide whisked me off to the next stop on a cultural itinerary which included the water village of Kampong Ayer and more mosques.

Bandar Seri Begawan is an understated capital, built on the riches of oil and gas reserves much like Dubai, with urban life centred on restaurants and designer shopping malls. Brunei is a tiny state with a population of just over 400,000, but it is the fifth-richest nation in the world. My guide encouraged me to apply for work at one of the city's international schools while extolling the singular virtue of Brunei life: it is tax-free as the state is rich enough. The tour was over in less than an hour (having been padded out with a stop at a local market), and I was glad of my return to the airport as I was closer to the exit. Places such as Bandar Seri Begawan compel me to revisit Bangkok, a city of life, where alfresco dining is interrupted by indelicate salespeople pushing cheap knockoff watches, or bracelets carrying sweet and romantic messages such as 'Lick my Smorstix,' 'I rape cunt' and 'Fuck dick me now.' I came to an understanding of why Thailand is an underachiever in the English Proficiency Index as I passed signs warning: 'No smoking alcohol.' I have seen worse, as a manicure in Xi'an was advertised as a 'ManiCunt' and an Indian eatery in Kuala Lumpur went by the name of ISHITA Restaurant.

Floating markets are ever-present in Thailand like conical hats in Vietnam, but those idyllic, and wonderfully photographic scenes are harder to find than you'd imagine, with many filed under yesteryear. In a land that's in with the new, out with the old, it is a way of life that is in decline when once upon a time, travel by water was central to daily life in Thailand. Bangkok's Taling Chan has an equal mix of local and tourist visitors, and while it doesn't have much scenic charm, it is about as close to the real deal as you'll get in the capital, catering to the needs of the local Thai communities it serves, not tourists. For a market which supposedly floats, there were not many boats or traders in the water and the same can be said of Bang Nam Phueng on Bang Krachao, which is a green oasis on the Chao Phraya River beside the city.

Damnoen Saduak is Thailand's best-known floating market and it is a frequent stop off on organised tours, but it was a disappointment of epic proportions as there's nothing authentic about it, as the number of western faces outnumbers Thais by ten to one. The historical and cultural charm it once held has floated downstream, and to all intents and purposes, it is Khao San Road on the water with its vendors selling counterfeit sunglasses and baggy fishermen's pants. It was lively, and it was colourful, but Amphawa, in the district of Samut Songkhram, was the bona fide floating market I was searching for, and it matched my cultural expectations.

Amphawa is a ninety-minute journey by taxi or minivan from Victory Monument, the transport hub of the capital. A local and quaint market, it caters primarily for Thais but also welcomes tourists. It is an enjoyable experience with vintage cafes, restaurants and wooden shop-houses neatly lined along the canal to sell sweets, antiques, and books. A favourite weekend getaway for Thais, I enjoyed sitting by the water as boats pulled alongside to tempt me with barbequed delights, freshly fished from the canals and the Mae Klong River. I couldn't resist the temptation of 'boat noodles' with grilled squid and river prawns, and I communicated my delight with friendly smiles and enthusiastic nods.

There is more to explore at Amphawa than a floating market, with river tours on long-tail boats passing traditional riverside communities, fruit orchards and the abandoned, mystical temple of Wat Khai Bang Kung. The temple is barely visible to the naked eye as it is ensnared within the roots and branches of several banyan trees, which have fingered their way through open windows to form a rooftop canopy. At night, Amphawa transforms into an enchanting world of fireflies as the trees and the river banks are decorated with nature's lights, but the Maeklong Railway Market was the unexpected highlight as it is one of the most surreal and yet highly organised places I have visited on my travels. It looks like a typical open-air market of Asia with baskets full of tropical fruits such as lychee, durian, and mango or brightly coloured dried spices, pastes and herbs, but it is anything but ordinary. Famous for all the wrong reasons, it gives a two-fingered salute to the concept of health and safety.

Several trains pass through the market each day, so the vendors habitually pack up their produce with haste when the siren sounds. Low-hanging awnings and umbrellas are pulled back just in time to clear a safe passage for the train, and the market is known locally as Talat Rom Hoop, which translates to 'Market Umbrella Close.' Now you see it, now you don't. As soon as a train has passed, the rooftop canopy falls back into place in a matter of seconds, and the tracks disappear under stalls which are wheeled back into position. It was a delightfully dangerous moment to stand by the tracks, and it is a relatively tight squeeze as the train was inches from my nose when it nonchalantly made its way through the market, running over stray lemons and limes. The market workers are a well-oiled machine, and everyone knows the role they perform in the transformation, which must be one of the world's greatest magic tricks in terms of number of participants.

In Bangkok, you are always a few feet away from something sublime or uniquely strange, with an Erawan Shrine, a modest pilgrimage site at a frenetic transport intersection, and an Elephant Tower, the world's largest elephant building which has legs, a trunk, eyes, ears, and tusks. There is even a David Beckham Temple - Wat Pariwat - with a golden statue of the icon in a traditional garuda pose, set into its altar. It was in Bangkok that I had my first encounter with the third gender on the BTS Skytrain, when an impossibly beautiful woman (with a face like Princess Leia in her pomp) shattered the illusion with a voice as deep and powerful as James Earl Jones. Some of the most attractive women in Thailand are, in fact, men, and the country's transgender population is the bullseye on a board of unconventional in Southeast Asia. They are a fascination for first-time visitors, as they challenge accepted ideas of gender by using medical advancements to modify, reverse or enhance human biology. Thailand's third sex is an accepted but much-maligned and marginalised group in Thai society, but rates of transgenderism are not - as you would expect - any higher in this country than they are anywhere else in the world.

GIRES (the UK organisation that sponsors research and education on gender identity) has reported that 'at least' 1% of the UK population is gender non-conforming, while the figure is *lower* at 0.5% in Thailand with a transgender population estimated at 300,000 of the total population. Often nicknamed 'ladyboys,' 'shemales' or 'kathoeys' (the Thai term for transgender), the difference in Thailand is not the prevalence but the visibility, as they tend to congregate in tourist areas where they can find work as a curiosity in cabaret shows or go-go bars, or freelance as prostitutes. The prettiest often find employment in modelling, and the educated tend to work in service industries, while the less convincing or uneducated head for the red lights of Soi Cowboy, Patpong and Nana Plaza. Spotting the difference between a lady and a ladyboy is something of a national pastime, and they are a fascinating subject worthy of world tours, as *The Ladyboys of Bangkok* entertain their audiences by singing Disney classics such as *Let It Go* and perform fashion show catwalks in fabulously decorated outfits. I wanted to get beyond the narrow clichés of the secret world of Thailand's third gender, so I bought a copy of *Ladyboys*, a book which offers insight through intimate portraits of celebrities, cabaret performers, a champion Muay Thai fighter and sex workers.

It is a small world in Thailand on occasion, and it didn't take me long to make the connection when I recognised a stranger's face at the top of an application form for the vacancy in my department. He featured as one of the chief guests and 'experts' on the Sky Living TV series *Ladyboys*, a documentary about love and relationships with Thailand's third gender, filmed in Bangkok. He would have been an interesting colleague to chat with over tea and biscuits, had he been short-listed for interview. I had a transitioning student in one of my iGCSE classes who styled his hair with feminine curls, grew his nails long and spoke with an affected voice. He would have suffered bullying to the point of suicide in a UK school, but his peers accepted him in a country where Buddhist teachings promote toleration and acceptance. Thailand also happens to be one of the most gay-friendly countries in the world, and Bangkok is the veritable hub of gay nightlife in Southeast Asia, with dedicated rainbow streets in the district of Silom brimming with bars, saunas, and go-go boy shows. One of my former colleagues was an aficionado of Sois 2 and 4 and heralded the streets of Silom as 'the capital of Gay World.'

Bangkok has its very own genre of fiction and non-fiction, with enough colourful titles to shelve a small library. Much of Bangkok's fiction is, predictably, crime-related and clichéd, leaning heavily on stereotypes and seedy sensationalism. They represent the capital as a cultural smear campaign with all their stories sharing red-light settings populated by prostitutes and trigger-happy desperados. Bangkok is one of the safest cities in the world (when the locals aren't protesting) and I am travel-wise enough to see past the bleakness of front covers and sordid print, to find beauty in a beast of disorder whose unrelenting energy pulsates through the streets like a bull in Pamplona. And while some of these books provide interesting insights, none of their authors are likely to win Nobel prizes for literature as debauchery, crime and corruption are narrow themes for a city associated with vice.

The extensive catalogue of non-fiction is vastly superior to the fictional works, but is often harrowing and hard-hitting. Warren Fellows' *The Damage Done* offers a cautionary tale - in the autobiographical form - of the twelve years he spent behind bars in Bangkok, with sewer rats and cockroaches the only nutritious foods available to him, while Chavoret Jaruboon's *The Last Executioner* contains the honest but disturbing memoirs of Thailand's last prison executioner. *Bangkok Boy* explores the hidden and taboo world of male prostitution in Thailand, while *Miss Bangkok* presents the vivid, powerful and moving memoirs of a Thai prostitute. Bua Boonmee compares her life and fate to an escape from a tiger in the country, only to be chewed up by a crocodile in the city. By reading these titles, I was at least able to develop empathy for the country's underprivileged and a partial understanding of Thailand from a Thai perspective.

Father Joe Maier's *Welcome to the Bangkok Slaughterhouse (The Battle for Human Dignity in Bangkok's Bleakest Slums)* introduced me to the capital's largest slum neighbourhood in the district of Klong Toey. As a Redemptorist priest from the United States, he has selflessly devoted his life to the poor, establishing the Human Development Foundation in 1972 to release families from the self-fulfilling cycle of drugs, violence, sexual abuse and prostitution which prevails in the squatter slums. Bangkok is a city of contrasts, and its slums are often hidden out of sight beneath bridges and multi-laned freeways, only a few stops on the metro from the five-star hotels and luxurious malls in the Sukhumvit area. The 'haves' and the 'have-nots' share horizontal space but find separation on the vertical axis, with middle class aspirations accommodated by high-rise apartments and condominiums. The wealthy, quite literally, look down on the poor and socially immobile.

There are 5,500 slum communities in Thailand, and I took (for want of better words) a 'poverty tour' of Klong Toey, which is home to 100,000 Bangkok residents. Guided by slum resident Saiyuud Diwong (known to her friends by her nickname, Poo, which she explained means 'crab'), I was given a tour of the slum as we sourced fresh ingredients for a cooking class in a chaotic conglomeration of fresh fruits, vegetables, and live produce. Passing buckets of jumping frogs, slippery eels, bowls of water bugs and platters of pigs' heads, I wondered what kind of cooking class I had signed up for. Poo did, however, show me how to cook three traditional Thai dishes from scratch (pomelo salad, chicken with basil and taro in coconut milk) while I proudly wore an apron with white-on-black print: 'I've cooked with Poo and I liked it.'

Poo has released a book of classic Thai recipes (*Cooking with Poo*, which won the 'World's Weirdest Book Title' award in 2012) and I continue to follow her instructions at home. Every sizzle and stir is a reminder of the people of Klong Toey who, despite their grinding poverty, poor housing, putrefying sewage and unmanaged waste, have access to the capital's freshest wet market ingredients. It is, perhaps, the thinnest of linings on an all-encompassing cloud. Spending time with Poo and her neighbours was like stepping through a portal to the capital's hushed and unseen worlds, but for a city with western pretensions, it is nothing more than an eyesore. The authorities prefer their tourists to focus on dazzling mosaics and grand temple complexes.

It is quite easy to get 'templed out' in Thailand as the country has 40,717 Buddhist temples, and some of these are Thailand's most celebrated attractions. The very best of Bangkok's temples are conveniently clustered in the area of Ko Rattanakosin (the old city) but, somewhat inconveniently, neither the BTS Skytrain nor the MRT underground serves this part of the city. I hopped off the BTS at Saphan Taksin for a scenic boat ride to Pier 8 (Tha Tien) and a short walk to the ever-popular Grand Palace. The palace houses

Wat Phra Kaew (commonly known as 'The Temple of the Emerald Buddha') which is the most sacred and visited temple in Bangkok. Inside it sits the Emerald Buddha ('borrowed' and returned by Laos), carved from a solid block of jade, which has been revered by the Thais for centuries as a palladium of Thai society. Only a king or a crown prince can touch it, when they change its seasonal costumes to mark the beginning of summer, 'winter' (as far as Thais know it) and the rainy season.

Close to the Grand Palace is Wat Pho ('The Temple of the Reclining Buddha'), a temple I frequently visited as it houses a gigantic, reclining Buddha. The beautiful, soft lighting and shimmering gold leaf surfaces of this 5-meter-high, 43-meter-long image are stunning to behold, and the interior temple walls showcase a thousand exquisite imaginings of Buddhist heaven, which are often ignored as eyes gravitate toward the magisterial elegance of the restful Buddha. Wat Arun ('The Temple of Dawn') is one of the most recognisable landmarks in Bangkok, and it is hard to miss it as it sits in a prominent position on the Thonburi bank of the Chao Phraya River. Wat Arun is a Khmer-style temple, uniquely decorated with seashells and broken porcelain. It is the city's second major landmark after the Grand Palace, and it offers an incredible view of the skyline from its upper platforms. Wat Saket supports a giant, golden chedi and was once the tallest building in the capital, with three hundred steps offering a vertical hike. Wat Traimit, Loha Prasat, Wat Mahatat, Wat Suthat, Wat Benjamabhopit and Wat Prayoon are all beautiful attractions, but it took me eight years to complete Bangkok's cultural trail and discover more unusual religious buildings, such as the Erawan and David Beckham temples.

As a tax and bill-paying resident, I explored all the tourist trails at least a dozen times. I found new ways to appreciate the city by taking to its fringes in up-and-coming Thai neighbourhoods, such as Udom Suk, or by relaxing in its green spaces such as the beautiful King Rama IX Park, or Mueang Boran with its miniatures of Thailand's temples and palaces. Green spaces fight for survival, but at least they are well-maintained and a welcome escape from the capital cacophony. The small pottery island of Ko Kret and Bang Krachao - Bangkok's green lungs - offer respite from the cultural overload. With boat crossings from Klong Toey pier to a small wooden dock at Bang Krachao, I hired a bicycle and followed cycle routes through orchards and gardens, stopping at village temples, Talad Nam Peung floating market and the lovely Sri Nakhon Khuan Khan Park. Some of my Thai colleagues had never heard of it, while those that had never ventured to set foot on the island (which may as well be invisible, despite its prominent placing on the Chao Phraya River).

Whenever it got too hot for comfort, I would escape to Snow Town at Dream World, an amusement park on the outskirts of the city. On Nut was my residential neighbourhood and its night market was an extended kitchen before it was bulldozed, as my apartment had every modern facility except an oven to cook. As time passed, I lived more like a local, stopping for street food on my commute with bottles of Coca-Cola poured into bags of ice at stalls that served barbequed tripe. I lived like a king in Thailand, and that is part of the appeal, as upmarket sky bars offer 'buy one, get one free' cocktails and five-star hotels come at budget rates in the low season. The country accommodates every wallet and purse from limos to songthaews, luxury hotels to homestays in slums, but it is a city changing by degrees.

The military government is overseeing a steady makeover of Bangkok's streets: improvised bars, flower and street markets are succumbing to red tape strangleholds as city aesthetics fall into line with those of the Asian Tigers. At least they'll never be able to take my memories away.

## Chapter 41: Politics and Protests

You don't often get the opportunity to stand in the middle of a breaking-news story, surrounded by live international media coverage, and spectate as each chapter of its bloody narrative unfolds. But there I stood on the embattled streets of Bangkok, as the anti-government protests of November 2013 to May 2014 engulfed the city in a political rage. It marked a period of seven months of turmoil and instability in Thailand, but it wasn't the first insurrection of its kind, as the Thais prefer their politics with a capital 'P.'

They are also rather fond of another eight-letter word beginning with the same initial consonant: protests. As more fuel poured onto a fire prodded by untold sticks, the conflict intensified and burnt a gaping hole in Thailand's tourism industry as worldwide embassies issued warnings to defer all travel to the country until the dust of political reform had settled. With the economy taking a series of damaging hits, something had to give, and it was the government that was eventually knocked out after several fiercely contested and lively rounds, despite its clever footwork, dodging, ducking and weaving.

The People's Democratic Reform Committee (the PDRC) was a meticulously well-organised pressure group led by former Democratic Party MP Suthep Thaugsuban, who is now held, indefinitely, as a political prisoner of Thailand. His anti-government campaign gathered considerable momentum under his charismatic leadership, and he reminded me of a fascinating study by Laurence Rees, which explores how Adolf Hitler's dark charisma enabled him to lead millions of people into the abyss. As I listened to the carefully crafted rhetoric of Thaugsuban's speeches at strategically placed rally points across the capital (where he whipped his supporters into a frenzy of disruptive intent), I was distracted by his incredibly long index fingers. He reminded me of ET the Extra-Terrestrial as he pointed from a makeshift stage to supporters armed with umbrellas, calling on them to make a stand for Thailand by shutting down the capital and ousting a corrupt government.

Thaugsuban's PDRC was unrelenting in its commitment to the cause, fixing the focus of its campaign on a single, but predictable, common enemy: Prime Minister Yingluck Shinawatra. The Shinawatras are a prominent and wealthy family but a politically distrusted dynasty; it was the actions of former Prime Minister Thaksin Shinawatra (a business tycoon and corrupt politician) that brought the Shinawatra family name into disrepute. When he sold more than a billion dollars of shares in his corporation to foreign investors without paying a single baht in taxes, a movement of the people (the People's Alliance for Democracy) revolted against perceived corruption and abuse of power, instigating a sequence of mass protests. The anti-Thaksin campaigners were identifiable by the bright yellow shirts they wore when they gathered to march, and the group was, consequently, labelled 'the yellow shirts.'

Thailand's politics are colour-coded, and the Thai people are as obsessed with colour schemes as they are with national and royal flags. The anti-Thaksin protesters usurped King Bhumibol Adulyadej's royal colour, so loyalists to the crown had to think twice about what they wore, especially on Mondays, as yellow acquired a new connotation. Bangkok is the only city in the world where I was anxious about making a fashion faux pas which could be misinterpreted as a political statement of allegiance. The Thai government issued warnings to foreigners that should they be spotted marching with and supporting the demonstrators (which I assumed to imply, by extension, wearing their colours), they would be arrested and deported. I didn't want to take my chances with deportation or a wounded government's wrath as I had too much to lose, but I still followed the protests with interest, taking on the role of an apolitical, non-participant observer as I performed a mime of journalistic disinterest from behind the lens of my Canon camera.

My first teaching year in Thailand was routinely disrupted by anti-government protests as schemes of learning were abandoned, the curriculum was modified and condensed, and exam schedules discarded. The Principal emailed repeated warnings to overseas staff to stay away from conflict zones and, better still, to stock up on essential provisions and lock up at home. He was concerned about the potential deaths and deportations of his staff, but I suspected he wanted to avoid an impromptu recruitment drive midway through the school year. It would have been a hard sell too, as not many sane and functioning adults choose to uproot and live and work in a conflict zone.

School closed for single days and weeks on end, with its central location in Phaya Thai District close to one of the key rally points at Victory Monument. Overseas staff made the most of this opportunity to leave Thailand 'for their safety' as they escaped to the sandy havens of the Maldives and Madagascar. A whole-staff email delivered the opportunity for an unexpected adventure: 'School will remain closed for the next two weeks, possibly longer. Please be safe.' Safe from what? The only protection I needed was sun cream and insect repellent. I emailed some work to my students, packed my rucksack and headed north to the historical kingdoms of Sukhothai and Si Satchanalai.

Hollywood actor Owen Wilson had a politically close shave with the Thai authorities while he was filming the thriller *No Escape* on location in Thailand, a story about an American family caught amid a bloody and violent coup which breaks out in an unnamed Asian country. The film's subject matter, and the timing of the location shooting, couldn't have been much worse, as scenes of fictional protesters clashing violently with the authorities raised a few eyebrows. Art and script had imitated life, before life imitated art when Wilson was inadvertently placed at risk of incarceration when a Thai fan put a whistle around his neck (with a ribbon showing Thailand's national colours) and posted a photo update to social media. The actor, unwittingly, posed with a symbol which identified him as a supporter of the anti-government movement. The production office received a phone call from the Thai Prime Minister threatening Wilson with immediate detention, but timing and happenstance were on his side as he had already left the country as the production had wrapped.

When interviewed by the *New York Post*, Wilson light-heartedly reflected on his time in Thailand and a sticky situation from which he may have had no escape: 'There's a fine line between being in a good story and being in a Thai prison.' Three of my devil-may-care colleagues made the most of the opportunity for self-promotion when their school band performed live at a protest site at the central Ratchaprasong Junction, with thousands of excited agitators mistaking a geography, art and primary teacher for a famous international boy band. The event and their faces were broadcast live on Thai television, so it was a high-risk gamble they got away with as they expanded their fan base and released their first single. They certainly knew how to profit from a protest.

Thailand is a country of confusions and contradictions. Having walked past 'fashionable' young Thais wearing T-shirts emblazoned with sequined Nazi swastikas, or a picture of Jesus Christ dressed in a bloody crown of thorns with the slogan 'Jesus is a cunt' (popularised by British extreme metal act Cradle of Filth, it is, quite possibly, history's most controversial casual wear), I frowned and shrugged my shoulders when a friend (wearing a pink T-shirt with an image of the Buddha wearing headphones) was stopped in her tracks and lambasted with angry words. I suggested she never wear it again in Thailand, where images of the Buddha are sacred and sacrilegious acts are punishable by a life behind bars, even when they are unintentional. The best course for the visitor is to tread lightly.

While preparing for my return to the UK in 2015, I wrapped and packed a silver statue of the Buddha that I had purchased as a tasteful souvenir of my travels. It was, however, seized at the airport as my luggage was scanned at the security gate; the customs official explained to me that all images of the

Buddha are sacred (even the ones manufactured in Sweden) and therefore belong to the Thais, not foreigners. I surrendered Buddha without complaint, and I suspect he now looks rather fetching on a shelf inside that customs official's house, instead of my own.

When friends ignored travel warnings to visit from the Netherlands in February 2014, the government and the demonstrators had reached a deadlock in their dispute, but neither side was ever going to back down and lose face, so the violence only escalated on both sides. I advised them not to pack any yellows or reds and suggested their country's national colour would be the ideal and neutral choice, as orange is a mixture of both. Orange was the new Switzerland. To my frustration, I couldn't wear some of my Manchester United football shirts as red was, initially, the colour of the pro-Thaksin supporters before his deposition; their support was transferred to Thailand's ruling Pheu Thai party when his younger sister, Yingluck, followed in his footsteps of power without responsibility.

Thaksin was thrown out of office in September 2006 by a coup d'état, and a military junta was installed to re-establish the rule of law on the streets and transparency in governance. I had just returned from my first holiday to Thailand, so I was transfixed to my television screen when I watched BBC news stories about riots and rampaging demonstrators, armed with wooden bats and iron bars, as they surged through police cordons to storm the sprawling terminals and lay siege to Suvarnabhumi International Airport. With all international flights cancelled, the timing of my exit was rather fortuitous, to say the least, but as I had been tucked away in the quiet southern district of Hua Hin for the last week of my holiday, I was completely oblivious to all the capital chaos. There is a thick line between a summer getaway and living as an expat in a foreign country.

Thaksin's party was eventually toppled, outlawed and barred from all political activity. To avoid any further sanctions, Thaksin boarded a private jet and now lives in self-imposed exile with his billions. It was a shrewd move as he was sentenced, in absentia, to two years in prison for political abuses of power and criminal corruption charges, though he is unlikely to serve a single day behind bars. He was smart enough not to insult the king's dog as that would have carried a far harsher sentence, and he was too busy socially for jail time as he sought political asylum in the UK and bought himself a Premier League football club with all those unpaid taxes: the sky blue shirts of Manchester City. The writing was, however, on the wall for future generations of the Shinawatra family (they remain tainted by his legacy a decade later).

Some Shinawatra family members brought misfortune and shame upon themselves, only to consolidate the Shinawatra association with familial corruption.

The Thai people regarded Yingluck Shinawatra as a political proxy - a puppet whose strings big brother Thaksin was pulling from afar. As such, they remained deeply sceptical and uncomfortable with the holding influence the Shinawatra family managed to maintain over the political landscape of their country. Yingluck was successful in business before she turned to politics, and she became Thailand's first female prime minister when she led her party to victory in the 2011 elections. She remained in post for three years, until she presided over the controversial decision to grant a blanket amnesty bill which would have pardoned corrupt politicians and absolved them of all their former charges (had it been passed into law). The tide turned against her as her brother would have been one of the beneficiaries of the proposed bill. It was rejected unanimously by the Senate of Thailand, and a flamethrower engulfed the blue touch paper.

Yingluck's political credibility dissolved faster than a gummy bear in hydrochloric acid as mass rallies called for her resignation and the dissolution of her Pheu Thai government. History was repeating itself, but she held onto power and its privileges with chipped polish and broken nails. As widespread violence resulted in twenty-eight deaths and eight hundred injuries, she declared a 'national state of emergency' in an opportunistic attempt to regain control of the streets. The protesters had other ideas: they were never going to return voluntarily to a Pandora's Box that she and her government had opened.

In Thailand's political pantomime, Yingluck Shinawatra was cast as the vilified public figure, while Suthep Thaugsuban took on the role of the people's hero whose 'cause' he championed with appeasing hyperbole. A ridiculous campaign image featured a professionally edited photograph and poster of Suthep, surrounded by journalists in military fatigues, as he punched the air with the flag of Thailand fluttering above his head. It heavily plagiarised the iconic 1945 photograph of six servicemen as they raised the American flag over Mount Suribachi during the battle of Iwo Jima in the Second World War, which I recognised immediately as I have visited the enormous statue of the same scene, the Marine Corps War Memorial in Washington DC. Suthep developed an elevated sense of self and his powers, delusions of grandeur, as throngs of protesters marched behind him through the capital, cheering, waving and whistling in a whirlwind of adulation. He believed in his hype and

God-like influence, as propagandist images of the people's leader outnumbered pictures of the king and even Tongdaeng the loyal, royal dog.

Political banners read more like theatre advertisements and some were quite extreme in their message, such as the dual-language notice in Thai and English - draped over a roadblock barrier at Asoke Interjunction - which demanded: 'Devil Shinawatra family go to the deepest hell.' For dramatic emphasis, the last five words were written in hell-red with a dripping-blood font. Some placards were more restrained with a simple 'NO MORE Shinawatras' or 'Yingluck Shinawatra GET OUT, GO AWAY from Thailand,' while others presented images of Thaksin and Yingluck dressed as blood-sucking vampires with ropes about their necks. Poster designers also used 'humour,' with a picture of Suthep's enlarged boot kicking Yingluck's ass out of Thailand and into Dubai where she could, presumably, join her brother in a state of exile. Intelligent and impersonal banners focused on the real issue at stake with 'All Thais against corruption!' while others had no message, subtlety or intelligence at all: 'Yingluck, FUCK YOU!'

The Constitutional Court removed Yingluck from office in May 2014, but the drama didn't end there, as the Thai Royal Army declared a state of martial law and followed this up with a coup and the ousting of her entire government. Like her brother before her, she was arrested and found guilty of abusing her power, and impeached for a controversial subsidy scheme which paid farmers well above market rates for their rice in - surprise, surprise - strongholds of party support. It was simple Math for Yingluck as she is an educated woman with a master's degree in the politics of public administration: she paid for the votes of the rural poor and bought her party's landslide victory and election to power. Incredibly, she had never run for office or held a government post before her rapid rise and appointment as Prime Minister of Thailand. She is banned from politics and faces criminal charges which could result in a prison term, but like her brother, she is unlikely to serve a single day behind bars. Thaksin and Yingluck have been cast as the toxic twins of Thai politics.

Army General and former Commander in Chief of the Thai Royal Army, Prayuth Chan-ocha, stepped into the breach as acting Prime Minister (and Head of the National Council for Peace and Order) when the military replaced a civilian government. Historian and moralist, John Emerich Edward Dalberg Acton, observed in 1887 that 'Power tends to corrupt, and absolute power corrupts absolutely,' so onlookers were wise to reserve judgement as a new military order, much like Myanmar's ousted military government, warmed its buttocks in the Thai socio-political driving seat. Having restored order to the streets, removed the entrenched protesters and revived Thailand's faltering economy and tourism industry, a military-dominated national legislature (Prayuth cherry-picked its members) voted him into power as Thailand's twenty-ninth Prime Minister in August 2014. He has since smothered all dissent, and he has no opposition party to contest his rule, having become the root and branch of Thailand's political system. What seems to be different in Thailand is quite often the same, *same but different*.

Some of my fondest memories of living in Thailand include, oddly, those anti-government campaigns and all the months of protesting, marching, and holidaymaking. The streets pulsated with a raw energy and carnival atmosphere as entrepreneurs made the most of their opportunity to turn the city into a giant, unlicensed open-air market selling all manner of protest merchandise like the musical memorabilia for sale at festivals such as Reading and Glastonbury. Groups of women sat on nylon sheets to craft handmade handbags, necklaces, bracelets and earrings as they struggled to meet the demands of protesters who were eager to display their support for the cause by wearing their national colours in every way imaginable.

At each rally point, huge PA systems were set up for live bands to entertain the crowds and keep them there, away from the air-conditioned comfort of their homes. The city transformed into a campsite with more tents than cockroaches; admission was free, and there was no requirement to wear a wristband so I could come and go as I pleased. Every detail of convenience was thoughtfully considered, with mobile toilet units, food stalls, and rice kitchens which fed the poor and kept them coming back for more, while rows of soft leather armchairs enticed the weary for post-march foot massages. Bottled water was handed out freely, and Bangkok was a community united by the spirit of political revolution. It was a festival of politics.

Thais tend to be conservative in public, especially when interacting with foreigners, but during periods of prolonged protest their social masks slipped and any divisions between rich and poor, young and old, Thais and foreigners, were lost in the crowds. Strangers wanted to talk to me, sit and eat with me and pose for selfies. It was the only time (except for the Songkran festival) that I felt genuinely accepted by the people of Thailand, rather than tolerated as a tax-paying expat. The disorder was a cultural icebreaker. I hadn't experienced anything remotely like it before, and the city was unrecognisable as I walked along main roads turned into improvised markets that would, ordinarily, clog with traffic. The occasional placard reminded me that a greater purpose was at work with messages such as 'This is Thai People's Revolution,' but I was unconvinced the crowds were as politically motivated as they claimed to be. They were having sanook and plenty of sabai, as the street encampments were full of sleeping Thais who only roused themselves for handouts, the next live act or a celebrity appearance.

The capital was awash in revolutionary rhetoric and the colours of the national flag decorated rally points and camping sites. Bangkok was the capital of smiles - genuine, unaffected smiles - as the people had taken it back for themselves and were bathing in the sunshine of their anarchy. The city certainly looked more appealing as Bangkok is cement-grey, and the protesters repainted it a rainbow of colours. The protests were a welcome escape from everyday drudgery and life's hardships, and it was a period of partying turmoil that was more Kafkaesque than a Franz Kafka novel.

On the morning of January 13th, 2014, the 'Shutdown Bangkok' campaign was officially launched as the protesters stepped up their efforts to overthrow Yingluck's government. I couldn't resist the fervour, so I bought a souvenir T-shirt with the catchy-clever slogan: 'Shutdown Bangkok: Restart Thailand.' As I was leaving my apartment, the building manager displayed a sign in the lift with the subject heading: 'Emergency Plan for Bangkok Shutdown.' As the marchers had disconnected water and electricity supplies, this apparently made him anxious as he advised: 'The building management would like to ask all residents to prepare some water and flashlight for water and electricity cut off.' It was an exciting time to be living in a city under siege, with major road intersections blocked off by thousands of demonstrators, and government buildings occupied by force as pressure mounted. It was also an unusual time to show friends and first-time visitors around the city.

The main protest sites were strategically located to cause maximum disruption to travel infrastructures, but the festival atmosphere was only a deception, as people were shot and killed on the streets as the music played on. Trudging along in the heat, I mingled with the marchers and found it hard not to be swept up by such proud patriotism and political devotion. In the UK, ballot box apathy is the antonym of Thai politics. While I was enjoying a relaxing foot massage, I heard an explosion and asked the masseuse if she could change the television channel to one of the international news outlets. As she fidgeted with the control, I asked her what she thought had created the noise. With all the dispassion her boredom could muster, she replied:

'Just bomb.'

Like 'penis' and 'shrine,' I never expected to hear 'just' and 'bomb' combined in the same sentence.

International embassies, not surprisingly, encouraged their nationals to desist with travel plans to Thailand, and a tragic episode served as a reminder of the thinly veiled dangers when two children lost their lives to an improvised explosive device at a protest site next to a busy intersection. Crowds were protesting peacefully, lost in the live music and political speeches, when a family pushed through the throng to return home from a meal at a KFC restaurant. They were victims of time and place, and as their son's brain matter leaked onto the streets of the capital, the pressure mounted on the military to intervene and act as decisively as it had done during the Thaksin revolt. The police were outnumbered, out-armed and powerless to prevent wave after wave of street violence as buses were set alight and police officers were confronted and killed. Explosions could be heard all over the city, and the targets included a politician's house, protesters and bystanders at rally sites. Television news cameras even captured the gruesome moment when a grenade was thrown by a demonstrator at a police line during clashes at Phan Fah Bridge. As one of the officers tried to kick it away, it exploded and blew his lower leg right off, live on air.

To maximise the fear and level of threat on the streets, trained snipers moved in and covertly took out their targets. These gunmen were labelled 'the popcorn shooters' as one of them was caught on camera taking aim, using an empty popcorn bag to disguise his rifle during a shootout at a shopping centre. Their targets were pro-government red-shirt supporters who were the perfect stand-out targets for anti-government snipers. My Manchester United home shirts remained in their drawer. Indefinitely. The army tried to maintain its neutrality as its troops became targets for bullets and bombs, but when grenades fired from shoulder-mounted launchers, its hand was forced and a military coup was inevitable. Pockets of violence had become widespread, as Bangkok turned into the setting for a violent computer game like *Manhunt*. With the world watching, the crisis was brought to a swift end. Political violence claimed the lives of three innocent children, including a five-year-old girl, which was a high price to pay for a political fallout.

Most my interactions with the protesters were positive; some were even keen to be photographed, perhaps wrongly assuming if I was a photojournalist working for some heady overseas publication. When the headquarters of the Royal Thai Police were infiltrated with the potential for violent clashes, I took an elevated position on the BTS Skywalk to ensure I was beyond the range of stray bullets. The police sat motionless behind railings, impotent and castrated by the masses before them, as unimaginative graffiti artists sprayed ill-thought abuse which included 'Suck Police!' and 'Fuck Thai Police.'

I feared, on just the one occasion, that my presence could lead to a confrontation with protesters, and that was at Democracy Monument, a key rally point and camp community which resembled a scene from a post-apocalyptic *Mad Max* film, with roadside bunkers formed of sandbags and stacked rubber tyres set on fire. Hostility was omnipresent, and I detected repeated mutterings of 'farang' as I made my way through worn-out encampments. I was confident that 'farang,' in this context, was an insult. Scowls replaced smiles, as this part of town lost its sense of humour and joie de vivre. I put my camera back in its carry case and moved on, preferring not to run my head into a noose of its making like Thanakorn Siripaiboon. Ominous graffiti guided me home as I passed the image of an empty chair with a hooded figure standing next to it, pointing with a sword dripping with blood. Above it, the words 'You're next' were spray-painted in blood-red.

The first rule for safe passage through Thailand is never to speak openly about the royal family. The second rule is not to discuss Thai politics, especially with Thais. Politics is a sensitive subject, and the military government has a strict policy of sending political dissidents to 'attitude adjustment' camps. How Orwellian is that? I kept my opinions to myself and avoided unnecessary run-ins with the Thought Police of Thailand.

# Chapter 42: Songkran Festival

The Songkran festival is the world's largest outdoor water fight and the liquid embodiment of the phrases 'organised chaos' and 'young at heart.' Jolly snipers stalk the streets with an arsenal comprised of a beaming smile, waterproofing and colourful, cheaply made water guns and blasters. I read about the festival in guidebooks and on travel websites, which forewarned their readers to be forearmed with aquatic pistols, machine guns and pump-action shotguns (ideally, the bigger, the better). I bought a fully automatic water-Uzi at a market stall on Sukhumvit Road and made my way through Bangkok's street parties with all the indestructible finality of Arnold Schwarzenegger's *Terminator*. Thais make the most of their opportunities for sanook, and with April the hottest month of the year, a combination of high spirits and intense tropical heat naturally equates to spraying cold water over every stranger who crosses your path. It makes perfect sense.

Thailand's Songkran, Germany's Oktoberfest and Mexico's Day of the Dead celebration are cultural events I serially missed, but I had an alternative - and entirely unexpected - Oktoberfest when I stumbled upon a small piece of Deutschland in the city of Yokohama. Japan's faithful drinkfest replica takes place on the waterfront in the historic Yokohama Redbrick Warehouse, with more than a hundred German beers available (including some of the official Munich Oktoberfest brews), Bavarian oompah bands, lederhosen and buxom bier maidens clutching fistfuls of empty steins.

An excursion to see Hikawa Maru - the famous wartime hospital ship - turned into a weekend of mirthfulness and drunken revelry, sauerkraut and sausages. My narrow perception of the Japanese people completely turned on its head as monochromatic, suited and serious city workers transformed in front of my eyes as they were dressed with smiles, unreserved friendliness, and comical beer hats. I was grabbed by the shoulders as strangers cajoled me to dance like my dad, and I stood shoulder-to-shoulder with Japanese beer buddies as we joined in choruses of *Ein Prosit* every fifteen minutes, raising our steins to answer the band's question (Are you having fun?) with an 'Oi! Oi! Oi!' I enjoyed my cultural pilgrimage to Japan, but this festival experience topped all the golden pavilions, imperial palaces and iconic mountains that came before it. For the very first time, I saw the Japanese people without the social mask. Prost!

I was determined to make my first Songkran and Thai New Year celebration an equally unforgettable experience, long before I had a single memory to forget. There is no better way to get to the heart of a foreign country than to observe its customs and traditions and, ideally, the stranger the better. Travel should be transformational, a break from daily routines, but it is all too easy to fall into the trap of ritualisation by taking holidays that lack any real sense of discovery. Passing out beside the pool with a book in one hand and a cocktail the other seems the obvious, effortless antidote to months of long hours in the office, but there is a limited return on the investment other than rest and bar bills.

Emile Durkheim, the late French sociologist and social psychologist, introduced the concept of a 'collective effervescence,' which is the notion that when people are in proximity to each other, they generate a social electricity. The individual finds transformation from a single pulse and outlook to a collective mindset and energy which, in turn, elevates the group to a higher level of euphoria. Collective effervescence erodes social barriers and prejudices and creates a shared space for foreigners and locals to mix and be together, enjoying their time celebrating and making memories with a focus that is bigger than themselves. Cultural festivals are the absolute of collective effervescence.

La Tomatina (the Tomato Throwing Festival), for example, is a popular annual event in the town of Bunol, near Valencia in Spain. With Songkran similarities, the festival takes place on the last Wednesday of August with thousands of people flocking, spilling and slipping into town from all over the world to participate in the world's leading food fight. The population of backcountry Bunol stands at just nine thousand, but this figure has swollen to more than fifty thousand during the festival week with the town, its guest houses and restaurants bursting at the seams. The authorities have since introduced a ticketing system to control the chaos and reduce visitor numbers, which are now capped at twenty thousand tomato throwers. With 175,000 metric tonnes of ripe tomatoes tossed through the air and bespattered all over streets and buildings in a single hour in 2015, the festival is a colourful and fabulous advert for the local tourism industry, but I doubt whether Bunol's street cleaners would agree with me.

The festival officially begins at 11 am once the tomato transports have deposited their weapons of mass discolouration in the town's centre, Plaza del Pueblo, and a brave soul has managed to mount a greased pole to claim the 'prize' of a joint of ham. When the coveted meat feast is successfully wrestled free and presented to the gods like a fleshy Jules Rimet trophy, water cannons douse the crowds to signal the commencement of a red-fruit bloodletting and it's every man, woman, and child for themselves. There are some 'rules' to be followed as participants are instructed to squash tomatoes in their hands before throwing them at strangers, as this lessens the impact of contact and potential injuries. The festival lasts for just the one hour before the carnage is brought to an abrupt end by a gunshot when everyone is expected to surrender their ripened grenades as red pulp drips from pedestrians and lamp posts. Conveniently, the mess cleans itself up, as the citric and malic acids disinfect the streets and pavements shine in the midday sun. Tourists and locals head for the showers before lunch, with a cultural memory that will not wash.

It is the remembrance of these exciting festivals that I tend to cherish and play on repeat months and years later, not the miles of beaches, parasols and cocktails with outlandish names and decorative umbrellas. You simply cannot compare the frenzy of La Tomatina with Sex on the Beach. La Tomatina has no political or religious significance; it is just good, old-fashioned and messy fun. What it does provide is the opportunity for an immersive cultural experience. I will forget, with time, a thousand beautiful churches and cathedrals I visited in this region of the world, but I will never forget that first tomato that hit a stranger's face, or that bucket of cold water that was poured over my head as I sat down to dinner on Khao San Road. American author Pat Conroy was right when he observed: 'Once you have travelled, the voyage never ends, but is played out over and over again in the quietest chambers. The mind can never break off from the journey.'

When I returned to the UK for my first New Year's Eve celebration for some time, I longed for the grip of a water gun in my hand as the chimes of Big Ben counted down to midnight and a spectacular firework display that was all over in eleven freezing-cold minutes. The Thais know how to stage a political protest, but they also know how to put the 'P' in a party when they countdown to a New Year.

Thailand's Songkran festival is the traditional New Year celebration, but it is also observed (with variations on the theme) in Myanmar, Cambodia, Laos, Yunnan Province in Southwest China and the states of Assam and Arunachal Pradesh in India. It is, without a doubt, the most important event of the calendar year though most Thais will, of course, cite King's Day (Father's Day) and National Mother's Day. Both are rather serious, stuffy affairs with the onus on ritual formality as the King and Queen of Thailand are the nation's ceremonial father and mother. Flags and portraits mark the occasion and dominate the visual spectrum, but during the festival days of Songkran, water is king and having fun is his decree.

Songkran marks the end of the dry season and takes place between the 12th and 15th of April. From a foreigner's point of view, it is a crazed celebration of early childhood years as adults behave like children, without fear of judgement, and strangers can be friends in an instant. The whole of Thailand is embroiled and saturated by a week-long water fight accompanied by music and dancing, and it is impossible to resist the urge to join in. Had Ebenezer Scrooge lived in Thailand, he would have left his counting house to take part in the splish-splashing jollity. There is a spiritual focus to the festival as 'making merit' is an essential element of Songkran, with the expectation that Thais will visit nine sacred temples during the festival period. On the first day of Songkran, Thais celebrate Rod Nam Dum Hua (National Elderly Day) with the younger generations of a family pouring fragrant water onto the palms of their elders in a gesture of humility, which doubles as a request for a blessing. The second day of Songkran, National Family Day, is all about quality time with loved ones and the ritual of bathing images of the Buddha, which again earns merit and blessings for the whole family. Once the formalities and the rites and rituals are out of the way, Songkran takes on a more festive note. Cue the tourists.

My introduction to Songkran took place on the waterpark streets of the capital, where the pavements would benefit from a La Tomatina-type cleaning. I had three weeks to get comfortable in my life's new shoes before I started the serious work of my new teaching post, and Songkran was the perfect ice-breaker. I wondered what my new employers would make of my neon combat fatigues when they last saw me wearing a three-piece suit on interview in London, where I was mindful of my Ps and Qs and just about every other letter of the alphabet. For my next Songkran, I travelled north to Thailand's second city: Chiang Mai. Famous for its New Year celebrations, a moat surrounds the city core - the perfect refilling station - and a ring road doubles as a circuit for the brave and daring, as tuk-tuk drivers are mercilessly sprayed and splashed as they pass gun-toting, kerbside water warriors. Motorcyclists are fair game too, and can have whole buckets of liquid thrown in their faces. It comes as no surprise that there is an annual spike in the death rate during Songkran, as alcohol fuels bravado with 442 Songkran-related deaths, 3,656 injuries and 3,447 accidents reported in 2016.

The wettest and most exuberant festival spots in the capital are Silom Road, where mostly Thais gather for a soapy frolicking at foam parties, and Khao San Road, which is popular with backpackers. The backpackers intermittently exchange bottles of beer for squirt guns and buckets of ice-cold water (the deadliest weapon) as they go in search of warm and unsuspecting victims (while completely forgetting about the harmful effects of the sun). The locals pass the intelligence test every year, as they celebrate Songkran beneath the platform shade of the BTS Skytrain. Wherever you are in Thailand, you don't have to be set on fire for a perfect stranger to pour a whole bucket of water over your head - a total lack of awareness of those around you will do the trick, even while you are eating. The festival fervour should be embraced with an open heart but a closed mouth, as the water is sourced wherever it is available. Dedicated Thais go to the extreme of literally filling up their pickup trucks with water so they can drive and slosh around the city uninterrupted, with a constant water supply, as friends and family sit in the depths of the flat tray, shielded behind hinged panels which also form an improvised mobile swimming pool.

It is hard to believe that Thailand's most important public holiday is a Buddhist festival; time has changed tradition with the custom of pouring scented water over statues of the Buddha usurped by neon super-soakers and foam machines. Thais welcome the break from the sun as Songkran allows them time off work to return to the provinces of their births for family reunions, to visit and worship at family temples and scrub clean the family home and shrine. The symbolic ritual of cleansing and purification washes away former sins and misfortunes to usher in optimism, renewal and the hoped-for prosperity of a fresh calendar year. The word 'Songkran' is derived from the Sanskrit word 'Sankranti' (which means 'astrological passage') and it refers to a period of transformation and change in the cycle of the seasons and the solar calendar. It reminded me of April Fools' Day as strangers played water-themed pranks, with westerners the target of choice as I had a seven-day target marker fixed to my head.

I will never forget the day I took a shortcut down Soi Cowboy to meet friends on parallel Sukhumvit Road. Unarmed and wearing a thick cotton shirt and even thicker cotton shorts, one of the working girls ran at me from behind to pour a whole bucket of near-frozen water over my head. With an ice cube lodged in my shirt pocket, my water nemesis pointed at my chest and smiled from behind teeth covered in wire dental braces. All I could see before me was a power chain with rubber bands, and I was disarmed by her impression of Jaws from the James Bond films *The Spy Who Loved Me* and *Moonraker*. The only reply I could think to make was to smile back, thankful for my saturation. I failed to correct a prior fashion mistake when I wore a pair of super-thin, white Manchester United shorts which soaked right through to reveal my Charlie and the Sperm Factory to the world. With my face covered in din sor pong (a sign of protection, it is a natural white powder Thais mix with water to create a paste which they smear all over strangers' faces, necks, and bare chests to ward off evil spirits), I made quite an entrance at The Black Swan.

Officially, the Songkran celebration should last three days, but it usually goes on for much longer than that as having fun is such an integral aspect of Thai culture and society. Friendly water fights can erupt almost anywhere and everyone's fair game, including uniformed police officers (except monks, the elderly and babies), with some of the street parties and hangovers lasting a whole week. I machine-gunned a Thai police officer on Silom Road, covering him with water wounds which seeped through his grey uniform, but he didn't even try to arrest me or extort money from my wallet. Nothing gets in the way of the party spirit, so most office buildings, banks, as well as family-run shops and restaurants, shut down completely. Songkran essentials include the obligatory water gun, shorts, flip flops and a waterproof bag to protect belongings such as cameras, wallets, and mobile phones. I packed a spare compact camera, which was repeatedly soaked on Khao San Road, but I didn't care about the last of my material possessions during all that frivolity and childishness. My compact was a festival casualty, but my memory card survived the battlefront onslaughts.

Bangkok experiences a mass exodus during Songkran week with as many as half its residents travelling to their hometowns. The capital is remarkably quiet, like the calm before the storm, before it erupts into happy anarchy every 12th April. Into the shoes of the Thais step the eager tourists, who fly to Bangkok to participate in one of Southeast Asia's most exciting festivals. I preferred the Silom Road celebrations as they contained the largest and wildest crowds, with thousands amassed under the shelter of the Skytrain as the fire brigade blasted water from powerful hoses on their trucks, which lay in wait at intersections to ambush the unwary. As I defended and fought alongside my Thai comrades, the whole area was alive with movement and colour and Thailand could genuinely claim to be a land of smiles. Silom Road was a walking street as traffic rerouted for the serious business of water fights and live bands, parades, street and foam parties. Songkran was a peaceful prequel to the Shutdown Bangkok protests in an alternative universe without politics, gunfire and explosions.

The Songkran festival revealed a face of Thailand that is usually screened by social politeness. During those festival days in the capital and the north, strangers were friends, allies, brothers in arms and the vibrancy of Songkran renewed my appreciation for travel by removing an invisible, cultural barrier between myself and the trigger-happy people of Thailand. I was reminded of the words of Maya Angelou as I sang and danced with strangers:

*Perhaps travel cannot completely prevent bigotry, but by demonstrating that all peoples cry, laugh, eat, worry, and die, it can introduce the idea that if we try and understand each other, we may even become friends.*

For just the one week every year, the streets of Thailand are a war zone of festivity, celebration and collective effervescence. Songkran is a cherished memory that will never fade with wear, and whenever I book a short holiday or plan a prolonged period of travel abroad, I always check the country's calendar of cultural events and festivals first, as there is no better way to get an understanding and appreciation of your hosts. Songkran returned me to childhood days and revived the spirit of my youth.

I witnessed the sound and visual spectacle of the Kecak in Bali, a traditional fire and trance dance (also known as the Ramayana Monkey Chant) when I explored the central village of Ubud. The experience was cultural opium. This unusual take on a Hindu epic is unique for the fact that the accompanying music is created by the human voice alone - without instrumental or technological aid - like that commercial for the Honda Civic in which the Hollywood Film Chorale Sound Effects Choir replicates every sound a car can make, from winding windows to skidding wheels.

The performance tells the story of Prince Rama and his battle to rescue Princess Sita. The gamelan suara (a choir composed of one hundred male performers) sit in a series of concentric circles, swaying, standing up or lying prone as the story develops, wearing the traditional checkered batik cloth while percussively chanting 'cak.' They enact scenes from Hindu folklore and mythology, and even though I didn't fully understand the story, this sui generis spectacle left a lasting cultural and spiritual impression of Bali and its islanders. I found myself chanting *cak* for the next few days, taking the performance with me to the annoyance of friends and colleagues when I returned to Thailand.

## Chapter 43: A Sanctuary for Elephants

One of the most enriching experiences of my travel life was giving a baby elephant an evening bath. For some, it might be hiking to an Incan citadel set high in the Andes Mountains or riding a bicycle through the lavender fields of Provence, but in the provinces of Ayutthaya and Kanchanaburi in Thailand, it was all about getting close to nature's greats and smalls. As Sugarcane splashed knee-deep in a baby-blue bathtub filled with muddy water, a smile formed on his elfin-grey face. Reaching upwards with a toddler's trunk to grab hold of jets of river water, I teasingly sprayed and hosed him down.

Wildlife tourism is one of Thailand's primary attractions, but I never imagined surpassing the experience of sunrise and sunset safaris at the Shamwari Game Reserve near Port Elizabeth in South Africa, where I observed the 'big five' in their natural habitat from the backseat safety of an open Land Cruiser. I got even closer to nature as a conservation volunteer in Thailand where I could feed, assist with medication, bathe and ride the elephants free of the harnesses and saddles strapped to their backs for the comfort of trekking tourists. Dolphinariums offer the costly 'once-in-a-lifetime' experience of swimming with mammals, but I could swim with a motley herd of elephants as the sun stooped low to admire its reflection in the gentle waters of the River Kwai. And I didn't have to part with a single baht for the privilege. Conservation is a dirty job, but hey, somebody's got to do it.

Thailand celebrates its elephants on National Elephant Day (March 13th) while World Elephant Day (August 12th) spreads awareness, shares knowledge and provides better solutions for the care and management of both captive and wild elephant populations. The human race has long-respected and revered the elephant as a species: they are the largest land mammal on earth, and we have an ingrained empathy for them as they share our strong sense of family ties and relationships, while displaying many of our 'human' behaviours and emotions. I watched a wildlife documentary featuring a baby elephant mourning the death of its mother in Kenya's Masai Mara; observing conservationists feared that if it continued to linger by its mother's corpse, it would die from its grief by forgetting to find a fresh water source. It was a touch-and-go and a very touching moment.

Elephants are one of the smartest animal species and are quick to learn and acquire new skills as their adult brains weigh, on average, five kilogrammes which, at birth, are the same size as a fully developed human brain. They are capable of painting portraits of their peers and have a penchant for abstract art, using their trunks to hold brushes and select colours, and some of their paintings have been compared to the works of famous expressionists such as Hans Hofmann and Jackson Pollock. Elephants are wonderfully complex creatures and the ancient Greek philosopher, Aristotle, gave high praise indeed when he described them as the animal '...which surpasses all others in wit and mind.'

Elephant artwork is a prospering cottage industry in Thailand and Laos with authentic trunk-made artworks selling at major international auction houses for many thousands of pounds. There have been accusations of cruelty and claims that the elephants are beaten into submission and forced to paint and create, but elephant artwork was available for sale at every conservation centre I visited in Thailand as a means for funding ongoing conservation work and the survival of this beast of burden.

Thailand's elephants have survived a troubled past. An unsympathetic logging industry utilised them as rough-and-ready trucks and heavy machinery, until a disastrous flood in 1988 killed hundreds of people and covered whole villages and farmland under uprooted trees and sand, prompting a government rethink and logging ban. It was agreed that trees are more useful as natural flood breakers when they are not chopped down for a quick timber sale. Conservation work wasn't all fun and games, though, as I witnessed first-hand some of the horrors of poaching and neglect at a rescue centre in Kanchanaburi Province, where I heard the tragic story of a male elephant named Pla-ra.

Pla-ra got his nickname from a freshwater mudfish, found in the north of Thailand, which is fermented with roasted rice for several months and thus has a rather pungent smell and flavour. Having worked his entire life dragging weighty loads through the jungles of Northern Thailand, poachers removed his tusks by cutting directly into his head with a chainsaw (to remove them from the root) leaving him to die in a bloody mess while they profiteered on the black market. He beat terrible odds by surviving such a savage assault, but his wounds were not treated adequately or quickly enough, and the resulting infection blinded him. As I listened to one of the volunteer vets explain his suffering and the dark world he now inhabits, my eyes welled with tears.

By the time Pla-ra arrived at the rescue centre, his infections had already spread to his eyes and he suffered the side effect and indignity of terrible bad breath (hence his nickname). He received a diet of specialist medical care, and his wounds were flushed out daily with a purple disinfectant which coloured his cheeks. The whole time I observed him at the rescue centre, he remained fixed to the one spot as white pus oozed from the corners of his eyes to attract a swarm of flies, which he half-heartedly swatted away with his trunk. He got used to my scent and raised his trunk expectantly for food whenever I approached, still finding trust in his dependence for the species that had subjected him to decades of abuse. Perhaps Aristotle was right, as I struggled to comprehend how one species could have such a total disregard for another.

Pla-ra died twelve months later.

Whenever I stood next to an adult elephant and looked it in the eye, behind those thick, wiry lashes I have sensed conscious and self-aware creatures. I was smacked in the face by a wary adult when its mahout left me alone to guide it back to its night spot, by holding the tip of its left ear and motioning it forwards. Elephants have an extraordinary sense of smell, and having spent most of the day perspiring profusely and shovelling muck, I had acquired a pungent odour. When it detected an unfamiliar, unappealing scent, it glanced down to register a stranger and blindsided, whipped me in the face with the full force of its trunk. I learnt a vital lesson in volunteer survival: always ensure an elephant is aware of your approach and do so from its right side, as many elephants have been trained to attack strangers approaching from the left.

That swipe was my cue to take a shower, and I no longer doubted the extent of an elephant's cognitive functioning. I was also acquainted with the incredible strength and versatility of an elephant's most important appendage, which is an extension of the upper lip containing forty thousand muscles. Elephants are skilled multitaskers as they can use their trunks to smell, drink, eat, wash and swim. They can also paint a masterpiece or two and, whenever the need arises, swat away bothersome foreigners needing a reminder of their status in the pecking order.

My wounds didn't take long to heal (a small cut and a swollen upper lip) and the fault was entirely my own, as familiarity had bred complacency. Having looked after a female retiree named Yitor for some days, she came to accept me as a surrogate mahout, but my boldness with an unknown male was slapped into place. I was reminded that while elephants are a popular and good-natured animal, they are responsible for hundreds of human deaths each year in Africa and Southeast Asia. The sanctuary's owner reprimanded Kyaw, its mahout, as his perceived laziness had put me at risk of harm. I found forgiveness quickly when a volunteer explained that he was a persecuted migrant (he fled over the mountains from the troubles in Myanmar) and besides, I have immense respect for mahouts as they dedicate their lives to their elephants, often staying with them day and night in a 365-day commitment. An unscrupulous mahout had an enforced stay at the rescue centre and slept in a barn with the dogs, as his baby elephant was confiscated by the authorities when he misused its cuteness to beg for money and food in Kanchanaburi Town. With its health checked, its owner fined by the local police and warned with arrest and permanent confiscation if caught again, it was released back to him.

The Thai government has banned elephants from walking the streets of its towns and cities as urban environments are detrimental to their health, but once upon a time in Thailand, they would have been a common sight on the streets of the capital. We all despair when we get caught in a traffic jam, but when I visited the city of Agra in India, it was one of the highlights of my short stay in a city with few places of interest. The rickshaw driver switched the engine off while we waited at a busy junction near the Taj Mahal, and just like that famous T-Rex scene from *Jurassic Park* (albeit in really slow motion), an enormous elephant picked and weaved its way through the traffic. As it passed on my right side, I leant out to look up at its sinewy frame which cast me into a shadow of awe. The Taj Mahal, by comparison, was a disappointment, and that is why the rich rewards of travel are quite often the unexpected sights, sounds, smells, tastes and experiences that can't be indexed within the pages of a travel guide.

American writer, Lawrence Block, explained: 'Our happiest moments as tourists always seem to come when we stumble upon one thing in pursuit of something else.' When I revised for my driving theory test, I memorised all the different road signs in *The Highway Code*, but when I approached a triangular warning sign on a quiet country road in South Africa, I was presented with a picture of an elephant with a small text box which carried the words 'Elephants crossing.' I wouldn't usually consider pulling over to stop and photograph a road sign for fear of a white-coat intervention, but that is what I did. And that is what travel does well: it springs surprises upon you when, and where, you least expect them.

American comedian W.C. Fields is credited with the line: 'Never work with children or animals.' He lived, joked and died long before I was born, so I failed to heed his warning, having worked with the former for twenty years and having had at least one of the latter in every class I have taught. I couldn't resist the golden ticket of an opportunity to work with and support mistreated and ailing animals at a rescue and rehabilitation centre in Kanchanaburi, and an elephant kraal in Ayutthaya. Animal conservation is an incredibly worthwhile cause and rewarding experience which allows volunteers to work hands-on with all kinds of animals from bears to lions, elephants to orangutans, or turtles to monkeys. When I received a certificate in recognition of my conservation efforts - which helped to create a sustainable future for Thailand's elephants - I bought a silver frame and displayed it with pride in my entrance hall.

On my return to work after a summer holiday in 2012, colleagues were interested to hear tales of my travels in Thailand and anticipated blissful recounts of idyllic islands and beaches. When I explained that I had spent a whole week of my holiday working up a serious sweat as a volunteer, hands raised to stroke chins, eyebrows arched with suspicion and lips pursed with disappointment. If they had thought bubbles floating above their heads, they would have shared the same rhetorical questions: 'What's wrong with you? Why weren't you sunbathing on white-sand beaches?' I tried to explain how working with these incredible creatures is a truly humbling experience and one that will live on within me for the rest of my days, but my colleagues did not share my concept of the perfectly rounded holiday.

At the elephant kraal in Ayutthaya, the new recruits were rounded up on arrival and seated together so the rules of our stay could be explained to us in what resembled a deleted scene from David Fincher's *Fight Club*. Paul, a resident volunteer, began:

'The priority of this camp is the care and welfare of its elephants. Our second concern is the well-being of our elephants. Please understand that tourists and volunteers are not our priority, but we do want you to be safe.'

We all laughed in reply, though somewhat nervously. Paul continued by informing us that he would be responsible for supervising our work and should we wish to avoid impalement or death by crushing, it would be wise to follow his instructions to the letter. We were reminded that it was a conservation centre for elephants, not a holiday camp for tourists, and before I was assigned a hut and sleeping quarters, I first had to sign a legally binding disclosure statement. I put ink to paper and agreed that in the event of being trampled to death by a herd of elephants, the fault would be entirely my own for failing to follow Paul's safety instructions.

I can understand the need for elephant sanctuaries to protect themselves from overexuberant volunteers as I met one in Kanchanaburi, who claimed to be an animal whisperer which, to my mind, is a claim to superhuman powers like Wolverine or Captain America. Having read *The Horse Whisperer* by Nicholas Evans, I had a vague idea how animal whisperers 'communicate' with their furry friends, but I never imagined meeting a real-life whisperer and self-proclaimed pet psychic. Animal Whisperer was, without a doubt, one of the strangest people I have ever met. I've met quite a few, including a middle-aged teacher (who worked in my department in Bangkok) who routinely added smut and spice to Monday morning staff briefings by sharing detailed accounts of his busy weekends in the capital's brothels. I didn't have to be within earshot to understand what he was talking about, as he had a horrible habit of pounding his fist into his palm to stress the power of his virility and the art of his lovemaking. With eleven countries and 620 million people squeezed into Southeast Asia, there are a few rotten eggs.

Animal Whisperer managed to convince me to film her 'talking' to the animals, like a shoestring version of Doctor Doolittle, but it was a one-way conversation. She got particularly excited about the elephant shrine where the skulls and bones of the deceased are collected up and displayed (there was a severed foot, still fresh with flesh and skin). As we approached, she closed her eyes, extended her arms and stood in silence while the camera recorded an impression of Jesus Christ. My arms ached, and I wondered whether she was trying to test my anger-management skills.

I spent the best part of a week working alongside (and for, in my role as camera operator) Animal Whisperer. I was forced to share breakfast, lunch and evening meals as she explained how her 'special gift' enabled her to commune with living animals and those that had, sadly, departed for the spirit world. While nodding, yawning and feigning mild interest, I scanned the roof of the dining hut for hidden cameras fearing an appearance on the next series of Impractical Jokers. People are strange, but the oddest I have met have been westerners exiled in Thailand. Animal Whisperer was an amusing distraction, an American with poor social skills travelling Southeast Asia for six months on her own (I could understand why) looking for heart-to-hearts with wild and dangerous animals. She asked for permission to approach an elephant - which had been chained up for killing its mahout - because she wanted to hear 'its side' of the story.

Politeness and tolerance have thresholds - even for volunteers - and mine were misplaced when I bathed two baby elephants and the contentment of the moment was interrupted. Animal Whisperer had to be at the centre of everything, so she decided it was high time for her evening bath as she climbed into the tub to embrace Sugarcane and Tee Gee in a vice-like grip about their necks. The late afternoon bathing ritual was important as it cooled the baby elephants from a day's exposure to the sun as they were too small to be trusted to swim and wash in the river. She spoilt the future memory, so I challenged her and disconnected the water supply as my duties did not extend to washing the insufferable. When she explained that she was communicating with them through inner hearing and sensing, it was probably just as well that she couldn't hear my unkind thoughts.

The personal needs of Animal Whisperer grew more demanding by the day, and she even claimed that she was filming a documentary for a 'major broadcaster' in the US (despite not having a crew and using only a cheap camcorder). She neglected her duties and the first two rules of Elephant Club, instead filming everyone else doing all the hard work scrubbing, cleaning, feeding, washing, and raking. Frustration mounted, and she was eventually asked to leave the kraal. She was a threat not only to herself, but the other volunteers, and the elephants were at risk of euthanasia should they have killed her out of kindness. She joined the sanctuary for herself, not the animals.

Paul could relax in her absence, and he explained how he had reinvented himself in Thailand as a bar owner (which is to put the 'C' in expat cliché) before he drank away his profits and lost his business to a Thai girlfriend. When expats return to Farangland to visit family and friends, they often boast about owning bars in exotica but the reality is that bar is usually a dirty, run-down hole in the wall and at least a million other enterprising expat entrepreneurs have had the same idea. When his business went belly up, he volunteered to work at the elephant kraal which is now a sanctuary for elephants, asylum seekers and expats.

Understandably, Paul didn't want to return home with just the clothes on his back to start over in his mid-fifties. Having found solace at the bottom of a bottle (until he couldn't afford another), he found some common sense and saved himself, from himself, by offering his time and energies as a volunteer in exchange for bed and board. He now lives in a tree hut, suspended over a stream, with just a few earthly possessions to call his own (including his beloved acoustic guitar), but he was happier than all my former colleagues combined, who were struggling from month to month to pay mortgages, childcare, loans and credit cards. He was a portrait of inner peace and contentment and he seemed to be having the last laugh, living the life of Riley with no more cares in the world other than elephants. Seven months later, I sold up and shipped out myself and with hindsight, perhaps he was an unlikely source of inspiration.

My travels introduced me to unconventional people, but I also continued my encounters with unusual meats and eats in Thailand. At the rescue centre in Kanchanaburi, I sampled the strangest barbequed meat I have ever tasted. One of the mahouts caught a medium-sized monitor lizard and with lunch fast approaching, a makeshift barbeque was erected and I was invited to share the 'dish of the day' with migrants from Myanmar (who were less fussy about their eating habits than I was). The monitor lizard's cooked flesh was painfully chewy so my jaw ached while my stomach anticipated the swallow, which probably accounts for why I have never seen it on a menu in Southeast Asia where dogs and snakes are fair game. The migrants seemed to love it and couldn't scoff it down fast enough, but one taste was enough to satisfy my curiosity.

Water monitors are unpopular creatures in Thailand and their local name - hia - is an insulting word which can be applied to almost anything that is deemed evil, including people. In traditional rural Thai villages, people still prefer to live in elevated, stilted houses with the ground floor set aside as a living space for domestic animals such as dogs, pigs and chickens. Monitor lizards are rather partial to a chicken dinner themselves, and have consequently received the nickname 'dtua gin gai' for their eating habits (it translates to 'chicken eater') as they sneakily poach their prey from under the roofs of sleepy Thai houses. When the lizard was caught, butchered and barbequed, three cheers filled the air and one of the volunteer vets explained why. Not surprisingly, the chicken eater tasted just like chicken. You are what you eat.

When I wasn't sampling the local wildlife, my daily duties included the dreaded trip to a field of sugarcane - on the back of a sputtering tractor - where I helped to plant and cut down the cane and bananas and gathered vegetables for the sick, old, disabled, abused and rescued elephants. It was sweaty, draining work but many hands made it lighter. The rescue centre functioned as a hospice and nursing home where elephants could rest and find some joy from their remaining months or years. Day-trippers were welcome to visit and donate, but the behaviour of some tourists was culturally insensitive, to say the least, and entirely unwelcome. A couple from Germany joined us, without invitation or a polite greeting, as we swam with some of the elephants in the river as a reward for our hard work. They turned the sanctuary and its elephants into a backdrop for a fashion photo shoot, as Miss World undressed by the water's edge to reveal one of the skimpiest bikinis I have ever seen, even though we were hundreds of miles from the nearest beach.

Miss World refined that perfect but clichéd porn-star posture as she threw her shoulders back and arched her lower back forwards, a look polished by bright-red lipstick, dramatic black eye shadow, and flashy false nails. Her presence was an affront to Thai culture. The elephants blushed, but a passing monk was not impressed when his eyes met overexposed flesh. They had no interest in the elephants, other than as props, and they didn't even try to conceal that fact as Miss World's doting assistant extended his tripod to flash-photograph her sitting and standing on an elephant or swimming beside them.

With the elephants bathed, cooled and scrubbed clean, we sat on their backs as they dipped us in and out of the water, or swam around them as they splashed their trunks and stood in the river like giant floats. Elephants are surprisingly agile swimmers, but it is hard to believe it, without seeing it, with all that body bulk. They love the water and can swim long distances, using their trunks as periscopes which also double as shower units to spray themselves and unsuspecting passers-by. I gripped onto hairy heads and tucked my feet behind leathery ears when it was my time for a bath, but on my return to the surface on one occasion, a huge ball of greenish dung lodged in my groin which a mahout removed and tossed in the river. Whatever it had eaten stained my shorts so badly, they needed industrial-strength cleaning.

In the late evenings, we returned the elephants to their night spots and prepared their meals by cleaning and boiling the fruit and vegetables we had gathered in the morning. We mashed some of the softer fruit, such as pumpkin, with sticky rice to form rice balls with which to feed the older elephants without teeth. It was a real honour to serve and care for these animals whose experiences of life had been painfully reduced. Some of the local women challenged my claim to masculinity when we unloaded trucks full of pineapples: my whole body wilted in minutes while they had more energy reserves stored in their fingers. I wasn't used to the physical activity; I was much better at keeping detailed records of animal care.

Thailand's conservation centres welcome the support of visiting volunteers. The country's elephants need as much help and protection as they can get, with their numbers having plummeted from 100,000 at the turn of the twentieth century to an estimated three thousand domestic and two thousand surviving wild elephants a century later. I followed the vets on their rounds and assisted as a fetcher and carrier as they medicated a range of infections. As you can imagine, working this closely with elephants was already rich reward, but settling down on the porch of a traditional Thai-style cottage in the evenings, with views of the river, the green mountains and the orchestral sounds of nature, was the perfect lullaby. I visited the Kanchanaburi rescue centre during the wet season when the most mobile elephants prefer to sleep and eat in the forests. I could walk with them and their mahouts to night spots and I was guided to the top of one of the lower mountains for a beautiful pre-dusk view of the valleys near the border with Myanmar.

My lodgings at the elephant kraal in Ayutthaya were less romantic and far more functional, as I shared a room with an invasion of insects and restless, sheltering geckos while a tethered adolescent elephant slept right outside my hut. When I settled down to sleep, my ears homed in on the heavy breathing of a sleeping giant and I wondered what elephants dream about at night. People allow their pet dogs and cats to sleep at the end of their beds, but I shared a sleeping space with an unlikely companion. If that wasn't a strong enough dose of the unconventional, the sanctuary kept a disabled monkey as a pet (its legs had been torn off during a savage attack by wild dogs) and caged it with a rabbit.

My experiences were getting stranger by the day, and while I didn't mind trying a sample of monitor lizard when offered to me in Kanchanaburi, I declined a mouthful of barbequed elephant placenta in Ayutthaya. As the leftovers simmered like bubble and squeak, one of the mahouts asked me if I would like to try it. I didn't have the guts. Mother Nature couldn't resist her moment in the sun either, as she revealed the optical phenomenon of a sun halo - a giant eye in the sky.

I had so many priceless moments as a volunteer, and they all came in exchange for elbow grease. I made the effort to learn fourteen basic elephant commands so that I could ride Yitor confidently and without the ever-watchful eye of her mahout, but first I had to perfect my pronunciation as Thai elephants speak only one language: Thai. Once I had mastered how to say 'go' (bai), 'stop' seemed the next logical step and with these verbal commands committed to memory, I was taught the essential foot commands for controlling Yitor's movements should my grasp of Thai suddenly desert me or get lost in translation with a wild animal. I got used to touching Yitor's rough skin with my bare feet, and I was able to drive her like a mahout using her primary operating system: to walk her forwards, I pressed my toes behind her ears; to walk backwards, I pressed back with my heels; to get her to raise her trunk, I used my toes to push upwards; to sit down, I pushed downwards with one of my heels and to get her to turn left or right, I would hold my heel backwards and press forward with either my left or right toes. It was much easier than learning how to drive a car and twice as much fun.

With so many sanctuaries and rescue centres to choose from in Thailand, I selected non-profit organisations where nature and conservation matters come first and foremost and where I could live with, care for and learn about the elephants. Thailand's elephants and their mahouts have been repurposed in a tourism industry in which elephant activities are a highly profitable business. Trekking camps and elephant circuses have a reputation for putting financial gain before animal welfare, and the tell-tale signs are obvious, as the elephants are forced to perform unnatural behaviours such as headstands when they put all their weight on their two front legs. The word 'elephant' comes from the Latin 'ele' and 'phant' which, combined, translate to 'huge arch.' Upon those arches wooden platforms are strapped to carry heavy tourist loads, which can cause the animal tremendous pain and harm (an elephant's back is not as muscular as its neck or trunk). Nature never intended for its elephants to carry human weights for up to ten hours a day, so the ethics of Thailand's elephant industry are open to debate and scrutiny.

For most tourists visiting Southeast Asia, riding an elephant will feature on their 'must do' lists as they are a unique photo opportunity to share with family and friends back home. When I first visited Thailand in 2006, I rode my bucket list with four legs through the wilds of Chiang Mai. The experience was, however, underscored by a nagging sense of the unnecessary discomfort I was causing the elephant, which was forced to carry me (and three others) over steep terrain with a wooden deck fixed by rope to its back, neck, and tail. Every time it stopped to rest and catch a breath, the mahout struck its head with a bull hook. When its wounds started to bleed, I noticed the scars of previous beatings and was filled with remorse. It was my first and last ride on a platform, but at the rescue centres, I could ride the elephants responsibly and ethically, bareback as a single rider.

Thailand has an abundance of nature-based activities and wildlife tourism pursuits with a staggering 127 national parks (twenty-two of which are marine parks). The first national park, Khao Yai, was my preferred retreat to the arms of nature when I needed a break from the city. It was honoured with UNESCO World Heritage status in 2005 in recognition of its valuable and delicate ecosystems, but its pricing system is a sensitive issue and is often the source of tourist anger as Thais are charged twenty baht for entry while foreigners must stump up four hundred. But that's life when you travel, you should suck it up or else stay at home and visit a zoo (which is bound to cost more). When I visited the Taj Mahal, local Indians were charged thirty rupees while I paid 750, but I was hardly going to refuse to pay out of principle and besides, western lifestyles should be able to afford the difference when they can afford to carry the cost of hotels and international flights.

Khao Yai is a three-hour drive northeast of Bangkok, and it is the country's third-largest national park. It stretches across four provinces peppered with a diverse range of incredible natural resources of ecological importance and unique natural beauty, with stunning waterfalls, a mountain valley backdrop and a wide variety of species from elephants to exotic birds (such as hornbills) in their natural habitat. I hired a local guide - Boonyarit - who accompanied me to all the key sites and took me on night safaris through tropical rainforest. He probably saved my life more than once as we made our way through evergreen forests and grasslands to Haew Suwat Waterfall: I needed a heat break and was tempted to dip my feet in a pool of water when he pointed to a sign warning of a crocodile.

I had another close and unexpected encounter with nature as we made slow progress through an area of thick jungle. Boonyarit whispered for me to stop in my tracks, before pointing to a poisonous snake that was reclining on a branch just a few feet ahead. I failed to notice the lurking threat (even though it had a bright-green body) as my eyes were focused on clumsy footings. I was glad he was with me for every step of the journey; he was a quiet companion, but at least he was observant. As we walked along a jungle pathway in the dark, he motioned for me to stand still as elephants came crashing through the jungle, clearly more aware of our presence than we were of theirs. We backed away, returned to the vehicle and continued safely on our way.

Thailand's north-eastern provinces rarely feature on tourist itineraries. Isan (or Isaan, Issan, Esan, it seems to have so many different spellings) shouldn't be missed as it is the home of spectacular Phu Phra Bat Historical Park and a wealth of tropical ice-age evidence. Udon Thani is one of four principal cities in Isan Province, and I used it as a travel hub to explore the region, visiting a vast archaeological site that features ancient constructions and objects of both prehistoric and historic times (including cave paintings).

The park's peculiarly shaped rock formations were the result of glacial movements millions of years ago, when an ancient man called this site his home. The area is surrounded by the Pa Khua Nam Forest with its pleasant walking routes, and I was surprised to see so few tourists had made the effort to visit. But that doesn't mean it is not worth seeing, it's just less well known and must compete with tropical temptations to the south. The Ban Chiang archaeological site and museum are compelling reasons for visiting this historical area (declared a UNESCO World Heritage site in 1992) and the pottery it displays indicates the ancient origins of civilisation in Southeast Asia.

Thailand appeals to its serial visitors for a host of reasons and motivations, from sex and medical tourism to heritage and ecotourism. Thailand can't match its neighbours' legacy interests, but it does have its fair share of cultural and historical UNESCO World Heritage sites, which are often overlooked - and perhaps overshadowed - by greater claims to dust and fame across its borders to the east and west.

# Chapter 44: Sukhothai and Ayutthaya

The concept of 'heritage tourism' has been classified by America's National Trust for Historic Preservation as 'travelling to experience the places, artifacts, and activities that authentically represent the stories and people of the past,' with a focus on a destination's 'cultural, historical and natural resources.' It is a desperately dull and long-winded definition and doesn't do it any justice at all. I have already shared my bemusement for the patrons of sex tourism and my fascination with dark tourism (I knew I had the dark type in my blood when my fondest memory of visiting the beautiful city of Prague was the Museum of Medieval Torture), but heritage tourism is my travel raison d'être. It is an opportunity to sift through a foreign country's dust and bones.

When you fly hundreds or even thousands of miles, there should be a significant return on the investment other than sun, sand and sea water. History, I have discovered, is a reliable wager and Thailand has a wealth of heritage neatly packaged within the walls of its historical parks at Sukhothai, Si Satchanalai, Kamphaeng Phet, Ayutthaya, Phanom Rung, Phimai and Muang Sing.

Not everyone will agree with me, though, as a friend visited Rome and completely disregarded the Colosseum, the symbolic heart of the Roman Empire. He argued his case with a technicality, claiming that as his taxi had passed it on the way to his hotel, he had, therefore, 'seen' it. A heritage-immune colleague who lived as a teacher in Beijing resisted the cultural lure of the Great Wall of China, summarily dismissing it with: 'It's a wall. So what? My garden has three of them.' It was voted one of the new Seven Wonders of the World in 2007, and I judged it with wonderment three years later, agreeing that it deserved its lofty status alongside the Taj Mahal, Petra, Machu Picchu, the Colosseum, Chichen Itza and Christ the Redeemer. The UK's annual Heritage Counts report concluded in 2014 that visiting heritage sites could have a positive impact on personal wellbeing, making people happier than when they play sports or visit art galleries. I couldn't agree more, but I would add that visiting Thailand's heritage sites offers a three-for-one value, as they often include a physical workout in outdoor art galleries.

When I planned a six-week tour of the islands of Indonesia, the Mahayana Buddhist temple of Borobudur - in Central Java - was my starting point. The highlight of a month's travels in Japan was meeting a geisha in Gion and sumo wrestlers in Tokyo, as both encounters were unexpected flashbacks to a feudal era. I wondered whether I had pressed the wrong button on the control panel of my Japanese wonder toilet and triggered a time machine into action.

The Arabic nation of Jordan was never likely to feature on my Bucket List 101, as capital Amman is regularly slammed on international travel polls as one of the world's ugliest ducklings, and it is, with its sprawling residential neighbourhoods resembling haphazardly stacked cardboard boxes which are all cut and paste imitations. It was like trying to navigate a giant 'find your way home' puzzle. The city is, at the very least, a convenient springboard from which to explore the incredible Roman ruins of Jerash, the salty waters of the Dead Sea and the ancient mysteries of the Nabataeans of Petra, who lost some of their mysteriousness when *Indiana Jones and the Last Crusade* was shot on location. My Amman hotel had a mosque for a noisy neighbour, so I didn't have to set my alarm to sightsee as the call to prayer blasted me bolt upright at 4:15 am every morning. It was the first time - in a lifetime of travels - that I made it down to breakfast, on time, every morning of my stay.

In South Korea, the cultural peak of my journey was the historic capital of Gyeongju, a coastal city with more than two thousand years of history secreted away in the country's south-eastern corner. The tombs and history of its Silla Kingdom kings are as absorbing and fascinating as Egypt's pharaohs in the Nile Valley. The city is often referred to as 'the museum without walls' as it has more palace ruins, temples, Buddhist statuary, pagodas, tombs and rock carvings than any other city in the country. I came, I saw, and I conquered its tourism trail, and I loved every footstep, even the exhausting climb of Namsan Mountain which is itself home to more temples, shrines, carvings and so on.

From Gyeongju, I travelled further south to the modern port city of Busan which was, by comparison, to exit a sophisticated dinner party by quaffing down a yard of ale. I couldn't wait to leave the cement and glass of Busan behind me and an urge for a satisfying slice of dark tourism tempted me to return north to visit the Demilitarised Zone, which separates North Korea from South Korea. If I were to choose just the one highlight from every country I have visited in East or Southeast Asia, heritage tourism would link them all together in a chain of interest.

The historical kingdoms of Sukhothai and Ayutthaya are Thailand's cultural near-equivalence of Cambodia's Angkor Wat or Myanmar's ancient city of Bagan. The city of Ayutthaya - in Ayutthaya Province - is a popular day trip from Bangkok with trains, public buses, minivans, tuk-tuks and boats plying the route by rail, road and river. I boarded a train at Bangkok's central

Hualamphong train station for the fifty-mile journey north (the cheapest and most scenic option) and a little over two hours later, I was exploring and photographing the temple ruins of a former empire in the valley of the Chao Phraya River.

Ayutthaya has a long-established tourism industry so it has been well and truly discovered, which led to some frustration as I struggled to get clear photographs of historic sites without the background noise of tourists and their accidental but continuous photobombing. Coaches cluttered the city's streets to offload their tour groups so they could rampage through history and form rugby scrums at every significant site, as guides explained their potted histories in seconds, but nobody listened or seemed to care. Experience has taught me that the more iconic a place, a painting or a view, the more annoying the tourists tend to be. As tour groups ran amok over ruins, cramming hundreds of years of history into sixty minutes of pixels, I was reminded of American novelist Sinclair Lewis' observation:

> *He who has seen one cathedral ten times has seen something; he who has seen ten cathedrals once has seen but little, and he who has spent half an hour in each of a hundred cathedrals has seen nothing at all.*

By comparison, not so many tourists make the effort to visit Sukhothai or its regional neighbour, Si Satchanalai, due to their out-of-the-way location in lower north-central Thailand. When my school closed for yet another week of anti-government marching, protesting and bombing in early December 2013, I read a book about the history of Thailand which was full of glossy photographs showcasing the ancient wonders of Sukhothai and Si Satchanalai. I had never heard of them until I turned those pages, not even from my Thai colleagues, and each photograph painted a thousand words of enticement. I decided to pay them a visit and my mind was made up like fast-setting jelly.

The extra-thick silver lining of Thailand's cloudy political situation provided unanticipated opportunities to travel. I booked a three-night stay at a hostel in central Sukhothai, and with my camera batteries charged and a small rucksack packed with neutrally coloured football shirts and shorts, half a tube of toothpaste and a single roll of toilet tissue, I was ready to set off and explore another UNESCO World Heritage site in Southeast Asia. Thailand, currently, has just five officially recognised UNESCO World Heritage sites (the Sukhothai region and Ayutthaya historical parks, the Khao Yai national park, the Ban Chiang archaeological site and the Thung Yai and Huai Kha Khaeng wildlife sanctuaries) when Spain has forty-two and the UK has twenty-eight. I had no excuse for not making the effort to get out and visit them all.

There was, however, an unforeseen delay to my travel plans as I was forced to earn my corn first. With images of a country on the brink of civil war broadcast all over the world, my school, not surprisingly, struggled to recruit a new English teacher for the vacancy in my department. I was about to board a bus to Sukhothai from Mo Chit Northeastern Bus Terminal but had to make an impromptu U-turn as my school Principal called me on my mobile phone and asked me to join him, within the hour, to Skype interview a candidate he had 'found' in Azerbaijan of all places. I couldn't believe my luck. I explained that I was too far from my apartment to return and change within the hour and that I was hardly dressed for an interview. It did not put him off in the slightest, so when I arrived at the front gate covered in sweat, I asked the security guard to hide my rucksack as I didn't want to make my intentions clear to the boss, having prioritised holidaying and sightseeing over planning and marking.

It is important to maintain a professional appearance in front of your employers and even more so in Thailand, where Thai colleagues ranked appearance ahead of every other workplace skill (and personal quality) during a training day exercise. Wearing a sharp suit and appearing to be good at your job is all that matters in a Thai workplace. Some of my colleagues tried their hardest to establish and maintain a good impression, even remaining in the school buildings for twelve hours a day before daring to sign out (and only doing so in the safety of numbers). The reality of that time and 'dedication' to their work included at least a dozen gossip and napping breaks, hours sifting through trivial social media updates, or sitting in the office staring at desktop monitors and catching up with low-grade Thai soap operas. The workplace functioned as a social and leisure space which was, occasionally, interrupted by the small matter of education. I had an awkward meeting with one of my former colleagues, whose idea of teaching a lesson was to set up an activity before swiftly returning to the staffroom for more coffee and cakes. I never imagined that I would have to explain - to a man in his late forties - that when you teach a lesson, it usually helps to be *in* the lesson.

With the interview concluded (the candidate later pulled out, having decided Bangkok was far too dangerous a city to live in), I agreed with the Principal that beggars couldn't be choosers and a body in the classroom is better than nobody at all. As he bemoaned the prolonged disruption to our students' learning, I nodded my head in all the right places, but I was more concerned and frustrated by his interruption of my travel plans. Sukhothai was waiting. With the polite chit-chat ended, I sprinted to the front gate and tipped the security guard fifty baht for his compliance (and silence) before making an ever-madder dash to the bus station. I didn't have time to grab drinks and snacks from one of Bangkok's billion 7-Eleven convenience stores, so I boarded the bus to Sukhothai drenched in sweat and spent the next eight hours shivering in air-conditioning and salivating every time one of my fellow travellers opened a bag of God-knows-what to eat. I was looking forward to a bed of roses for a few days as Bangkok was full of nail bombs, but that journey severely tested my patience and tolerance for confined spaces. I paid the hard-seat price for penny-pinching, as my ticket cost 250 baht (£5) when a budget flight with Bangkok Airways was priced at 2,300 baht (£46) and would have got me there in less than an hour.

My first three holidays in Thailand, when combined, totalled three months of travelling, but I failed to cross paths with Sukhothai or rustic Si Satchanalai. They eluded my footsteps as travel inclinations led me southwards for island escapes on the Gulf and Andaman coasts (I blame the guidebook photographers). The Sukhothai, Si Satchanalai, and Kamphaeng Phet parks were combined as one site by UNESCO and awarded World Heritage status in 1991. Many of Thailand's tourists depart the country having never heard of them (as did I), and if they have, they struggle to pronounce their names or find time away from pool and beach itineraries. Sukhothai and Si Satchanalai (and Ayutthaya, to a lesser extent) were the heritage highlights of my travels in Thailand. Sukhothai's glorious ruins are the postscript of an ancient capital which existed from 1238 until 1438, and it is the province's must-see attraction for history and art enthusiasts.

I leisurely explored Sukhothai and Si Satchanalai from the worn seat of a peddle bicycle, though Si Satchanalai was a thirty-minute public bus ride north with its sites scattered rather than grouped. The natural scenery provided pleasant distraction and a superb backdrop for my photographs, with the sky permanently set to a clear blue. If I were asked to recommend just the one ancient site in Thailand, it would be the old city of Sukhothai. My brothel-bothering colleague had lived in Thailand for ten years, and when he asked me how I spent my protest time off, his face was full of puzzlement as he had never heard of Sukhothai or Si Satchanalai. His interests, it seemed, were horizontal and sprung from mattresses, not history books.

Sukhothai was the first capital of Siam (the country's historical name, before it was changed to 'Thailand' in 1949) and was founded in the thirteenth century in the year 1238. Its name carries good omens for travellers as it translates to 'The Dawn of Happiness,' a fact Heritage Counts should use as evidence in their next annual report. Sukhothai was a cosmopolitan kingdom of the central plains which stretched over much of modern-day Thailand except the north, which was controlled by the Khmers. This period was the golden age of Thai history: arts and culture prospered under the rule of nine benevolent kings who played host to a variety of cultures from Borneo, Sri-Lanka, and China, which combined to produce a melting pot of architectural designs and a rich diversity of monuments, with some set before serene lakes carpeted with sacred flowers.

The kingdom's greatest ruler, King Ram Khamhaeng, has been credited with the creation of the Thai alphabet and for establishing Theravada Buddhism as the state religion, and his historical importance has been recognised and honoured with a grand monument at the park's entrance. The kingdom fell into decline when it surrendered some of its territorial gains, and it was usurped by Ayutthaya which was founded in 1350 and established as the second Siamese capital before it was invaded, sacked and looted by Burmese invaders and moved south to what is now modern-day Bangkok.

Old Sukhothai has a small population of just thirty-five thousand inhabitants, and they benefit directly from the 193 ruins they inherited from their ancestors, spread over forty-three miles of antiquity (tuk-tuk drivers provide a necessary alternative to the peddle option during the fiercely hot summer months). There are no inhabited buildings inside the rectangular old city walls (most of which have fallen into complete ruin, as well as the former city gates), but just outside the park's boundary is a collection of modest guesthouses and restaurants which still have roofs and a welcome. Modern New Sukhothai has nothing of cultural or historical interest, except for a few places to stay and eat. Quite by chance, I found a fantastic, family-run restaurant named Poo (after the owner) which serves incredible western and Thai dishes and an unexpected selection of bottled Belgian beers, including Kwak with its wooden handle and yard-of-ale-shaped glass.

Sukhothai's heritage and prestige have been painstakingly restored and proudly present one of the finest collections of Buddhist statuary and architecture in the world, with separate admission charges for each of the city's five archaeological zones (reasonably priced at 100 baht for seven hundred years of Thai history). With experience having taught me to be selective with sightseeing, I did some research before I left Bangkok. Starting with the twenty-six temples and monuments inside the remains of the palace and old city walls, the most impressive and historically significant of these ruins is Wat Mahathat. Only the base survives and a royal temple which contains two hundred separate structures (including a chedi which features a lotus-bud motif and a frieze with 111 images of the Buddha). From all angles, the beauty of history was revealed to my eyes in every stone and blade of grass. From the historic core, I peddled to the nearby temples of Wat Sa Sri and Wat Chana Songkhram. I tested my thigh muscles by cycling north to Wat Phra Phai Luang and Wat Si Chum, and west to Wat Saphan Hin and the temples of the forest. The further I peddled, the more ruined the ruins.

With a map of the park in my pocket and the wind in my hair, I appreciated the car-free freedom and pleasure of riding a bicycle through Sukhothai's beautiful rural landscapes, over wooden canal bridges and along dusty back roads. It was the highlight of my time away from the concrete and chaos of the capital. To hire a bicycle for a whole day cost just 30 baht (60p) which was an absolute steal, and with the sun on my face and a cold beer in my hand, I could soak up history's ruins in a truly picturesque setting. I was guilty of drunk cycling on more than one occasion as my refreshment pit stops were frequent in the heat, and bottles of Chang Beer were the catch of the day. I cycled further distances at Si Satchanalai Historical Park, located on the bank of the Yom River at Tambon Muang Kao, as some of the temple ruins are remote and difficult to find, even with a tourist map in hand. Climbing steep hills in Indian Jones mode, they were worth the effort of discovery with ruins set against leafy backdrops. I had some temples to myself with not a single tour bus in sight.

Si Satchanalai is often overlooked for Sukhothai, or briefly visited as an afterthought, but its temples have been touched less by the hands of restoration, and consequently their old-world charm remains crumbled but intact. Si Satchanalai has nineteen monuments inside the city wall, with the highlights and most accessible temple ruins being Wat Chang Lom, Wat Chedi Chet Thaeo, and Wat Phra Sri Rattana Mahathat. But again, it was all about the sense of serenity and escape as I rode through fields of pampas grass and quiet rural villages, disturbed only by birdsong and two squeaking wheels. My visit coincided with the late king's birthday celebrations, so the town was awash with yellow flags, banners and flowers as villagers marched through the streets carrying portraits of the monarch. When I found the courage to join the procession, strangers placed jasmine garlands around my neck.

I returned to Sukhothai for Loy Krathong, the festival of lights, which is celebrated annually in the month of November when the country's waters come alive as the staging area for a cultural and spiritual performance set to candlelight. Sukhothai has found credit as the birthplace of this festival; it is the country's prime location for witnessing this incredible spectacle with lakes and temples incandescent and aglow. Sukhothai celebrates the tradition for two whole weeks and the days are long, with evening concerts and firework displays. It has similarities with Songkran, but the festival is a peaceful and altogether more refined celebration with traditional parades, concerts, beauty pageants and family get-togethers. Millions of floating rafts (made from a combination of bamboo leaves, lotus flowers, candles, and incense) are released and set sail on every body of water in Thailand, even puddles, to carry away bad luck and misfortune.

The ancient ruins of the Sukhothai, Si Satchanalai, and Ayutthaya historical parks are impressive reminders of Thailand's cultural past. The value of the latter's temple ruins was granted UNESCO World Heritage status in 1981, but Ayutthaya offers only a reduced glimpse of a once-impressive city. Few historical remains have endured the ravages of time or the hammers of eighteenth-century invaders, who gleefully beheaded the majority of its four thousand sacred statues to assert their dominance and power. Once considered the most spectacular city on earth, its impressive features include reliquary towers and monastery grounds which give some hint to the splendour of its past when gilded temples and treasure-laden palaces marked it out as one of the world's wealthiest, powerful and cosmopolitan cities. Ayutthaya is compact enough to navigate on foot, but having visited on a scorching-hot day, I hired another bicycle and let the wheels take the strain.

My budget remained untroubled in Ayutthaya as entrance fees for historical sites were priced from low to very low at 20 baht (40p), while renting a bicycle for the day set me back a wallet-whopping 40 baht (80p). Some of Europe's attractions and heritage sites are outrageously overpriced when compared to Southeast Asia, with a weekend in London likely to trigger bankruptcy. The most expensive UNESCO World Heritage site that I have visited is the ancient city of Petra, in Jordan. As the country's cultural highlight, the greedy authorities squeeze every drop of milk they can extract from its teats with oily, grasping hands (a standard entrance ticket cost £50 in 2012). For that sum, I expected my admission to include a knowledgeable guide or, at the very least, an audio guide, transport and a map, but all I received was a torn ticket stub which I couldn't even keep as a souvenir. There was hardly any tourist information to guide me around the site, so I had absolutely no idea what I was looking at until I recognised the treasury building (Al Khazneh) which featured in *Indiana Jones and the Last Crusade*. Thailand regularly reminded me why millions of travellers faithfully return to Southeast Asia each year.

The most iconic image of Ayutthaya is that of a Buddha's head entangled within the roots of a bodhi tree at Wat Mahathat. A standard postcard and guidebook image, it is one of the most recognisable tourism images of Thailand. Little remains of the temple, and it is a complete mystery how the head of a statue found itself encased in the body of a tree, with one theory suggesting that when the temple was abandoned and reclaimed by nature, the tree respectfully grew around it. Another theory proposes that it was hidden by a casual thief or treasure hunter. Whatever the truth may be, it is an enigmatic and sacred site guarded around the clock. There are numerous heritage highlights awaiting discovery, though Wat Yai Chaya Mongkol is Ayutthaya's most photogenic temple with hundreds of its statues dressed in yellow robes, while Wat Lokayasutharam's main feature is the colossal sculpture of a reclining Buddha. Viharn Phra Mongkol Bophit is a copy of the Grand Palace in Bangkok and is famous for a giant statue of the Buddha, reportedly the largest of its kind in Thailand.

On my return to the capital, I took a detour to the district of Bang Pa-In in Ayutthaya Province to visit the Summer Palace. The palace dates to the seventeenth century and is an eclectic collection of Thai and European-style buildings, which are used for state occasions rather than as a place of residence. It is a beautiful area to wander and explore with artificial ponds, a lake full of turtles and an elegant Thai-style pavilion. There is a similar royal palace in the old city of Phetchaburi to the south-east of the capital, built on a hill by King Rama IV and named Phra Nakhon Khiri, which is visited by fewer tourists but is besieged by monkeys that seem to delight in harassing visitors so they never return. I visited the nearby Khao Luang Cave, which is a holy site full of images of the Buddha and an asylum for wild monkeys wanting to feed, as they stealthily skim and scan passing tourists for edible plunder. The mischief-makers (they stand like statues on the stairs leading down to the cave) scared the life out of me when they hissed and showed their teeth at every step. Returning to the security of daylight, I abandoned a friend who still hasn't forgiven me for leaving her to the clawing clutches of pestiferous monkeys.

I should have paid more attention to titles when I explored the temples of the Sacred Monkey Forest in Bali. I knew, instinctively, that I was close to the forest as I could sense dark, furtive eyes watching from the branches and masking foliage of trees. I understood immediately why the forest had been given this name, as dozens of bold and mischievous Balinese long-tailed, grey-haired macaques run around feet and jump over tourists' heads. The Sacred Monkey Forest is a nature reserve and a sacred Hindu temple complex and it is very easy to locate, as it sits at the lowermost section of Monkey Forest Road. Signs warn visitors to be mindful of their belongings as the monkeys are not backwards at coming forward, but I was there to visit three sacred temples within the forest: Pura Dalem (the Death Temple), the Madya Mandala (the Holy Bathing Temple) and Pura Prajapati (the funerary or Cremation Temple).

I enjoyed exploring these ancient sites in their *Raiders of the Lost Ark* settings and I half expected to be chased by a giant boulder or, at the very least, be shot down by a dozen poison darts. To visit the Holy Bathing Temple, I first had to descend a long flight of sacred stairs next to a sacred stream (everything is sacred), and the experience was like stepping into a lost world in a secret valley. Giant statues of moss-covered Komodo dragons poked their heads out of thick jungle vegetation at the bottom of the stairs, and they reminded me of the vicious Velociraptors in Steven Spielberg's *Jurassic Park*. The only living terrors in this forest are the monkeys, and they are more frightening than the child-eating Rangda demons which, per traditional Balinese mythology, led armies of evil witches against the Barong, a lion-like creature, and king of the spirits and forces of good.

The monkeys, not surprisingly, are also considered to be sacred as locals believe they protect the area from evil spirits when they are the very embodiment of those evil spirits and a persistent nuisance. It is not easy to relax and enjoy the forest, or its heritage, as the unwelcome attention of hundreds of monkeys is a source of continual annoyance and distraction. I have encountered temple monkeys all over Southeast Asia, but I have never gotten used to them, as their unpredictability usually puts me on my guard. There are two simple rules to follow: never stand still (unless you want to roleplay as a climbing frame) and never show fear. I find the latter harder to observe as my body often betrayed my mind, like a peripatetic thesaurus for nervousness.

Wild monkeys are an entirely different prospect to temple monkeys, and I love nothing better than venturing into the wild with them when on safari in South Africa. Asia's temple monkeys, by contrast, exist on a diet of human leftovers, and they have consequently become an irksome bunch of lazy opportunists and conniving kleptomaniacs. They will confront you, grab at you and, given half the chance, steal from you. Macaques are the most common breed in Asia, but they also happen to be the naughty child of the primate world. They give monkeys a bad name.

In Bali, there have been reports of tourist scams involving these innocent-looking but crafty creatures. There are claims that some of the monkeys have been trained by locals to steal valuables such as handbags, mobile devices and anything that glitters from unsuspecting tourists. For their light-fingered services, they are rewarded with fresh fruit. While this may sound a little absurd and far-fetched, observe their keen interest in sunglasses, jewellery (especially earrings) and anything made of plastic or metal, and you may well be convinced. There is nothing sacred about the sly and stealthy inhabitants of the Sacred Monkey Forest.

Thailand's Lopburi is synonymous with macaques and is overrun with them. The Old Town (nicknamed Monkey Town) is a long-tailed version of *Dante's Inferno* where the ever-present demon on all nine circles of hell is a primate. Even the main temple attraction - Prang Sam Yot - is more commonly known as The Monkey Temple. The town's menacing residents steal from unlocked vehicles and zip-line on electricity cables and so badly behave, they are the rock stars of the animal kingdom and could double as mischievous sprites in *Gremlins*. They hang from trees and wires to watch their victims' movements with telescopic eyes or gather in gangs on rooftops and ledges, like a primate Mafioso. The town hosts an annual Lopburi Monkey Festival and Banquet which is a mass feeding frenzy as the servants of the city - the people - feed their macaque masters. Visitors are warned to avert their eyes as the monkeys have developed some rather nasty toilet habits, which includes the use of tourists as chamber pots.

Heritage sites are a portal for tourists to go back to their future. As we marvel at and consider the legacies of the cultures of human past, what made them great or contributed to their fall, it is a poignant reminder that our own time on earth is sacred for being short. How will we be remembered? Whenever I see a photograph of Hitler, I wonder what he would think - and how he might react - if I went back in time, whispered in his ear and told him that his name and face would live on in history as a representation of humanity's capacity for cruelty and evil.

Exploring the past allows us to examine ourselves and our small place in the world; it is a reminder to make the most of the time that has been given to us, before others consider and discuss our stories and the world we left behind.

## Chapter 45: All's Well that Ends Well

When is a massage not a massage? *When it's not a massage.* Nudge, nudge (wink, wink). Most stories tend to have happy endings but so too do some varieties of massage. I have had dozens of massages in Thailand where it shouldn't be assumed (but if often is) that he or she who works in a massage shop, may also double as a sex worker. During my first trip to Thailand, I struggled with the heat and a massage was a daily Formula One pit stop. I could escape the humidity and the hustle for an hour, with access to toilet and shower facilities, and the air conditioning was reliably fixed on its coldest setting. The healing hands of massage therapists rejuvenated my body and mind before sending me on my way, patched up and ready for the next lap of my adventures. Having a foot massage at the end of a busy day of sightseeing was the closest I have come to believing a heaven exists.

The Thais have exported their massage services around the world, but a typical aromatherapy massage will set you back at least £50 in mainland Europe when I never paid more than £4 in Thailand. Thai massage has cultural and historical roots as an ancient healing system and the practice is, essentially, a form of assisted yoga. Traditional massage doesn't use oil or lotions, and the recipient remains fully clothed while the masseuse pushes and pulls, compresses, rocks and stretches the body. My first traditional Thai massage was delivered by a robust woman the size of Giant Haystacks, the late professional wrestler, and I feared for my life when she raised me in the air and balanced me on her feet like a circus performer, before horribly twisting and contorting my body. When the massage was over (once she had cracked every joint in my fingers and toes), I was saturated in fear sweats and did my best impression of a sufferer of hyperhidrosis.

Thais enjoy taking a massage because it is part of their sabai pursuit of leisure and relaxation. It can reduce stress and relieve health issues and at the very least, it is a social activity as massages are often performed in public places, with recliners lining the streets in popular tourist areas such as Khao San Road. Massage venues are easy to spot, especially in the capital, as groups of uniformed men or women sit and wait on the steps and try to entice clients to wander in and relax. I noticed they often put their youngest and prettiest staff at the entrance, while Macbeth's three witches waited inside the massage rooms.

Perceptions of massage blur, however, when hands become oily. I enjoyed aromatherapy massages as I could lie down and fall asleep as soothing music piped into the room. Aromatherapy uses fragrant oils extracted from herbs, fruits, and flowers, so I often left smelling better than when I arrived, dripping with sweat and diffusing the most unpleasant odours. Most spas display certificates claiming their staff trained at the famous Wat Pho Thai Traditional Medicine and Massage School in Bangkok, with origins dating back to King Rama III, who feared the ancient art of Thai massage was in decline. He had the foresight to establish what is now regarded as Thailand's first university at the temple of Wat Pho, preserving this traditional aspect of Thai culture for future generations of Thais and tourists, and it is still going strong. In the land of counterfeiting, however, accredited certificates from Wat Pho should be taken with a pinch of salts like all those TripAdvisor ratings displayed in almost every empty restaurant and run-down hostel.

Thai massage might be one of Southeast Asia's greatest exports but in Thailand itself, it is a saturated market where supply exceeds demand by a thousand to one. When I explored the nooks and crannies of the city, some streets were massage-only with every shop front overcrowded with bored masseurs. Entrepreneurs have diversified the oil and hands market by creating niche interests with, for example, a Banana Club offering massages just for men, by men, with a shopfront sign carrying - ahem - the image of a slow-peeled, smiling cartoon banana. Thailand, and the capital especially, is a breeding ground for strangeness with phallic shrines, forensic museums and buildings shaped like elephants and robots, but that strangeness extends to its healing arts.

With ladyboy-only massage parlours, a venue advertising a 'Lady of the Night Massage' and another where the staff wear flight attendant uniforms (to each his own, I guess), the concept of what constitutes a 'massage' is somewhat blurred in Thailand. Annie's Soapy Massage Parlour claims to be famous for adding soap and suds to its services, but it's a brothel. I passed a massage venue in 2006 named Miss Puke, which hardly set the tone for pleasure and relaxation. Some establishments advertise prostate massages, and I took pity on their poor staff who, quite understandably, looked thoroughly depressed. I wondered how many boxes of rubber gloves they get through in a year and whether a life of poverty is preferable.

Nuru massages are erotic, body-to-body massages, during which a masseuse slides her (or his) naked body over the client using special gels derived from seaweed. It is claimed the tactile sensations 'relieve stress,' but that sounds like a sloppy euphemism. A massage in Thailand comes with the unfortunate association of the 'happy ending' and to be asked if you would like to have one sounds like a rhetorical question. Why would you choose the unhappy alternative? A happy ending is, however, the lazy man's attempt at masturbation, described as a 'special' massage by the men and women who offer them as they gladly make some money on the side for a few minutes of intimate touching. If asked whether you would like 'boom boom' during the massage and you make the mistake of responding politely in the affirmative, your massage 'therapist' will take off her clothes as 'boom boom' is urban slang for penetrative sex. When a Thai woman calls you 'handsome man,' assume that she thinks you are hideously ugly but at the right price, she'll pretend you are Robert Patterson for three minutes.

How can you tell the difference between a legitimate spa and a knocking shop? It's all in the name. Cockatoo, I was right to assume, is a ladyboy bar while Sexy Night and Shag Bar, not surprisingly, are frequented by willing ladies with individual price tags. At Spanky's there's a lot of spanking. Massage parlours are subtle and more discrete (with the exception of establishments such as Naughty Girls) and keywords often give the game away, by implying the potential for naughty goings-on ('dream,' 'heaven,' 'paradise,' 'happy,' 'love teen,' 'pretty,' 'candy,' 'cherry,' 'honey' and 'sensual,' for example). Their services are as offbeat as their customers with a menu that includes bondage, rape play, hot wax, blindfolding, face sitting, body worshipping, and just about any other deviance you can imagine. If there is someone willing to pay, there will always be someone willing to provide. Intercourse is the 'full service' which sounds like a visit to the dry cleaners or the mechanical services of a Kwik Fit garage.

For those who like to get straight down to business with minimal fuss, there's Dr BJ's Salon on Sukhumvit Road, which is a 'clinic' where the nurses and consultants offer mouth-to-member relief. There is an actual term for these places in Thailand - 'blowjob bars' - and there are hundreds of them in the capital.

For a massage without the extras, Wat Pho is the surest and safest bet. Only in Thailand.

## Chapter 46: Tiger Tempers, Tiger Temple

Tyger tyger, burning bright… in the chains and enclosures of Kanchanaburi Province.

Wat Pha Luang Ta Bua Yanasampanno (the 'Tiger Temple' in tourist parlance), was one of Thailand's 'top' visitor attractions before it was raided and closed down in May 2016. The Thai government sanctioned its Department of National Parks, Wildlife, and Plant Conservation to make a stand for wildlife by sending in five hundred of its officers, wildlife officials and vets to seal the temple's fate and confiscate its 137 'tamed' tigers. It was the nation's temple of controversy for two decades as it leant heavily on an unlikely symbiosis to get away with murder, marketing itself as a union of the natural and spiritual worlds as ochre-clad monks lived in seemingly perfect harmony with endangered animals and their adorable, cutesy cubs. Tourists were welcome to join them, albeit at the right price, in one of the few places in the world where you could pet deadly beasts while they 'slept.' Curiosity was, however, killing the cats and scarring some of their unfortunate admirers for life.

Following some awkward, high-profile standoffs with the wealthy and powerful temple abbot and his monks (they acquired Mafiosi status in the province), the Thai government claimed a considerable scalp when it succeeded in putting the Tiger Temple out of business. There are plans afoot to create a new sanctuary for the relocated tigers which, it must be hoped, does not include an exorbitant entrance fee and tiger merchandise. The Thai government erred when it put the cart in front of the horse, as it would have made more sense to have built the sanctuary before confiscation. The Tiger Temple was a money-spinning enterprise as hundreds of day-trippers flocked to its grounds, from all over the world, to enjoy close encounters with 'wild' and exotic creatures - the picture-perfect subjects for Facebook updates (and worth a six-hour round trip from the capital). The temple was a staple part of the South-east Asian backpacking experience, its unique selling proposition the rare opportunity to cuddle nature's largest cat species at an 'attraction' controlled by Buddhist monks. It was a two birds with one stone bargain: wildlife and religion.

Plagued by years of allegations of abuse, neglect, corruption, illegal breeding and wildlife trafficking, something had to give. The monks were the perfect face and robes to front what was, essentially, a niche enterprise with FTSE 100 potential (had it been relocated to London). The temple was a sweet shop behind which a secret society of gamblers made hay with game room casinos and slot machines. It may have convinced some of its visitors that it was an animal sanctuary, their fees contributing to the conservation of the species, but in practise, it was a poorly managed zoo. It wasn't the holy place I expected it to be, but not all monks are as holy as you would expect them to be either. All that glitters may not necessarily be gold, and he who wears orange may be a con artist soliciting unwarranted donations.

In September 2014, a story broke like a cherished Ming vase when eighteen 'fake monks' were arrested in Suphanburi Province for posing as holy men so they could finagle donations which, reporters claimed, they used to fund their gambling addictions and purchase pornography and hard drugs. I stumbled upon some novice monks enjoying a cigarette break in the shade of a temple in Thonburi, a quiet district of Bangkok, when I followed the route of one of the circuits in Kenneth Barrett's *22 Walks in Bangkok*. I was more embarrassed by their indiscretions than they were, and they even offered a cigarette from a packet of Krong Thip, which is a popular brand in Thailand. Like gangster wannabes of the cloth, they posed for a group photograph with cigarettes in hands and mouths.

As an aside, if you want to give up smoking but can't find the resolve, I suggest you ignore your doctor's advice, plan a short holiday in Thailand and attempt to buy a packet of cigarettes when you get that first craving for nicotine. In western countries, packets come with restrained warnings such as 'Smoking kills' and 'Smoking is highly addictive, don't start,' but in Thailand they carry gratuitously offensive images like miniature posters for gore and splatter movies, taking the graphic label concept into the territory of Wes Craven nightmares. Whenever I popped into a 7-Eleven to buy bread and milk, I had to avert my eyes from the shelves or else vomit all over the assistant.

In 2013, the greatest religious scandal of my time in Thailand hit the front pages when a jet-setting monk (with a hi-so lifestyle) had a Harrison Ford moment and became an unlikely fugitive. Luang Pu Nen Kham, who now goes by his pre-monastic name of Wirapol Sukphol, sucked all the credibility out of his role as a monk when he was hotly pursued across the globe by the Thai authorities to face accusations of statutory rape, money laundering and drug trafficking. He was photographed aboard a private jet with Louis Vuitton hand luggage and aviator sunglasses, fingering a thick wad of cash like Harry Enfield's *Loadsamoney*. He was too cool for monkhood, with thug life excesses and designer luxury winning over his monastic vow to lead a simple life.

He was defrocked in absentia when the authorities issued a warrant for his arrest, and there are claims that he accumulated personal assets worth a billion baht. If crime doesn't pay, religious lifestyles can be rewarding. Wearing the colours of a monk's robes also pays dividends at Thailand's airports, with specially reserved seats in waiting lounges and priority boarding over first class passengers. Wirapol Sukphol has found a new lease of life - without a life sentence - in the US, where he has sought permanent residency and even plans to open a new 'monastery.' Corruption abounds like lubricant in Thailand, penetrating even the holiest of places.

The Tiger Temple was the photo opportunity, par excellence, for trophy hunters and gatherers. I visited the temple in June 2013, but I was oblivious to all the controversy. When I returned to Bangkok, I shared the exploits of my weekend in Kanchanaburi with colleagues, and before I had a chance to offer an opinion, they formed a picket line of animal rights activists. I was a man condemned, guilty of sinning against the natural world. Having seen the temple with my own eyes, I could offer an informed opinion. And I agreed with them, it was horribly exploitative, so there was no need to hold placards with bold print messages: 'He's been to the Tiger Temple!' My morality was on trial and I understood how the witches felt during their trials of the mid-1640s, but I did not regret my decision as I was curious about my host nation, warts and all.

When I ordered shark fin soup in Bangkok's Chinatown district (where every restaurant window has a display of fins like a row of oversized teeth), I acquired the status of a serial killer. I was Si Quey Mk II; my arc was complete. I could not eat the tiny portion of fin that was floating in the bowl as the taste of the broth was unappealing, and trying to eat a dorsal fin is like chewing on a rubber flipper. The consumption of this soup dates back to Ming Dynasty China and for the Chinese, it is one of the eight treasured foods from the sea. But it is a delicate and controversial delicacy, and I now understand why, having watched a documentary titled *Shark Bait* presented by popular chef Gordon Ramsey (a proud patron of Shark Trust, though he probably shouldn't be).

In the Channel 4 documentary, Ramsey exposes and rallies against the gruesome process of 'finning,' when the fins are mercilessly separated from the body. Once removed, the shark is tossed back into the ocean, still alive, but unable to swim freely (which usually results in rapid sinking and slow suffocation or, worse still, being eaten alive by other predators). I was sickened to the pit of my stomach by the moving images on the screen, and I wouldn't have ordered that bowl of soup had I seen that documentary first. But unlike Gordon Ramsey, I can't be accused of hypocrisy: I did not enter into a foul-mouthed crusade to describe the indiscriminate slaughter of the world's shark population as 'cruel,' 'sick' and 'barbaric' having been filmed sport fishing and capturing a rare breed off the Florida coast (which a taxidermist turned into a trophy of his derring-do). Ramsey preferred to catch and kill, instead of release, and to use his words from the documentary: 'Fucking leave them alone and respect their beauty!' The same can be said of some of Thailand's captive tigers; they are long overdue a return to the forests of the night.

Visitors to the Tiger Temple enjoyed proximity with wild animals that would never be permitted in the health and safety conscious countries they call home, where zoo animals are observed from afar with dangerous animals kept behind bars or reinforced glass. But as Southeast Asia readily breaks with convention, you can probably have a sit-down lunch with a shark before eating it for supper. The utterly unusual experience the Tiger Temple offered was a golden opportunity for the monks to make millions as satisfied selfie-snapping tourists queued around the block to part with their money, the majority unaware of the national and international controversy the temple courted. In their defence, I was blissful in my ignorance for about five minutes, until I observed passive creatures that did not behave remotely like wild animals.

The natural instincts of the tigers seemed to have deserted them; they were more like lambs without bleats. I was reminded of the cats I rehomed when I watched full-grown predators roll on their backs to have their tummies tickled. My senses were on high alert, and I was in a state of continuous nervous tension for the whole hour I spent on the temple's grounds, no matter how hard volunteer staff tried to reassure me that as the tigers had been reared by hand, they were 'completely tame.'

Tigers are naturally active creatures, but without exercise, they tend to get fat and lazy like humans. They feed on a diet of red meat which contains the taurine enzyme and other essential vitamins for muscle development and the promotion of their long-term health. But what they received at the Tiger Temple was an American diet of chicken for breakfast, lunch and dinner as white meat is cheaper than red (though I am sure the monks could have afforded the latter with all those donations). Many of the tigers were placid, docile creatures that could barely be bothered to move an inch. The exception was a separate enclosure where in exchange for another fee, tourists could 'play' with adult tigers by holding long poles with bags of air attached, which the tigers seemed to enjoy jumping for and clawing at as did my cats when I used a similar toy. It was a high-risk game to play, to stimulate and agitate wild animals in their enclosure with no protection other than hands and sticks. Two months after my brief visit in August 2013, a university student was knocked to the ground and mauled by an adult when she tried to wash its back, which should have been a strong deterrent and reminder of the latent but ever-present dangers, but it didn't put the tourists off.

The tigers don't care too much for religious persuasions either, as one of the monks was admitted into intensive care when he was attacked in May 2015 and suffered a broken arm, a broken tooth, and scratches to his face. He was walking a tiger on a lead but slipped and fell over, which startled the animal and triggered its aggression. When I reflect on my visit, I accept that it was foolish to walk openly and freely with tigers having been reassured that I would be safe; my actions defied common sense and betrayed an evolution of survival instincts in a country where animals and tourists are not as protected as they should be. There was something rotten in the idylls of Kanchanaburi Province, and William Blake must have been somersaulting in his grave as he observed his fellow man turn one of nature's finest creations into a theme park attraction. As almost anything can be counterfeited in Southeast Asia, I wondered if some enterprising monks had created the tigers' fearful symmetry by painting a few strokes of orange on complicit stray dogs that had come begging for food, but got more than they bargained.

Stupid is as stupid does, which includes taking a full-grown, unpredictable and wild animal for an unsupervised walk. I did not dare to tug on its leash so the tiger, effectively, took me for a walk on the wild side. If it led me to lunch and I was the main course, it would have been my fault. I have already mentioned how finding reliable health and safety precautions in this region is an Abominable Snowman in a paddock of unicorns, so there I was, leash in hand, walking beside an adult tiger which could have torn out my throat had I stepped on its tail. I wouldn't have stood much of a chance against a four-hundred-pound animal, and when I nervously glanced down at the furry companion by my side as he led the way to the tiger canyon, I realised how ridiculous I must have looked and cringed.

Man's best friend should not have the capacity to dine on his companion, but it also occurred to me that I had not seen any sign of a temple at the Tiger Temple, and I couldn't detect any religious or conservation value in my visit. It was a highly profitable attraction disguised as something wholesome. Entrance fees were 'welcome donations' which had to be paid to enter the site or feed, walk and cuddle the big cats. Even as I write these words, the absurdity of what I am describing is not lost on me. I didn't know what to expect on arrival, but on exit, I understood that I had entered one of the most unethical tourist traps in the world. I could escape it, but the tigers remained trapped, waiting for liberation.

Despite making promises not to breed or make commercial use of the animals, baby tigers were the star attraction as they could be held and cuddled while fed bottle-after-bottle of formula milk, which seemed to be the must-have phototrophy for visitors to collect, like a stamp in a passport to brag about later. As more and more cubs were born and hand-reared by the monks, the temple was accused of being a breeding farm with the cubs a cash cow guaranteeing high returns, as tourists queued to join the morning and afternoon feeding programme with the cubs fed on repeat to the point of bursting.

Tempers flared, and the flames of anger were fanned by former long-term veterinarian Dr Somchai Wisetmongkolchai, who rediscovered his conscience and medical ethics and spilled the milk. He claimed three 'missing' tigers were sold for butchering and medical harvesting on the Chinese market, with the body of an adult cat having an estimated wholesale worth of five million baht (about £100,000). The murky world of the Tiger Temple found exposure to the sun. The presiding abbot, Phra Jakkit Sanhakitteko, calmly denied all claims of wrongdoing with a passable impression of Arsene Wenger when one of his players commits a serious foul, or his team has benefitted from an unfair refereeing advantage: 'I didn't see anything happen here.'

With Thailand's national animal at severe risk of extinction, tigers were fair game, and I saw all manner of wild animals on Thailand's streets where in exchange for a few baht, you can handle them as much as you like (whether they like it or not). In Kanchanaburi Town, I passed a wooden shophouse which had a leopard cub chained in a fixed position for the attention of passing tourists. For twenty baht (40p), visitors could touch and stroke it or pose and grin for selfies. Like tiger cubs, they are usually taken from their mothers during the first few weeks of their lives so they can be socialised with humans and be readied to net considerable gains. Because of this withdrawal and heavy petting (in the wild a cub will live with its mother for up to two years), they fail to form the natural predatory instincts they would need for survival if released. When the shopkeeper noticed me photographing the sad and sorry state of his leopard, he was insistent that I should pay for the shot, rubbing his thumbs and index fingers together. I held my ground and refused, suggesting that it might be a good idea to give the poor creature a bowl of water as it was exposed all day to the sun and was panting heavily.

When I visited Phuket, I had a Slow Loris thrust in my face every night as their handlers complete nightly circuits of all the tourist bars and clubs.

They are unimaginably cute creatures, like living teddy bears, and while they are conveniently nocturnal, they are a shy, endangered and protected species, but that doesn't seem to carry much weight when there is money to be made. They are poisonous too so they often have their teeth pulled before handling so they can't bite their owners or the tourists who stroke them. As a species ourselves, we are programmed from birth to have a fascination with cute and cuddly animals. We anthropomorphise them in children's books and films so when given the opportunity, we can't resist cuddling up to dolphins, baby elephants, monkeys and tiger cubs, but it is unlikely they ever feel the same way about us.

There was a photo and molestation set list at the Tiger Temple: bottle-feeding; sitting with and holding a tiger's tail; walking one on a leash and laying down for a group photo with 'sleeping' tigers (by which I mean heavily sedated). And they were sedated, without question. I observed the monks walk among the tigers in a small canyon they have created, as one of the volunteers tried to distract us with precise instructions on how to 'safely interact' with them. There was no need for an explanation as they were completely lifeless lumps of meat, once the monks had fingered their nostrils and magically induced a state of sedation. I failed to understand how such mistreatment and hollow interaction with one of nature's apex predators could be described or reviewed as an enjoyable 'attraction.' The monks did, however, make some considerable investments at the site with a Tiger Island opened in 2011 to house twenty-eight open enclosures, though the cynic in me regards it as an opportunistic attempt to offset external pressures and appease a throng of vociferous critics. When the temple was raided, the monks deserted it like a sinking ship, and when forty frozen cub carcases were discovered in a freezer (and twenty more preserved in jars of formaldehyde), the ship found its way to the bottom of the ocean with all those finless sharks.

The Tiger Temple was a Tiger Business first and foremost. I seriously doubt my 'donation' was ever used to support conservation efforts (though some of the monks wore nifty sunglasses) as the monks were busy building themselves a penthouse crib with the proceeds, with giant statues of tigers and their cubs and Loadsamoney gilding. I should have picked up on the Playboy Mansion tell-tale signs when I was driven through the open mouth of a giant tiger at the entrance to the compound. When I returned to my waiting taxi, the driver was curious to know whether I had enjoyed myself as he couldn't detect a smile on my face:

'You have fun time?'

It was neither entertaining nor educational, and it wasn't fun. Instead, I was left with a strong urge to make merit and atone for my visit, and if this chapter encourages readers to think twice about wildlife tourism and question whether it is always ethical and animal-friendly, merit will be made.

## Chapter 47: Muay Thai and National Sports

National sports and pastimes are intrinsic to the history, culture and identity of all nations. For many western countries, the national sport will involve a ball of some kind and a bat, but in Southeast Asia, they are very much hands-on. Muay Thai (or Thai Boxing) is the cultural sport of Thailand, a hard form, close-combat martial art from the rural heartlands that is so heavily ritualistic, it is like watching and waiting for a flower to bloom on the first day of spring. And just like the water-throwing festival of Songkran, Muay Thai is not exclusive to Thailand as there are variations on the boxing and kicking theme in Cambodia, where they enjoy Pradal Serey ('free boxing'), Lethwei in Myanmar, Tomoi in Malaysia, and Lao Boxing in Laos. But why is Muay Thai such a popular sport at home and abroad?

King Bhumibol was an avid fan, which in part explains its domestic appeal and growth in the last century, while the mixed martial arts industry - which has exploded globally - has positioned Muay Thai as a premium product. For the people of Thailand, it is more than a sport: a way of life, it provides a means by which to make a modest living, with up to sixty thousand professional fighters competing at any one time. A network of gyms shares a common mantra: *Train like a Thai to fight like a Thai.*

Muay Thai is a unique form of martial art and is commonly referred to as the 'Art of Eight Limbs.' Taekwondo and Karate forbid the use of the elbow and knee, but when confronted with a real life self-defensive situation, we use them instinctively. Muay Thai opponents are licensed to strike with punches, kicks, elbows and knees, thus creating eight points of contact. The whole body is, effectively, weaponised: hands mimic the movements and cuts of swords and daggers; shins and forearms shield against blows like protective armour; challengers are felled with elbow strikes like a heavy hammer, while legs and knees function as axe and staff as they probe for an opening to disarm and engage.

Muay Thai's origins can be traced back to the Sukhothai period, a time of warring kingdoms, when soldiers were instructed in hand-to-hand combat and weapons handling (Krabi Krabong) to protect the first capital of Thailand from invaders. What was ingrained in the culture of the early Siamese people has evolved into a modern-day competitive game and pastime which, subconsciously, connects the Thai people with the traditions of their past, while consciously providing a platform for serious gambling.

Modern Muay Thai found exposure and international recognition from an unlikely source: The Second World War. Fascinated overseas soldiers coined the term 'Siam Boxing' due its unique rules of engagement, while the French dubbed it 'Le Sport Orient.' Keen to have a go themselves, they were taught the fundamentals and traditions by their Thai counterparts, word spread and the sport adapted to the modern age with rings replacing open courtyards, gloves preferred to rope or leather bindings, and female and foreign fighters welcomed. It is now a governed, organised sport and the rubber stamp of approval will come with its inclusion as an Olympic sport, a campaign spearheaded by the World Muaythai Council.

My first experience of Muay Thai came in the summer of 2006 at the legendary Lumpinee Boxing Stadium in Bangkok. A former mecca for boxing enthusiasts, it opened its doors in March 1956 but closed for demolition and relocation in 2014, transferring to a swanky, air-conditioned venue on the other side of town. It marked the end of an era for leaky Lumpinee which had outlived its run-down, rusty mess of a structure with a circular roof bolted together with sheets of tin. It did, however, have a special sense of charm and history as it harkened back to the capital's golden days before the incursion of modernity with skyscrapers and supermalls. Lumpinee's central staging ring provided a platform upon which fifty years of champions contended their status as Thailand's greatest Muay Thai fighter.

As a foreigner on fight night and with its dual pricing policy, I paid two thousand baht (£40) for a ringside seat and an uninterrupted view. Hundreds of Thai devotees gathered outside the stadium, spilling out onto busy Rama IV Road and surrounded by an equal number of mobile food stalls. Pushing my way through the crowd, giant advertising hoardings stared me down as the heroes of the day raised their gloves and flexed their muscles. Within the inner confines of Lumpinee, I wondered whether I had taken a wrong turn as bare-chested men were rubbed down with liniment to glisten beneath spotlights, while herbal aromas filled the air to mask the odour of dampness. Ringside, I was at the heart of the cultural mothership. The air crackled with energy as spectators shouted into phones or wildly gesticulated with their hands to place bets on favourites, while rhythmic drums set the pace to frenetic. Not a single seat was occupied, and faces were obscured by hands as the stadium and spectators transformed before me into a Wall Street trading floor during the stock exchange collapse of 1929. I was a time traveller with one foot in the present and one in the past as conditioned fighters entered the ring to perform the wai kru ram muay - a ritual dance rooted in Buddhist spirituality - before the main event of hard kicking, knee and elbow strikes.

Boxers wear sacred headpieces (the 'mongkol,' which is fashioned from woven rope, thread and silk) and these are presented to them by trainers in recognition of their dedication to training, their understanding of the culture and traditions of Muay Thai, and their readiness for combat. Headpieces are traditionally blessed by monks for good luck, and foreign fighters have been known to honour the tradition. The mongkol also holds symbolic importance, recognising as it does the roles 'significant others' have played and contributed to a fighter's journey and success in the ring, such as hometown gyms, coaches and a cast of supportive family. Before the fighting begins, the trainers ceremoniously remove the mongkol and say a short prayer, but the 'prajioud' (optional arm bands) remain tied in place as additional charms for protection. Traditionally, the prajioud was made from a piece of fabric torn from a sarong, a throwback to times of war when mothers blessed their sons before they set off for national or regional conflicts.

Thais love their tattoos, but for Muay Thai fighters they are more than flesh art as the traditional sak yant tattoo has a history of some two thousand years. Sak yant tattoos are hand-etched onto the skin by Buddhist monks using simple, bamboo needles. They feature a mixture of Buddhist prayers and ancient geometric designs, which are believed to bestow upon the fighter sacred and magical powers associated with luck, strength, healing and protection. Bangkok's Wat Bang Phra Temple has become something of a pilgrimage site for Thai people, backpackers and Muay Thai fighters as they join to sit in a peaceful queue and wait their turn for the magic ink. I have resisted late-night inducements to get tattoos of Manchester United legends and logos, but I was seriously tempted to get a magic-infused tattoo in Thailand. And who would have thought a boxing match would reveal so much about a country's history, culture and spirituality? Festivals and national sports are golden tickets to cultural appreciation.

My first trip to Japan was, likewise, made more memorable for sporting reasons when I sat ringside to watch an elite sumo wrestling competition at the Ryogoku Kokugikan in Tokyo (the National Sumo Hall). Japan captured my childhood imagination, appealing to me as some mythical creature with one foot in our world and the other in some ethereal elsewhere. Images of ladies with painted faces, dressed in kimonos, were more like their Manga counterparts than actual living, breathing human beings, and when I watched my first televised sumo wrestling competition, I could only assume that the television camera was invented a thousand years ago. Who were those flickering, flabby behemoths? What was all that pre-bout ceremony for, all that effort, just to push each other out of a giant ring? As I entered the arena some thirty years later, the Japanese flag hovered above the dohyo (the sumo ring) with its solitary red dot catching my eye, and I observed a displaced scene from Japan's feudal past as men in traditional costumes raked the mud to prepare the dohyo for the first tournament bout.

I always travel in pursuit of cultural difference, and there is no better place to find it than Japan. Japanese culture is as distinct as it gets, having been closed off from the rest of the world for the best part of two centuries. Japan developed independently, removed from the cultural interchange and influences of its Sinosphere neighbours in East Asia. Geographically, it sits on the edge of the world, and this is the perfect metaphor for its remoteness. Japan has an unbroken history of independence: it was never colonised or influenced by foreign powers so it is no surprise, therefore, that for most of the modern, western world, Japan continues to evoke images of deadly ninjas, noble samurai and sumo wrestlers. It can only be expected that the Japanese do things differently and they don't disappoint (try using one of their toilets).

Sporting pursuits continue the trend as we usually admire athletes for their athleticism, but in Japan, it is all about the bulk and brawn. *Bigger* is *better*. Sumo wrestlers are the equivalent of Hollywood film stars and, despite their size, they can move with astonishing agility as their initial charges are all about pace, positioning and power. In the United States, WWE wrestling is an icon of American popular culture with all its modern showbiz glamour, but Sumo wrestling is Japan's national sport, having originated in ancient times as a performance to entertain the Shinto deities. Many rituals with religious contexts are still performed to this day, such as the symbolic purification of the ring with salt and the stamping of feet to disperse evil forces.

In Japan, sumo wrestling is considered a martial art (or 'gendai budo') and in line with tradition, only men are permitted to practise the sport professionally. They must comply with a strict set of rules for lifestyle and public conduct (as defined by the Sumo Association) and are required to live in a 'heya' which is the communal training stable. Highly regimented lifestyles and codes of honour include rules for meals and how to dress. This ancient sport has hardly changed over hundreds of years, and the wrestlers' iconic hair style (a topknot of hair called a 'chonage') is a symbolic connection with the past, as it is the same style the samurai of the Edo Period used to wear. I am not a fan of wrestling at all - in fact, I am more likely to volunteer to put toothpaste back in its tube - but there is no denying that watching a sumo tournament is at the apex of cultural experiences in Asia.

Ryogoku is a fascinating district in Tokyo where the Ryogoku Kokugikan, famous sumo stables, chanko restaurants and other sumo-related attractions are located. I wanted to try the sumo diet, so I set aside a couple of hours at a chankonabe restaurant where I ate as much Japanese stew as my body could hold (sumos eat it in vast quantities to help them gain extra weight). To work off the calories, I visited the sumo 'beya' or training stables where aspiring champions hone their skills in preparation for the annual tournaments. The Ryogoku seats over ten thousand visitors and hosts three of the six annual sumo tournaments (in January, May and September). Bouts are scheduled throughout the day and usually last a few intense seconds with lots of ritual posturing, stretching, stamping and salt-tossing. I was surprised to see two western wrestlers compete and this is, perhaps, the sport's first step towards a global audience. In recent years, non-Japanese competitors have attained the sport's highest rank of 'yokozuna' (Grand Champion).

Simplicity is the key to sumo. Some sports have complex rules and football is the obvious example, with its 'Laws of the Game' having been published by FIFA, its governing body. Almost every week of the football calendar, pundits debate the laws of the offside rule and what constitutes a 'professional foul' (there is even a rule for the colour of artificial surfaces). A bout of sumo wrestling, by contrast, is won when one opponent pushes the other out of the inner circle or throws him over in the dohyo (the loser need only put a toe or heel over the straw bales marking the circle and its game over). Should a wrestler stumble and touch the ground with any part of his body (which includes the tip of a finger or his top-knot), he loses the match. Striking opponents with fists, hair pulling, eye gouging, choking and kicking in the stomach or chest are prohibited, and it is against the rules to seize the part of the band covering the vital organs. As there are no weight limits, it is possible for a sumo to find himself pitted against an opponent twice his weight. Who cares about fairness? It's all about the spectacle and it is fat-tastic to behold.

Sumo wrestlers are the very embodiment of Japan's traditional values: dignity, discipline and respect. The Japanese name these collective virtues 'hinkaku' and the wrestlers are a reminder to modern Japan of the values it should still hold dear. The solitary dot on the national flag reminded me of the cultural separateness of this fascinating sport and people as I tucked into my bento box full of warm rice, fish, fresh vegetables and meat. I wondered what a Thai or Japanese holidaymaker would make of my own country's national sport and cringed at the thought of vile terrace chants and images of players surrounding the referee to contest a decision.

In the Philippines, they prefer a more immediate and bloodthirsty variety of ringside combat: cockfighting. I had the opportunity to visit the La Loma Cockpit in Quezon City, one of the oldest arenas in the Philippines (established in 1902), which is both legal and fully licensed and has a seating capacity of 3,500. Local expert and cockfighting enthusiast - Nympha Flores - was my guide for the day and she welcomed me to an unfamiliar world, offering fascinating insights into Filipino psychology, tradition, and culture.

A wise traveller will always look beyond the postcard and travel guide depictions to seek and find, if he can, what it is that makes the country visited different from his own. Reflecting on his time living and travelling across the subcontinent of India, Rudyard Kipling observed: 'The first condition of understanding a foreign country is to smell it.' I was curious to witness and understand the Filipino love affair with cockfighting, the cultural equivalent of Spanish bullfighting. Before I set off to visit new places and experience other cultures, I try not to pack any prejudices with my socks and underwear; any sense of self-righteousness should be left at home. A traveller should observe and resist judging his hosts. Differences should be celebrated, even when they challenge the gravitational pull of one's moral compass. After all, if the world were all the same, we would never present our boarding passes, and our garden fences would be the limit of our experiences.

Cockfighting is the unofficial national sport of the Philippines and a quasi-religion, as gambling denizens gather in their bloody temples to participate in the world's oldest blood and spectator sport (mosaics from ancient Rome have been unearthed with depictions of fighting cocks). The Philippines hosts the World Slasher Cup, which is a biannual tournament regarded as the supreme cockfighting event in a multi-million-pound business. The sport is regulated and legitimised, so the government takes its share of the spoils, much like the red light scene in the Netherlands. Rules will always be broken, so while freelance sex workers walk the streets of the Dutch capital, illegal cockfights take place in every Filipino community. I could hear crowing cocks everywhere, and I was never far away from a fighting arena, official or otherwise.

At the La Loma Cockpit, Nympha explained the daily routines of the handlers as sparring partners are weighed and matched and their curved fighting blades attached by the fitters (or 'gaffers'). If a fitter's blade is attached to a winning cock, they get paid by the handler. I was quite surprised by the passivity of the birds in their feathery shades of brown, red and gold, as they gently nestled in their handlers' arms like boats on a calm sea before a storm. When she was a child, Nympha's father used to breed and fight birds in the backyard of the family home. She recounted stories of how he excluded her from those feathery duels (called 'sabong' in the Philippines) as cockfighting is a pastime for men and serious gamblers. She recalled how she would climb a tree and watch in secret, fascinated by the frenzy and heated activity as bets were placed, won and lost below. I visited La Loma on a Sunday, the busiest day of the week with up to a hundred bouts. I was warmly welcomed by curious arena veterans and kindly offered a VIP seat with a literal birds-eye view, right up against the glass by the ringside entrance where the handlers queue for their turn, cock-in-hand (so to speak).

It was a truly authentic glimpse into Filipino culture, and a highly ritualistic, brutal and bloody 'sport.' I wasn't put off by the sign on entry which demanded spectators deposit their guns, and I was the only westerner in attendance. My status was bumped up to the 'celebrity minor' category, and the crowds obliged me when I photographed their frenzied hand signals as they placed bets. The cockerels that are selected to fight in the arenas are 'gamecocks' as they have been bred by their handlers over generations to be highly aggressive, their lineage carefully managed. A famous joke (attributed to national hero, Jose Rizal) pokes fun at the breeders for spending more time with their cocks than they do with their wives and children. At the La Loma Cockpit, Nympha showed me the purpose-built R&R rooms where the cocks rest and relax before tournaments begin, adding that their owners sometimes join them. Even the family's rice money is not sacred and could be spent on expensive vitamins to condition and strengthen the birds.

La Loma is a modern-day gladiatorial arena: cocks thrust and cut with razor-sharp steel blades attached to their legs, fighting instinctively for territorial dominance and survival, while the excited and animated crowds bay and cheer, having chosen their champion and placed their bets. The pre-bout betting fever is an incredible spectacle for a foreign visitor to behold; when the bell rings, the pantomime of yelling, roaring, and wild gesticulation begins. Amid all the apparent chaos and confusion, the bet-takers ('kristos') casually scan the terraces to mentally take note of every hand signal with each one connoting a separate betting amount. It was the purest form of brain gym I have ever witnessed. The cocks are the epitome of passive-aggressive as they transform - in an instant - to tear each other to pieces until one of them resembles the spilt contents of a pillow. Their training is evident as they lull each other into a false sense of security, appearing more interested in displaying their feathers or pecking the ground for invisible seed, when suddenly their aggressive, territorial instincts take effect, spiked by adrenaline. Sometimes, within just a few seconds, a fatal blow is landed.

At the end of each contest, the referee declares the winner, money changes hands (or is thrown) and the next bout begins. The vanquished featherators exit the arena in a plastic bucket - an ignoble end - only to be plucked and gutted outside and sold for their very fresh meat (no commercial opportunity is wasted). The signs of suffering are dotted on paths in red blotches, and the victors are carried off to a cock-medic in a makeshift bird surgery behind the arena, where they are hastily patched up for a small fee so they can live to fight another day. The cocks are not the only victims, as there have been instances when handlers (and spectators) have been cut open by pumped up feathered cutthroats. If you were to stand and directly face a cockerel, they would regard you as a challenger and the locals will place a bet on the cock. The cocks are so fierce the arena perimeter is made of Plexiglas - the same glass used for commercial aircraft windows.

Watching animals fight, suffer and die is not my idea of a pleasurable pastime (in truth, I found it quite disturbing at times, despite the consuming enthusiasm all around me), but there is no denying the role of cockfighting in the social and cultural spectrum for Filipinos. Social scientists have speculated that its popularity is borne of the Filipino mentality, a national personality trait and passion for brevity called 'ningas kugon,' which is a reference to wild cogon grass which burns hot and fast. Filipinos enjoy cockfighting because it is a short-lived enthusiasm.

Cockfighting is not burdened by the social class prejudices of other animal sports such as horse riding or fox hunting so that anyone can take part, politician or farmer. It is a form of escapism from the drudgery of daily life in a country where poverty is at the forefront of the national consciousness. In Roman times, emperors hoped to distract the poor from their poverty and quell any thoughts of revolt; the gladiatorial games were more spectacular, expensive and elaborate over time, often involving numerous participants or outlandish features such as exotic wild animals and re-enactments of famous battle scenes. Ultimately, they were a strategic opiate for the masses, and in modern-day Manilla, if you can't feed the poor, you may as well distract them.

# Chapter 48: Thai-Burma Death Railway

I was surprised to discover how much Second World War history traces back to Southeast Asia. Harbour defences shielded Corregidor Island from Japanese invasion in the Philippines, and a Death Railway network connected Thailand to neighbouring Myanmar. Kanchanaburi Province is western Thailand's unlikely setting for war, aerial bombing campaigns, prisoner-of-war encampments and crimes against humanity. It is one of Southeast Asia's classically original locations, full of extraordinary beauty and grand scenery with dense forests, lush wetlands, limestone caves, waterfalls, rugged hills and enough flourishing wildlife to fill the pages of Rudyard Kipling's *The Jungle Book*. The unrelenting Japanese war machine found its way to peaceful Kanchanaburi Province, which, in turn, found worldwide recognition when a bridge was built over its river before it was immortalised by celluloid strips in David Lean's *The Bridge on the River Kwai*.

Kanchanaburi Province has a broad range of natural and man-made delights to engage and entertain its tourists. And much like modern-day Vietnam, there is more to this province than war. Kanchanaburi Town is comfortable with its association with the Second World War as this is the primary draw for the mass of tourists filling its restaurants, museums, hotels and guesthouses. With the Tiger Temple wiped from the tourism map, elephant sanctuaries offer genuine retreats for volunteers to help protect and conserve a threatened species. For those with interest in hydroelectric power, there is day-trip potential in the Srinakarin Dam in the Si Sawat district of Kanchanaburi, a rockfill dam with a clay core and a total generating capacity of 720mw. It is the third-largest dam of its kind in Thailand, and it spans the Kwai Noi River, but it is also a great spot for those in search of death by creeping boredom.

I visited the dam on what must have been the worst school trip of my career and childhood combined. My Thai colleagues organised a science discovery project so our students could learn about the dam and power plant, which are 'landmarks' of Kanchanaburi Province I never wanted to see, in this life or the next. The dam is a blot on rural Thailand and to compound the lack of interest it held for me, it was a weekend visit. I felt sorry for my students as we wasted a whole day of our lives - time we will never get back - traipsing around a power plant learning about hydroelectric power, pressing knobs and buttons while men in hard hats offered exhaustive explanations about how this panel or that lever worked.

Overseas teachers rarely volunteer to join Thai school trips as they are bone-dry and formal affairs, but at least I had some fun with my students when we gathered for shared meals at the hotel. Some Thai words and names have unfortunate English meanings and associations. I had students with colourful names such as Porn (which means 'blessing'), Pornthip (a 'splendid' blessing) and Pornpiss ('full' of blessings) which are cute names from their parents' perspectives, but rather awkward for a polite foreigner. Thai children are often aware of the unfavourable connotations of their names, but they respect the fact that their parents chose them. When I asked one of the boys to explain what he was eating (he was devouring his food like a prisoner on day release), he replied:

'Fuktong!'

*Excuse me?* Fuk Tong Pad Khai is stir-fried pumpkin with egg with the 'fuk' referring to any gourd or squash, with fuktongs and fukmeaws aplenty. Language, like politics, is a blindfolded walk through a cultural minefield in Thailand. How should you react to a woman who tells you her name is Fukmee? My cultural awkwardness provided my students with much amusement, so I played along and asked Terdsak to pass me the bowl of pricks on his table. 'Prick' is the Thai word for chilli peppers.

The popular Erawan Waterfalls (of the impressive Erawan National Park) are, by a country mile, the best falls I have enjoyed in all Southeast Asia. Mother Nature layered the falls over seven platforms, and I could swim in emerald pools which doubled as complimentary fish spas as Garra rufa (nicknamed 'the fish doctor') nibbled away contentedly on my dead skin. Tanks of these fish can be seen on the streets of most resort towns where they are a novelty and cultural curiosity for tourists. They offer a cut-price pedicure, but at the Erawan National Park, they have developed into full-grown adults. It took me a while to get used to their ticklish lips as they sucked and tugged on my nipples and just about everything else below water (I didn't have the courage to skinny-dip). It took me four hours to climb to the top of the falls with pool breaks, but there wasn't much wildlife to witness as the tourists scared it all away as they hollered from branches and dive-bombed in paradise.

Kanchanaburi Province does not have a regular taxi service like the capital. To reach sites of interest, I either booked a driver through my hostel when I had a clear destination in mind (such as the Tiger Temple), or hitchhiked from site to site on the backs of strangers' pickup trucks (which was great fun, aside from the flies that hitched a ride on the back of my throat). On my first outing to the province in 2011, I took the budget travel option when I boarded a train from Bangkok's Thonburi Station which bumped me all the way to my destination - stopping at every platform - on hard and splintered wooden seats. Those five hours felt like fifty, and I could have drowned on the humidity inside the carriage as I rubbernecked for countryside views and desperately inhaled the slithers of fresh air that slipped through broken rubber seals. I have travelled around the world in eighty trains, so the romance of rail escapes me. Whenever I returned to this province, I used the capital's faster-than-speeding-light minivan services which could beat the Millennium Falcon in a race to the Death Star.

The region's iconic attraction is easy to find, as Kanchanaburi Town expands around the bridge over the Kwai Noi River. It was popularised by French author Pierre Boulle when his novel *Le Pont de la Rivière* published in 1952, and a film adaptation followed five years later with memorable performances by Alec Guinness, Jack Hawkins and William Holden: *The Bridge on the River Kwai*. In 2014, the history of the bridge and the Thai-Burma Railway it served, was refreshed for modern audiences with the release of *The Railway Man*. The film stars Colin Firth as surviving British serviceman Eric Lomax, who revisits his nightmares when he returns to Kanchanaburi Province to meet and confront the man who caused him so much pain, Nagase, a Japanese officer and translator. It is a true story, but it didn't throw new light on one of the darkest chapters in military history.

The horrors of the Second World War are inescapable in the small town. I was returned to the classroom to fill in the blanks of my knowledge as well as the realms of dark tourism with a 'Death Railway' reminding me of all those terrifying rides you find at amusement parks with carriages carrying screams through over-haunted houses. But there was nothing at all amusing about the Death Railway, or the suffering inflicted on the Allied POWs, who had to endure psychological as well as physiological torment as they toiled in the tropics and served the whims of their sadistic captors. Two deactivated bombs flank the entrance to the town's mostly reconstructed bridge, and they set the tone for serious reflection. The bridge stands as a symbolic reminder of the terrible traumas the Japanese army inflicted on its prisoners of war in this region, where they exploited forced labour to create a strategic supply line to carry their troops and supplies from Thailand into British-colonial Burma, to expedite their expansion into Southeast Asia.

I could walk across the black iron bridge and pass from the east bank to the west, and I enjoyed some low-level thrills as crossings on foot have to be timed with passing trains in mind. I was mindful of my step as there are a few unguarded drops and of the original bridge, only two central pairs of girders remain. The POWs would never have imagined that the bridge they built would endure to become a tourist attraction with annual re-enactments of their suffering. They deliberately bungled its construction whenever they could as this delayed its completion, and the British Royal Air Force finished the job when they bombed it. There is a grim but informative Death Railway Museum and Research Centre which is a short walk from the bridge. It contains artefacts, survivor accounts and graphic photos which are hard evidence of the forced labour, malnutrition and the conditions the POWs were forced to overcome and survive. The JEATH Museum (an acronym for the main countries that participated in the historical events that occurred in this region: Japan, England, Australia, Thailand and Holland) houses one of the most impressive exhibits - an original Japanese transport train.

Further down the line at Tham Krasae, I boarded a train so I could ride the Death Railway over the Tham Krasae Bridge to Nam Tok, a two-hour journey through nature and history. It was the third and last service of the day, and I had the carriage all to myself which was a pleasant surprise as I expected it to be heaving with tourists. The journey began with the picturesque but hair-raising section of the track at Tham Krasae, where a wooden trestle viaduct curves with the Kwai Noi and clings onto the cliff for dear life; I hoped it would hold firm and let the train pass while I was on it. It was a peaceful end to an eventful day, with the train grinding its way past fields and mountains in the Kwai Noi Valley and stations decorated with frangipani and jasmine. When I leant out the window to view the river and the floating tourist bungalows below, I could imagine the difficulties of building such an awkward section of the line where nature was an opposing force. As the train squeezed its way through solid rock cuttings which the prisoners cleared for the railway, I was blown away by such an extraordinary feat of engineering. The Japanese planned the route of the railroad, but credit must go to the blood, sweat and tears of the men who made the impossible possible.

The Japanese didn't care about the health and safety of their captives, whose high mortality rate worsened with malnutrition, tropical diseases, and torture. When the soldiers survived savage beatings with bamboo or other merciless methods of torture, malaria, dysentery and cholera waited patiently in the wings. Camp conditions were dreadful, and maggots were a vital source of protein. Some prisoners went to extreme lengths to survive, even collecting undigested beans from Japanese officers' latrines. Allied prisoners were rounded up in Malaysia, Singapore, Borneo and Indonesia and deposited in Kanchanaburi Province where they were joined by an army of press-ganged Asian labourers (the Romusha) whom the Japanese deemed even more

320

expendable than their POWs. You must break a few eggs to make an omelette, but the Japanese smashed 116,000.

In August 1942, Thailand's prime minister - Field Marshal Phibun Songkhram - signed an agreement allowing the Japanese commanders to build their railway. It resulted in the deaths of some 16,000 POWs - and an estimated 100,000 labourers - during the process of its construction, which equates to one death per sleeper laid along the entire route of a line which stretches 250 miles across some of the region's most inhospitable and impenetrable terrain (dynamite eventually found a way through). I finally understood how and why the railway acquired its grave nickname, with heavy manual work supported by elephants tasked with the role of carrying away the loads of rock and fallen trees. The Red Cross dropped food and medical aid, but the spiteful Japanese officers often left it where it landed to rot in the humidity, preferring to watch their prisoners reduce to skeletal frames, while the sick were forced to work as they coughed up blood from tropical ulcers. Medical equipment was improvised and crafted from bamboo (almost everything was made of bamboo), and Garra rufa fish came to their aid by cleaning out wounds and nibbling away infected flesh.

The survivors lived in the shadow of death for months before liberation came in August 1945. The dead have since been honoured at three war cemeteries (and a Japanese war memorial) with the Thanbyuzayat Cemetery in Myanmar (the final stop on the line) and two more in Kanchanaburi Town, on either side of the river. The cemetery gardens are well-tended with alphabetical registers pinpointing the graves of individual soldiers, with simple headstones inscribed with poignant messages about war and loss. It is a beautiful place to be buried, but considering how very far from home these brave soldiers remain to this day, I found myself touched by their sacrifices.

While the ghosts of the past will forever haunt and hover over Kanchanaburi Town, it has been developed into a modern resort with first-rate hotels and restaurants. Sitting by the riverside late one evening, I enjoyed a tranquil view of the bridge until my peace was disturbed by discos which floated upriver on specially designed party rafts. I would have joined them had I been invited, so I spent the evening watching bats skim the river like stones, as passing partygoers waved and the natural world reverberated to *Gangnam Style*. The town is similar in appearance to every urban space outside the capital as it is characterised by bland egg box designs, but it is the perfect provincial springboard to outlying areas of interest with Highway 323 leading to the Three

Pagodas Pass, the border with Myanmar and one of Thailand's better museums: The Hellfire Pass Memorial Museum.

The Hellfire Pass Memorial is a small but world-class museum. Founded and maintained by the Australian government since it opened in 1998, its Peace Vessel serves to remind visitors of the positive values of human life in an area that was once ravaged by war. The museum sits above the Hellfire Pass (Konyu Cutting) which was a notoriously difficult section of the line to construct, as the labourers and POWs slaved their way through sheer rock for up to eighteen hours a day. As the Japanese overseers were frustrated by their progress, they beat some of their captives to death at this site while others died from exhaustion over a period of six weeks of drilling, digging and blasting. The memorial is funded by donations, and the audio guide was one of those rare recordings that shared both entertaining as well as informative comment, alongside the haunting recounts of surviving prisoners. It is one of the world's most sobering and evocative destinations for travellers with interest in history and war, and it was rated the best museum in Thailand by TripAdvisor in 2014 (which also ranked it the fifth-best museum in Asia).

From the museum, which briefly introduces visitors to the site with historical information and model reconstructions, there is a boarded walkway leading down to the walking trail which follows the route of the railway's tracking bed for a couple of miles through the Tenasserim Hills. Trains no longer run along this section of the line as most of the single-metre-gauge track has been removed, with only a few sleepers surviving in place. At the beginning of the trail, there is a memorial - a black stone pyramid - dedicated to all 'who suffered and died' here between 1942 and 1945. As I walked through the first Konyu Cutting, I tried to picture the scene, the noise and the terrible hardships of the men as they cleared this area, hacking open the masses of solid rock before them. It wasn't too difficult to imagine, as I came across a broken drill bit stuck within a steep rock wall, and I was surrounded by rough surfaces, the result of continuous drilling and dynamiting, with several cuttings along the route leading to Hintok Station.

I will never forget that railway as I shared in its misery and memories, while the summer sunshine belied its history and did its best to raise my spirits. It was the POWs who coined the tourist names 'Hellfire Pass' and 'Death Railway' that we use today but in their day, they captured how a corner of the jungle in Thailand was transformed into hell on earth, as campfires licked rocks while the Japanese tormented their captives like biblical sinners. For three long years, Kanchanaburi Province was Dante's *Inferno*.

322

## Chapter 49: Sin and the City: Pattaya

When God passed divine judgement on the biblical cities of Sodom and Gomorrah, he consumed their impenitent sinners in a rain of fire and brimstone (he wasn't taking any chances). The legend of Pattaya is also well-documented. The city should be a mandatory field trip and curriculum case study for every religious studies student, as a weekend in this popular seaside resort is a three-dimensional journey through the *Book of Genesis* in *The New Testament*. The residents of Sodom and Gomorrah have found sanctuary on the sands of Thailand's eastern Gulf coast in Pattaya Bay, and God has turned a blind or lazy eye to their late-night recreations (in his defence, it does get rather hot during the summer months from March to June). I was introduced to Pattaya by the TV series *Sin Cities* when appropriately named presenter Grub Smith took a cultural tour of the city's sleazy underbelly. The global appeal of Pattaya's high-yielding super niche has since been captured by an unofficial tourism slogan, printed on souvenir T-shirts: *Good guys go to heaven; bad guys go to Pattaya.*

Pattaya is a no-holds-barred city full of neon lights and exposed flesh, but it also holds a dark tourism appeal. At the mention of 'Pattaya,' the immediate connotation is red-light seediness, which is a legacy with roots in the Vietnam War. The city has romantic origins: Pad Tha Ya is named after the welcome sea breezes which usher in the rainy season, and it was once popular with Thai holidaymakers travelling from Bangkok for weekend staycations in beach huts and bungalows. As its popularity grew, it acquired city status in 1978 and an unfortunate reputation that it has since been unable to shake off, as Pattaya is Thailand's sin city and the sin of choice is lust.

Pattaya attracts a disproportionate number of sexpats and sex tourists from all over the world, whose idea of the perfect holiday getaway involves sweat and heavy breathing. Pattaya promises the sun, sand, sea, and a plentiful supply of sex for sale. It is a buyers' market too with a dedicated Walking Street where workers parade their fleshy wares to attract pleasure-seekers. Fans of the late Amy Winehouse should beware, as I saw her transgender lookalike playing pool at a sports bar (with a pinched face covered in thick black eyeliner and that trademark exaggerated beehive). She had Amy's signature look down to a tee, with a tight-fitting pink dress barely concealing her breast and butt implants.

There are more sex workers per square mile in Pattaya than anywhere else on planet Earth. The city also has its fair share of cunning linguists, especially when it comes to bar names and slogans. The 'Fcuk Inn' on Soi LK

Metro (a deliberate spelling error, accompanied by a bent-over-barrel, topless cartoon woman) impressed me the most with its delightfully clever use of paronomasia in a bar sign advertising 'Liquor in the front' and 'Poker in the rear.' By contrast, and without much imagination or intelligence of thought, there is garish Pussy Beer Bar with bold red lettering beside the image of a squatting, braless dancer sucking suggestively on her index finger. Pattaya has a street named Drinking Street for the lost and inebriated, but what confused me the most in this city of confusion, was the prominent placing of a neon sign - at the end of Walking Street - with a gold-framed portrait of the late King Bhumibol Adulyadej and the words 'Long Live the King!' To celebrate his kingship at the entrance to a notorious red light area is a bold-as-brass decision.

Pattaya is a stranger to subtlety, and its gigantic beachfront PATTAYA CITY sign is the first indication, aping as it does the iconic Hollywood landmark but with alternating colours which welcome visitors to what is, essentially, an erotic theme park where the rural poor have been turned into slot machines and pendulum rides. Pattaya and prostitution go together like itching and scratching, but there is more to this controversial town than carnal discovery, decadence and debauchery. It rightly deserves its reputation as a sex capital (densely populated by beer bars, massage parlours and go-go clubs) and it even introduced me to the concept and not-so-secret world of the 'short time' room.

As I passed the gaudy signs of grubby hotels that advertised their value-for-screwing rates, I noticed three hundred baht was the generally agreed fixed price for a small space in which to make the beast with two backs. When I sat with a friend at Hanrahans Irish Bar on Bangkok's infamous Soi Nana, having returned from a weekend in Pattaya, I watched a thousand girls in halter tops and mini-skirts entice their usual crowd of balding and bloated middle-aged men for a spot of 'how's your father.' I overheard their heartfelt promises to pot-bellied punters, how they will 'love' them 'for long time' as they were led away by hand to the nearest short-time room with a poorly sprung mattress thrown on the floor. The wreckage of humanity often finds comfort and company in Thailand.

The working girls of Thailand's red light districts are the subject, par excellence, of people watching. A 'lady' in red caught my attention one evening in Nana District, the second largest red light area in Bangkok after Patpong, as she wore an elegant but incongruous evening dress which clung to her implants like poison ivy. She evidently wanted to be seen and heard as she cavorted excitedly with a young, athletic and good-looking backpacker at the opposite

Hillary Bar (he was a welcome break from her usual Falstaffian clientele). Every cell of her being was calculated to make a premium sale, and she stood at the perfect angle from the ceiling fan to create that windswept effect of shampoo adverts, casually tossing her hair over her shoulder and turning her whole body into an animated billboard poster. Seduced and intoxicated by her natural charms (sex does sell), he chugged down a full pint of overpriced cheap beer to showcase his virility, grabbed her by the waist like Captain Caveman, and carried her off to a short-time hole in the wall hidden by the darkness of an insalubrious backstreet.

The lady in red returned, alone, about twenty minutes later and immediately attached herself to the next willing sperm and baht donator. She had a sound business model as she micromanaged all the logistics from demand to supply, while enjoying a continuous flow of complimentary drinks which, I presumed, doubled as mouthwash. Other bar girls relied on their acting skills to broker a deal, and I was the audience of one such curious performance when I had the misfortune to sit at a table - the same bar, but a different night - next to one of the drunkest Brits I have ever witnessed abroad. His motor skills had completely deserted him, but his chosen lady of the night could stagger to the kerb to stop a taxi into which they both fell in an entangled heap. It is a social taboo for Thais to get drunk in public, so I watched her behaviour and intoxicated state with some interest and a wry smile.

Thailand is a confounding nation. Soliciting on a street corner is perfectly acceptable as male, female and transgender prostitutes line up outside the Nana Hotel like a selection for a school football team, while being tipsy in public is socially unacceptable and insulting the king's dog is punishable by incarceration. Drunk Thai had not broken any social taboos though (but she could have won an Academy Award for the Best Supporting Actress category), as she returned to the bar thirty minutes later - completely sober - to target her next easy victim with a reduced libido and poor memory recall.

Lost in the schadenfreude, I wondered whether that unsuspecting sex tourist had his wallet stolen or would even remember *not* having sex with his purchase from one of Bangkok's wholesale meat markets. Nana doesn't beat around the bush when it comes to sexual etiquette, as the Nana Plaza is fronted by an enormous sign declaring free entry to 'The World's Largest Adult Playground.' The Plaza's primary concerns are mixing drinks and bodily fluids, so it doesn't bother to mix its words. As the capital's naughty central, it certainly puts the 'Bang' and 'kok' in the capital.

Amsterdam is Europe's leading sin city, and like Bangkok, it will never match Pattaya for scale. Gluttony is Amsterdam's sin as it celebrates life's excesses in the form of sex, drugs and rock 'n' roll with hedonistic hash cafes and 'erotic' live sex shows. The Dutch capital was compared to Dante's *Inferno* by French author and philosopher Albert Camus, who likened its concentric canals to the circles of hell, its legendary red light district the sinful epicentre and ninth circle which, in the verse of Dante, is full of treachery. Amsterdam's flesh industry has been legalised and fully regulated with taxpaying sex workers contributing to the economy; Pattaya, on the other hand, is another anarchistic Crazy Town of the Wild East. My first impressions of this 'beachside paradise' took a severe knock when I arrived at my resort. The straight-talking manager thought it prudent to display a rather forthright notice (in a lovely, handmade teak frame) on the main reception desk to remind his guests that: 'Child sex is a crime in Thailand. If found guilty, you will be sentenced to the maximum extent of the law.' The subtext of his warning implied: 'Welcome to Pattaya! The management assumes YOU are a degenerate!'

Guilt is a terrible burden to carry, especially when you have done absolutely nothing wrong, and I have often felt the guilty fear of a shoplifter while passing the scrutinous eyes of security guards. Upon my arrival in Pattaya, I was a suspected paedophile! I thought I had passed the sufferance test when I tried to find my 'exclusive' resort from the thousands of hotels littering Pattaya's coastline. My taxi driver insisted he had never heard of it (The Rabbit Resort, which, I hoped, had nothing to do with a certain brand of sex toy) as we drove up and down the same street for more than an hour. Google Maps said it was there, so there it must be. Many Thais struggle to pronounce the 'R' sound, so they often substitute it with an 'L' or drop it entirely from a consonant cluster, but I discovered this language difficulty once I had arrived, exasperated, outside the main reception building and the driver repeated 'Labbit! Yes, Labbit Lesot! Labbit Lesot!' as if all of his numbers had come up at once in a lottery draw. If looks could kill and he was a cat, he would have lost all nine lives in a single blink.

It is hard to imagine Pattaya as a small, quiet and humble fishing village, cut off from the outside world before it was thrust into the limelight during the years of the Vietnam War between 1961 and 1975. During that war, Thailand obliged the United States Air Force by allowing it to deploy its combat aircraft to Thai military air bases from which an estimated 80% of all US air strikes over North Vietnam were launched. America reduced its enemy count and made an exotic, erotic and obliging new friend; Thailand gained a powerful trading ally. With national pride and 'face' coming before war and bloodshed, the Thai government reached a gentlemen's agreement with the US that its air bases would remain Royal Thai Air Force bases commanded by Royal Thai officers. As the US military presence expanded into Thailand, American servicemen were exposed to the country's beaches and beauties (which included the local women) away from the shells and shrapnel of Vietnam. Pattaya soon became the military byword for rest and recuperation, and it was transformed from a sleepy village into one of Thailand's premier, liveliest and most successful beach resorts where the sharks no longer patrol the waters, they walk the streets. There is even a bar and club named Shark, which is full of willing victims.

A quick search on Google Images will reveal photographs of idyllic Pattaya Bay with its quaint fishermen's huts and palm trees before they were all bulldozed and covered with a thick layer of cement. Rapid urban development turned Pattaya into a dusty building site strewn with rubbish, and for a time, the waters were unswimmable due to inadequate wastewater treatment systems, with raw sewage pumped directly into the bay for swimmers to compete against yesterday's dinner. Pattaya is no longer a tropical idyll, but it does have sun, sand and watersports aplenty, and its saving grace is that it can be reached by road in less than two hours from Bangkok. It is the star attraction of Chonburi Province (few tourists ever visit Chonburi Town), and it has tried, but failed, to rebrand itself as a family getaway while the locals have tired of their city's sordid, but justified, reputation. Ultimately, it doesn't matter how long or hard you polish or paint a turd, it's still a turd. Tourists see Pattaya for what it is and embrace it with gloves, lubricants, and extra-thick condoms.

Holidaymakers that arrive on package holidays leave Thailand with very little sense of what the rest of the country has to offer. There is not much in the way of traditional Thai culture to be found in Pattaya, so unfavourable and narrow impressions of the people are formed and shared with folks back home, who should be forgiven for thinking that every woman in Thailand is a sex worker. Rampant tourism, unchecked development, prostitution and crime (drug trafficking, murder, and theft) have combined to create modern perceptions of Pattaya City, an artificial construct where sleaze in inescapable. There are more natural, sin-free alternatives on Pattaya's coastline with the islands of Ko Sak, Ko Lin, and Ko Pai. Divers can enjoy coral reefs and the tropical sea life that survived dynamite fishing, but travellers seeking a two-week slice of paradise should look elsewhere, as the only aspect Pattaya has in common with paradise is that first consonant.

Pattaya is a city awash with Russians, and their vocabulary forms the second language of the city, not English. Simple economics led to the influx of Russian tourists and expats as flights were cheaply priced, and the rouble had been strong against the baht before the economic crash of late 2014 when falling oil prices and uncertainties over the Ukraine stemmed the flow of vodka and kvass. The local people welcomed the Russians and their vast spending power with open arms, accommodating them with dual language signs and a plethora of Russian restaurants, shops and tour providers. There are even dedicated strip clubs with Eastern European women dancing and catering to their needs at the right price. Property development has been hit the hardest by the crisis, with projects left unfinished as Russian investors abandoned their condominiums as they could no longer afford the monthly instalments. Pattaya reminds me of the sugar daddy football clubs such as Chelsea and Manchester City, which are owned by benevolent billionaire investors. The clubs' undeserved riches have provided instant and unprecedented short-term success, but if their owners were ever to tire of their toys and walk away, their fans would be the ones left to feel the pinch as trophy cabinets fill with dust.

Pattaya has a split personality and in its defence, there is an awful lot of wholesome fun to be had on its streets for couples and families, as the Tourism Authority of Thailand has encouraged Chonburi Province and Pattaya's city planners to shoehorn savoury entertainments alongside red light interests. Walking Street might be crammed full of vice, but there is no denying that the live music scene is first-rate, and it caters for classic rockers as I could punch the air and make devil horns in Rolling Stone and Hot Tuna Bar. There is even a Hard Rock Café where I pretended to be a multi-millionaire for an hour and the staff, not surprisingly, treated me like a member of the Thai royal family before I parted with a small tip. There is an ice bar too (The Ice Bar V20) and tropical Thailand is the natural host for such a venue, unlike the ice bars in Scandinavia where I escaped from the cold and paid for the privilege of getting colder. Pattaya's ice bar is the size of a desktop goldfish bowl, and its glass frontage faces straight onto the thousands of passing tourists on Walking Street. It is made of ice, but it's an icebox for physical space, which I shared with a ladyboy (dressed in a polar bear costume) who persistently nagged me to buy her cocktails while I shivered in a wafer-thin T-shirt and shorts. I couldn't drink my ice bar vodka, so I gave it to the alcoholic polar bear and suggested we swap outfits.

There are numerous activities for thrill-seekers to enjoy by day (in addition to those late-night cheap thrills), but I made the costly error of booking online and paying in advance for an unlikely hangover cure: skydiving over Pattaya Bay. The company failed to pick me up from my resort at the designated time, so my hotel receptionist called to enquire on my behalf. Having apologised profusely for my inconvenience when all I had done was sit in an air-conditioned lobby, they explained that they were having a slight problem with their plane. They didn't have one. I considered taking a bungee jump as an alternative, but remembering that I was in Thailand, I feared the moment I dropped, a megaphone would announce the lack of a bungee rope with a belated apology.

I took to the sands of Jomtien Beach with the kind of grimace fixed to my face that is only achievable the moment you accidentally soil your pants in public. When I walked through Boyztown, I had a similar expression, as I didn't know what to make of it at all as leathered Lotharios (who prefer men to women) covered themselves from head to toe in sticky baby oil and offered deep-tissue anal massages. Why had they oiled themselves? Where were they planning to insert their bodies? A typical foot or body massage lasts an hour, so that is a rather small and delicate spot to rub and prod for a whole hour. The mind boggles at the thought.

Pattaya's beaches are everything I fear and loathe about seaside holidays in Europe. Jomtien Beach is overcrowded with holidaymakers wearing union jack or hammer and sickle tattoos, a million deckchairs and umbrellas covered in Pepsi or Coca-Cola logos which blot out the sun. There was no escape from the grating sounds of roaring jet skis, banana boats, and parasailing, windsurfing and kiteboarding enthusiasts. The beachside restaurants were unremarkable, and whenever I tried to find some peace, vendors interrupted my sleep to sell silk scarves and handicrafts on white-sand beaches that looked like a giant's outdoor ashtray. I could have saved money and flight hours had I stayed closer to home and holidayed in the Mediterranean.

Hat Pattaya is the more famous of Pattaya's two beaches and even though it stretches for two miles, tropical paradise deserted its sands long ago, and it has since acquired the nickname 'Patpong by the sea' (a reference to Bangkok's infamous red light area, it is not an endorsement). When I strolled along Beach Road, I passed all the losers of every Miss World pageant since its creation by Eric Morley in 1951. Thailand's finest lined themselves along the promenade and offered their sex for sale, with an opening gambit of 'Hey, sexy man' or a flirtatious wink and smile. Even if you are not buying, it's a great walk if only to appease the male ego lurking inside.

I did not know it at the time, but the part of Jomtien Beach where I settled down and attempted to sunbathe is Dong Tan or 'gay beach.' The clues should have been obvious when I passed the six-pack torso of a Thai teenager, who could have bulldozed an apartment complex with his abdominal muscles but had chosen to wear a fetching pair of lilac and see-through French knickers. He resisted the crotchless thong option, which was a relief, as he probably reserved that for Friday night outings. I thought it was unusual that men - and only men - were giving oily beachfront massages to other men (usually much older, inflated westerners with Chewbacca-hairy backs) and some were completely naked with the sun bouncing off their shiny buttocks. The penny dropped in slow motion, and I considered applying for the role of village idiot in Dong Tan.

I was too afraid to sunbathe on Pattaya's beaches, but I did enjoy Mini Siam, an enormous miniature park with copies of Thailand's famous landmarks (such as The Grand Palace in Bangkok) and world icons which include the Eiffel Tower and the Sydney Opera House. For a cultural break from the red-glow smut, I climbed a hill to visit the Big Buddha at King Rama IX Park and visited one of Thailand's most impressive and ornate temples with an incredible view of the Gulf of Thailand: The Sanctuary of Truth. For a break from the neon and to find some peace and quiet, I visited the Nong Nooch Botanical Garden and to stimulate my senses, I spent an hour inside the Ripley's Believe It or Not! museum before my senses were further confuddled by the excellent 3D Art in Paradise exhibition. Pattaya has a zoo and crocodile farm, an elephant village, an artificial floating market, a teddy bear museum, waxworks, a night bazaar, a sheep farm, ATV off-road tours, water and theme parks, upmarket shopping centres and exclusive spas, so there really is more to the city than the sins of the flesh. The provincial authorities have made every effort to branch out and redefine Pattaya's tourism profile, but all roads lead, inevitably, to prostitution as the flesh trade remains Pattaya's platinum commercial activity.

Pattaya's sex industry may yet be destroyed by the wrath of God, though I would imagine overseas economic crises are more likely to curtail its activities and keep it in check. With millions of annual arrivals, Pattaya must be doing something right. It has struggled with its identity as it tried to find a middle ground between a long-established reputation as a factory outlet for sex tourism and an upmarket, family-oriented resort with first-class golf courses and glitzy cabaret shows. Ultimately, it doesn't matter how brightly coloured the authorities paint the city, as Pattaya's dominant strokes will always be red.

Before I left the sin and sexploitation for the last time, I took a walk up Pratumnak Hill to the Khao Pattaya View Point to the south of Beach Road. It offers an elevated view of Pattaya's sweeping crescent bay, which stretches all the way north to the headland that separates Pattaya Beach from Naklua Beach. The viewing area is hidden by Wat Khao Phra Bat, another temple which claims to hold a piece of the Buddha, and an impressive monument dedicated to Kromluang Chomphonkhetudomsak, the founding father of the Thai navy. It is a busy area as holidaying Thais are dropped off by the coachload to point, pose and click before returning to the coach to hastily upload social media updates.

The views of Pattaya reminded me of the cheap holiday resorts of Spain, such as Majorca and Andalucia, and as clouds crawled across the blue sky to hover over the bay like B-52 bombers, I wondered whether God's stockpile of fire and brimstone was ready to provide my camera with a colourful, biblical panorama.

## Chapter 50: Island Escapes

Tropical islands and sun-drenched beaches are Thailand's primary enticements for tourists, but 'paradise' is not as easy to find as you would expect, and neither is a cocktail umbrella beneath a stack of parasols. I tried to unearth the travel brochure yardstick of white sands, languid palm trees, and unforgettable sunsets - a mythical quest more suited to the Greeks and Romans. The deserted island of Tom Hanks' *Castaway* was my benchmark for paradise, a sandy haven without parasols, jet skis or the physical and emotional trials of survival. The meaning of 'paradise' has been stretched beyond the elasticity of Hooke's law by all-night, Full Moon parties. Thailand's party islands explode into frenzies of psychedelic trance as jugglers and fire-eaters entertain neon partygoers hell-bent on drowning themselves in buckets of cheap beer and diluted spirits. It is a rite of passage experience - with permed and frizzy origins - on the once-quiet island of Ko Phangan where, in the mid-1980s, a handful of tourists danced and drank the night away beneath the moon, which doubled as a giant disco ball and energy-efficient night light.

Popularised by Danny Boyle's *The Beach* and word-of-mouth recommendations, trouble has found its way to paradise with tens of thousands of tourists flocking to full moons from all over the world, with depravity and debauchery their bywords for 'fun' without inhibition or restraint. Paradise should be uncluttered, unpopulated and unspoilt; Ko Phangan, however, is the real-life setting for Robinson Crusoe's Island of Despair. With Half Moon and Quarter Moon parties supplying the demand for alcohol, drugs, and casual sex on the beach, the military government cracked down on the revelry in 2014 when it curtailed the noise and environmental pollution by restricting the range of parties to the Full Moon variety. The island's innocence and romance have drowned in a tsunami of testosterone, with every inch of Ko Phangan's once-beautiful beaches jam-packed with painted faces and near-naked bodies. As a venue for unceasing bacchanals, few visitors have any interest or concern for the island itself. The islanders sold their souls to the devil and lived off the profits, so bending the knee or begging for mercy is unlikely to offer a reprieve. When Mephistopheles forewarned Doctor Faustus about the horrors of hell and the consequences of using his soul as a bargaining chip, he ignored him and - surprise, surprise - a host of devils appeared.

The Kingdom of Thailand is, fittingly, shaped like an elephant's head; its elongated trunk reaches southwards to a border with Malaysia and parts the Gulf of Thailand from the Andaman Sea. It is a country blessed with a glorious bounty of beautiful beaches and tropical islands with the capital city placed as the geographical gateway and dividing line, separating northern plains from exotic strands to the south. Thailand's long and diverse coastline (which extends for more than two thousand miles) spoils its visitors for choice. I went in search of island escapes on the Gulf and Andaman coasts and found paradise ten years later, once I had circumnavigated all the Full Moon parties and island-hopped my way by boat and plane to the country's six regional coastlines. With Ko Phangan and Pattaya at the insalubrious end of the paradise spectrum, Ko Chang and Ko Phi Phi offered a glimpse into tropical paradise without the aid of red lights or moon glow. Ko Samet is a popular weekend retreat for Thais, expats and backpackers and it sits in the middle of the spectrum with sedate and secluded beaches to the island's south, and fire shows, beach barbeques and bucket huggers in the north. It is a beautiful island, relatively undeveloped as a protected national park, and I enjoyed my weekend escapes to Ko Samet once I had survived the speed merchants and their taxi speedboats.

Taking a speedboat from the mainland to the islands can be a hair-raising experience as their captains audition for the World Powerboat Racing Competition. Several tourists were injured and drowned in May 2016 when their boat was overturned by a wave off the coast of Ko Samui. The captain, Sanan Seekakiaw, was accused of reckless endangerment as he defied the currents - and common sense - by speeding his way through rough waters and high winds. Whenever I boarded a speedboat at Ban Phe Pier to reach Ko Samet, I had to throw my bags onto the open bow and jump on afterwards, hoping not to slip over the edge for a face-to-face with the propellers. I dreaded journeys across the channel, as passengers reliably vomited all over themselves as the boat smashed its way through high waves at speed. I am not a strong swimmer, and there were never enough life vests for all the passengers, so had we capsized and survived death by drowning, a passing boat may well have finished me off and smashed my head to a pulp. My spine survived repeated attempts at herniation as the boats bounced and thumped against the waves.

My island adventures began on Ko Samui, Thailand's third largest after Phuket and Ko Chang (the Thai word for island is 'ko' and 'hat' means beach). It was a fabulous introduction as it has everything from quiet beaches to noisy beer bars, elephant treks, and secret Buddha gardens. The island is an hour's flight south of the capital and found its place in tourism folklore in the 1970s when it became a haven for Thailand's first wave of backpackers. It has since developed into a tourism and spa mecca with palm trees making way for international hotel chains, but it is large enough to accommodate foreign influences and retain its paradisiacal elements. The island's south-west corner offers a peaceful retreat from the capital, while its north-east corner - Hat Chaweng - is Bangkok by the beach. From Samui, I joined a snorkelling and kayaking tour of the Ang Thong Marine National Park, but my first (and last) attempt at snorkelling was brought to an abrupt end by embarrassment and broken fingers, when I tried to launch myself from the back of the speedboat and forgot to let go of the ladder. I spent the next two hours nursing fingers and a bruised ego, while the rest of my tour group enjoyed unparalleled views of coral reefs and marine life.

Ang Thong Marine Park is paradise found with its cerulean waters and golden sands encircling the marine park's jungle islands, limestone cliffs, and hidden lagoons. Like a broken emerald necklace with fragments clustered around the main islands of Ko Tai Plao, Ko Mae Ko and Ko Wua Talap to the south, I was able to enjoy incredible views of the Green Lagoon. It is a hidden lake formed by rainwater which seeped through the limestone to erode a huge cavern in the centre of the rock. When the roof of the cavern eventually collapsed, nature begrudgingly revealed her beauty in the form of an emerald lagoon surrounded by steep cliffs. Ang Thong is a pristine archipelago of forty-two islands with white-sand beaches, waterfalls, fertile mangroves and a rich variety of exotic wildlife and sea creatures. It is a protected postcard-perfect image of a tropical paradise.

Maya Bay, by contrast, was as disappointing as Manchester United in the post-Ferguson era. It is a horribly overcrowded enclave on the coastline of Ko Phi Phi Leh near the diving, snorkelling and surfing 'haven' of Koh Phi Phi. The bay and its beach found worldwide acclaim in *The Beach* (filmed on location), but since its release in 2000, it has been flooded by sightseers searching for a glimpse of the paradise described by Alex Garland, the main character (played by Leonardo DiCaprio):

> *You fish, swim, eat, laze around and everyone's so friendly. It's such simple stuff, but If I could stop the world and restart life, put the clock back, I think I'd restart it like this. For everyone.*

Sadly, it is not like that anymore. I visited the bay as part of an organised tour of paradise, and I couldn't wait to get back on the boat as the air filled with the sputtering sounds of power engines, the beach a line of boats bobbing in the water like floats on fishing lines. It is more Mayhem than Maya as a small beach of two hundred metres is trampled by thousands of frustrated

334

tourists every day, all desperately trying to capture the same photograph of 'me in paradise' as hundreds of strangers loiter in the background while they, themselves, linger in someone else's background. Paradise should be quiet and private, and while Maya Bay is a stunning beach cove surrounded and sheltered by high cliffs, a teeming reef of colourful coral, exotic fish, and exceptionally clear waters, the experience failed to deliver. On my return to Krabi, the capital of southern Krabi Province, the captain stopped for an hour at Coral Island's Banana Beach. My steps were haunted by ominous signs reminding tourists that they were holidaying in a tsunami hazard zone, while my head filled up with images of Boxing Day 2004. As boats tailgated offshore to offload their tourists for an enforced walk along the beach, it suddenly occurred to me that I would never find paradise on an organised trip.

Bustling Krabi Town is a convenient transport hub for the Andaman Sea with popular day trips including 'James Bond Island' at Ko Khao Phing Kan, a famous landmark in Phang Nga Bay as it featured in *The Man with the Golden Gun* as Scaramanga's tropical hideout. Phang Nga Bay is Thailand at its stunning best, and its topography reminded me of Halong Bay in northern Vietnam as limestone cliffs emerged from pea-green waters. James Bond Island's signature rocky pinnacle stands at the island's entrance and earned the rather literal name of Ko Tapu, which translates to 'Nail Island.' I enjoyed visiting this film set, but the experience was very much in line with Maya Bay as hundreds of tourists wrestled for position with tripods and cameras, when the island simply isn't broad enough to accommodate them all. The highlight of my trip to Phang Nga Bay was exploring the islands on a long-tail boat and stopping for lunch at Ko Panyee, a Muslim fishing village where everything from the school to the market is propped up on stilts and floats.

The longer I lived in Thailand, the more I yearned for less touristic islands and beaches popular with Thai holidaymakers, such as Ko Si Chang and Bang Saen. Bang Saen has been a favourite weekend getaway for Thais for decades, and it is a short drive south of the capital in the eastern province of Chonburi. It is a charming village resort which attracts few foreign tourists. When I pulled over on Beach Road wearing a full Manchester United kit and riding a customised Manchester United scooter, I was greeted with mutterings of 'farang' which I interpreted as genuine surprise to see a foreigner in these parts (I stood out like a sore thumb on a giant's hand). I enjoyed walking along Bang Saen's main beach and sharing fresh seafood with the locals while they drank whisky, played cards, listened to music and swam in the Gulf of Thailand. There weren't many sunbathers clogging the beach as Thais shun the sun, but there were plenty of kite flyers as it was kite flying season (it is an ancient sport in Thailand, dignified by rules and regulations with a heritage shared by commoners and kings). Bang Saen introduced me to the less-dignified but very strange world of the Buddhist Hell Garden at Wang Saen Suk, a short walk from the beach front and one of the most extraordinary places I have visited in Southeast Asia.

Ko Si Chang, the closest island to Bangkok, is a small and lovely island getaway; I enjoyed rugged coastlines and visited quiet fishing villages which offered a peaceful retreat from city life. There is no sex tourism or bar scene (I could only find one restaurant with a bar on the island), and there are no high-rise or luxury condo developments either. It is a low-key, homestay island with a sabai sabai vibe and royal associations (the kings of the Chakri Dynasty holidayed here). The island's natural beauty, its nesting seabirds, royal palaces and Chinese temples restored peace to my mind without the A-Z of tourist beach life. Ko Chang is one of the remotest, distant islands from the capital and getting to it required a tediously long drive in a minivan, but like Ko Si Chang, it has resisted package-tour makeovers to retain a laid-back atmosphere and charm, with hiking trails to waterfalls, a national park, quiet beaches, offshore coral reefs and a fishing village (Bang Bao) propped up on stilts.

The resort of Cha-am, in Phetchaburi Province, is a cheap and cheerful beach town. Popular with local working class families, Thai-style beach parties have more in common with their Full Moon counterparts with banana boats and food and drinking marathons. Hua Hin is a resort further along the coast, which used to be the holiday destination of the Thai royal family (they built summer palaces and helped to establish the area as a seaside resort). But what was once a quiet fishing village is slowly transforming into the sister city of Pattaya with crowded, polluted beaches and an open sex industry. Hua Hin was unrecognisable from my first visit in 2006, but its out-of-town vineyards were the saving grace of my return when I tasted varieties of the locally produced Monsoon Valley wines. The main town of Patong - in Phuket - underwhelmed in equal measure with its wild nightclubs, soapy massage parlours and super-busy beachfront, but its western shore edged me closer to postcard idylls with mountains and rainforests and high-end resorts with private beaches.

'Paradise,' I discovered, is a way of life, not a place. It is all about movement and discovery. When I returned home to settle in Northwest England, I completed the final step of my journey of a thousand miles, but I was a stranger in my own land. Standing in the middle of Manchester's Piccadilly Gardens, I was surrounded by shadowy figures disguised by heavy winter coats, hunched beneath umbrellas like an animated Renoir painting. I was a character in a film, emotionally dislocated from my environment, as the world passed by in fast motion. The spell of invisibility broke when a teenager pointed at my feet, sniggered, and commented to his friend: 'He's hard-core.' I was still wearing my Havaianas flip flops. Why was everyone in such a hurry? Thais never rush, they meander from Point A to Point B, which of course makes perfect sense when you live in the tropics. I was out of rhythm with my former life and would need time to readjust.

My voyage across Southeast Asia was greater than the sum of its parts; it opened my eyes and all my senses, as well as my wallet. It tested my opinions, values and worldview. American historian Miriam Ritter Beard captured the transformational aspects of travel when she observed: 'Travel is more than seeing the sights; it is a change that goes on, deep and permanent, in the ideas of living.' How could I not be affected by the journey, having stood before a stupa displaying five thousand neatly stacked human skulls, walked across killing fields and witnessed a social revolution?

Travel made me examine my life and how I want to live it, and I finally understood what it means to have enough when I visited the slums of Manila and Bangkok. For two years, I carried a light backpack of essentials, and it was all that I needed; those possessions I sold on eBay were unnecessary and not important after all. The memories collected, and the thousands of photographs amassed, will always hold more value over material things. Travel is the university of life: I learned so much about history and culture, myself and other people. Travel also made me feel small: it is a huge world out there, and I have only scratched the surface.

Memories of Thailand never fail to put a smile on my face as they transport me to islands on the Gulf and Andaman coasts, flights over mountains and buses, trains, cars and motorbikes across borders to Vietnam, Cambodia, Myanmar and Laos. Thailand's nickname makes perfect sense on reflection: as an industrialised nation, its greatest export is a smile. It was my 'home from home' and if a home is truly where the heart is, mine is beating some 5,900 miles away.

Southeast Asia is no longer a distant region but a close relation, and while I look forward to seeing her again, like all family relationships there are moments of joy and times of challenge. With my mind stretched by new experiences, I typed a single word on a blank digital page to fulfil the second stage of historian John Hope Franklin's travel commandment:

> *We must go beyond textbooks, go out into the bypaths and*
> *untrodden depths of the wilderness and travel and explore and tell*
> *the world the glories of our journey.*

Printed in Great Britain
by Amazon